MITI AND THE JAPANESE MIRACLE

It is only managers—not nature
or laws of economics or governments—that
make resources productive.

Peter F. Drucker, *Managing in Turbulent Times*

MITI

AND THE JAPANESE MIRACLE

The Growth of Industrial Policy, 1925-1975

CHALMERS JOHNSON

Stanford University Press, Stanford, California

Stanford University Press, Stanford, California
© 1982 by the Board of Trustees of the Leland Stanford Junior University
Printed in the United States of America
Cloth ISBN 0-8047-1128-3
Paper ISBN 0-8047-1206-9
Original edition 1982
Last figure below indicates year of this printing:
92 91 90 89 88

To the memory of

WILLIAM W. LOCKWOOD
(1906–1978)
who pioneered this subject

PREFACE

P ERHAPS the oldest and most basic subject in the study of political economy is the relationship between governmental institutions and economic activity. The distinctions in this field lie at the heart of all modern political analysis: free trade versus mercantilism, socialism versus capitalism, laissez faire versus social goal setting, the public sector versus the private sector—and, ultimately, a concern with procedures (liberty) versus a concern with outcomes (equality). Japan occupies a preeminent place in this discussion as both a model and a case. Japan's postwar economic triumph—that is, the unprecedented economic growth that has made Japan the second most productive open economy that has ever existed—is the best example of a state-guided market system currently available; and Japan has itself become a model, in whole or in part, for many other developing or advanced industrial systems.

The focus of this book is on the Japanese economic bureaucracy, particularly on the famous Ministry of International Trade and Industry (MITI), as the leading state actor in the economy. Although MITI was not the only important agent affecting the economy, nor was the state as a whole always predominant, I do not want to be overly modest about the importance of this subject. The particular speed, form, and consequences of Japanese economic growth are not intelligible without reference to the contributions of MITI. Collaboration between the state and big business has long been acknowledged as the defining characteristic of the Japanese economic system, but for too long the state's role in this collaboration has been either condemned as overweening or dismissed as merely supportive, without anyone's ever analyzing the matter. With this book I hope to contribute to such an analysis.

The history of MITI is central to the economic and political history of modern Japan. Equally important, however, the methods and achievements of the Japanese economic bureaucracy are central to the continuing debate between advocates of the communist-type command economies and advocates of the Western-type mixed market economies. The fully bureaucratized command economies misallocate resources and stifle initiative; in order to function at all, they must lock up their populations behind iron curtains or other more or less impermeable barriers. The mixed market economies struggle to find ways to intrude politically determined priorities into their market systems without catching a bad case of the "English disease" or being frustrated by the American-type legal sprawl. The Japanese, of course, do not have all the answers. But given the fact that virtually all solutions to any of the critical problems of the late twentieth century— energy supply, environmental protection, technological innovation, and so forth—involve an expansion of official bureaucracy, the particular Japanese priorities and procedures are instructive. At the very least they should forewarn a foreign observer that the Japanese achievements were not won without a price being paid.

As a particular pattern of late development, the Japanese case differs from the Western market economies, the communist dictatorships of development, or the new states of the postwar world. The most significant difference is that in Japan the state's role in the economy is shared with the private sector, and both the public and private sectors have perfected means to make the market work for developmental goals. This pattern has proved to be the most successful strategy of intentional development among the historical cases. It is being repeated today in newly industrializing states of East Asia—Taiwan and South Korea—and in Singapore and other South and Southeast Asian countries. As a response to the original beneficiaries of the industrial revolution, the Japanese pattern has proved incomparably more successful than the purely state-dominated command economies of the communist world. Since the death of Mao Tse-tung even China has come to acknowledge, if not yet emulate, the achievements of the capitalist developmental state.

This study proceeds historically for reasons that are elaborated in Chapter 1. Its time frame of 1925 to 1975 is significant in that it begins with the creation of the official industrial-policy bureaucracy, covers the period in which the main issues of industrial policy were discovered and debated, and reflects the direct continuity that exists between the prewar and postwar periods in terms of personnel and organizations. As a prologue to this history, the first two chapters are devoted to an explication of the controversies surrounding industrial policy itself and Japan's bureaucratically dominated government. In a final chapter I sketch some of the broader themes raised throughout the book and attempt to abstract a model of the Japanese political economy.

In this history and analysis I attempt also to reveal some of the Japanese language of bureaucracy—its concepts, euphemisms, and slogans. For readers who do not know Japanese, the parenthetical recurrence of Japanese terms in romanization may be annoying. If so, I apologize, but it must be stressed that the language of all bureaucracy is euphemistic and often opaque; students of Japan who have mastered the language will want to know precisely what I have translated, particularly since titles of laws and organizations in Japan are often rendered in English in several different ways. At the same time, for the reader who is interested in Japan but does not read Japanese, all terms, laws, book titles, and names of associations have been translated into English. Japanese personal names are given in the Japanese manner, surname followed by given name. A full list of cabinets and of ministers and vice-ministers of MITI for the period 1925 to 1975 is presented in Appendix A. Some readers may also have difficulties in distinguishing among the numerous names of Japanese people that occur in this book. Nakamura, Nagamura, Nakayama, and Nagayama are all quite distinctive names when written in Japanese, but in English they tend to blur. I do not apologize for this. Too many studies of bureaucracies and state policies read as if they were dealing with disembodied abstractions with little reference to the way things actually happened. This book is in part about working bureaucrats, and their names naturally occur often.

Numerous individuals and organizations have helped me with this study. In Japan my primary debts are to Professors Masumi Junnosuke and Akagi Suruki of Tokyo Metropolitan University, who have guided me to materials, discussed the subject with me extensively, and indicated which topics were of greater and lesser significance. Yokokawa Hiroshi of MITI studied at Berkeley during the year 1978–79 and made many important contributions to my seminar on Japanese politics. In obtaining the sometimes fugitive materials on MITI's past, I have received invaluable assistance from Yutani Eiji of the East

Asiatic Library, University of California, Berkeley, and Murata Shirō of the Murata Bookstore, Takaban 3–9–8, Meguro-ku, Tokyo. The Center for Japanese studies of the Institute of East Asian Studies, University of California, Berkeley, has supported my research with funds, a travel grant to Japan, and a superb collegial setting in which to try out some of my ideas. Since beginning this study in 1972, I have had the research assistance of several graduate students at Berkeley, including Fujimoto Tetsuya, Yasuda Ryūji, Kawamoto Chizuko, Gotoda Teruo, Mikumo Akiko, Matsumoto Yoko, and Chang Dal-joong. My thanks also to Pauline D. Fox of Palm Springs, California, for her eight years of clipping the *Los Angeles Times* for me.

My greatest debt is to Sheila K. Johnson for her professional editing of my prose and her typing of the entire manuscript.

Despite all the generous assistance I have received, I remain responsible for all matters of fact or interpretation in this analysis of MITI and the Shōwa era in Japan.

Berkeley   C.J.
December 1980

CONTENTS

TABLES

ABBREVIATIONS

AML	Antimonopoly Law
BOT	Board of Trade
Butsudō	Materials Mobilization Plans
CPB	Cabinet Planning Board
EDA	Economic Deliberation Agency
EPA	Economic Planning Agency
ESB	Economic Stabilization Board
FILP	Fiscal Investment and Loan Plan
FTC	Fair Trade Commission
GATT	General Agreement on Tariffs and Trade
GNP	Gross National Product
IMF	International Monetary Fund
ITB	International Trade Bureau
JDB	Japan Development Bank
JETRO	Japan External Trade Organization
Keidanren	Federation of Economic Organizations
LDP	Liberal Democratic Party
MAC	Ministry of Agriculture and Commerce
MCI	Ministry of Commerce and Industry
MITI	Ministry of International Trade and Industry
MM	Ministry of Munitions
MSEA	Medium and Smaller Enterprises Agency

NREA	Natural Resources and Energy Agency
OECD	Organization for Economic Cooperation and Development
RFB	Reconstruction Finance Bank
SCAP	Supreme Commander for the Allied Powers
SMRR	South Manchurian Railroad
TIRB	Temporary Industrial Rationality Bureau
TMCB	Temporary Materials Coordination Bureau

MITI AND THE JAPANESE MIRACLE

ONE

The Japanese "Miracle"

B Y COMMON agreement among the Japanese, the "miracle" first appeared to them during 1962. In its issues of September 1 and 8, 1962, the *Economist* of London published a long two-part essay entitled "Consider Japan," which it later brought out as a book that was promptly translated and published in Tokyo as *Odorokubeki Nihon* (Amazing Japan). Up to this time most Japanese simply did not believe the rate of economic growth they were achieving—a rate unprecedented in Japanese history—and their pundits and economists were writing cautionary articles about how the boom would fail, about the crises to come, and about the irrationality of government policy.[1] Yet where the Japanese had been seeing irresponsible budgets, "overloans," and tremendous domestic needs, the *Economist* saw expansion of demand, high productivity, comparatively serene labor relations, and a very high rate of savings. Thus began the praise, domestic and foreign, of the postwar Japanese economy—and the search for the cause of the "miracle."

First, some details on the miracle itself. Table 1 presents indices of industrial production for the entire period of this study, 1925 to 1975, with 1975 as 100. It reveals several interesting things. The miracle was actually only beginning in 1962, when production was just a third of what it would be by 1975. Fully half of Japan's amazing economic strength was to be manifested after 1966. The table also shows clearly the "recessions" of 1954, 1965, and 1974 that spurred the government to new and even more creative economic initiatives; and it demonstrates the ability of the Japanese economy to come back even more strongly from these periods of adversity. Intersectoral shifts are also recorded: the decline of mining as coal gave way to oil and the move-

TABLE 1

Indices of Japanese Mining and Manufacturing Production, 1926–1978

(1975 = 100)

Year	All industry	Public utilities	Mining and manu- facturing	Mining	All manu- facturing	Manufacturing industries										
						Iron and steel	Non- ferrous metals	Metal finished goods	Ma- chinery	Ceramics and cement	Chem- icals	Petro- leum and coal products	Pulp and paper	Textiles	Wood and wood products	Food
1926		2.5		54.5		1.5	4.0				1.5	0.7	4.9	17.4		
1927		2.8		59.7		1.7	4.1				1.7	0.8	5.3	18.8		
1928		3.3		62.0		2.0	4.6				1.8	1.0	5.8	18.1		
1929		3.6		63.2		2.2	4.6				2.2	1.0	6.4	18.9		
1930	5.5	3.9	5.8	62.0	5.3	2.1	4.8		1.4	8.4	2.5	1.0	5.5	21.8	15.8	21.0
1931	5.0	4.0	5.2	58.8	4.7	1.8	4.4		1.1	8.5	2.6	1.1	5.3	23.0	15.2	19.0
1932	5.3	4.3	5.5	60.0	5.0	2.3	4.9		1.0	9.2	3.2	1.2	5.3	24.9	16.0	20.8
1933	6.4	4.9	6.7	68.6	6.1	3.1	5.7		1.4	10.3	3.7	1.4	5.8	28.6	18.8	22.3
1934	6.9	5.3	7.2	75.1	6.5	3.7	5.6		1.4	10.0	4.3	1.7	5.4	31.5	24.0	22.5
1935	7.3	6.0	7.6	81.0	6.9	4.4	6.7		1.4	11.6	5.2	1.8	5.9	33.4	26.4	22.5
1936	8.2	6.5	8.6	89.6	7.8	4.9	7.4		1.7	12.0	6.2	2.1	7.0	35.8	27.6	23.0
1937	9.6	7.1	10.0	97.5	9.2	5.7	8.7		2.3	12.7	7.1	2.5	8.0	40.8	27.9	25.2
1938	9.9	7.7	10.3	103.8	9.4	6.5	9.1		2.5	13.5	8.1	2.7	7.2	33.6	27.5	25.5
1939	10.9	8.1	11.4	108.8	10.5	7.2	10.3		3.1	14.2	8.6	3.2	8.3	33.6	32.2	26.1
1940	11.4	8.3	12.0	116.7	11.0	7.3	10.1		3.8	14.7	8.5	3.4	8.3	30.4	26.8	22.7
1941	11.8	9.1	12.4	117.1	11.3	7.5	9.6		4.4	13.1	8.5	4.0	8.5	24.6	33.5	19.7
1942	11.5	9.1	12.0	114.4	11.0	7.9	10.9		4.5	10.8	7.1	4.0	6.7	19.5	31.7	17.5
1943	11.7	9.2	12.1	115.5	11.1	8.9	13.3		5.0	9.6	6.1	4.0	5.7	12.7	28.0	14.5
1944	11.9	9.0	12.4	105.1	11.4	8.3	14.7		5.8	7.5	5.7	3.2	3.3	6.8	24.8	11.9
1945	5.2	5.4	5.3	55.5	4.8	2.9	5.5		2.5	2.9	2.3	0.9	1.6	2.6	14.8	7.9
1946	2.3	6.9	2.2	40.9	1.8	1.0	2.9		0.8	3.1	1.4	0.4	1.7	4.3	22.7	7.0
1947	2.9	7.8	2.7	54.0	2.3	1.3	4.0		0.9	3.8	1.9	0.5	2.4	5.8	29.9	6.3
1948	3.8	8.5	3.6	66.2	3.0	2.1	5.5		1.4	5.8	2.5	0.8	3.5	6.6	34.7	7.7

1949	4.8	9.6	4.6	75.7	4.0	3.7	6.3		1.7	7.6	3.5	0.9	4.9	8.9	34.8	11.7
1950	5.9	10.3	5.7	80.0	5.1	5.1	7.3		1.8	9.0	4.7	1.7	6.7	12.6	36.5	13.1
1951	8.0	11.0	7.8	91.4	7.1	6.9	8.8		2.9	12.5	6.3	2.8	9.1	17.9	54.7	16.8
1952	8.6	11.9	8.4	94.4	7.7	7.1	9.3		3.0	13.0	6.9	3.6	10.4	20.3	58.2	17.2
1953	10.4	12.7	10.2	101.2	9.5	8.4	9.9		3.8	15.4	8.6	4.6	13.3	24.4	55.7	26.3
1954	11.2	13.5	11.1	97.5	10.4	8.8	11.5		4.3	17.5	9.8	5.4	14.5	26.5	54.6	28.5
1955	12.1	14.5	11.9	98.0	11.3	9.8	12.2		4.3	17.7	11.3	6.2	16.6	29.6	54.4	30.3
1956	14.9	16.7	14.6	108.3	13.9	12.0	14.7		6.2	21.5	13.6	8.0	19.2	35.2	60.8	32.0
1957	17.3	18.6	17.3	119.3	16.5	13.6	16.4		8.7	25.3	16.0	9.6	21.7	38.9	64.1	30.7
1958	17.4	19.7	17.3	115.7	16.6	12.8	16.0	15.6	9.3	23.9	16.0	10.0	21.3	34.8	61.8	35.6
1959	20.9	22.6	20.8	114.6	20.1	17.0	21.0	19.2	12.0	28.3	18.5	12.4	27.9	40.6	65.9	37.7
1960	26.0	26.5	25.9	125.2	25.3	22.4	27.8	24.4	16.5	25.7	22.3	15.8	33.6	47.9	73.2	39.9
1961	31.0	30.8	31.0	134.0	30.4	28.3	33.3	28.8	21.4	41.5	25.5	19.0	40.5	51.7	77.5	43.1
1962	33.5	32.9	33.6	137.0	32.9	28.3	32.5	30.3	24.0	45.3	29.2	21.4	43.4	54.5	79.3	46.6
1963	37.3	36.0	37.4	135.9	36.7	31.9	37.2	34.0	26.5	48.1	32.2	25.6	48.0	58.6	83.8	57.8
1964	43.2	40.6	43.3	137.1	42.6	39.7	45.6	39.6	32.3	55.5	36.6	30.3	54.5	64.8	88.9	62.7
1965	44.9	43.3	44.9	135.2	44.3	40.8	45.3	40.5	32.8	57.1	40.1	34.8	55.7	69.4	90.0	66.7
1966	50.7	47.6	50.8	143.1	50.2	47.2	51.0	48.0	38.1	62.2	45.3	40.0	62.5	76.4	95.4	73.1
1967	60.5	54.0	60.7	141.0	60.2	61.1	61.6	58.6	49.6	72.8	53.0	48.1	69.6	83.3	102.5	76.8
1968	69.7	59.6	70.1	142.1	69.6	68.4	74.3	71.0	61.5	81.4	62.6	56.9	76.9	88.4	107.0	78.7
1969	80.7	67.0	81.3	142.9	80.9	82.6	86.6	84.0	74.8	90.3	73.7	67.9	86.6	97.0	113.9	83.6
1970	91.8	75.9	92.5	139.2	92.2	94.2	93.8	96.9	87.7	101.0	86.8	79.8	98.2	105.2	118.7	89.9
1971	94.3	80.6	94.9	131.6	94.6	91.2	95.7	100.1	89.8	102.6	91.6	87.4	100.6	109.4	117.1	92.6
1972	101.1	87.4	101.8	121.9	101.6	98.7	108.4	111.0	87.3	109.5	97.2	91.5	106.7	110.8	120.7	97.8
1973	116.2	97.4	117.0	112.8	117.0	118.8	128.6	133.4	117.4	126.5	110.2	106.6	119.3	118.5	122.1	98.6
1974	111.7	97.3	112.3	105.8	112.4	116.9	112.6	123.0	116.2	117.0	109.9	104.4	113.7	106.1	109.1	97.5
1975	100.0	100.0	100.0	100.0	100.0	100.0	100.0	100.0	100.0	100.0	100.0	100.0	100.0	100.0	100.0	100.0
1976	111.0	108.5	111.1	100.0	111.2	109.5	119.3	116.8	113.7	110.4	111.5	102.7	113.3	108.4	106.8	101.1
1977	115.6	113.7	115.7	103.1	115.7	108.1	125.0	124.9	121.3	115.2	117.2	104.7	115.3	106.7	104.4	104.6
1978	122.7	119.9	122.8	105.9	123.0	110.1	135.0	134.9	131.5	121.0	131.0	104.0	120.8	107.7	107.0	106.1

SOURCE: Mainichi Shimbun Sha, ed., *Shōwa shi jiten* (Dictionary of Shōwa History), Tokyo, 1980, p. 457.

ment from textiles to machinery and finished metal products, a movement the Japanese call heavy and chemical industrialization (*jūkagaku
kōgyōka*).

If we use a slightly different base line—for example, if we take
1951–53 to be 100—then the index of gross national product for 1934–
36 is 90; for 1961–63, 248; and for 1971–73, 664; and the index of manufacturing production for 1934–36 is 87; for 1961–63, 400; and for 1971–
73, 1,350. Over the whole postwar era, 1946 to 1976, the Japanese
economy increased 55-fold.[2] By the end of our period Japan accounted
for about 10 percent of the world's economic activity though occupying only 0.3 percent of the world's surface and supporting about 3
percent of the world's population. Regardless of whether or not one
wants to call this achievement a "miracle," it is certainly a development worth exploring.

Many voyagers have navigated these waters before me, and a survey of their soundings is a necessary introduction to this study and to
my particular point of view. The task of explaining Japanese economic
growth—and its repeated renewals after one or another set of temporary advantages had been exhausted or removed—is not easy, as the
frequent use of the term "miracle" suggests; and the term cannot be
isolated and applied only to the high-speed growth that began in 1955.
As early as 1937 a much younger Prof. Arisawa Hiromi (b. 1896), one of
the people who must be included on any list of the two or three
dozen leading formulators of postwar industrial policy, used the
phrase "Japanese miracle" to describe the increase of 81.5 percent in
Japanese industrial output from 1931 to 1934.[3] Today we know why
that particular miracle occurred: it resulted from the reflationary deficit financing of Finance Minister Takahashi Korekiyo, who at 81 was
assassinated by young military officers on the morning of February
26, 1936, for trying to apply the brakes to the process he had started.

This earlier miracle is nonetheless problematic for scholars because
of what Charles Kindleberger refers to as "the riddle" of how Japan
"produced Keynesian policies as early as 1932 without a Keynes."[4]
Some Japanese have not been overly exercised by this riddle; they
have simply settled for calling Takahashi the "Keynes of Japan."[5] As I
hope to make clear in this book, this kind of sleight of hand will not
do; there was more to state intervention in the thirties than Keynes-
ianism, and Arisawa and his colleagues in the government learned
lessons in their formative years that are quite different from those that
make up what has come to be known in the West as mainstream governmental fiscal policy.

Kindleberger's "riddle" does serve to draw attention to the projectionists, one major category among modern explorers of the Japanese economic miracle. These are writers who project onto the Japanese case Western—chiefly Anglo-American—concepts, problems, and norms of economic behavior. Whatever the value of such studies for the countries in which they were written, they need not detain us long here. This type of work is not so much aimed at explaining the Japanese case (although it may abstract a few principles of Japanese political economy) as it is at revealing home-country failings in light of Japan's achievements, or at issuing warnings about the possible effects of Japan's growth on other parts of the world. Even the *Economist's* brilliant little tract of 1962 might better have been called *Consider Britain in Light of What the Japanese Are Doing*, which was in any case its true purpose. Successors to the *Economist* include Ralph Hewins, *The Japanese Miracle Men* (1967), P. B. Stone, *Japan Surges Ahead: The Story of an Economic Miracle* (1969), Robert Guillain, *The Japanese Challenge* (1970), Herman Kahn, *The Emerging Japanese Superstate* (1970), and Hakan Hedberg, *Japan's Revenge* (1972). Perhaps the most prominent work in this genre, because it is so clearly hortatory about what Americans might learn from Japan rather than analytical about what has caused the phenomenal Japanese growth, is Ezra Vogel's *Japan as Number One: Lessons for Americans* (1979). My study does not follow these earlier works in advocating the adoption of Japanese institutions outside of Japan. It does, however, try to lay out in their full complexity some of the main Japanese institutions in the economic field so that those who are interested in adopting them will have an idea of what they are buying in terms of the Japanese system's consequences—intended, unintended, and even unwanted.

A second and entirely different set of explanations of the Japanese miracle belongs to the socioeconomic school, or what I have sometimes called the "anything-but-politics" approach to "miracle" research. This broad school includes four major types of analysis that often overlap with each other but that are clearly isolable for purposes of identification, although they rarely appear in pure form. These are the "national character–basic values–consensus" analysis favored by humanists in general and the anthropologically oriented in particular; the "no-miracle-occurred" analysis, chiefly the work of economists; the "unique-structural-features" analysis promoted by students of labor relations, the savings ratio, corporate management, the banking system, the welfare system, general trading corporations, and other institutions of modern Japan; and the various forms of the "free-ride" analysis, that is, the approach that stresses Japan's real but transitory advantages in launching high-speed growth in the postwar world.

Before proceeding to sketch the qualities of these types of analysis, let me say that to a certain extent I can agree with all of them. My interest is not in disputing the facts that they have revealed nor in questioning their relevance to the miracle. However, I believe it can be shown that many of them should be reduced to more basic categories of analysis, particularly to the effects of state policy, and that they need to be weighed according to standards different from those used in the past, thereby giving greater weight to the state and its industrial policy.

The national-character explanation argues that the economic miracle occurred because the Japanese possess a unique, culturally derived capacity to cooperate with each other. This capacity to cooperate reveals itself in many ways—lower crime rates than in other, less homogeneous societies; subordination of the individual to the group; intense group loyalties and patriotism; and, last but not least, economic performance. The most important contribution of the culture to economic life is said to be Japan's famous "consensus," meaning virtual agreement among government, ruling political party, leaders of industry, and people on the primacy of economic objectives for the society as a whole—and on the means to obtain those objectives. Some of the terms invented to refer to this cultural capability of the Japanese are "rolling consensus,"[6] "private collectivism,"[7] "inbred collectivism,"[8] "spiderless cobweb,"[9] and "Japan, Inc."[10]

My reservations about the value of this explanation are basically that it is overgeneralized and tends to cut off rather than advance serious research. Consensus and group solidarity have been important in Japan's economic growth, but they are less likely to derive from the basic values of the Japanese than from what Ruth Benedict once called Japan's "situational" motivations: late development, lack of resources, the need to trade, balance of payments constraints, and so forth.[11] Positing some "special capacity to cooperate" as an irreducible Japanese cultural trait leads inquiry away from the question of *why* Japanese cooperate when they do (they did not cooperate during almost half of the period under study here), and away from the probability that this cooperation can be, and on occasion has been, quite deliberately engineered by the government and others. David Titus's research into the use of the Imperial institution in prewar Japan to "privatize" rather than to "socialize" societal conflict is one creative way to look at this problem of consensus.[12]

Many instances to be discussed later in this study illustrate how the government has consciously induced cooperation among its clients—with much better results than during the Pacific War, when it sought to control them. In the final analysis it is indeed probable that Japanese basic values are different from those of the Western world, but this needs to be studied, not posited; and explanations of social behavior in terms of basic values should be reserved for the final analysis, that is, for the residue of behavior that cannot be explained in other more economical ways. Actually, the explanation of the Japanese economic miracle in terms of culture was more prevalent a few years ago, when the miracle had occurred only in Japan. Now that it is being duplicated or matched in the Republic of Korea, Taiwan, Hong Kong, and Singapore—and perhaps even in some non–East Asian nations—the cultural explanation has lost much of its original interest.[13]

Exemplars of the "no-miracle-occurred" school of analysis do not literally assert that nothing happened to Japan's economy, but they imply that what did happen was not miraculous but a normal outgrowth of market forces. They come from the realm of professional economic analyses of Japanese growth, and therefore in their own terms are generally impeccable, but they also regularly present extended conclusions that incorporate related matters that their authors have not studied but desperately want to exclude from their equations. Hugh Patrick argues, "I am of the school which interprets Japanese economic performance as due primarily to the actions and efforts of private individuals and enterprises responding to the opportunities provided in quite free markets for commodities and labor. While the government has been supportive and indeed has done much to create the environment for growth, its role has often been exaggerated."[14] But there is a problem, he concedes. "It is disturbing that the macro explanations of Japanese postwar economic performance—in terms of increases in aggregate labor and capital inputs and in their more productive allocation—leave 40 percent plus of output growth and half of labor productivity growth unexplained."[15] If it can be shown that the government's industrial policy made the difference in the rate of investment in certain economically strategic industries (for instance, in developing the production and successful marketing of petrochemicals or automobiles), then perhaps we may say that its role has not been exaggerated. I believe this can be demonstrated and I shall attempt to do so later in this study.

Many Japanese would certainly dispute Patrick's conclusion that the government provided nothing more than the environment for economic growth. Sahashi Shigeru, former vice-minister of MITI (the Ministry of International Trade and Industry), asserts that the government is responsible for the economy as a whole and concludes, "It is an utterly self-centered [businessman's] point of view to think that the government should be concerned with providing only a favorable environment for industries without telling them what to do." [16] There have been occasions when industries or enterprises revolted against what the government told them to do—incidents that are among the most sensational in postwar politics—but they did not, and do not, happen often enough to be routine.

Discussions of the Japanese economy in purely economic terms seem to founder on their assumptions rather than on their analyses. It is assumed, for example, that the Japanese developmental state is the same thing as the American regulatory state. Philip Trezise argues, "In essentials, Japanese politics do not differ from politics in other democracies." [17] But one way they differ is in a budgetary process where appropriations *precede* authorizations and where, "with the single exception of 1972, when a combination of government mishandling and opposition unity led to small reductions in defense spending, the budget has not been amended in the Diet since 1955"; before that there was no pretense that the Diet did anything more than rubber-stamp the bureaucracy's budget. [18]

Another difference between Japan and the United States is to be found in the banking system. Before the war the rate of owned capital of all corporations in Japan was around 66 percent—a rate comparable to the current U.S. rate of 52 percent—but as late as 1972 the Japanese rate of owned capital was around 16 percent, a pattern that has persisted throughout the postwar period. Large enterprises obtain their capital through loans from the city banks, which are in turn over-loaned and therefore utterly dependent on the guarantees of the Bank of Japan, which is itself—after a fierce struggle in the 1950's that the bank lost—essentially an operating arm of the Ministry of Finance. The government therefore has a direct and intimate involvement in the fortunes of the "strategic industries" (the term is standard and widely used, but not in the military sense) that is much greater than a formal or legal comparison between the Japanese and other market systems would indicate. MITI was not just writing advertising copy for itself when in 1974 it publicly introduced the concept of a "plan-oriented market economy system," an attempt to name and analyze what it had been doing for the previous twenty years (the twenty years before that it had spent perfecting the system by trial and error). [19] The plan-oriented market economy system most decidedly includes some differences from "politics in other democracies," one of them being the care and feeding of the economic miracle itself.

The "no-miracle-occurred" school of miracle researchers agrees that Japanese economic growth took place but insists that this was because of the availability of capital, labor, resources, and markets all interacting freely with each other and unconstrained in any meaningful ways. It rejects as contrary to economic logic, and therefore as spurious, all the concepts that the Japanese have invented and employed continuously in discussing and managing their economy—such concepts as "industrial structure," "excessive competition," "coordination of investment," and "public-private cooperation." Most seriously, from a historical point of view, this explanation short-circuits attempts to analyze what difference the government's intervention has actually made by declaring in advance and as a matter of principle that it made no difference. The result is, as John Roberts has put it, that Japan's "'miraculous' emergence as a first-rate economic power in the 1960s has been described exhaustively by Japanese and foreign writers, and yet very little of the literature provides credible explanations of how it was done, or by whom."[20] This study is an attempt to answer these questions.

The third prevalent type of analysis of the Japanese miracle—stressing the influence of unusual Japanese institutions—is by far the most important of the four I have isolated, and the one that has been most thoroughly discussed in Japan and abroad. In its simplest form it asserts that Japan obtained a special economic advantage because of what postwar Japanese employers habitually call their "three sacred treasures"—the "lifetime" employment system, the seniority (*nenkō*) wage system, and enterprise unionism.[21] Amaya Naohiro of MITI, for example, cites these three institutions as the essence of what he terms Japan's *uchiwa* (all in the family) economic system; and in reporting to the Organization for Economic Cooperation and Development's Industry Committee during 1970, the former MITI vice-minister Ōjimi Yoshihisa referred to various "typically Japanese phenomena" that had helped Japan to obtain its high-speed growth—the phenomena again being the three sacred treasures.[22] Because of these institutions, the argument goes, Japan obtains greater labor commitment, loses fewer days to strikes, can innovate more easily, has better quality control, and in general produces more of the right things sooner than its international competitors.

This argument is undoubtedly true, but it has never been clearly formulated and is, at best, simplistic. There are several points to be made. First, the three sacred treasures are not the only "special institutions," and they are certainly not the most sacred. Others include the personal savings system; the distribution system; the "descent from heaven" (*amakudari*) of retired bureaucrats from the ministries into senior management positions in private enterprises; the structure of industrial groupings (*keiretsu*, or the oligopolistic organization of each industry by conglomerates); the "dual economy" (what Clark usefully terms the system of "industrial gradation"[23]) together with the elaborate structure of subcontracting it generates; the tax system; the extremely low degree of influence exercised over companies by shareholders; the hundred-odd "public policy companies" (public corporations of several different forms); and, perhaps most important of all, the government-controlled financial institutions, particularly the Japan Development Bank and the "second," or investment, budget (the Fiscal Investment and Loan Plan).[24]

It is unnecessary here to describe each of these institutions. Most of them are quite familiar even to novice Japan watchers, and others will be analyzed in detail later in this book since they constitute some of the primary tools of the government for influencing and guiding the economy. What needs to be stressed is that they constitute a system— one that no individual or agency ever planned and one that has developed over time as ad hoc responses to, or unintended consequences of, Japan's late development and the progrowth policies of the government. Taken together as a system, they constitute a formidable set of institutions for promoting economic growth (a "GNP machine," in Amaya's metaphor), but taken separately, as they most commonly are, they do not make much sense at all.[25] And this is the primary reservation that one must make about the unique-institutions explanation: it never goes far enough and therefore fails as anything more than a partial explanation.

Let us take one example. As a result of the recognition of the Japanese miracle around the world, some American professors of business administration have begun to recommend to American entrepreneurs that they experiment with one or all of the three sacred treasures. Sometimes Japanese practices, suitably modified, travel well.[26] However, an American businessman who really attempted to institute "lifetime" employment without the backing of the other institutions of the Japanese system would soon find himself bankrupt. Among other things, lifetime employment in Japan is not for life but until the middle or late fifties; and although wage raises are tied to seniority, job security is not: it is those with most seniority who are the first fired during business downturns because they are the most expensive. Lifetime employment also does not apply to the "temporaries," who may spend their entire working lives in that status, and temporaries constitute a much larger proportion of a firm's work force than any American union would tolerate (42 percent of the Toyota Motor Company's work force during the 1960's, for example).[27]

Even if these problems could be taken care of, the American employer still would not have below him the extensive enterprise sector of medium and smaller subcontractors that his Japanese counterpart can squeeze in difficult times. Tomioka calls the subcontractors the "shock absorbers" of the Japanese business cycle—the smaller firms on the receiving end when large firms find they can no longer carry the fixed costs of their labor force and must "shift the strain" (*shiwa-yose*).[28] On the other hand, the American employee would not have Japan's extensive if redundant distribution system to fall back on in case he did get laid off. The distribution system in Japan serves as a vast sponge for the unemployed or underemployed when economic conditions require it. As testimony to the layers of middlemen in Japan, the volume of transactions among Japanese wholesalers in 1968 exceeded the total of retail sales by a ratio of 4.8 to 1, whereas the United States figure was 1.3 to 1.[29] It is not surprising that many knowledgeable Japanese do not want to change the distribution system, despite protests from foreign salesmen who have trouble breaking into it, because it performs other functions for the society than distribution, not the least of which is reducing the tax burden necessary to provide adequate unemployment insurance.

Lifetime employment, Japanese style, offers many advantages from the point of view of economic growth: it provides a strong incentive to the employer to operate at full or close to full capacity; it inhibits a horizontally structured trade union movement; and, in the words of Ohkawa and Rosovsky, it gives the Japanese entrepreneur "a labor force without incentives to oppose technological and organizational progress even of the labor-saving type."[30] But it does not exist in isolation and would not work without the rest of the system of "unique institutions."

The second main point about these special institutions concerns the date of their origins and how they are maintained. It is here that this school of explanations of the miracle sometimes blends imperceptibly with the first school, which says that Japanese culture and the Japanese national character support the economy. Amaya, for example, traces the three sacred treasures to the traditional world of family (*ie*), village (*mura*), and province (*kuni*), which he believes have all been homogenized and reincarnated today within the industrial enterprise.[31] It has to be stated that assertions of this type are a form of propaganda to defend these special institutions from hostile (often foreign) critics. Extensive research by scholars in Japan and abroad has demonstrated that virtually all of the so-called special institutions date from the twentieth century and usually from no earlier than the World War I era.

Lifetime employment, for example, has been traced to several influences, including the efforts during World War I to inhibit the growth of a left-wing social reform movement; the introduction of large numbers of Korean and Taiwanese laborers during the 1920's, which caused Japanese workers to seek job security at all costs; and the wartime munitions companies, which had to guarantee the jobs of their best employees in order to keep them. R. P. Dore, one of the leading authorities on Japanese industrialism, summarizes the state of research on this subject as follows: "Japan's employment system in 1900 was pretty much as market-oriented as Britain's. It was conscious institutional innovation which began to shape the Japanese system in the first two decades of this century, perfected the system of enterprise familism (or what one might call corporate paternalism) in the 1930s, and revamped the system to accommodate the new strength of unions in the late 1940s to produce what is called [by Dore] the 'welfare corporatism' of today."[32]

Nakamura Takafusa finds the roots of a whole range of important institutions in the wartime control era—including the bank-centered keiretsu (industrial groups based on the Designated Financial Organs System of the time) and the subcontracting system, which though it existed before the war was greatly strengthened by the forced mergers of medium and small enterprises with big machinery manufacturers (the so-called *kigyō seibi*, or "enterprise readjustment," movement discussed in Chapter 5).[33]

There are several ways in which the government has influenced the structure of Japan's special institutions. Many of these institutions it created directly in the course of its "industrial rationalization" campaigns of the 1930's or in the prosecution of the Pacific War. When the government did not create them directly, it nonetheless recognized their usefulness for its own purposes and moved to reinforce them. The savings system is an example. It is possible, as many commentators have urged, that the savings of private Japanese households—the highest rate of savings as a share of GNP ever recorded by any market economy in peacetime—is due to the natural frugality of the Japanese. But there are some strong external pressures that encourage the Japanese to save: a comparatively poor social security system; a wage system that includes large lump-sum bonus payments twice a year; a retirement system that cuts a worker's income substantially before he reaches the age of 60; a shortage of new housing and housing land, as well as a premium on university education for one's children, both of which require large outlays; an underdeveloped consumer credit system; a government-run postal savings system with guaranteed competitive interest rates; the lack of a well-developed capital market or other alternatives to personal saving; and a substantial exemption from income taxes for interest earned on savings accounts. The government is quite aware of these incentives to save and of the fact that money placed in the postal savings system goes directly into Ministry of Finance accounts, where it can be reinvested in accordance with government plans. Innate frugality may indeed play a role in this system, but the government has worked hard at engineering that frugality.

The theory of the "free ride," our fourth category of explanations, argues that Japan is the beneficiary of its postwar alliance with the United States, and that this alliance accounts at least for the miraculous part of Japan's rapid economic growth, if not for all of it. There are three ways in which Japan is said to have enjoyed a free ride: a lack of defense expenditures, ready access to its major export market, and relatively cheap transfers of technology.

Although it is true that Japan has not had to devote much of its national income to armaments, this factor cannot have influenced its growth rate significantly. If Japan's overall rate of investment had been very low—as low, for example, as it was in China—then the demands of defense could have had a retarding effect. But in Japan, where capital formation exceeded 30 percent of GNP during high-speed growth, the effect of low defense expenditures was negligible. The cases of South Korea and Taiwan, which have been pursuing the high investment strategy of the Japanese with equal or even more spectacular results, illustrate this point: their very high defense expenditures have had little or no impact on their economic performance.

The case of exports is more important. Japan profited enormously from the open trading system that developed throughout the world after World War II, and Japanese government leaders have repeatedly acknowledged the favorable effects for them of such institutions as the General Agreement on Tariffs and Trade, the International Monetary Fund, and, until 1971, stable exchange rates—all institutions that they had no role in creating. In fact, in their more pessimistic moods MITI leaders have speculated on the historical observation that Japan's great economic achievements came in the relatively open periods of world commerce—from the Meiji Restoration to World War I and from 1945 to 1970—and they have expressed concern that the post-1970's era could look like 1920–45 when seen in historical perspective.[34]

Nonetheless, the important point for our discussion is that Japan's growth did not depend nearly so much on exports as it did on the development of the domestic market (a market half the size of the

United States' in terms of population). Eleanor Hadley notes that although Japan's economy in the early sixties was roughly three times the size of the 1934–36 economy, exports as a proportion of GNP were only about two-thirds what they had been in the mid-1930's.[35] By the late 1960's Japan's exports were only 9.6 percent of GNP, compared for example with Canada's 19.8 percent.[36] From 1953 to 1972 Japan had a consistently lower dependency on exports and imports as a percentage of GNP at constant prices than France, Germany, Italy, Britain, or OECD Europe as a whole. Japan's exports ran at about 11.3 percent of GNP, and its imports at 10.2 percent, whereas the OECD European figures were 21.2 percent and 20.9 percent respectively.[37] There is no question that Japan, as a heavily populated resource-deficient country, has to export in order to pay for its vital imports, but foreign sales were not the main factor driving its economic activity during high-speed growth.

Home demand led Japan's growth for the twenty years after 1955. The demand was there, of course, before 1955, but with the coming to power of the Ishibashi government in December 1956 and Ikeda Hayato's return to the post of minister of finance, Ishibashi and Ikeda launched the policy of "positive finance." Under the slogan "a hundred billion yen tax cut is a hundred billion yen of aid" as the basis for the fiscal 1957 budget, Ikeda opened up domestic demand as it had never been opened before.[38] Balance of payments problems slowed positive finance during the "bottom-of-the-pot" recession (with its trough in June 1958), but the economy responded quickly to government discipline and rebounded in the Iwato Boom (July 1958–December 1961), during which Ikeda became prime minister and launched the Income-doubling Plan. The propelling force of the economy in this and later periods was private corporate investment nurtured by favorable expectations for the longer term that were created by the government; it was not export sales.

Technology transfers—the third alleged "free ride"—were not exactly free, but there can be no question that they were crucial to Japanese economic growth and that the prices paid were slight compared with what such technology would cost today, if it could be bought at any price. Japan imported virtually all of the technology for its basic and high-growth industries, and it imported the greater proportion of this technology from the United States. But it is trivial and misleading to refer to this movement of patent rights, technology, and know-how across the Pacific and from Europe as a "free ride." It was, in fact, the heart of the matter.

The importation of technology was one of the central components of postwar Japanese industrial policy, and to raise the subject is to turn the discussion to MITI and the Japanese government's role. Before the capital liberalization of the late 1960's and 1970's, no technology entered the country without MITI's approval; no joint venture was ever agreed to without MITI's scrutiny and frequent alteration of the terms; no patent rights were ever bought without MITI's pressuring the seller to lower the royalties or to make other changes advantageous to Japanese industry as a whole; and no program for the importation of foreign technology was ever approved until MITI and its various advisory committees had agreed that the time was right and that the industry involved was scheduled for "nurturing" (*ikusei*).

From the enactment of the Foreign Capital Law in 1950 (it remained on the books for the next thirty years), the government was in charge of technology transfers. What it did and how it did it was not a matter of a "free ride" but of an extremely complex process of public-private interaction that has come to be known as "industrial policy." MITI is the primary Japanese government agency charged with the formulation and execution of industrial policy.

Thus I come to the final school, in which I place myself, the school that stresses the role of the developmental state in the economic miracle. Although the rest of this book is devoted to this subject—and to some of the nonmiracles produced by the developmental state in its quest for the miracle—several further points are needed by way of introduction. What do I mean by the developmental state? This is not really a hard question, but it always seems to raise difficulties in the Anglo-American countries, where the existence of the developmental state in any form other than the communist state has largely been forgotten or ignored as a result of the years of disputation with Marxist-Leninists. Japan's political economy can be located precisely in the line of descent from the German Historical School—sometimes labeled "economic nationalism," *Handelspolitik*, or neomercantilism; but this school is not exactly in the mainstream of economic thought in the English-speaking countries. Japan is therefore always being studied as a "variant" of something other than what it is, and so a necessary prelude to any discussion of the developmental state must be the clarification of what it is not.

The issue is not one of state intervention in the economy. All states intervene in their economies for various reasons, among which are protecting national security (the "military-industrial complex"), insuring industrial safety, providing consumer protection, aiding the weak, promoting fairness in market transactions, preventing monopolization and private control in free enterprise systems, securing the public's interest in natural monopolies, achieving economies of scale, preventing excessive competition, protecting and rearing industries, distributing vital resources, protecting the environment, guaranteeing employment, and so forth. The question is how the government intervenes and for what purposes. This is one of the critical issues in twentieth-century politics, and one that has become more acute as the century has progressed. As Louis Mulkern, an old hand in the Japanese banking world, has said, "I would suggest that there could be no more devastating weakness for any major nation in the 1980s than the inability to define the role of government in the economy."[39] The particular Japanese definition of this role and the relationship between that role and the economic miracle are at once major components and primary causes of the resurgent interest in "political economy" in the late twentieth century.

Nowhere is the prevalent and peculiarly Western preference for binary modes of thought more apparent than in the field of political economy. In modern times Weber began the practice with his distinction between a "market economy" (*Verkehrwirtschaft*) and a "planned economy" (*Planwirtschaft*). Some recent analogues are Dahrendorf's distinction between "market rationality" and "plan rationality," Dore's distinction between "market-oriented systems" and "organization-oriented systems," and Kelly's distinction between a "rule-governed state" (*nomocratic*) and a "purpose-governed state" (*telocratic*).[40] I shall make use of several of these distinctions later, but first I must stress that for purposes of the present discussion the right-hand component of these pairs is *not* the Soviet-type command economy. Economies of the Soviet type are not *plan rational* but *plan ideological*. In the Soviet Union and its dependencies and emulators, state ownership of the means of production, state planning, and bureaucratic goal-setting are not rational means to a developmental goal (even if they may once have been); they are fundamental values in themselves, not to be challenged by evidence of either inefficiency or ineffectiveness. In the sense I am using the term here, Japan is plan rational, and the command economies are not; in fact, the history of Japan since 1925 offers numerous illustrations of why the command economy is not plan rational, a lesson the Japanese learned well.

At the most basic level the distinction between market and plan refers to differing conceptions of the functions of the state in economic affairs. The state as an institution is as old as organized human society. Until approximately the nineteenth century, states everywhere performed more or less the same functions that make large-scale social organization possible but that individuals or families or villages cannot perform for themselves. These functions included defense, road building, water conservancy, the minting of coins, and the administration of justice. Following the industrial revolution, the state began to take on new functions. In those states that were the first to industrialize, the state itself had little to do with the new forms of economic activity but towards the end of the nineteenth century the state took on *regulatory* functions in the interest of maintaining competition, consumer protection, and so forth. As Henry Jacoby puts it, "Once capitalism transformed the traditional way of life, factors such as the effectiveness of competition, freedom of movement, and the absence of any system of social security compelled the state to assume responsibility for the protection and welfare of the individual. Because each man was responsible for himself, and because that individualism became a social principle, the state remained as almost the only regulatory authority."[41]

In states that were late to industrialize, the state itself led the industrialization drive, that is, it took on *developmental* functions. These two differing orientations toward private economic activities, the regulatory orientation and the developmental orientation, produced two different kinds of government-business relationships. The United States is a good example of a state in which the regulatory orientation predominates, whereas Japan is a good example of a state in which the developmental orientation predominates. A regulatory, or market-rational, state concerns itself with the forms and procedures—the rules, if you will—of economic competition, but it does not concern itself with substantive matters. For example, the United States government has many regulations concerning the antitrust implications of the size of firms, but it does not concern itself with what industries ought to exist and what industries are no longer needed. The developmental, or plan-rational, state, by contrast, has as its dominant feature precisely the setting of such substantive social and economic goals.

Another way to make this distinction is to consider a state's priorities in economic policy. In the plan-rational state, the government will give greatest precedence to industrial policy, that is, to a concern with the structure of domestic industry and with promoting the structure that enhances the nation's international competitiveness. The very existence of an industrial policy implies a strategic, or goal-oriented, approach to the economy. On the other hand, the market-rational state usually will not even have an industrial policy (or, at any rate, will not recognize it as such). Instead, both its domestic and foreign economic policy, including its trade policy, will stress rules and reciprocal concessions (although perhaps influenced by some goals that are not industrially specific, goals such as price stability or full employment). Its trade policy will normally be subordinate to general foreign policy, being used more often to cement political relationships than to obtain strictly economic advantages.

These various distinctions are useful because they draw our attention to Japan's emergence, following the Meiji Restoration of 1868, as a developmental, plan-rational state whose economic orientation was keyed to industrial policy. By contrast, the United States from about the same period took the regulatory, market-rational path keyed to foreign policy. In modern times Japan has always put emphasis on an overarching, nationally supported goal for its economy rather than on the particular procedures that are to govern economic activity. The Meiji-era goal was the famous *fukoku-kyōhei* (rich country, strong military) of the late nineteenth and early twentieth centuries. This was followed during the 1930's and 1940's by the goals of depression recovery, war preparation, war production, and postwar recovery. From about 1955, and explicitly since the Income-doubling Plan of 1960, the goal has been high-speed growth, sometimes expressed as "overtake Europe and America" (*Ōbei ni oikose*). Amaya lists the goals of the past century in detail: *shokusan kōgyō* (increase industrial production), *fukoku-kyōhei* (rich country, strong military), *seisanryoku kakujū* (expand productive capacity), *yushutsu shinkō* (promote exports), *kanzen koyō* (full employment), and *kōdo seichō* (high-speed growth).[42] Only during the 1970's did Japan begin to shift to a somewhat regulatory, foreign-policy orientation, just as America began to show early signs of a new developmental, industrial-policy orientation. But the Japanese system remains plan rational, and the American system is still basically market rational.[43]

This can be seen most clearly by looking at the differences between the two systems in terms of economic and political decision-making. In Japan the developmental, strategic quality of economic policy is reflected within the government in the high position of the so-called economic bureaucrats, that is, the officials of the ministries of Finance, International Trade and Industry, Agriculture and Forestry, Construction, and Transportation, plus the Economic Planning Agency. These official agencies attract the most talented graduates of the best universities in the country, and the positions of higher-level officials in these ministries have been and still are the most prestigious in the society. Although it is influenced by pressure groups and political claimants, the elite bureaucracy of Japan makes most major decisions, drafts virtually all legislation, controls the national budget, and is the source of all major policy innovations in the system. Equally important, upon their retirement, which is usually between the ages of 50 and 55 in Japan, these bureaucrats move from government to powerful positions in private enterprise, banking, the political world, and the numerous public corporations—a direction of elite mobility that is directly opposite to that which prevails in the United States.[44] The existence of a powerful, talented, and prestige-laden economic bureaucracy is a natural corollary of plan rationality.

In market-rational systems such as the United States, public service does not normally attract the most capable talent, and national decision-making is dominated by elected members of the professional class, who are usually lawyers, rather than by the bureaucracy. The movement of elites is not from government to the private sector but vice versa, usually through political appointment, which is much more extensive than in Japan. The real equivalent of the Japanese Ministry of International Trade and Industry in the United States is not the Department of Commerce but the Department of Defense, which by its very nature and functions shares MITI's strategic, goal-oriented outlook. In fact, the pejorative connotations in the United States of terms such as "Japan, Inc." are similar to those surrounding the domestic expression "military-industrial complex" referring to a close working relationship between government and business to solve problems of national defense. (Not to be outdone, some Japanese have taken to calling the Japanese government-business relationship a "bureaucratic-industrial complex.")[45] American economic decisions are made most often in Congress, which also controls the budget, and these decisions reflect the market-rational emphasis on procedures rather than outcomes. During the 1970's Americans began to experiment with industrial policy bureaucracies such as the Department of Energy, but they are still rather wary of such organizations, whose prestige remains low.

Another way to highlight the differences between plan rationality and market rationality is to look at some of the trade-offs involved in each approach. First, the most important evaluative standard in market rationality is "efficiency." But in plan rationality this takes lower precedence than "effectiveness." Both Americans and Japanese tend to get the meanings of efficiency and effectiveness mixed up. Americans often and understandably criticize their official bureaucracy for its inefficiency, failing to note that efficiency is not a good evaluative standard for bureaucracy. Effectiveness is the proper standard of evaluation of goal-oriented strategic activities.[46] On the other hand, Japanese continue to tolerate their wildly inefficient and even inappropriate agricultural structure at least in part because it is mildly effective: it provides food that does not have to be imported.

Second, both types of systems are concerned with "externalities," or what Milton Friedman has called "neighborhood effects"—an example would be the unpriced social costs of production such as pollution. In this instance, however, the plan-rational system has much greater difficulty than the market-rational system in identifying and shifting its sights to respond to effects external to the national goal. The position of the plan-rational system is like that of a military organization: a general is judged by whether he wins or loses. It would be good if he would also employ an economy of violence (be efficient), but that is not as important as results. Accordingly, Japan persisted with high-speed industrial growth long after the evidence of very serious environmental damage had become common knowledge. On the other hand, when the plan-rational system finally shifts its goals to give priority to a problem such as industrial pollution, it will commonly be more effective than the market-rational system, as can be seen in the comparison between the Japanese and American handling of pollution in the 1970's.

Third, the plan-rational system depends upon the existence of a widely agreed upon set of overarching goals for the society, such as high-speed growth. When such a consensus exists, the plan-rational system will outperform the market-rational system on the same benchmark, such as growth of GNP, as long as growth of GNP is the goal of the plan-rational system. But when a consensus does not exist, when there is confusion or conflict over the overarching goal in a plan-rational economy, it will appear to be quite adrift, incapable of coming to grips with basic problems and unable to place responsibility for failures. Japan has experienced this kind of drift when unexpected developments suddenly upset its consensus, such as during the "Nixon shocks" of 1971, or after the oil shock of 1973. Generally speaking, the great strength of the plan-rational system lies in its effectiveness in dealing with routine problems, whereas the great strength of the market-rational system lies in its effectiveness in dealing with critical problems. In the latter case, the emphasis on rules, procedures, and executive responsibility helps to promote action when problems of an unfamiliar or unknown magnitude arise.

Fourth, since decision-making is centered in different bodies in the two systems—in an elite bureaucracy in one and in a parliamentary assembly in the other—the process of policy change will be manifested in quite different ways. In the plan-rational system, change will be marked by internal bureaucratic disputes, factional infighting, and conflict among ministries. In the market-rational system, change will be marked by strenuous parliamentary contests over new legislation and by election battles. For example, the shift in Japan during the late 1960's and throughout the 1970's from protectionism to liberalization was most clearly signaled by factional infighting within MITI between the "domestic faction" and the "international faction." The surest sign that the Japanese government was moving in a more open, free-trade direction was precisely the fact that the key ministry in this sector came to be dominated by internationalistic bureaucrats. Americans are sometimes confused by Japanese economic policy because they pay too much attention to what politicians say and because they do not know much about the bureaucracy, whereas Japanese have on occasion given too much weight to the statements of American bureaucrats and have not paid enough attention to Congressmen and their extensive staffs.

Looked at historically, modern Japan began in 1868 to be plan rational and developmental. After about a decade and a half of experimentation with direct state operation of economic enterprises, it discovered the most obvious pitfalls of plan rationality: corruption, bureaucratism, and ineffective monopolies. Japan was and remained plan rational, but it had no ideological commitment to state ownership of the economy. Its main criterion was the rational one of effectiveness in meeting the goals of development. Thus, Meiji Japan began to shift away from state entrepreneurship to collaboration with privately owned enterprises, favoring those enterprises that were capable of rapidly adopting new technologies and that were committed to the national goals of economic development and military strength. From this shift developed the collaborative relationship between the government and big business in Japan. In the prewar era this collaboration took the form of close governmental ties to the zaibatsu (privately owned industrial empires). The government induced the zaibatsu to go into areas where it felt development was needed. For their part the zaibatsu pioneered the commercialization of modern technologies in Japan, and they achieved economies of scale in manufacturing and banking that were on a par with those of the rest of the industrial world. There were many important results of this collaboration, including the development of a marked dualism between large advanced enterprises and small backward enterprises. But perhaps the most important result was the introduction of a needed measure of competition into the plan-rational system.

In the postwar world, the reforms of the occupation era helped modernize the zaibatsu enterprises, freeing them of their earlier family domination. The reforms also increased the number of enterprises, promoted the development of the labor movement, and rectified the grievances of the farmers under the old order, but the system remained plan rational: given the need for economic recovery from the war and independence from foreign aid, it could not very well have been otherwise. Most of the ideas for economic growth came from the bureaucracy, and the business community reacted with an attitude of what one scholar has called "responsive dependence." [47] The government did not normally give direct orders to businesses, but those businesses that listened to the signals coming from the government and then responded were favored with easy access to capital, tax breaks, and approval of their plans to import foreign technology or establish joint ventures. But a firm did not have to respond to the government. The business literature of Japan is filled with descriptions of the very interesting cases of big firms that succeeded without strong governmental ties (for example, Sony and Honda), but there are not many to describe.

Observers coming from market-rational systems often misunderstand the plan-rational system because they fail to appreciate that it has a political and not an economic basis. During the 1960's, for example, when it became fashionable to call the Japanese "economic animals," the most knowledgeable foreign analysts avoided the term because, in Henderson's words, there was "no doubt that Japan's center of gravity is in the polity not the economy—a source of puzzlement for Japan's numerous economic determinists of various Marxist stripe in academia and opposition politics." [48] One did not have to be an economic determinist or a Marxist to make this error; it was ubiquitous in English-language writing on Japan.

J. P. Nettl's comment on Marx is relevant to this point: "The notion that 'the modern state power is merely a committee which manages the common business of the bourgeoisie' is one of the historically least adequate generalizations that Marx ever made." [49] It is not merely historically inadequate; it obscures the fact that in the developmental state economic interests are explicitly subordinated to political objectives. The very idea of the developmental state originated in the situational nationalism of the late industrializers, and the goals of the developmental state were invariably derived from comparisons with external reference economies. The political motives of the developmental state are highlighted by Daniel Bell's observation—based on Adam Smith—that there would be little stimulus to increase production above necessities or needs if people were ruled by economic motives alone. [50] "The need for economic growth in a developing country has few if any economic springs. It arises from a desire to assume full human status by taking part in an industrial civilization, participation in which *alone* enables a nation or an individual to compel others to treat it as an equal. Inability to take part in it makes a nation militarily powerless against its neighbors, administratively unable to control its own citizens, and culturally incapable of speaking the international language." [51]

All of these motives influenced Meiji Japan, and there were others that were peculiar to Japan. Among these was one deriving from the treaties Japan was forced to conclude after its first contacts with Western imperialism in the nineteenth century: Japan did not obtain tariff autonomy until 1911. This meant that Japan was not able to aid its developing industries by the protective duties and other practices recommended by the market-oriented theories of the time, and the Meiji government consequently concluded that it had to take a direct hand in economic development if Japan was ever to achieve economic independence. [52]

A second special problem for Japan lasted until the late 1960's, when it temporarily disappeared only to return after the oil crisis of the 1970's; this was a shortage in its international balance of payments and the resultant need for the government to manage this most implacable of ceilings in a country with extremely few natural resources. As early as the 1880's, Tiedemann writes that in order to keep foreign payments in balance with customs receipts, "all agencies were required to prepare a foreign exchange budget as well as their normal yen budget." [53] Such a foreign exchange budget came into being again in 1937 and lasted in one form or another until 1964, when trade liberalization was carried out. In the era of high-speed growth, control of the foreign exchange budget meant control of the entire economy. It was MITI that exercised this controlling power, and foreign currency allocations were to become its decisive tool for implementing industrial policy.

The political nature of plan rationality can be highlighted in still other ways. MITI may be an economic bureaucracy, but it is not a bureaucracy of economists. Until the 1970's there were only two Ph.D.'s in economics among the higher career officials of the ministry; the rest had undergraduate degrees in economics or, much more commonly, in public and administrative law. Not until Ueno Kōshichi became vice-minister in June 1957 was modern economic theory even introduced into the ministry's planning processes (Ueno studied economics during a long convalescence from tuberculosis before assuming the vice-ministership). Amaya Naohiro reflects this orientation of the ministry when he contrasts the views of the scholar and of the practitioner and notes that many things that are illogical to the theorist are vital to the practitioner—for instance, the reality of nationalism as an active element in economic affairs. Amaya calls for a "science of the Japanese economy," as distinct from "economics generally," and pleads that some things, perhaps not physics but certainly economics, have national grammars.[54] One further difference between the market-rational state and the plan-rational state is thus that economists dominate economic policy-making in the former while nationalistic political officials dominate it in the latter.

Within the developmental state there is contention for power among many bureaucratic centers, including finance, economic planning, foreign affairs, and so forth. However, the center that exerts the greatest *positive* influence is the one that creates and executes industrial policy. MITI's dominance in this area has led one Japanese commentator to characterize it as the "pilot agency," and a journalist of the *Asahi* who has often been highly critical of MITI nonetheless concedes that MITI is "without doubt the greatest concentration of brain power in Japan."[55] MITI's jurisdiction ranges from the control of bicycle racing to the setting of electric power rates, but its true defining power is its control of industrial policy (*sangyō seisaku*). Although the making and executing of industrial policy is what the developmental state does, industrial policy itself—what it is and how it is done—remains highly controversial.

Industrial policy, according to Robert Ozaki, "is an indigenous Japanese term not to be found in the lexicon of Western economic terminology. A reading through the literature suggests a definition, however: it refers to a complex of those policies concerning protection of domestic industries, development of strategic industries, and adjustment of the economic structure in response to or in anticipation of internal and external changes which are formulated and pursued by MITI in the cause of the national interest, as the term 'national interest' is understood by MITI officials."[56] Although this definition is somewhat circular—industrial policy is what MITI says it is—Ozaki makes one important point clear: industrial policy is a reflection of economic nationalism, with nationalism understood to mean giving priority to the interests of one's own nation but not necessarily involving protectionism, trade controls, or economic warfare. Nationalism *may* mean those things, but it is equally possible that free trade will be in the national economic interest during particular periods, as was true of Japan during the 1970's. Industrial policy is, however, a recognition that the global economic system is *never* to be understood in terms of the free competitive model: labor never moves freely between countries, and technology is only slightly more free.

There are two basic components to industrial policy, corresponding to the micro and macro aspects of the economy: the first the Japanese call "industrial rationalization policy" (*sangyō gōrika seisaku*), and the second, "industrial structure policy" (*sangyō kōzō seisaku*). The first has a long history in Japan, starting from the late 1920's, when it was quite imperfectly understood, as we shall see later in this book. MITI's *Industrial Rationalization Whitepaper* (1957) says that industrial rationalization subsumes a theory of economic development in which Japan's "international backwardness" is recognized and in which "contradictions" in the areas of technology, facilities, management, industrial location, and industrial organization are confronted and resolved.

Concretely, according to the *Whitepaper*, industrial rationalization means: (1) the rationalization of enterprises, that is, the adoption of new techniques of production, investment in new equipment and facilities, quality control, cost reduction, adoption of new management techniques, and the perfection of managerial control; (2) the rationalization of the environment of enterprises, including land and water transportation and industrial location; (3) the rationalization of whole industries, meaning the creation of a framework for all enterprises in an industry in which each can compete fairly or in which they can cooperate in a cartellike arrangement of mutual assistance; and (4) the rationalization of the industrial structure itself in order to meet international competitive standards.[57] (The last element of the definition was included before the concept of "industrial structure" had been invented by MITI. After about 1960 it was no longer included in the concept of industrial rationalization.)

The short definition is that industrial rationalization means state policy at the micro level, state intrusion into the detailed operations of individual enterprises with measures intended to improve those operations (or, on occasion, to abolish the enterprise). Nawa Tarō says that in its simplest terms industrial rationalization is the attempt by the state to discover what it is individual enterprises are already doing to produce the greatest benefits for the least cost, and then, in the interest of the nation as a whole, to cause all the enterprises of an industry to adopt these preferred procedures and techniques.[58]

Industrial rationalization in one form or another is an old and familiar movement going back to Frederick W. Taylor's system of "scientific management" of the progressive era in the United States (1890–1920); it exists or has appeared in every industrialized country, although it probably lasted longer and was carried further in Japan than in any other country.[59] Industrial structure policy, on the other hand, is more radical and more controversial. It concerns the proportions of agriculture, mining, manufacturing, and services in the nation's total production; and within manufacturing it concerns the percentages of light and heavy and of labor-intensive and knowledge-intensive industries. The application of the policy comes in the government's attempts to change these proportions in ways it deems advantageous to the nation. Industrial structure policy is based on such standards as income elasticity of demand, comparative costs of production, labor absorptive power, environmental concerns, investment effects on related industries, and export prospects. The heart of the policy is the selection of the strategic industries to be developed or converted to other lines of work.

Robert Gilpin offers a theoretical defense of industrial structure policy in terms of a posited common structural rigidity of the corporate form of organization:

The propensity of corporations is to invest in particular industrial sectors or product lines even though these areas may be declining. That is to say, the sectors are declining as theaters of innovation; they are no longer the leading sectors of industrial society. In response to rising foreign competition and relative decline, the tendency of corporations is to seek protection of their home market or new markets abroad for old products. Behind this structural rigidity is the fact that for any firm, its experience, existing real assets, and know-how dictate a relatively limited range of investment opportunities. Its instinctive reaction, therefore, is to protect what it has. As a result, there may be no powerful interests in the economy favoring a major shift of energy and resources into new industries and economic activities.[60]

Whether this is true or not, MITI certainly thinks it is true and considers that one of its primary duties is precisely the creation of those powerful interests in the economy that favor shifts of energy and resources into new industries and economic activities. Like Gilpin, MITI is convinced that market forces alone will never produce the desired shifts, and despite its undoubted commitment in the postwar era to free enterprise, private ownership of property, and the market, it has never been reticent about saying so publicly (sometimes much too publicly for its own good).

Although some may question whether industrial policy should exist at all in an open capitalist system, the real controversy surrounding it concerns not whether it should exist but how it is applied. This book is in part devoted to studying the controversy over means that has gone on in Japan since industrial policy first appeared on the scene. The tools of implementation themselves are quite familiar. In Japan during high-speed growth they included, on the protective side, discriminatory tariffs, preferential commodity taxes on national products, import restrictions based on foreign currency allocations, and foreign currency controls. On the developmental (or what the Japanese call the "nurturing") side, they included the supply of low-interest funds to targeted industries through governmental financial organs, subsidies, special amortization benefits, exclusion from import duties of designated critical equipment, licensing of imported foreign technology, providing industrial parks and transportation facilities for private businesses through public investments, and "administrative guidance" by MITI (this last and most famous of MITI's powers will be analyzed in Chapter 7).[61] These tools can be further categorized in terms of the types and forms of the government's authoritative intervention powers (its *kyoninkaken*, or licensing and approval authority) and in terms of its various indirect means of guidance—for example, its "coordination of plant and equipment investment" for each strategic industry, a critically important form of administrative guidance.

The particular mix of tools changes from one era to the next because of changes in what the economy needs and because of shifts in MITI's power position in the government. The truly controversial aspect of these mixes of tools—one that greatly influences their effectiveness—is the nature of the relationship between the government and the private sector. In one sense the history of MITI is the history of its search for (or of its being compelled to accept) what Assar Lindbeck has called "market-conforming methods of intervention."[62] MITI's record of success in finding such methods—from the founding of the Ministry of Commerce and Industry (MCI) in 1925 to the mid-1970's—is distinctly checkered, and everyone in Japan even remotely connected with the economy knows about this and worries about MITI's going too far. MITI took a long time to find a government-business relationship that both enabled the government to achieve genuine industrial policy and also preserved competition and private enterprise in the business world. However, from approximately 1935 to 1955 the hard hand of state control rested heavily on the Japanese economy. The fact that MITI refers to this period as its "golden era" is understandable, if deeply imprudent.

Takashima Setsuo, writing as deputy director of MITI's Enterprises Bureau, the old control center of industrial policy, argues that there are three basic ways to implement industrial policy: bureaucratic control (*kanryō tōsei*), civilian self-coordination (*jishu chōsei*), and administration through inducement (*yūdō gyōsei*).[63] Between 1925 and 1975 Japan tried all three, with spectacularly varied results. However, at no time did the Japanese cease arguing about which was preferable or about the proper mix of the three needed for particular national situations or particular industries. The history of this debate and its consequences for policy-making is the history of MITI, and tracing its course should give pause to those who think that Japanese industrial policy might be easily installed in a different society.

What difference does industrial policy make? This, too, is part of the controversy surrounding MITI. Ueno Hiroya acknowledges that it is very difficult to do cost-benefit analyses of the effects of industrial policy, not least because some of the unintended effects may include bureaucratic red tape, oligopoly, a politically dangerous blurring of what is public and what is private, and corruption.[64] Professional quantitative economists seem to avoid the concept on grounds that they do not need it to explain economic events. For example, Ohkawa and Rosovsky cite as one of their "behavioral assumptions . . . based on standard economic theory and observed history . . . that the private investment decision is mainly determined by profit expectations, based among other things on the experience of the recent past as affected by the capital-output ratio and labor-cost conditions."[65]

I cannot prove that a particular Japanese industry would not or could not have grown and developed at all without the government's industrial policy (although I can easily think of the likely candidates for this category). What I believe can be shown are the differences between the course of development of a particular industry without governmental policies (its imaginary or "policy-off" trajectory) and its course of development with the aid of governmental policies (its real or "policy-on" trajectory). It is possible to calculate quantitatively, if only retrospectively, how, for example, foreign currency quotas and controlled trade suppress potential domestic demand to the level of the supply capacity of an infant domestic industry; how high tariffs suppress the price competitiveness of a foreign industry to the level of a domestic industry; how low purchasing power of consumers is raised through targeted tax measures and consumer-credit schemes, thereby allowing them to buy the products of new industries; how an industry borrows capital in excess of its borrowing capacity from governmental and government-guaranteed banks in order to expand production and bring down unit costs; how efficiency is raised through the accelerated depreciation of specified new machinery investments;

and how tax incentives for exports function to enlarge external markets at the point of domestic sales saturation. Kodama Fumio has calculated mathematically the gaps between the real trajectory and the policy-off trajectory of the Japanese automobile industry during its infant, growing, and stable phases (the data are of course not yet available for a future declining phase).[66] His measures are also tools for analyzing the appropriateness and effectiveness of the various governmental policies for the automobile industry during these phases.

The controversy over industrial policy will not soon end, nor is it my intention to resolve it here. The important point is that virtually all Japanese analysts, including those deeply hostile to MITI, believe that the government was the inspiration and the cause of the movement to heavy and chemical industries that took place during the 1950's, regardless of how one measures the costs and benefits of this movement. A measurement of what MITI believes and others consider to be its main achievement is provided by Ohkawa and Rosovsky: "In the first half of the 1950s, approximately 30 percent of exports still consisted of fibres and textiles, and another 20 percent was classified as sundries. Only 14 percent was in the category of machinery. By the first half of the 1960s, after the great investment spurt, major changes in composition had taken place. Fibres and textiles were down to 8 percent and sundries to 14 percent, and machinery with 39 percent had assumed its position of leading component, followed by metals and metal products (26 percent)."[67]

This shift of "industrial structure" was the operative mechanism of the economic miracle. Did the government in general, or MITI in particular, cause it to occur? Or, to put it more carefully, did they accelerate it and give it the direction it took? Perhaps the best answer currently available is Boltho's comparative appraisal: "Three of the countries with which Japan can most profitably be compared (France, Germany, and Italy) shared some or all of Japan's initial advantages— e.g., flexible labor supplies, a very favorable (in fact even more favorable) international environment, the possibility of rebuilding an industrial structure using the most advanced techniques. Yet other conditions were very dissimilar. The most crucial difference was perhaps in the field of economic policies. Japan's government exercised a much greater degree of both intervention and protection than did any of its Western European counterparts; and this brings Japan closer to the experience of another set of countries—the centrally planned economies."[68]

If a prima facie case exists that MITI's role in the economic miracle

was significant and is in need of detailed study, then the question still
remains why this book adopts the particular time frame of 1925–75.
Why look at the prewar and wartime eras when the miracle occurred
only in postwar Japan? There are several reasons. First, although industrial policy and MITI's "national system" for administering it are
the subjects of primary interest in this study, the leaders of MITI and
other Japanese realized only very late in the game that what they
were doing added up to an implicit theory of the developmental state.
That is to say, MITI produced no theory or model of industrial policy
until the 1960's at the earliest, and not until the creation of the Industrial Structure Council (Sangyō Kōzō Shingikai) in 1964 was analytical
work on industrial policy begun on a sustained basis. All participants
are agreed on this. Amaya quotes Hegel about the owl of Minerva
spreading her wings at dusk. He also thinks that maybe it would have
been just as well if the owl had never awakened at all, for he concludes with hindsight that the fatal flaw of MITI's prized but doomed
Special Measures Law for the Promotion of Designated Industries of
1962–63 (a major topic of Chapter 7) was that it made explicit what
had long been accepted as implicit in MITI's industrial policy.[69]

As late as 1973 MITI was writing that Japan's industrial policy just
grew, and that only during the 1970's did the government finally try
to rationalize and systematize it.[70] Therefore, an individual interested
in the Japanese system has no set of theoretical works, no locus classi-
cus such as Adam Smith or V. I. Lenin, with which to start. This lack
of theorizing has meant that historical research is necessary in order
to understand how MITI and industrial policy "just grew." Certain
things about MITI are indisputable: no one ever planned the ministry's course from its creation as the Ministry of Commerce and Industry (MCI) in 1925, to its transformation into the Ministry of Munitions
(MM) in 1943, to its reemergence as the MCI in 1945, down to its reorganization as MITI in 1949. Many of MITI's most vital powers, including their concentration in one ministry and the ministry's broad
jurisdiction, are all unintended consequences of fierce intergovern-
mental bureaucratic struggles in which MITI sometimes "won" by losing. This history is well known to ministerial insiders—it constitutes
part of their tradition and is a source of their high esprit de corps—
but it is not well known to the Japanese public and is virtually unknown to foreigners.

Another reason for going back into history is that all the insiders
cite the prewar and wartime eras as the time when they learned *how*
industrial policy worked. As will become clear in subsequent chap-

ters, there is direct continuity between prewar and postwar officials in this particular branch of the Japanese state bureaucracy; the postwar purge touched it hardly at all. The last vice-minister during the period of this study, Komatsu Yūgorō, who held the office from November 1974 to July 1976, entered the ministry in the class of 1944. All postwar vice-ministers previous to him came from earlier classes, going back to the first postwar vice-minister, Shiina Etsusaburō of the class of 1923. Wada Toshinobu, who became vice-minister in 1976, was the first without any experience of the Ministry of Munitions era.

Nakamura Takafusa locates the "roots" of both industrial policy and administrative guidance in the controlled economy of the 1930's, and he calls MITI the "reincarnation" of the wartime MCI and MM.[71] Arisawa Hiromi says that the prosperity of the 1970's was a product of the "control era," and no less a figure than Shiina Etsusaburō, former vice-minister, twice MITI minister, and vice-president of the Liberal Democratic Party, credits the experiences of old trade-and-industry bureaucrats in Manchuria in the 1930's, his own and Kishi Nobusuke's included.[72] Tanaka Shin'ichi—who was one of the leading officials of the Cabinet Planning Board (Kikaku-in) before it was merged with MCI to form the MM, and who became a postwar MITI official—argues that wartime planning was the basis for the work of the postwar Economic Stabilization Board (Keizai Antei Honbu) and MCI.[73] And Maeda Yasuyuki, one of Japan's leading scholars of MITI, writes that "the heritage of the wartime economy is that it was the first attempt at heavy and chemical industrialization; more important, the war provided the 'how' for the 'what' in the sense of innumerable 'policy tools' and accumulated 'know-how.'"[74]

Even more arresting than these comments from participants and analysts is the fact that the Japanese economy began to change in quite decisive ways around 1930. It is true that industrial policy in one form or another goes back to the Meiji era, but it is also true that after the turn of the century the government moved progressively away from its former policies of interference in the domestic economy (if not in those of the colonies or dependencies), and that for about thirty years an approximation of laissez faire was in vogue. Rodney Clark's observation is startling but true: "The organization of Japanese and Western industry was probably more similar in 1910 than in 1970."[75]

MITI and modern Japanese industrial policy are genuine children of the Shōwa era (1926–), and the present study is for that reason virtually coterminous with the reign of Emperor Hirohito. To carry the story back any further is to lose focus on the postwar economic miracle, but to fail to incorporate the history of the prewar MCI is to ignore MITI's traditions and collective consciousness. MITI men learned their trade in MCI, MM, and the Economic Stabilization Board. These were once such fearsome agencies that it was said the mere mention of their names would stop a child from crying. Admirers of the Japanese miracle such as I have a duty to show how the disastrous national experiences of the 1940's gave birth to the achievements of the 1950's and 1960's.

TWO

The Economic Bureaucracy

WHEN the analyst discovers in the course of political research a persistent discrepancy between the stated principles and actual practices of a society, he has a strong impulse to ring the critical alarm bells to warn of a lack of legitimacy, of the operation of covert powers, or of simple hypocrisy. The end product is usually a muckraking or critical book, and the subject of Japanese politics has produced a plethora of them, by both Japanese and foreigners. I myself shall add a few items to the list of anomalies in Japanese bureaucratic life, but my purpose is not criticism. Instead, I am concerned to explain why the discrepancy between the formal authority of either the Emperor (prewar) or the Diet (postwar) and the actual powers of the state bureaucracy exists and persists, and why this discrepancy contributes to the success of the developmental state.

Japan has long displayed a marked separation in its political system between reigning and ruling, between the powers of the legislative branch and the executive branch, between the majority party and the mandarinate—and, in the last analysis, between authority and power. As a result, a discrepancy exists between the constitutional and the actual locus of sovereignty that is so marked the Japanese themselves have invented terms to discuss it—*omote* (outer, in plain view) and *ura* (inner, hidden from sight), or *tatemae* (principle; Edward Seidensticker once proposed the word should be translated "pretense") and *honne* (actual practice).[1]

Japanese and foreign observers are aware that the discrepancy generates a degree of hypocrisy or euphemism, and they often enjoy criticizing this hypocrisy. Kakuma Takashi, for example, argues that in the postwar world the business community likes to pretend that it is

"yielding under protest" to the powers of MITI when it is actually doing nothing more than pursuing its traditional relationship with the
bureaucracy.[2] Gōshi Kōhei is irritated by the senior business leaders
who refer their decisions for approval to government section chiefs
often not much older than their own grandchildren and then speak ill
of them back at the Industrial Club.[3] Obayashi Kenji believes that the
numerous "deliberation councils" (what Berger calls "policy councils," or *shingikai*), in which officials and entrepreneurs coordinate
policies, are really covers for MITI's "remote control" of the industrial
world; and he speaks somewhat cynically of "Japanese-style free com
petition."[4] And a foreign analyst, John Campbell, shrewdly draws
attention to the fact that "nearly everyone involved with Japanese
budgeting finds it in his interest to magnify the role played by the majority party."[5]

The origins of this separation between power and authority are to
be found in Japan's feudal past and in the emergence of the developmental state during the Meiji era. For reasons that will be made clear
in a moment, Japan in the late nineteenth century adopted for its new
political system a version of what Weber called "monarchic constitu-
tionalism," the form of government that Bismarck gave to imperial
Germany. The Bismarckian system is described by Weber's editors as
follows: "The prime minister remained responsible to the king, not to
parliament, and the army also remained under the king's control. In
practice, this arrangement gave extraordinary power first to Bismarck, then to the Prussian and Imperial bureaucracy, both vis-à-vis
the monarch and the parliament."[6] Japan had some reasons of its
own, in addition to Bismarck's personal influence on a few key Meiji
leaders, for finding this arrangement preferable to the other models it
looked at in the course of its "modernization." One of the most serious consequences for Japan of adopting this system was its decision
in 1941 to go to war with the United States and Great Britain—a decision in which neither the monarch nor the parliament participated.
But what is perhaps most important more than a generation after the
Pacific War is that the system persisted and became even stronger,
even though it was formally abolished by the Constitution of 1947.

The ancestors of the modern Japanese bureaucrats are the samurai
of the feudal era. During the two-and-a-half centuries of peace that
the Tokugawa shogunate enforced, the feudal warriors slowly evolved
into what one group of scholars has called a "governmentalized class"
or a "service nobility."[7] Constituting some 6 to 7 percent of the population, these samurai did not yet form a modern bureaucracy, if by
this one means what Weber has called the most rational and imper-

sonal form of state administration. For Weber true bureaucratic power is vested in an "office," and bureaucratic power in this sense "does not establish a relationship to a *person*, like the vassal's or disciple's faith under feudal or patrimonial authority, but rather is devoted to *impersonal* and *functional* purposes."[8] During the Tokugawa period the samurai became administrative officials rather than warriors, but they still occupied a status for which they received a stipend, rather than offering a particular competence for which they were paid a salary.[9] This emphasis on status rather than on the performance of an occupation was passed on under the Meiji Constitution to the bureaucrats, who enjoyed such a position legally until the Constitution of 1947 ended it, and to *their* successors, who still enjoy it informally more than thirty years later because of the persistence of tradition and bureaucratic dominance in postwar Japan.

The Meiji leaders did not plan to perpetuate samurai government under a new guise, nor for that matter were they much interested in creating a modern state officialdom. Their reasons for creating a "nonpolitical" civil bureaucracy were, in fact, highly political. They were trying to respond to strident public criticism of the monopoly of power by the two feudal domains (Satsuma and Chōshū) that had led the successful movement against the Tokugawa shogunate, and the corruption that this domination was generating. They also hoped to demonstrate their "modernity" to the West in order to hasten revision of the unequal treaties that had been forced on Japan. And, most important, they wanted to retain authoritarian control after 1890, when the new parliament (National Diet) opened and political parties began public campaigning for a share of power.[10]

The state bureaucracy and the cabinet both preceded the Meiji Constitution, the Diet, and the formation of political parties in Japan by some five to twenty years. The results were predictable. In seeking to forestall competitive claims to their own power by the leaders of the political parties, the Meiji oligarchs created a weak parliament and also sought to counterbalance it with a bureaucracy they believed they could staff with their own supporters, or at least keep under their personal control. But over time, with the bureaucracy installed at the center of government and with the passing of the oligarchs, it was the bureaucrats—both military and civilian—who arrogated more and more power to themselves.[11]

The bureaucrats of prewar Japan were not liked, but they were respected. Many Japanese had resented the persistence of Satsuma and Chōshū privilege after Japan became a unified nation, and the new bureaucracy, expertly trained and open to all men who had demonstrated their talent in impartial examinations, was clearly an improvement over Satsuma and Chōshū dominance. The political parties were an alternative to state officialdom, but they always suffered from the weakness of having arrived second on the political scene. The bureaucracy claimed to speak for the national interest and characterized the parties as speaking only for local or particular interests. As Japan industrialized, the parties slowly gained clout as representatives of zaibatsu and other propertied interests, but they never developed a mass base. One reason was the careful control exercised over the enlargement of the franchise (see Table 2). Another reason was that one house of the Diet, the House of Peers, was dominated by the bureaucracy, which arranged for the direct Imperial appointment of its senior retired members to the Peers, where they easily outclassed the titled members in political skill.[12] In short, whether the military and civilian bureaucrats of the post-Meiji era were really the most capable leaders of the nation became a moot question: they had effectively preempted most of the centers of power from which they might be challenged. There were many fights, and the final outcome was not a foregone conclusion, but ultimately a bureaucratic career became the most important route to political power. For example, not a single minister of the Tōjō cabinet, installed in October 1941, had served in the Diet as an elected member.

Prewar bureaucrats were not "civil servants" but rather "officials of the Emperor" (*tennō no kanri*) appointed by him and answerable only to him. Imperial appointment bestowed on them the status of *kan*, the primitive meaning of which in its Chinese original is the residence of a mandarin who presides over a city, and which still retains some of this early meaning in its contemporary usage to refer to judges (according to one legal authority, kan connotes officials with power who are not highly constrained by law).[13] This high social status linked them back in time to the samurai and forward to the postwar bureaucrats in their possession of intrinsic authority rather than extrinsic, or legal-rational, office. It meant that they were largely free of external constraints. "The present-day bureaucrat," writes Henderson, "is not, of course, identical with the warrior bureaucrat of the Tokugawa regime or even the new university-trained Imperial bureaucrat of prewar Japan. But they have all, until recently, been largely above the law in the sense of independent judicial review." Rather than a rule of law, Henderson finds that "a rule of bureaucrats prevails."[14] Isomura and Kuronuma concur. Even in the postwar world, they argue, Japan has had an administration "for the sake of the citizenry" and not an administration carried out with the "participation of the citizenry." In

TABLE 2

Changes in the Size of the Japanese Electorate, 1890–1969

Election	Date	Qualified voters (millions)	Population (millions)	Percent	Voting requirements
1	July 1, 1890	.45	39.9	1.3%	Males, over 25, who pay more than ¥15 in direct, national taxes[a]
7	August 10, 1902	.98	45.0	2.18	Same, except ¥10 in direct taxes
14	May 10, 1920	3.1	55.5	5.50	Same, except ¥3 in direct taxes
16	February 20, 1928	12.4	62.1	19.98	Same, except tax requirement abolished
22	April 10, 1946	36.9	75.8	48.65	All men and women 20 years and above
25	October 1, 1952	46.8	85.9	54.45	Same
29	November 20, 1960	54.3	93.2	58.30	Same
30	November 21, 1963	58.3	95.8	60.82	Same
31	January 29, 1967	63.0	99.8	63.11	Same
32	December 27, 1969	69.3	102.7	67.47	Same

SOURCE: Isomura Eiichi, ed., *Gyōsei saishin mondai jiten* (Dictionary of current administrative problems), Tokyo, 1972, p. 705.

[a]¥15 was the equivalent of about U.S. $12.30 in 1890. Since it was paid as a direct tax it meant, in essence, that only property owners or the wealthy could vote.

their view, this constitutes "administration through law," which is different from the "rule of law."[15]

In addition to their status, the bureaucrats of modern Japan also inherited from the samurai something comparable to their code of ethics and their elite consciousness. Kanayama Bunji draws attention to the frank elitism and sense of meritocracy associated in contemporary Japan with young men (and a few women) who pass the incredibly competitive Higher-level Public Officials Examination and then enter a ministry. He cites the long hours of work they are expected to perform without complaint, their being sent abroad for postgraduate education in elite universities, the theme of "sacrifice for the public good" that runs through most ministries, and the lectures to new recruits during their early years in a ministry by their "seniors," including those who have retired from public service and have moved to powerful positions in industry or politics. He believes that these customs add up to a "way of the bureaucrat" (*kanryōdō*) comparable to the old "way of a warrior" (*bushidō*).[16] Of course, many prewar bureaucrats actually came from samurai families, where the ethos of service persisted for decades after the samurai as a class had been broken up. As Black and his colleagues observe, "With the disbandment of samurai administrations throughout Japan, a civilian bureaucracy was formed, roughly one-tenth as large as the total number of former samurai household heads. For the most part drawn initially from the samurai class, and enjoying high status as the loyal representatives of the emperor, rather than the shogun or daimyo as before, these bureaucrats acquired some of the aura previously reserved for samurai."[17]

This "aura" formerly attached to samurai can still be found in some of the terminology now associated with bureaucrats. For example, the common term for governmental authorities is "those above" (*okami*). It is also said that Japanese do not normally question the authority of the government because they respect its "samurai sword" (*denka no hōtō*), which refers directly to a samurai family's heirloom sword. Such a jeweled sword symbolized the status of a samurai household rather than being a weapon designed for killing people. Yamanouchi says that use of the term reflects the popular consciousness of the law as being a symbol of authority, not something that the possessor of authority need actually use. The change from the old constitution to the new, Yamanouchi argues, did little to change this attitude. For example, the effectiveness of MITI's informal administrative guidance is said to rest in the final analysis on its "samurai sword": both the government and industry find it more convenient to work on this basis rather than through the actual swords of litigation and penalties.[18]

During the 1930's, when the political parties were under strenuous attack from the militarists, both the civilian and military bureaucracies extended the scope of their activities into areas they had previously left untouched. Given the sociological weakness of the parties in the 1920's despite their political prominence, Duus and Okimoto suggest that "the 1930s represented not a breakdown of 'democratic' government, but the stabilization of bureaucratic government"—a confirmation of tendencies that had been latent since the Meiji era.[19] Craig proposes that the 1930's saw the "indigenization" of the values and institutions that had been borrowed from the West during the Meiji era.[20] However one evaluates the decade and a half from 1930 to 1945, Japan's government was much more bureaucratic and state dominated at the end of this period than it had been at the beginning.

At the war's end this bureaucratic government had to face fierce domestic criticism for the disasters it had brought to the nation, as well as undergo the efforts of the Allied occupation to reform it in a democratic direction. But an unusual thing happened to the bureaucracy under the occupation: it did not by any means escape the Allied reforms unscathed, but a part of the bureaucracy—the economic ministries—emerged with their powers enhanced. In fact, the occupation era, 1945–52, witnessed the highest levels of government control over the economy ever encountered in modern Japan before or since, levels that were decidedly higher than the levels attained during the Pacific War. This is a subject I shall consider in detail in Chapters 4 and 5, but the "reform" of the bureaucracy during the occupation is a necessary preface to any understanding of the prominence of bureaucrats in and out of the ministries in postoccupation Japanese politics.

For reasons that are still none too clear, the occupation authorities, or SCAP (Supreme Commander for the Allied Powers), never singled out the civilian bureaucracy as needing basic reform. However, SCAP eliminated completely from political life one major rival of the economic bureaucracy, the military; and it transformed and severely weakened another, the zaibatsu. Both of these developments propelled the economic bureaucrats into the vacuums thus created. Equally important, SCAP broke up the prewar Ministry of Home Affairs (Naimu-shō), which had been the most prestigious and powerful of ministries under the Meiji Constitution. The powers of the old Home Ministry were distributed primarily among the new ministries of Construction, Labor, Health and Welfare, Home Affairs (at first called "Local Autonomy"), and the Defense and Police agencies. But the loss of power by the Home Ministry also offered new jurisdictions into which the economic bureaucrats could expand; for example, the Home Ministry's wartime regional bureaus and its police power to enforce rationing passed, respectively, to the Ministry of Commerce and Industry and the Economic Stabilization Board.

SCAP also included the civilian bureaucracy under its purge directives, that is, its campaign to exclude from various public and private positions of responsibility persons designated by category as having been partly responsible for the war.[21] A major purpose of the purge was to bring new, younger people into the government. Once again, however, the purge had little effect on the economic ministries. It is hard to calculate exactly how many economic bureaucrats were purged because many appealed on grounds that they were indispensable to the economic recovery effort, but one estimate is that only 42 higher officials (bureau chiefs and above) were purged from the Ministry of Commerce and Industry—the wartime Ministry of Munitions—and only 9 from the Ministry of Finance. Of the 1,800 civilian bureaucrats purged, 70 percent were police and other officials from the Home Ministry.[22]

Amaya Naohiro of MITI feels that the purge of business leaders, if not of bureaucrats, was very helpful to the postwar economy; he compares it to the purge of feudal leaders that actually accompanied the Meiji Restoration.[23] The postwar economic purge eliminated from industrial life the rentier class—what Weber calls the "property classes" (*Besitzklassen*) as distinct from the "professional classes" (*Erwerbklassen*), which includes entrepreneurs and highly qualified managers— and thereby greatly rationalized the zaibatsu, as well as allowing for the creation of new zaibatsu. Perhaps the most important rentier interest eliminated from economic life was the Imperial Household itself, which had been a significant owner of shares in the prewar and wartime "national policy companies."[24] But the purge did not really touch the economic bureaucrats themselves.

SCAP's attempts at positive reform of the bureaucratic system as a whole are widely acknowledged to have failed. Foster Roser, a member of the Blaine Hoover Mission, which wrote the National Public Service Law (law 120 of October 21, 1947) on the basis of then current American civil service legislation, concludes: "The proposed civil service law was submitted to the Diet in the fall of 1947. Unfortunately, the nucleus of feudalistic, bureaucratic thinking gentlemen within the core of the Japanese Government was astute enough to see the dangers of any such modern public administration law to their tenure and the subsequent loss of their power. The law which was finally passed by the Diet was a thoroughly and completely emasculated instrument compared with that which had been recommended by the mission."[25]

Blaine Hoover, former president of the Civil Service Assembly, knew nothing of the efforts made by the military during the 1930's and during the war to bring the ministries under centralized control and take personnel selection and promotion matters out of their hands—nor did he know of the successful efforts by the Home and Finance ministries to block these earlier attempts. The ministries had years of experience in sabotaging civil service reform movements.[26] Hoover's law did set up a National Personnel Authority attached to the cabinet to conduct examinations, set pay scales, and hold grievance hearings. But the law did not establish in either the cabinet or the prime minister's office the powers and staff necessary to control the ministries; in particular, the powers of budget-making remained in the Ministry of Finance (contrast the U.S. Office of Management and Budget attached to the President's staff).[27]

An amendment to the National Public Service Law enacted during 1948 compelled the reexamination of all officials from assistant section chiefs up to and including administrative vice-ministers. Despite protests from older officials, this examination took place on January 15, 1950—and instantly became known as the "Paradise Exam," since officials could smoke, drink tea, and take as long as they wished (some stayed all night). As a result, about 30 percent of incumbent officials failed to be reappointed, but the government simultaneously undertook a matching 30 percent reduction in force, so the net result was that no new blood entered the bureaucracy except through regular recruitment channels.

Aside from its enhanced status, however, the rapid rise of the economic bureaucracy during the occupation was primarily due to circumstances. First and foremost was SCAP's decision to conduct an indirect occupation, working through and giving orders to the Japanese government rather than displacing it. In the eyes of many Japanese this was probably a desirable decision, but it opened the way for the bureaucracy to protect itself. Seven years of bureaucratic *menjū fukuhai* (following orders to a superior's face, reversing them in the belly) is the way one commentator has put it.[28]

Prof. Tsuji Kiyoaki, Japan's most prominent authority on the public service, believes the two key reasons for the perpetuation of what he calls the "Imperial (tennō) system," meaning not the Imperial institution itself but the structure of a state bureaucracy unconstrained by either the cabinet or the Diet, were indirect rule and the prompt acceptance by the government of the new American-drafted constitution. The latter forestalled MacArthur's threat to take his constitution to the people in a plebiscite if the government continued to balk. Tsuji acknowledges that the Constitution of 1947 provides for a highly responsible, democratic government—the constitution was, in fact, the most important act of positive democratization carried out by the occupation. But he believes the important point was seen by the bureaucrats: the need to avoid direct participation in politics by the people if bureaucratic power was to be preserved. The Constitution of 1947, as liberal as it unquestionably is, was bestowed on the society from above just as was the Meiji Constitution of 1889.[29]

A comment made by a Ministry of Finance official to John Campbell elucidates Tsuji's point. Japan, he said, "has never undergone a 'people's revolution,' which would have created a feeling among citizens that 'the government is something we made ourselves.'" [30] Tsuji feels that an opportunity was missed during the occupation for such a popular revolution, despite the considerable degree of social mobilization that was achieved in the social, labor, industrial, and farming sectors. Nevertheless, it must be pointed out that the effective operation of the developmental state requires that the bureaucracy directing economic development be protected from all but the most powerful interest groups so that it can set and achieve long-range industrial priorities. A system in which the full range of pressure and interest groups existing in a modern, open society has effective access to the government will surely not achieve economic development, at least under official auspices, whatever other values it may fulfill. The success of the economic bureaucracy in preserving more or less intact its preexisting influence was thus prerequisite to the success of the industrial policies of the 1950's.

The bureaucracy did not simply preserve its influence, it expanded it—in two ways. First, the requirements of economic recovery led to a vast ballooning of the bureaucracy. Wildes offers figures showing that during the first three postwar years the size of the bureaucracy increased 84 percent over its highest wartime strength.[31] Whether or not SCAP saw the irony in this, the Japanese people certainly did. In a famous lead editorial in *Chūō kōron* in August 1947, the editors wrote:

The problem of the bureaucracy under present conditions is both complex and paradoxical. On the one hand, the responsibility for the war clearly must be placed on the bureaucracy, as well as on the military and the zaibatsu. From the outbreak of the war through its unfolding to the end, we know that the bureaucracy's influence was great and that it was evil. Many people have already censured the bureaucrats for their responsibility and their sins. On the other hand, given that under the present circumstances of defeat it is impossible to return to a laissez-faire economy, and that every aspect of economic life necessarily requires an expansion of planning and control, the functions and significance of the bureaucracy are expanding with each passing day. It is not possible to imagine the dissolution of the bureaucracy in the same sense as the dissolution of the military or the zaibatsu, since the bureaucracy as a concentration of technical expertise must grow as the administrative sector broadens and becomes more complex.[32]

It was not just a matter of an increase in the number of tasks for the bureaucracy; even more important was SCAP's insistence that economic functions previously shared between the government and the zaibatsu should now be placed exclusively in governmental hands. As we shall see in Chapter 4, this was a development that the prewar bureaucracy had fought for with passionate enthusiasm but had never achieved due to the resistance of the private sector. Tsuji thinks that SCAP never fully appreciated the implications of what it was doing when it forced the transfer of the zaibatsu's share of power to the government because SCAP, in accordance with American governmental theory, regarded the bureaucracy as a "nonpolitical instrument," not a political body. Moreover, SCAP was itself an official bureaucratic organization—the U.S. Army—and disinclined to question institutions comparably based on professional, if not necessarily politically accountable, service to the nation.

The second reason for the expansion of bureaucratic influence was the relative incompetence of the political forces SCAP had fostered to replace the old order. Cadres of the old political parties brought again to leadership of the government by the new constitution had never (or not for almost twenty years) exercised political power. Moreover, some of the most competent among them had been purged. The American-style tradition in which party leaders become deeply involved in administrative affairs and the drafting of legislation had never been well established in Japan in any case. Under the Katayama government, created on May 24, 1947, the cabinet ministers were so lacking in expertise and so unfamiliar with legislation that everyone had his vice-minister sitting next to him in the cabinet room in order to advise him on what to do.[33] This state of affairs ended in January 1949 with the establishment of the third Yoshida government. Yoshida Shigeru (1878–1967) was himself a former high-ranking bureaucrat of the Ministry of Foreign Affairs, and he established the "bureaucratic leadership structure" (*kanryō shudō taisei*) that has formed the mainstream of Japanese politics to the present day.

The twenty-fourth general election of January 1949 brought into the Diet 42 new members who were former bureaucrats; in most cases they were also protégés and allies of Yoshida, who had encouraged them to run. Among this new class of politicians were Ikeda Hayato (1899–1965), recently retired as vice-minister of finance, who became Yoshida's new finance minister, and Satō Eisaku (1901–1975), recently retired as vice-minister of transportation and soon to become chief secretary of Yoshida's Liberal Party. Shortly before the election, on December 24, 1948, Kishi Nobusuke (b. 1896) was released from Sugamo Prison as an unindicted class A war criminal. He had served as vice-minister of commerce and industry under the Abe, Yonai, and Konoe cabinets and as minister of commerce and industry and vice-minister of munitions in the Tōjō cabinet. On April 29, 1952, he was depurged, and a year later he was also elected to the Diet. These three former bureaucrats, each of whom had had a full and very successful career in his respective ministry, dominated Japanese politics from 1957 to 1972: Kishi was prime minister from February 1957 to July 1960, Ikeda from July 1960 to November 1964, and Satō from November 1964 to July 1972. Yoshida himself, a former vice-minister of foreign affairs and ambassador to Great Britain, served as prime minister from May 1946 to May 1947 and from October 1948 to December 1954.

In addition to these leaders, many middle-ranking Diet members were also drawn from the ranks of state officialdom. In 1946 Liberal Party (conservative) ex-bureaucrat Diet members accounted for only 2.7 percent of the total. Yoshida raised the number to 18.2 percent in 1949, and this proportion has held firm ever since. As of 1970, 69 members of the House of Representatives (23 percent) and 50 members of the House of Councillors (37 percent) were ex-bureaucrats belonging to the Liberal Democratic Party (LDP). In 1977 the respective figures were 27 percent and 35 percent.[34]

Party politicians holding a safe electoral base (*jiban*) in one of the prefectural constituencies did not take this intrusion of bureaucrats with equanimity. Many of them believed, and still believe today, that bureaucrats were not so much becoming politicians as they were displacing politicians and contributing to a dangerous blurring of functions between the executive and legislative branches. In the election of October 1952 approximately 40 percent of some 329 prewar and wartime politicians recently released from the ban against their holding public office were reelected to the Diet. They held about 30 percent of the seats. From that point on, the main configuration of postwar Diet politics was established: the so-called mainstream of the conservative forces was occupied by retired bureaucrats, and the antimainstream by old (later called "pure") politicians who did not come from a background in the state apparatus. In 1955 the two main conservative parties, successors to the Seiyūkai and Minseitō of the prewar era, united in order to confront the growing strength of the opposition socialists. They created the huge coalition Liberal Democratic Party that has controlled the Diet without interruption ever since.

Within the LDP the bureaucratic mainstream and the party politicians' (*tōjinha*) antimainstream factions compete with each other, with the bureaucrats usually dominant; but for the sake of party unity neither group is ever totally excluded. The second Kishi cabinet of 1958 established bureaucratic supremacy when eight of the twelve ministries were headed by ex-bureaucrats. Former bureaucrats also held many influential positions in the party's Policy Affairs Research Council and on the key standing committees of the Diet, where the plans and budgets of the ministries are ratified. Given their skills and background in government, former bureaucrats also advanced more rapidly to the cabinet level of power within the LDP: according to one calculation, a former bureaucrat turned politician must be elected an average of seven times to reach this level, whereas an ex-journalist or a representative of an economic interest group will require nine successful elections, and a local politician ten.[35]

Not surprisingly, the influence of former bureaucrats within the Diet has tended to perpetuate and actually strengthen the prewar pattern of bureaucratic dominance. Spaulding notes that 91 percent of all laws enacted by the Diet under the Meiji Constitution (1890–1947) originated in the executive branch and not in the Diet.[36] The pattern is similar in the postwar Diets. For example, in the first Diet under the new constitution, May 20 to December 9, 1947, the cabinet, which acts on behalf of the bureaucracy, introduced 161 bills and saw 150 enacted, while members of the House of Representatives introduced 20 bills and saw 8 enacted. In the 28th Diet, December 20, 1957, to April 25, 1958, the cabinet introduced 175 bills and saw 145 enacted, while members of the House of Representatives introduced 68 bills and saw 15 enacted.[37] This pattern more and more has become unfavorable to private members' bills. Cabinet bills originate and are drafted exclusively within the ministries. They are then passed to the LDP for its approval and introduction in the Diet. As a matter of routine, ministerial officials are also present in the Diet to explain their legislation and answer questions.

Genuine deliberation on laws takes place within and among the ministries before they are sent to the cabinet, and civilians do play some role. A kind of ministry-dominated quasi deliberation occurs in the 246 (as of 1975) "deliberation councils" (*shingikai, shinsakai, kyōgikai, chōsakai,* and *iinkai,* known collectively as shingikai) that are attached to the ministries. These are official standing organs created by a minister and composed of civilian experts selected by him to inquire into and discuss policies and proposed legislation of his ministry. In 1975 the largest number of deliberation councils (51) was attached to the Prime Minister's Office, but MITI operated the next largest number (36).

To the extent that laws are scrutinized and discussed at all in Japan by persons outside the bureaucracy, it is done in the councils. Even such critical matters for a parliament as tax and tariff laws are merely rubber-stamped by the Diet after having been considered by the deliberation councils. For example, the Tax System Deliberation Council (Zeisei Chōsa Kai) annually recommends revisions of the tax laws and tax rates with no input from the Diet, and usually no Diet changes in its recommendations. Similarly, the Customs Duties Deliberation Council (Kanzeiritsu Shingikai) sets tariff rates and procedures, and the Diet then approves them without change.[38] There is no question that the deliberation councils handle some very important matters; the problems relate to the selection, procedures, and degree of independence from the bureaucracy of the councils.

And on those questions there is considerable debate. Do the councils actually provide civilian input to the bureaucracy's decisions, or are they merely covers for bureaucratic power, intended to provide the public with a façade of consultation and consensus? Former MITI Vice-Minister Sahashi said in an interview that as far as he was concerned deliberation councils were important primarily as a device to silence in advance any criticism of the bureaucracy.[39] Kawanaka Nikō believes that deliberation councils are actually important weapons of the bureaucracy in the struggles that occur within and among ministries to promote particular policies: the important names that appear as members of a council are not so much intended to impress the public as they are to influence and warn off rival bureaucrats, one ministry's clients serving to counterbalance those of another ministry.[40]

Some Japanese journalists are even harsher. A group of *Mainichi* economic specialists calls the deliberation councils "gimmicks," noting that the councils do not have independent staffs and that all proposals submitted to them have been approved in advance by the sponsoring ministry. On the other hand, they believe that the most important councils in the economic sphere—the Economic Council (Keizai Shingikai) attached to the Economic Planning Agency, the Industrial Structure Council (Sangyō Kōzō Shingikai) attached to MITI, and the Foreign Capital Council (Gaishi Shingikai) attached to the Ministry of Finance—are not mere "ornaments."[41] Concerning one of these, the Foreign Capital Council, the MITI Journalists' Club disagrees, suggesting that at least before capital liberalization it was a *kakuremino*—a magic fairy cape thrown over something (in this case MITI's influence over all foreign capital ventures in Japan) in the hope of making it invisible.[42]

If these criticisms are at all valid, we may ask why the Diet itself does not perform the vital tasks of writing and deliberating laws. The answer is that the Japanese Diet is not a "working parliament" in Weber's sense, "one which supervises the administration by continuously sharing in its work."[43] The most important work of the government is done elsewhere and is only ratified in the Diet. As we have already stressed, the Diet's dependent relationship with the bureau-

cracy originated in the prewar structure. It persisted and was reinforced because of the harsh period of postwar reconstruction. During
the late 1940's and early 1950's the bureaucracy fought for its policies,
and against interference by the none-too-competent political parties
of the time, by invoking the old idea that the bureaucracy speaks for
the national interest and the political parties only for local, particular,
or selfish interests. General wisdom was said to reside in the state and
only particular wisdom in the society, a political philosophy that was
not at all alien to Japan, in contrast to some of the democratic institutions founded by SCAP. Kojima Akira traces this ideology to the
state's monopoly in the Meiji era of the power to establish the "orthodoxy of the public interest," everything not so designated being, by
definition, part of the private interest and therefore subordinate.[44]

Interest groups exist in Japan in great numbers, but there is no theory of pluralism that legitimates their political activities. The parties
developed what strength they had before the war by representing private interests to the government, and this heritage too was passed on
to their postwar successors. One of the reasons that there are so few
private members' bills passed is that virtually all of them are based on
appeals from constituents or are intended to serve some special interest. Many party politicians themselves accept the orthodoxy of a vertical relationship between the state's activities and their own activities. "They tend," writes Campbell, "to perceive voters as animated
almost solely by particularistic, pork-barrel desires rather than by
concern over issues of broad social policy."[45]

Although Japan's fused relationship between the executive and legislative branches may be disappointing to liberals, from the point of
view of the developmental state it has some hidden advantages. In
the postwar world the Diet has replaced the Imperial institution in
the role of what Titus has called "the supreme ratifier," the agency
that legitimates decisions taken elsewhere.[46] Like the emperor under
the Meiji Constitution, the Diet is the public locus of sovereignty, but
the same discrepancy that existed earlier between authority and
power is still maintained, and for at least some of the same reasons.
There is, however, one major difference: the Diet performs these vital
functions much more safely, effectively, and democratically than the
Imperial institution ever did. For the bureaucracy to have mobilized
resources and committed them to a heavy industrial structure as it did
in postwar Japan, the claims of interest groups and individual citizens
had to be held in check. Although the high-growth policies of the bureaucracy ultimately raised the economic level of all citizens and may
thereby have served their diverse interests, the citizens themselves

were not consulted. The funds, legislation, and institutions the bureaucracy needed for its programs were enacted by what Wildes has
called the "puppet Diet."[47]

This "puppet Diet," working through its LDP majority, has nevertheless served as a mediator between the state and society, forcing the
state to accommodate those interests that could not be ignored—
agriculture and medium and smaller enterprises, for example—and,
on occasion, requiring the state to change course in response to serious problems such as pollution. At the same time, it has held off or
forced compromises from those groups whose claims might interfere
with the development program. By and large, it has done so equitably, maintaining a comparatively level pattern of income distribution
and of hardships.[48]

The Diet's unproclaimed mediating role has been the subject of
much scrutiny and analysis in Japan. Although there are many different formulations, most of them end up dividing Japanese society
into two sets of social groups and institutions, those that are central
and those that are peripheral (or privileged and ordinary, first class
and second class), with the central groups operating the developmental state for the sake of the society as a whole and not just for their
own particular interests. The central institutions—that is, the bureaucracy, the LDP, and the larger Japanese business concerns—in turn
maintain a kind of skewed triangular relationship with each other.
The LDP's role is to legitimate the work of the bureaucracy while also
making sure that the bureaucracy's policies do not stray too far from
what the public will tolerate. Some of this serves its own interests, as
well; the LDP always insures that the Diet and the bureaucracy are
responsive to the farmers' demands because it depends significantly
on the overrepresented rural vote. The bureaucracy, meanwhile,
staffs the LDP with its own cadres to insure that the party does what
the bureaucracy thinks is good for the country as a whole, and guides
the business community toward developmental goals. The business
community, in turn, supplies massive amounts of funds to keep the
LDP in office, although it does not thereby achieve control of the
party, which is normally oriented upward, toward the bureaucracy,
rather than downward, toward its main patrons.

This triangular relationship sometimes looks conflict ridden and
sometimes consensual, but both impressions are deceptive according
to Kawanaka Nikō, who maintains that interest groups representing the strategic industries—he calls them the "prime contractor
groups"—always hold a privileged relationship with the bureaucracy.
The two will sometimes be in conflict, however, with private indus-

trial groups or enterprises asking for flexible execution of governmental policies or for partial or technical changes in policies that will benefit one or another of them. The government will be forthcoming, seeking compromises, brokering mergers, offering financial incentives, confronting foreign competitors, and so forth, but the government will also impose on the industries new conditions that are conducive to the government's goals. This conflict is important and time-consuming, but according to Kawanaka it should always be understood as *miuchi* (among relatives).

In the case of outsiders—for example, consumer groups, local conservationists, or groups hostile to the alliance with the United States—the government's policy is to ignore them, or if they become very powerful, to seek a compromise with them through the LDP. The Japanese people understand these relationships and support them not as a matter of principle but because of the results they have achieved. They have developed what Kawanaka labels a "structure of organizational double vision," by which he means the tendency for subordinate or dependent parts of the structure to perceive the intentions of the dominant or guiding parts and to formulate their own policies as if the superior's policies were their own. It all looks like consensus to outsiders, but it is, in fact, dictated by a calculation of the balance of forces and a sense of Japan's vulnerability. Rather than consensus, Kawanaka proposes the concept of "interlocking decision-making," which acknowledges the symbiotic relationships among the bureaucracy, LDP, and the business community. The characteristics of such interlocking decisions, he suggests, are bureaucratic leadership, obscured responsibility, and fictive kinship ties.[49]

An even more important characteristic for our purposes is a differential access to the government by various groups: the "prime contractors" and vital political support groups have ready access, the less strategically placed groups little access—although more than they had under the Meiji Constitution. The channels of preferential access are not formalized, but they exist in the deliberation councils, in a circulation of elites from the bureaucracy to both the political and industrial worlds, and in a vast array of other "old boy" networks to be discussed below. The result is a developmental state much softer and more tolerable than the communist-dominated command economies (with much better performance, too) but with a considerably greater goal-setting and goal-achieving capability than in the market-rational systems.

Personal relations between bureaucrats and politicians in this subtle, malleable system can be quite complex. In each ministry there is only one genuine political appointee, the minister, who is named by the prime minister and is a member of the cabinet. The minister is normally but not invariably a member of the Diet (articles 67 and 68 of the Constitution of 1947 require that the prime minister be elected by and from the members of the Diet, but only a majority of the other ministers must be members). All other officials in a ministry are non-political, the most senior being the administrative vice-minister (*jimu jikan*, which I have rendered simply as "vice-minister"). The Japanese prime minister thus has the power to name only about 20 ministers, plus 4 party officials, whereas the American president, for example, appoints at least 1,000 people to posts in the bureaucracy (one Japanese analyst counted 916 bureaucratic appointments made by President Carter during early 1977).[50] The prime minister is also guided by the political need to balance factions within the LDP and only rarely by the qualifications of a politician for a particular ministerial post.*

The Japanese bureaucracy jealously guards the practice of making no political appointments below the ministerial level; the bureaucrats believe that this helps establish their claim to be above politics and to speak only for the national interest. One of the bureaucracy's greatest fears is "political interference" in its internal affairs or, worse, a ministry's being made subservient to a party or a politician. Even though the minister is legally in command of and responsible for everything that happens in a ministry, a delicate relationship between him and the vice-minister inevitably exists from the outset. The norm is for the minister to fear his bureaucrats and to be dominated by them; one journalist suggests that the only time a minister ever enjoys his post is on the day he is photographed in formal dress at the Imperial Palace as part of the cabinet's investiture ceremony.[51] If this norm prevails, the bureaucrats are satisfied. But what they really want is a minister who will leave them alone while at the same time taking responsibility for the ministry and protecting it from intrusion by other politicians or

---

*The secretary-general of the LDP—one of the 4 party leaders under the party president (who is simultaneously the prime minister)—appoints an additional 24 parliamentary vice-ministers, 2 (1 for each house) in the ministries of Finance, Agriculture and Forestry, and International Trade and Industry, and 1 in each of the other ministries. These vice-ministers are supposed to provide liaison between the ministries and the Diet, but "the posts' chief attraction is that they furnish the politicians a chance to use the ministry's facilities to do favors for their constituents (thus bettering themselves in the elections), and for other politicians (thus bettering themselves in the party)." See Nathaniel B. Thayer, *How the Conservatives Rule Japan* (Princeton, N.J.: Princeton University Press, 1969), p. 279. The *Mainichi* observes that, like an appendix in a human body, the parliamentary vice-ministers do not seem to perform a vital function. They are invariably appointed with an eye to rewarding factions within the party and not to the effective functioning of either the bureaucracy or the Diet. See *Japan Times*, May 7, 1974, and December 27, 1975.

outside interests, particularly business interests. And this requires that a minister be a powerful politician—who may have ideas of his own. If he is also a former bureaucrat, perhaps even one from the ministry to which he has been appointed, the relationship can get quite complex.

Ministry of Finance officials claim to fear powerful ministers from their own service, men such as Kaya Okinori, Ikeda Hayato, or Fukuda Takeo.[52] Ikeda, in particular, was always an activist minister in whatever ministry he headed; and he became famous for shaking up the Ministry of Finance in order to remove fiscal conservatives who were blocking his plans for rapid economic growth, and also in order to enlist the ministry in support of his own political ambitions.[53] The trade and industry bureaucrats generally liked Ikeda when he was MITI minister, largely because they agreed with him, but when they disagreed—as for example over the pace of trade liberalization in 1960—he won. He also once gave orders that MITI men could not talk to the press without his approval because he was tired of reading in the newspapers about new economic initiatives that he knew nothing about.[54] He did not, however, interfere in ministerial personnel affairs.

Ikeda represented the unusual case of an ex-bureaucrat being an activist minister. Although somewhat trying for bureaucrats, such types do not pose a real threat to them. Much more serious are activist ministers from a party politician's (tōjinha) background. Their efforts to exert influence over a ministry can set off shock waves throughout Japanese politics that reverberate for years; details of cases in which this has occurred are repeated in every Japanese book on the central government. Probably the most famous case is that of Kōno Ichirō (1898–1965) and his efforts to bring the Ministry of Agriculture and Forestry under his personal control.

Kōno was an old follower of Hatoyama Ichirō in the prewar Seiyūkai. After his depurge in 1951 he returned to politics as an opponent of Yoshida's bureaucratic mainstream. With the unification of the two conservative parties into the LDP, he served as minister of agriculture and forestry in the first Hatoyama cabinet, as director-general of the Economic Planning Agency in the first Kishi cabinet, and as agriculture minister and then construction minister in the second and third Ikeda cabinets. As minister of construction in 1964, he was in charge of the Tokyo Olympics, Japan's debut on the postwar world scene as a rising economic power. After Ikeda's death Kōno led a major effort by the combined tōjinha to seize control of the party, but he was defeated by Satō Eisaku and died shortly thereafter.

When Kōno first became minister of agriculture in December 1954, he intervened powerfully in the internal personnel affairs of the ministry. His instrument was a bureaucrat named Yasuda Zen'ichirō, whom he promoted to the post of chief of the Secretariat (in the Ministry of Agriculture, the last step before the vice-ministership and the position responsible for all ministerial appointments) over the heads of many of his seniors. Yasuda then transferred or demoted bureaucrats who did not support Kōno. Yasuda was a willing participant in these operations because he hoped to have a political career himself, after retirement, as Kōno's protégé. He ended his bureaucratic service as chief of the Agriculture Ministry's Food Agency (July 1961 to January 1962), and then stood for and lost election to the lower house as a member of the Kōno faction.[55] Other ministries point to him as a prime example of the disasters that can befall a bureaucrat and a ministry if its members break ranks and allow a politician to use one of them for his own purposes.

Agriculture is often said to be the first ministry to have been "politicized" by the LDP because of the LDP's dependence on the farm vote. However, agriculture ministries are rarely "nonpolitical" in any country. At least one other ministry in Japan, Education, has always been under tight LDP control because of the party's ideological struggle with the communist-dominated teachers' union; there has never been even a pretense of bureaucratic independence at Education. As for MITI, over the years since its creation in 1949, prime ministers and ministers have attempted to gain control and use it for political purposes. MITI bureaucrats have been implacable in their resistance to these efforts, often citing the negative example of Kōno and agriculture. We shall analyze some of these MITI cases in detail later in this book, since they have often influenced the basic industrial policies of the ministry.

Some party politician ministers, even activist ones, have been welcomed at MITI because of their effectiveness in getting things done in the Diet: Tanaka Kakuei, Nakasone Yasuhiro, and Kōmoto Toshio are examples. Even when relations are good, however, the bureaucrats have in the back of their minds the danger of corruption when dealing with nonbureaucratic party politicians (corruption charges have been brought in postwar Japan against ex-bureaucrat politicians, but they have usually been make to stick only in the case of tōjinha politicians). If a minister should attempt to name the vice-minister (by custom the outgoing MITI vice-minister names his own successor) or otherwise alter the internal norms of bureaucratic life, warfare is inevitable. MITI officials have been known to cancel ministerial conferences or to declare them private gatherings when parliamentary vice-ministers insisted on attending.[56] From MITI's point of view, the ideal minister was someone like Shiina Etsusaburō (1898–1979), an old trade and industry bureaucrat who had no desire to intervene in ministerial affairs and who was also a powerful LDP politician and an effective Diet debater (in the Japanese context, this means a politician who can speak politely and at length without actually saying anything of substance—an art that Shiina had mastered). In general, prewar ministers had more influence over their ministries than postwar ministers, a change that again reflects the rise in bureaucratic power in the postwar era.

Although relations between bureaucrats and politicians are understandably delicate in the Japanese political system, the focus of bureaucratic life is within the ministry itself—and there informal norms and their occasional violation generate real passion. Landau and Stout remind us that "bureaucracies are fusions of artificially contrived and naturally developed systems. Apart from their formal properties, they are characterized by interest groups, personal networks, patron-client relations, brokers, and derivative coalitions."[57] These informal ties sustain an organization's "culture," helping it to function effectively by inspiring loyalty, easing communications problems, socializing newcomers, generating new ideas in the clash of values and so forth. Throughout this book I shall be dealing with MITI's fabricated properties—above all with the famous industry-specific vertical bureaus that were its formal organization from 1939 to 1973—but it is the informal practices and traditions that give life to an organization and that make its formal organization interesting.

Kusayanagi Daizō argues that all human relations in Japanese society are based on four kinds of "factions" (*batsu*): *keibatsu* (family and matrimonial cliques), *kyōdobatsu* (clansmen, or persons from the same locality), *gakubatsu* (school and university classmates), and *zaibatsu* ("factions based on money," an indefinite use of the term that should not be confused with its specific reference to the family-dominated industrial empires, or zaibatsu, of prewar Japan).[58] All of these occur in the bureaucracy, but the first two are of minor significance and can be dealt with speedily.

Evidence of keibatsu can be found in MITI. To cite a few examples, Hatoyama Michio, formerly a physicist in MITI's Industrial Technology Institute and after retirement head of Sony's technical department, is married to the second daughter of former Prime Minister Hatoyama Ichirō. The wife of Takashima Setsuo, who retired from MITI in 1969 after serving as vice-minister of the Economic Planning Agency, is the daughter of Kuroda Nagamichi, a former Imperial chamberlain. And Masuda Minoru, director-general of MITI's Natural Resources and Energy Agency in 1975, became a nephew through marriage of Nagano Shigeo, former president of Fuji Steel and one of the great industrial leaders of postwar Japan. Many other examples could be cited.

Before the war the Ministry of Commerce and Industry included in its ranks such high-status figures as Baron Itō Bunkichi, who was the illegitimate son of the Meiji oligarch Itō Hirobumi and who became the patron of Yoshino Shinji, one of the two or three most important figures in the history of MITI. Kidō Kōichi, of noble ancestry, was in the Ministry of Commerce and Industry before the war and became the wartime Lord Keeper of the Privy Seal. Shiina Etsusaburō was the nephew of Gotō Shimpei, the chief administrator of Taiwan in the Meiji era, president of the South Manchurian Railroad, and the rebuilder of Tokyo after the earthquake of 1923.

These connections and possible influences are important in Japan, and they are not necessarily accidental. A great many young bureaucrats ask their section chiefs to arrange their marriages, and a section chief will often have keibatsu considerations in mind when he promotes a match. Nonetheless, most informed observers conclude that keibatsu is not as important in the postwar bureaucracy as it was before the war.[59] Still, some MITI officials report that it is better for one's career to have a good keibatsu than a poor one, and Kubota notes that "on the average the 1949–1959 higher civil servants [the group that he studied in depth] more often had prominent fathers-in-law than prominent fathers."[60] It appears that bureaucrats in Japan are good catches as husbands.

Kyōdobatsu are similarly present among bureaucrats but of comparatively slight influence. A former MITI vice-minister, Tokunaga Hisatsugu (executive director of New Japan Steel after retirement), notes that when he was vice-minister, the minister was Ishii Mitsujirō, one of the major figures of postwar conservative politics. Ishii was not only his "senior" (*sempai*), but they both came from the same area of Fukuoka prefecture—that is, they both belong to what is called the same *kyōtō* (literally, "village party"). According to Tokunaga, this factor somewhat inhibited him in his relations with Ishii.[61] Kishi Nobusuke, Matsuoka Yōsuke, and Ayukawa Gisuke all were natives of Yamaguchi prefecture, and each has said that this contributed to their collaboration in the industrial development of Manchuria during the 1930's (Kishi is also the true elder brother of Satō Eisaku, although Kishi was adopted into a different lineage). The career of Kogane Yoshiteru, a major figure in the prewar Ministry of Commerce and Industry and an ex-MITI bureaucrat turned politician in the Diet during the 1950's and 1960's, illustrates both keibatsu and kyōdobatsu. He was born in 1898 into a commoner family in Odawara, Kanagawa prefecture, but as a young official he married the daughter of the sister of Mori Kaku's wife and thereby acquired the prewar secretary-general of the Seiyūkai party as his uncle. Through this connection and his background as a native of Kanagawa, he later succeeded to Mori's secure constituency in the Kanagawa third electoral district, which he represented in the Diet for about twenty years.[62]

Keibatsu and kyōdobatsu are part of any large Japanese organization, but gakubatsu is without question the single most important influence within the Japanese state bureaucracy. The cliques of university classmates are inseparable from bureaucratic life, because it is their university degrees and their success in passing the Higher-level Public Officials Examination that set bureaucrats apart from other elites in the society. Gakubatsu also forms the most pervasive "old boy" network throughout the society as a whole.

On March 1, 1886, the government issued an Imperial Ordinance stating that "the Imperial University has the objectives of giving instruction in the arts and sciences and inquiring into abstruse principles required by the state." This order established Tokyo Imperial University—or Tōdai, as it is known in abbreviation—as an institution to train an administrative service that would replace the samurai of Chōshū and Satsuma within the government. Tōdai graduates were always preferred by the government, but in the twentieth century, with the establishment of other modern universities, the government adopted the practice of examining all prospective state officials, including Tokyo University graduates. These higher civil service entrance examinations were extremely difficult; Spaulding calculates that the failure rate on the main exam during the period 1928–43 was 90 percent.[63] The entrance examination system continued after the war with little change. During 1977 about 53,000 people took the Higher-level Public Officials Examination, and only about 1,300 passed, a ratio of 1 passer to 41 applicants. Because of its original orientation toward education for government service, as well as its general excellence, Tokyo University has always provided the greatest number of applicants who pass the examinations (see Table 3).

Not all officials in a ministry must be certified through the civil service examinations, however. Before the war those who passed the examinations received Imperial appointments; those who did not take the examinations received ordinary (*hannin*) appointments. The distinction is roughly equivalent to that between commissioned and

TABLE 3

*Numbers and Universities of Passers of the Higher-Level
Public Officials Examinations, 1975 and 1976*

University	Number passing examination	
	1975	1976
Tokyo University	459	461
Kyoto University	172	193
Tōhoku University	67	51
Nagoya University	34	42
Kyūshū University	29	41
Tokyo Industrial University	44	38
Waseda University	28	32
Osaka University	44	32
Hokkaidō University	45	31
Tokyo University of Education	24	22
Nagoya Industrial University	7	19
Tokyo Agricultural University	18	15
Yokohama University	19	14
Chiba University	14	12
Kobe University	14	12
Hitotsubashi University	22	10
Keiō University	6	10

SOURCE: *Shūkan asahi*, July 15, 1977, pp. 21–23.
NOTE: No other university had as many as ten passers in either year.

noncommissioned officers in the military. In contemporary Japan all government officials must pass entrance examinations, but the old system is perpetuated by a differentiation between the difficulty and comprehensiveness of the examination taken. Today prospective bureaucrats must sit for either the class A (*kō*) or the class B (*otsu*) examinations; those who pass the first and are accepted by a ministry may advance to the highest executive levels of the career service, including the position of vice-minister, but those who pass the second cannot be promoted beyond the section chief level, and usually not that high.

University students hoping to enter government service take the class A examinations during their last year in the university. Those who pass and are selected by a ministry then become part of an entering class within the ministry. This identification with an entering cohort becomes the bureaucrat's most important attribute during his entire bureaucratic life, and it follows him long after he leaves government service. Entering classes establish vertical relationships among all high-level, or "career" (*kyaria*), officials—or what are called relations between *sempai* (seniors, those of earlier classes) and *kōhai* (juniors, those of later entering classes). Both promotion to the level of section chief and retirement are in accordance with strict seniority. This age grading (*nenkō joretsu*) and "respect for seniority" (*nenji sonchō*) among bureaucrats influences everything they do, not just their activities in a ministry. For example, as an aged man and a former prime minister, Kishi Nobusuke still habitually referred to Yoshino Shinji as his sempai, recalling their earliest relationship in the old Ministry of Agriculture and Commerce.[64] More poignantly, when Ōba Tetsuo, a former official of the Transportation Ministry and later president of All Nippon Airways, was hauled into the Diet to testify as a witness in the investigation of the Lockheed corruption case (1976), the press wrote that he shook with barely controlled anger under questioning. The explanation, the journalists said, was that the Diet member interrogating him was his former junior at the Transportation Ministry, and he was overcome by the impudence of a junior questioning a senior.[65]

In place of the term gakubatsu, some Japanese analysts prefer *Tōdaibatsu* (cliques of Tokyo University classmates) because of the predominance of Tokyo University graduates in the bureaucracy and in the upper echelons of the banking and industrial worlds. Even among the Tōdaibatsu, there is the batsu of all batsu—the alumni of the Tokyo University Law School. In order to understand their influence it is necessary to know that when an entering class joins a ministry, its members are permanently divided into two career paths—the path of "administrative officials," or generalists (*jimukan*), and the path of "technical officials," or specialists (*gikan*). This distinction differs from that between career (class A exam) and noncareer (class B exam) officials, but it has almost equally serious consequences. It is based on academic specialization in the university.

Only one ministry promotes technical officers to the top position— the vice-ministership—and that is the Ministry of Construction. It was created after the war around the nucleus of the old Home Ministry's Civil Engineering Bureau, plus many jimukan officers drawn from the Home Ministry's regular ranks. The struggle by the technicians to achieve equal treatment in Construction was both famous and fierce. It fell to the socialist government of Katayama Tetsu during the occupation to name the first vice-minister of the new Ministry of Construction. The old Home Ministry cadres proposed as their candidate the jimukan official Ōhashi Takeo, a former police officer; and the engineers put forward as their candidate the gikan official Iwasawa Tadayoshi. The unions of the various segments of the old Home Ministry put intense pressure on the Katayama government to favor one side or the other. Nishio Suehiro, chief cabinet secretary and an old socialist, chose Iwasawa. He explained that he personally had been victimized by the police in Okayama during the militarist era, precisely at the time when Ōhashi had served as chief of the Okayama police. As a result of Nishio's choice, the Construction Ministry bureaucrats forged an unwritten rule that the vice-ministership would alternate between administrative and technical officials, a practice that has prevailed to the present day.[66]

Within MITI only the head of the Mine Safety Bureau is open to a gikan officer—in fact, only to a graduate of the School of Engineering, Department of Mining, Tokyo University—and even here a pattern of alternation between generalists and specialists has developed. All other major posts in MITI and the other ministries, excluding the Construction Ministry and detached research institutes and other specialized organs, are monopolized by administrative officers. And the greatest source of administrative officers is the University of Tokyo's Law School.

According to a calculation of the National Personnel Authority, as of July 1, 1965, among 483 officials at the level of department chief (*buchō*) and above—all of whom had university degrees from law, economics, or literature departments—some 355 (or 73 percent) were graduates of Tōdai Law.[67] But Tōdai Law students do not go just to the government—only the best of them do. The rest go to top positions in the most important businesses in the country, and their affiliations with each other are legendary. Table 4 details the initial placement of the Tōdai Law classes of 1975 and 1976. Each class numbered around 690, of whom from 150 to 250 did not seek employment because they were continuing on in graduate work or had failed the Higher-level Public Officials Examination and were waiting to take it again the following year. Some 130 graduates of each class entered government service, choosing ministries in accordance with their own attainments and a rough rank ordering of the ministries in terms of their prestige—Finance, MITI, and Foreign Affairs on top; Welfare, Education, and Labor near the bottom. According to the *Mainichi*, "Before graduation, the Tokyo University counselors direct students to proper jobs— good enough for the Finance Ministry, or maybe not good enough for that but quite suitable for the Health and Welfare Ministry, or if this is undesirable, perhaps a leading business firm."[68]

Tōdai classmates in and out of government keep in touch with each other, and one reason private businesses are glad to get them is for purposes of liaison with the government. Perhaps more important, the Tōdai connection means that both government offices and board

TABLE 4
Placement of Graduates of the University of Tokyo Law School Classes of 1975 and 1976

Where graduate was placed	1975	1976
1. Central Government		
Ministry of Finance	17	15
MITI	13	14
Ministry of Foreign Affairs	10	11
Ministry of Justice	4	N.A.
Ministry of Posts and Telecommunications	12	13
Police Agency	7	12
Ministry of Home Affairs	13	10
Ministry of Agriculture and Forestry	11	9
Ministry of Transportation	9	9
Ministry of Construction	8	9
Ministry of Education	4	8
Ministry of Welfare	11	7
Ministry of Labor	5	4
Board of Audit	2	2
Supreme Court	1	2
Prime Minister's Office	1	1
Environment Agency	1	1
Defense Agency	1	1
National Tax Agency	0	1
Hokkaido Development Agency	0	1
SUBTOTAL	130	130
2. Prefectural governments	3	18
3. Public corporations	12	37
4. Banks, commercial and governmental	92	117
5. Securities and brokerage firms	4	8
6. Casualty and life insurance firms	26	27
7. Real estate firms	4	2
8. Shipbuilding companies	8	3
9. Automobile manufacturing companies	0	5
10. International trading companies	26	27
11. Electrical equipment manufacturers	5	4
12. Steel industry	20	22
13. Chemical industry	3	4
14. Textile industry	3	4
15. Construction industry	1	1
16. Warehousing and transportation industry	4	4
17. Public utilities	3	9
18. Mass communications	7	10
19. Other (family businesses, etc.)	c. 100	c. 111
TOTAL	451	543

SOURCE: *Shūkan yomiuri*, Apr. 3, 1976, pp. 156–59.

rooms are staffed by men who share a common outlook—one that is neither "legal" in the sense used in American law schools nor "entrepreneurial" in the sense used in American schools of business administration. Tōdai law offers a superb education in public and administrative law of the continental European variety, a subject much closer to what is called political science than to law in the English-speaking countries. Tōdai students also study economics—compulsory principles of economics in the first year, optional economic policy in the second year, and compulsory public finance in the third year. The resulting homogenization of views between the public and private sectors began before the war. As Rodney Clark observes from the point of view of corporate management: "By the 1920's higher education, particularly at certain great state and private universities, most especially the University of Tokyo, was coming to be seen as the most natural qualification for the management of major companies. . . . The emphasis on such [public law] studies argued (and, of course, promoted) a view of management as a bureaucratic and cooperative venture: the government of a company rather than the imposition of an entrepreneurial will on a market place and a work force by superior skill, courage, or judgment."[69]

Once in the bureaucracy, the Tōdai group in an entering class in a ministry works together to ensure that its members prosper and that others are frozen out of choice positions. Sakakibara Eisuke, a bureaucrat turned professor, recalls that his entering class at the Ministry of Finance in 1965 had a total of 18 members, 16 of which were from Tōdai and 2 from Kyoto University. Among the 18, 5 had economics degrees while the rest had law degrees. More usual was the class of 1966, with 21 members, of whom 20 were law graduates.[70] Under such circumstances a young official not from Tōdai will have difficulties in being promoted much beyond the section chief level. As the *Mainichi* reported, "When a Waseda University man was appointed to a bureau chief's post in the Ministry of Agriculture and Forestry some time ago, the event was played up prominently in all the newspapers."[71]

Who becomes a bureau chief, a director-general, or ultimately the one vice-minister is a source of intense competition among classes in a ministry. A new class of officers begins its life by circulating among different jobs in the various sections, moving every year or two (the bureaucrats call this *sotomawari*, or "going around the track"). Within MITI, in recent years most members of a class will also be posted overseas for a year in a consulate, an embassy, a university, or an office of JETRO (Japan External Trade Organization). Not all sections or posts in a ministry are equal. The general affairs section of each bureau is the most important section in the bureau, and the three main sections in the Minister's Secretariat (Daijin Kanbō)—those for personnel, general coordination, and budget and accounts, as they are known in MITI—are the most important sections in the ministry. A member of a class who passes through or heads several of these on his sotomawari is said to be on the "elite course" (*erīto kōsu*).

Nonelite class B exam bureaucrats do not circulate nearly so frequently. The pattern among them is to settle down in one section for years and become what is called a "walking dictionary" or "human encyclopedia" (*iki-jibiki*), the common term for those who do the detailed work of a section and who show the new career officers the ropes. Occasionally a walking dictionary will be promoted to section chief, but this is rare, and it never occurs in a key policy-making section.*

Promotion to section chief is virtually guaranteed to every career officer who does not make some major mistake. Table 5 shows the relative speed of promotion as of the end of 1975 for the various classes in the five economic ministries. It reveals that although both the Finance and MITI vice-ministers were from the classes of 1944, Finance was three years slower than MITI in making its new officers chiefs of section (in 1975, the class of 1958 at Finance was just getting their sections while at MITI the class of 1961 was already at that point). Competition over promotion begins beyond the section chief level.

There are only a limited number of bureau chief positions in a ministry, and obviously not every member of an entering class can have one. Those who are promoted are still in the running for the vice-ministership; those who are not are compelled to resign—or, as it is known in the Japanese government, to "descend from heaven" (amakudari) into a lucrative job in a public corporation or private industry. Ultimately everyone must "descend" because of the implacable pres-

---

*In MITI, for example, Abe Shinshichi, a former army paymaster who entered MITI service without taking the higher officials exam, rose to head the Vehicles Section in the Heavy Industries Bureau and ultimately became chief of the Shikoku regional bureau before retirement. Neither, however, is an important post. The Vehicles Section is avoided by career officers because it supervises bicycle and auto racing; it is said to be the only office in MITI with a regular subscription to the sports newspapers. During the last years of the occupation, criminal elements came to dominate bicycle racing in Japan; and after many public protests, the government turned bicycle racing over to MITI to clean up and to generate income from gambling at the tracks for public utilities and local finance. The Vehicles Section manages this; it should be distinguished from the Automobile Section in the same bureau, which is an important post. See Policy Review Company, ed., *Tsūsan-shō, sono hito to soshiki* (MITI: its personnel and organization) (Tokyo: Seisaku Jihō Sha, 1968), pp. 205–6.

TABLE 5

Relative Rates of Promotion by Entering Class (as of December 1, 1975)

Ministry	Vice-minister	Director-general, external bureau	Chief, internal bureau	Deputy chief, bureau; or department head	Chief, the three Secretariat Sections	Chief, General Affairs Section in bureau or agency	First appointment, section chief	Chief, regional bureau
Finance	1944	1946	1946–1948 (I)	1948 (II)–1950	1951–1952	1951–1952	1958	1948–1952
MITI	1944	1945–1947 (II)	1947 (I)–1948 (II)	1948 (II)–1951	1952	1952–1953	1961	1949–1951
Agriculture	1945	1945–1947 (I)	1946–1948	1948–1953	1952–1954	1953–1954	1960	1948–1951
Transportation	1943	1946	1946–1948 (II)	1948 (I)–1951	1953	1953–1955	1961	1952–1954
Construction	1944	1945	1945–1949	1949–1952	1951–1952	1952–1953	1958	none

SOURCE: Watanabe Yasuo, "Kōmuin no kyaria" (Careers of officials), in Tsuji Kiyoaki, ed., *Gyōseigaku kōza* (Lectures on the science of administration), Tokyo, 1976, 4: 191.
NOTE: The economic ministries recruited spring (I) and autumn (II) classes during 1947 and 1948 to meet their expanded duties under economic control.

sure from new entering classes advancing from below, and the usual retirement age for the vice-minister himself is slightly over 50. The practice is dictated by the rigid seniority system of the bureaucracy, but as we shall explain below, it has been turned to the advantage of the state as another very important channel of communication with the society.

The process of separating out those who will resign early and those who will stay in the ministry is called *kata-tataki* (the tap on the shoulder) or *mabiki* (thinning out). It is the responsibility of the vice-minister and the chief of the Secretariat, who are also responsible for finding the soon-to-be-retired officials good new positions on boards of directors. The final weeding out comes at the vice-ministerial level, when one man from one class is chosen by the outgoing vice-minister as his own replacement and when all the new vice-minister's classmates must resign to insure that he has absolute seniority in the ministry. The new vice-minister in turn devotes his efforts to seeing that these high-ranking retirees (and fellow classmates) get good amakudari landing spots. New positions for retiring vice-ministers are found for them by the minister and by the ministry's elder statesmen (sempai).

Competition in the maneuvering for high positions in a ministry normally occurs among classes and not individuals. For example, the 25 members of the class of May 1947 in the Ministry of Finance organized themselves as a club, the Satsuki Kai (May Club), which continued in amity for 31 years until 1978, when it had only one member left, Ōkura Masataka, the director of the Tax Bureau.[72] Even if not formally organized as a club, a class will sometimes meet and caucus as a body during periods of stress within a ministry in order to agree on common policies (the various classes in MITI met separately in 1963, at the time of Sahashi's initial failure to be appointed vice-minister, one of the big crises in MITI history, which I shall describe fully in Chapter 7).

Not every class can produce a vice-minister; if it did he could occupy the office for only a few months, which would greatly damage the effectiveness of a ministry's chief executive officer. Therefore, some classes have to be passed over. As a result of this factor, a chief of personnel in the Secretariat will sometimes attempt to remove promising members of rival classes from the competition in order to keep his own class in the running. Many of Sahashi's opponents have accused him of using his years as the personnel section chief to rig the succession. Whatever the case, the classes of 1935 and 1936, which lay between that of the outgoing vice-minister (1934) and Sahashi's own

(1937), found their members all occupying terminal positions. The "loser years" in MITI were 1935, 1936, 1938, and 1942.

Each class has its "flowers" (*hana*)—that is, candidates with strong credentials for the vice-ministership—and members of the class take pride in one of their comrades representing them at the top. For example, the *jū-huchi-nen gumi no hana* (flowers of the class of 1943) at MITI were Shō Kiyoshi, Yajima Shirō, Miyake Yukio, and Yamashita Eimei. During 1973 Shō ended his MITI career as director-general of the Medium and Smaller Enterprises Agency, Miyake as director-general of the Patent Agency, Yajima as chief of the Heavy Industries Bureau, and Yamashita made it to the top as MITI vice-minister from July 1973 to November 1974. Needless to say, when one class produces two vice-ministers—as happened twice in MITI (Ishihara Takeo and Ueno Kōshichi, both of the class of 1932, succeeded each other as vice-minister between 1955 and 1960; and Imai Zen'ei and Sahashi Shigeru, both of the class of 1937, succeeded each other as vice-minister between 1963 and 1966)—great strains are imposed on the internal norms of ministerial life.

Before the war age grading existed, but it was not as rigorously enforced as after the war. When Yoshino Shinji (class of 1913) became vice-minister of the Ministry of Commerce and Industry in 1931 (he served in that office until 1936), he was only 43 years old and was promoted over several of his seniors. Moreover, at his personal request, one of his seniors (Nakamatsu Shinkyō, class of 1908) remained on in the ministry as chief of the Patent Bureau for another five years. Within MITI the practice of all classmates or seniors resigning when a new vice-minister takes over appears to have originated in October 1941, when Kishi became minister and appointed Shiina vice-minister. Kishi and Shiina represented the Manchurian faction of pro-military bureaucrats in the ministry, and they had very definite ideas of what they wanted to do. Kishi asked all of Shiina's superiors, with whom both had disagreed on policy, to resign, and they did so.[73]

In the postwar world "respect for seniority" developed concomitantly with the tremendous expansion of the bureaucracy. It was needed to bring some definite order to the bureaucracy's internal personnel administration as well as to provide security for officials, who were significantly less well paid than before the war. As one measure of the bureaucracy's expansion, Watanabe calculates that whereas between 1894 and 1943 some 9,008 individuals passed the Higher-level (class A) Public Officials Examination, between 1948 and 1973 some 18,998 individuals did so.[74]

Not all bureaucrats like or approve of the system of age grading and forced early retirement. Sahashi has often denounced it as irrational, even though he was a past master at manipulating it. By the 1970's both the bureaucrats and the public were showing signs of irritation with the system. In 1974 an official rocked MITI by refusing to resign after he had been tapped and told it was time to go. Hayashi Shintarō, spring class of 1947 and a Ph.D. in economics, had been chief of the Industrial Location and Environmental Protection Bureau for less than a year when he was asked to resign. Even though he had excellent job offers from private industry, he refused them on the grounds that his current work was important and that it was poor administration to change officials before they could even begin to be effective in their posts. Hayashi was liked in the ministry; he had become famous for developing the postwar Japanese sewing machine industry into a thriving export business, and he had served for several years in the JETRO office in West Germany, where he had studied—as MITI habitually puts it—"how American capital overran the Western European economy."[75] His refusal to resign won praise from some younger MITI officials and from the press. Nonetheless, he was reassigned to the Secretariat with no work to do and took a cut in pay. Shortly thereafter he resigned and became vice-president of Jasco Corporation, a big chain of retail stores in the Osaka and Nagoya regions.

In contrast to the views of Sahashi and Hayashi, Ōjimi Yoshihisa, a vice-minister, defends the system. He argues that strict rules of seniority and early retirement make Japan's top bureaucrats more youthful and energetic than those of other countries, and that because of their vigor they can generate more good new ideas. At the same time, the system of senior-junior (sempai-kōhai) relations, which extends beyond the period of bureaucratic service, ensures that their actions are watched by men with great experience.[76] It should be added that an additional result of the system of early retirement and subsequent reemployment in big business or politics is another link between a ministry and its main clients. The practice of bureaucratic descent from heaven thus generates one more kind of factional tie among the central groups of Japanese society—factions based on financial considerations (zaibatsu, in the nonspecific sense of the term).

As we have already seen, state bureaucrats in Japan retire early from government service and then obtain new employment in big business, public corporations, or politics. This practice is obviously open to abuse, and many Japanese commentators have charged that it has been abused. MITI reporters, for example, argue that a wise bureaucrat will use his years as a section chief to generate new ideas and put pressure on the business community to adopt them, but that as a bureau chief he should become submissive toward the ministry's clients with a view to enhancing his own amakudari.[77] Misonō Hitoshi asserts that the combination of early retirement and inadequate pensions has made government service "only an apprenticeship for favorable employment after retirement."[78] And Takeuchi Naokazu, a disgruntled former Ministry of Agriculture bureaucrat who quit and became active in the consumer movement, charges that the Budget Bureau of the Ministry of Finance has been known to increase the budget shares of ministries that were willing to find positions for retiring finance officers in the public corporations those ministries control, or among their clients.[79]

Actual corruption among higher officials in Japan has occurred but is uncommon. In general, the Japanese public places greater trust in the honesty of state officials than in the honesty of politicans or business leaders. Such petty corruption as does occur— gifts from businessmen, golf club fees, dinner parties, junkets—is more common among noncareer officials than among the higher bureaucrats, and was more common in the period of shortages in the 1950's than in later years.[80] When such incidents do involve higher officials, the press and public are quick to condemn them. For example, charges of the misuse of public funds in several public corporations and efforts to apprehend the guilty were national causes célèbres during 1979 and 1980.[81] And the press and opposition parties are very watchful. The *Mainichi*, for example, reports that "toward the end of November of 1973, Nozue Chimpei, a member of the House of Councillors, conducted a unique study. He and his staff examined the trash cans at the construction and transport ministries to study how conservation policies were being carried out. After seven days of investigation, they found that the trash cans at the two ministries were filled with empty bottles of Johnny Walker and other expensive foreign liquor, and empty gift boxes bearing the names of senders."[82]

The serious issue in Japan is not the occasional abuse of office by a higher official but a pattern of cooperation between the government and big business that may have unintended consequences. Throughout its modern history Japan has experienced a series of major governmental corruption scandals, the most famous of which are the Siemens case of 1914, the Yawata state steel works case of 1918, the Teijin case of 1934, the Shōwa Denkō case of 1948, the shipbuilding bribery case of 1954, the Tanaka "money politics" case of 1974, and the Lockheed case of 1976. These are only the most sensational; numerous others have occurred, and four resulted in the fall of governments.[83]

Less flagrant but possibly more important have been incidents of seeming wholesale payoffs by the government to business interests with preferential access or advance knowledge: the "dollar-buying scandal" of 1931, the payments to munitions companies immediately following the defeat in 1945, and the Bank of Japan's dollar-buying policies at the time of the August 1971 "Nixon shock" (in the face of certain knowledge that the yen would be revalued). On August 27, 1971, alone the government paid out some $1.2 billion—six times the amount involved in 1931—to purchase dollars that had already been devalued on the rest of the world's foreign exchange markets. Total Bank of Japan dollar purchases in 1971 came close to $6 billion at ¥360 = $1 instead of ¥308 = $1; this represented a gift to business concerns of almost $1 billion. Some writers have called this "institutionalized corruption"; others have argued that it was the government's attempt to soften the blow for industries that would henceforth be selling their products at less advantageous prices.[84]

The reemployment of retired government bureaucrats on the boards of industries currently designated as economically strategic also creates many opportunities for hand-in-glove relationships. A classic case was the so-called Hakone railroad war of the late 1950's between two big private railroad systems, Seibu and Tōkyū. The issues involved the development of tourist railroads and bus franchises in and around the Mount Fuji area, a rail route from Itō to Shimoda, and tourist boats between Atami and Ōshima Island. In every instance the Ministry of Transportation gave approval or issued licenses to Tōkyū. The explanation of informed observers was that the president of Tōkyū, Gotō Keita (1882–1959)—one of the pioneers of the railroad, hotel, and department store businesses in Japan—was also a former official of the government railways and a minister of transportation in the Tōjō cabinet. The vice-president of Tōkyū and president of the Tōkyū-backed Tōei Film Company was Ōkawa Hiroshi, also a veteran of the Japanese National Railways. The executive director of Tōkyū and also president of Tōkyū Rolling-Stock Company was Yoshitsugu Toshiji, who had served in the old Railroad Ministry for more than twenty years. In addition, Karasawa Tsutomu, the Tōkyū managing director; Kawahara Michimasa, president of the Tōkyū-affiliated Keihin Rapid Transit Company; Torii Kikuzō, vice-president of the Tōkyū-affiliated Sagami Railroad Company; Shibata Ginzō, president of the Tōkyū-affiliated Hakone-Tōzan Railroad Company; Kajiura Kōjirō, president of the Tōkyū-affiliated Enoshima-Kamakura Electric Railway Company; and Kawai Kentarō, president of the Tōkyū-affiliated Shizuoka Railway Company, were all former officials of the Ministry of Railways or its postwar successor, the Ministry of Transportation. It has been suggested that these "seniors" might have had some influence over the transportation officials who had to review Tōkyū's plans. Some incumbent officials might even have been thinking of entering the Tōkyū empire when they retired.[85]

Thus one reason for the private sector's participation in amakudari is the extensive licensing and approval authority (kyoninkaken) of the government. Companies believe that having former bureaucrats among their executives can facilitate obtaining licenses from the ministries. The Ministry of Construction exercises licensing authority over the building industry, the Ministry of Transportation over rail and air transport and the bus and taxi business, the Ministry of Finance over the banks, and MITI over the key industries—steel, electric power, and chemicals in the 1950's, automobiles and appliances in the 1960's, advanced electronics in the 1970's, computers, robots, and new sources of energy in the 1980's. With this in mind it becomes understandable that whereas during the 1950's and 1960's very few ex-MITI officials joined foreign-affiliated firms, during the 1970's, with MITI's new commitment to the "internationalization" of the Japanese economy, ex-MITI officials began to appear in Matsushita-America, IBM Japan, and Japan Texas Instruments.[86]

It is misleading to consider this type of government-business relationship a form of "corruption"; it is, rather, an adaptation by private business to a particular governmental environment. The same adaptation occurs in other countries, although in the United States the preferred insiders are ex-congressmen rather than ex-bureaucrats (except in the defense industries). Thus, during the 1970's Albert Gore, Sr., a former senator, became a lawyer for Occidental Petroleum; Paul Rodgers, former chairman of a House public health subcommittee, became a member of the board of Merck and Company; and Brock Adams, former congressman and secretary of transportation, became a lawyer for Trans World Airlines.[87] This preference for congressmen rather than bureaucrats in the United States merely reflects the market rationality of the American system as contrasted with Japan's plan rationality.

Preferential access to the government for the strategic industries in Japan is not an unintended consequence of the developmental state; it is in fact an objective of the developmental state. This is the true significance of amakudari. A cost of the system is occasional misuse of access to gain some private advantage. Nonetheless, from the Japanese point of view, the advantages of amakudari for smooth policy formulation and execution outweigh this cost. The Japanese refer to consultations between ex-bureaucrat seniors and their incumbent juniors as "digging around the roots" (*nemawashi*), that is, preparing the groundwork for a government-business decision. To outsiders it often looks like "consensus."

The most senior amakudari positions—for example, the postretirement landing spots of MITI's vice-ministers (see Table 6)—are bases from which to coordinate the strategic sectors. At this level the Western distinction between public and private loses its meaning. As Eleanor Hadley remarks about the prewar zaibatsu, "The combines' strength was regarded as national strength but their profits were seen as private property."[88] In the postwar world this relationship persists, except that the weight of the government is much stronger. Satō Kiichirō, former president of the Mitsui Bank, observes that "during and after the war, . . . Japan's economy was controlled until it has become second nature with us to uphold a planned, controlled economy."[89]

At the level of the supreme leadership of the business community, the primary concern is that the relationship between government and business be managed effectively for the good of all. Amakudari is significant here only in that it contributes to a common orientation—as does education at Tōdai, golf club memberships (MITI's Amaya acknowledges that "they do other things than play golf at golf courses"), and the common experience of the war and its aftermath.[90] Of the five postwar presidents of Keidanren (the Federation of Economic Organizations)—Ishikawa Ichirō (1885–1970), Ishizaka Taizō (1886–1975), Uemura Kōgorō (1894–1978), Dokō Toshio (b. 1896), and Inayama Yoshihiro (b. 1904)—three are former bureaucrats (one at Communications, two at Commerce and Industry) and four are graduates of Tōdai (one in engineering, one in economics, and two in law). It would be difficult, however, to correlate their backgrounds with their policies, except to say that all five worked closely with the government. Ishikawa (a nonbureaucrat engineer), Uemura (an ex-bureaucrat), and Inayama (an ex-bureaucrat) were most cooperative; Dokō (a non-Tōdai engineer) was less so; and Ishizaka (a Tōdai law ex-bureaucrat), perhaps surprisingly, was the least cooperative.

Amakudari provides one more channel of communication for the government, the business community, and the political world. Nakamura Takafusa believes it is the main channel of liaison between the business world and the bureaucratic world.[91] Nonetheless, its influence is tempered by the similar but also cross-cutting influences of school ties, marital alliances, clan networks, deliberation councils, senior-junior relations, and the ministerial clubs of all retired bureaucrats (for example, MITI's Kayō-kai, or Tuesday Club, had some 588 members in 1963).[92] The human element also enters. Some bureau-

TABLE 6

MITI Vice-Ministers and Their Amakudari Positions (as of 1978)

(Parentheses under names indicate years of active service in MITI)

Name	Vice-minister dates	Amakudari position(s)
1. Yamamoto Takayuki (1929–1952)	5/49–3/52	Vice-president, Fuji Iron and Steel; died May 17, 1961.
2. Tamaki Keizō (1930–1953)	3/52–11/53	President, then chairman, Tōshiba Electric Co.
3. Hirai Tomisaburō (1931–1955)	11/53–11/55	President, then adviser, New Japan Steel Corp.
4. Ishihara Takeo (1932–1957)	11/55–6/57	Vice-president, then auditor, Tokyo Electric Power Co.
5. Ueno Kōshichi (1932–1960)	6/57–5/60	Vice-president, then adviser, Kansai Electric Power Co.; president, Kansai Oil Co.
6. Tokunaga Hisatsugu (1933–1961)	5/60–7/61	Vice-president, New Japan Steel Corp.; then president, Japan Petroleum Development Corp.
7. Matsuo Kinzō (1934–1963)	7/61–7/63	Chairman, Nippon Kōkan Steel Co.
8. Imai Zen'ei (1937–1964)	7/63–10/64	President, Japan Petrochemical Corp.
9. Sahashi Shigeru (1937–1966)	10/64–4/66	Sahashi Economic Research Institute; chairman, Japan Leisure Development Center.
10. Yamamoto Shigenobu (1939–1968)	4/66–5/68	Executive director, Toyota Motor Co.
11. Kumagai Yoshifumi (1940–1969)	5/68–11/69	President, Sumitomo Metals Corp.
12. Ōjimi Yoshihisa (Spring 1941–1971)	11/69–6/71	President, Arabian Oil Co.
13. Morozumi Yoshihiko (Autumn 1941–1973)	6/71–7/73	President, Electric Power Development Company.
14. Yamashita Eimei (1943–1974)	7/73–11/74	Managing director, Mitsui Trading Co.; president, Iran Chemical Development Co.
15. Komatsu Yūgorō (1944–1976)	11/74–7/76	Director, Kobe Steel Corp.

crats simply do not like amakudari because they feel that it is beneath them as officials to become involved in business for profit or because they do not want to come back to their old ministry to lobby their younger colleagues. Iwatake Teruhiko, for example, joined Kobe Steel after retirement from MITI, but he did not approve of amakudari. When a Ministry of Finance official, Inoue Yoshimi, beat him out as president of Kobe Steel, he was offered the presidency of a satellite company, but he resigned instead and became a lecturer in literature at Tōdai, something he had wanted to do for many years.[93]

The Japanese government-business relationship does not always work as smoothly as it appears to on the surface. A major check to its effectiveness, one that often alters the various relationships within the establishment in unforeseen ways, is competition among ministries—what the Japanese call "sectionalism." Some observers believe that it is the most important characteristic of the Japanese government, either limiting its potential effectiveness or mitigating its enormous powers.[94] To judge by the Japanese term commonly used to describe it—*gun'yū kakkyo* (the rivalry of local barons)—one would think that the Japanese believe sectionalism is an inheritance from the samurai era. Certainly one demonstrable cause of sectionalism was the Meiji Constitution of 1889, with its provisions for "independent responsibility to the throne," meaning that ministers and their ministries were not accountable to the prime minister, the cabinet, or the Diet, but only to the Emperor—and hence to no one but themselves. The drafters' intent was to prevent rivals to the oligarchs from coming to power and using the government against them, but the actual result was numerous instances in which the military ministries used their radical independence to defy all authority. And many scholars believe that the lack of coordination between the army, the navy, and the rest of the government during the Pacific War was a major cause of Japan's overwhelming defeat.[95]

The Constitution of 1947 states that "executive power shall be vested in the Cabinet" (art. 65), and that "the Cabinet, in the exercise of executive power, shall be collectively responsible to the Diet" (art. 66). Nonetheless, the cabinet has no coordinating organs, and executive power has remained, as it was before the war, in the ministries. (Neither the Board of Audit nor the Cabinet Legislation Bureau, the two main staff organs attached to the cabinet, has supervisory or coordinating powers over the ministries.) A minister can no longer bring down a government simply by resigning, but the old traditions of intense independence and of rivalry persist. Sahashi Shigeru, a former MITI vice-minister, contends that on this score the cabinet system of 1885 continues unchanged in its essentials to the present. He concludes, "Bureaucrats are officials of the various ministries first and only second are they servants of the nation." [96]

The postwar expansion of the bureaucracy followed by efforts to reduce its size reinforced this tradition. A bureaucrat's security and livelihood became dependent on maintaining or expanding his ministry's jurisdiction. Shrinking jurisdictions threaten not only the bureaucrats' active-duty positions but also their amakudari prospects, since a ministry needs clients and captive organizations to hire those of its retired members who do not have readily marketable skills. Tradition and circumstances thus produce an intense "territorial consciousness" (*nawabari ishiki*), punctuated—in Sakakibara's words—by "gangster-like struggles over jurisdiction" (*yakuza no nawabari arasoi*) throughout the state bureaucracy. [97]

Whatever the issue, bureaucrats' willingness to fight to defend the interests of their service has a marked delaying and distorting effect on Japanese governmental policy. Many decisions of the Japanese government are incomprehensible to the outside observer unless he or she understands the bureaucratic interests at stake and the compromises that these interests necessitate. In 1974, for example, when Prime Minister Tanaka proposed the creation of an overseas economic cooperation ministry, warfare among the existing ministries burst into the open. MITI had already tried to get written into the 1974 budget a proposal for a "mining and manufacturing overseas trade development corporation," and Agriculture wanted an "overseas agriculture and forestry development corporation." They were actively competing with each other for a share of what looked like an expansion of Japan's economic aid activities. Foreign Affairs promptly objected that it already had two agencies under its jurisdiction that had purposes similar to the proposed ministry. Prime Minister Tanaka ultimately decided on a ministry that would incorporate the two Foreign Affairs agencies but include MITI and Agriculture in their management. Foreign Affairs fought on and finally accepted the new International Cooperation Agency of August 1974 only when it was agreed that it would *not* be a ministry and that a foreign office official would head it. [98]

When Tanaka was prime minister he also promised in his reelection campaign to create a Medium and Smaller Enterprises Ministry, just as a few years later Prime Minister Fukuda promised to create an Energy Ministry and a Housing Ministry. Regardless of whether this proliferation of ministries would have been a good idea, the reason that none of them ever saw the light of day was not substantive objections but ministerial resistance. MITI mobilized the Agriculture and

Welfare ministries to stop the medium and smaller enterprises proposal by arguing that they, too, would lose some jurisdiction, to say nothing of MITI itself. MITI and the Ministry of Construction stopped the energy and housing ideas by utilizing their old boy networks, since neither ministry wanted to lose the petroleum and housing businesses as places for their officials to retire.

The longest continuing struggle in the Japanese government, dating from well before the war, has been over the attempt to take control of the budget away from the Ministry of Finance in order to lodge it in the cabinet or some supraministerial coordinating agency. In 1955 Kōno Ichirō conceived of an independent budget bureau; in 1963 the Temporary Administrative Investigation Council recommended creation of a system of cabinet assistants to oversee the budget; and in 1970 Kawashima Shōjirō called for the establishment of an Overall Planning Agency (Sōgō Kikaku-chō). The Ministry of Finance successfully beat back all these proposals. Regardless of what the constitution says, the coordinating power of the Japanese executive branch is exercised through the three annual budgets (general account, special accounts, and government investment), and control over them is in the hands of the Budget Bureau and the Financial Bureau of the Ministry of Finance.

The *Asahi* argues that, because of ministerial rivalry, in foreign affairs Japan can never create a monolithic negotiating position—which is not necessarily a bad thing. Contention often develops among Foreign Affairs, Finance, and MITI during any major international negotiations. Each of them maintains its own overseas communications network—Foreign Affairs through the regular foreign office cable system, Finance through the telex system of the Bank of Tokyo, and MITI through the telex system of JETRO. According to the *Asahi*, Japan actually has three foreign services, each of them with different policies and each represented overseas. The Ministry of Foreign Affairs is the most internationalist, MITI has historically been protectionist, and the Finance Ministry is fairly internationalist but stingy about spending money for defense or foreign aid. Policy is a result of compromises among these positions, and the compromises change as the power positions of the three ministries shift with political developments.[99]

The headquarters of a ministry engaged in interministerial struggles is, of course, its home office in the Kasumigaseki district of Tokyo. But in addition to its home office staff and its various old boy networks, client organizations, deliberation councils, and public corporations, each ministry has "assets" (*kabu*) spread throughout the government in the form of transferees, or what the French call *dé-*

tachés. The old-line ministries engage in a relentless contest to capture and control the more vulnerable agencies of the government through the sending of *détachés*. Their primary targets are the independent agencies attached to the prime minister's office, each of which is headed by an appointed minister of state (*kokumu daijin*): The Defense Agency, the Economic Planning Agency, the Science and Technology Agency, the Environment Agency, the National Land Agency, and a few others. The transferees who staff these agencies make up what the press calls expeditionary armies, which are quite regularly committed by their ministries to the "battles for the outposts" that are a serious part of the Japanese policy-making process.

The case of the Economic Planning Agency (EPA) has been the most widely studied and reported.[100] Suffice it to say that MITI and the Ministry of Finance both hold strong positions at the EPA—MITI controls its vice-ministership (since the 1960's a prestigious terminal appointment within the MITI personnel hierarchy) and the head of its Coordination Bureau, together with several section chief positions; Finance names its chief secretary and some important section chiefs. The positions MITI controls are valuable to it because through them it is able to place its own representatives on the Bank of Japan's Policy Board and on the deliberation council that supervises the Ministry of Finance's trust fund accounts, which are used to fund the investment budget.

As for the EPA itself, it has come to be known as a "colony agency," or a "branch store of MITI." It has no operating functions, but only writes reports—hence its other nickname of the "composition agency."[101] EPA's forecasts and indicative plans are read not so much for their accuracy or econometric sophistication as for official statements of what industries the government is prepared to finance or guarantee for the immediate future. Some Japanese economists believe that it is precisely this EPA function of indicating the government's intentions regarding the economy that gives rise to the "typically Japanese phenomenon" of excessive competition: excessive competition does not exist in all industries but only in those industries in which the government has expressed an interest—and in which, as a result, the risks are greatly reduced.[102] However, the quality of the EPA's main product, the annual Economic White Paper, has been affected by its colony status: in 1970 MITI prevented it from saying that the Yawata-Fuji steel merger (which produced New Japan Steel) could lead to monopolistic price increases, and in 1971 the Finance Ministry stopped any mention of the inflationary effects of the Bank of Japan's dollar buying following the Nixon shocks.[103]

The Defense Agency illustrates a different facet of the struggle for the outposts. Japan's postwar armed forces originated late in the occupation era as the National Police Reserve Force; in 1954 the Police Reserve was expanded, placed under the newly created Defense Agency, and renamed the Self-Defense Forces. In the same year a new national Police Agency was established. Since the civilian leaders of the Police Reserve had come from the old Home Ministry line of descent, and since the new Police Agency inherited the old Home Ministry's national police functions, it was natural that the Police Agency should continue supplying the civilian bureaucrats to staff the new Defense Agency. The first chief of the Police Reserve and the first vice-minister of the Defense Agency was Masuhara Keikichi, who held the post from August 1952 to June 1957. Masuhara was an old Home Ministry bureaucrat (Tōdai law, 1928; chief of the Yamagata prefectural police in 1940). The top positions in the uniformed service of Japan's new armed forces went to former military officers, but until the 1970's all the top Defense executive positions were held by Police Agency transferees.

However, the Police Agency ran into trouble holding on to its bureaucratic turf because its predecessors did not recruit many new officials during the key class years of 1948 to 1952. The Ministry of Finance, on the other hand, took in about 50 successful examinees in 1947 and 1948 each, and from 40 to 50 during each of the years 1949–53. By the middle of the 1970's the Finance Ministry was under heavy pressure to find positions for some of these now high-ranking officials, and the Defense Agency looked promising. In June 1974 the Finance Ministry finally succeeded in placing Tashiro Kazumasa, formerly of the Finance Ministry's Secretariat, as the vice-minister of defense. Even though defense issues were becoming increasingly important to the Japanese during the 1970's, the Defense Agency itself was preoccupied by the Police-Finance struggle. The real losers in this fight, as at the EPA, were the pure defense bureaucrats, those who went to the Defense Agency directly from the university.[104] MITI maintains a modest but choice portfolio at Defense: it controls the chief of the Equipment Bureau position and the main defense equipment section. The Welfare, Postal Services, Labor, and Foreign Affairs ministries also have one or two section chief positions under their control in the Defense Agency.

The case of the Environment Agency (Kankyō-chō), set up in 1971 after the famous "pollution Diet" of 1970 had greatly strengthened the environmental protection laws, is a classic of the established ministries staking out claims in newly opened-up territory. The Environment Agency's staff was fixed initially at 500 officials, and some twelve different ministries and agencies supplied them. The Welfare Ministry headed the list with 283, then Agriculture with 61, MITI with 26, the Economic Planning Agency with 21, and so forth. The fighting over the leadership posts was fierce. Welfare won it when the vice-minister of Welfare himself transferred to the new agency as its vice-minister. Welfare also captured two bureau chief positions and the position of chief of the Secretariat. Finance and Agriculture split the two remaining bureau directorships, and MITI got only a councillor's slot (*shingikan*). Of the 21 sections in the Environment Agency, Welfare names the chief of 7, MITI 3, Economic Planning and Agriculture 2 each, and Finance, Construction, Home, Labor, Police, Transport, and the Prime Minister's Office 1 each.[105] Watanabe notes that "this pattern is true for all newly created agencies."[106]

The struggle for nawabari (literally, "roped-off areas") is one of the passions of the Japanese bureaucracy. However, this may well be one of the hidden, if unintended, strengths of the Japanese system. As Hollerman argues, "If 'the government' of Japan were actually a highly coordinated set of agencies, its powers could be applied with overwhelming force. Instead, partly as a result of sheer ambition for status and partly as a result of divergent interests within the society itself, there is intense rivalry and jealousy among the ruling agencies and their personnel. In competing for power, they tend to neutralize one another's authority to some extent."[107]

On the other hand, Sakakibara, himself an ex-bureaucrat, defends what he calls the vertical organization of the bureaucracy because of the discipline and solidarity it instills in officials. Rather than committing themselves to some abstract ideal, they join a "family" when they enter an old-line ministry. Given its semilifetime employment system and its vertical organization, each ministry must create sufficient public corporations, affiliated associations of clients (*gaikaku dantai*), and colonial outposts for its retired and soon-to-retire seniors. These commitments cause a ministry to become a "welfare community," which in turn becomes an object of affection for its members and not merely an impersonal office.[108] Efforts at administrative reform in Japan have occasionally produced a reduction in personnel or the abolition of a grossly superfluous unit, but they have never affected the vertical structure.

MITI itself, as the descendant of one of the original ministries dating back to 1881, is certainly a "welfare community," but it also has several characteristics that distinguish it from the other economic bureaucracies. It is the smallest of the economic ministries in terms of personnel, and it controls the smallest share of the general account budget. This last feature is important because it frees MITI from the commanding influence of the Finance Ministry's Budget Bureau, which all the other ministries must cultivate. MITI exercises control over money through its ability to approve credit or authorize expenditures by the Japan Development Bank, the Electric Power Development Company, the Export-Import Bank, the Smaller Business Finance Corporation, the Bank for Commerce and Industrial Cooperatives, the Japan Petroleum Development Corporation, and the Productivity Headquarters, all of which are public corporations that it controls—or in which its views are decisive.[109] Although MITI's official budget in fiscal 1956, for example, was only ¥8.2 billion, the MITI Press Club concluded that the ministry actually supervised the spending of some ¥160.9 billion.[110]

MITI's internal pecking order is different from that in other ministries. Although most of its vice-ministers have served as chiefs of one of the sections in the Secretariat, the Secretariat itself is not the final spot—or "waiting room" (*machiai-shitsu*)—for the vice-ministership, as it is in other ministries. The internal MITI rank order is as follows:

1. vice-minister
2. chief, Industrial Policy Bureau (before 1973, the Enterprises Bureau, which was created in 1942)
3. director-general, Natural Resources and Energy Agency
4. director-general, Medium and Smaller Enterprises Agency
5. director-general, Patent Agency
6. chief, International Trade Policy Bureau
7. chief, Machinery and Information Industries Bureau
8. chief, Minister's Secretariat
9. chief, Basic Industries Bureau
10. chief, Industrial Location and Environmental Protection Bureau
11. chief, Consumer Goods Industries Bureau
12. chief, Trade Bureau (the old Trade Promotion Bureau)[111]

The high status of the Industrial Policy Bureau is a reflection of the internal factional fighting that has gone on continuously within the ministry since it was reorganized in 1949. In this fighting, which was between the industrial faction (also called the "control" or "domestic" faction) and the international faction (also called the "trade" or "liberal" faction), the industrial faction and its policies dominated the ministry until 1966, and its headquarters was the Industrial Policy Bureau. During the 1970's a new breed of internationalists took over the ministry and ended the earlier disputes, but the management of industrial policy has remained the hallmark of MITI. It is because of this that the directorship of the Industrial Policy Bureau is the last step before the vice-ministership.

MITI also differs from other ministries in the degree of internal democracy it supports and in the authority it gives to younger officials. The ministry believes that the most fertile time in the life of a bureaucrat for generating new ideas is when he serves as assistant section chief (*kachō-hosa*). MITI tries to tap this capacity through a unique institution known as the Laws and Ordinances Examination Committee (Hōrei Shinsa Iinkai). It is composed of the deputy chiefs of the General Affairs or Coordination sections in each bureau throughout the ministry. All major policies of the ministry are introduced and screened at this level, and no new policy can be initiated without its approval. For a young assistant section chief to be named chairman of this committee is a certain sign that he is on the "elite course" toward becoming a bureau chief and, possibly, the vice-minister.

Above this committee are review groups at the section chief level—the General Affairs Section Chiefs' Conference (Shomu Kachō Kaigi)—and at the bureau director level—the Operational Liaison Conference (Jimuren). The bureau director level is the court of last resort for approval of a policy initiated by the assistant section chiefs; anything that must go up to the vice-minister's and minister's level is by definition political. But the most substantive of all these internal coordinating groups is still the first.[112]

In addition to these formal groups, there are numerous informal brainstorming institutions in MITI. During the late 1960's one was called the "Komatsu Bar," the conference room and liquor cabinet of Komatsu Yūgorō when he was chief of the General Coordination Section in the Secretariat. Young officials gathered there around 10 o'clock at night for a drink and lively discussion—often about OECD, GATT, and European developments, topics that had interested Komatsu since his service as first secretary in the embassy in Germany. Komatsu, of the class of 1944, became vice-minister in 1974. In addition to the Komatsu Bar, a young MITI bureaucrat could also visit the "Yoshimitsu Bar" (Director Yoshimitsu Hisashi of the Medium and Smaller Enterprises Agency) and the "Takahashi Bar" (Chief Secretary Takahashi Shukurō).[113]

Japanese analysts usually characterize the basic outlook of MITI officials as "nationalistic." Kakuma observes that they like to use expressions such as *jōi* (expulsion of the foreigners) and *iteki* (barbarians) that date from the last decades of the Tokugawa shogunate. They see their function in life as the protection of Japanese industries from "foreign pressure."[114] When he was chief of the Trade Promotion Bureau from November 1969 to June 1971, Gotō Masafumi liked to use the derogatory term *ketō* ("hairy Chinese," by extension "unpleasant foreigner") to refer to Japan's competitors.[115] A different perspective is suggested by the former vice-minister Sahashi Shigeru's habitual use of the literary prefix *hei*, meaning "our" in a humble sense—a form of expression associated with an *ōbantō*, the chief clerk of an old mercantile house or a prewar zaibatsu holding company. When Sahashi spoke of *heikoku* (our country) as if he were a clerk referring to *heisha* (our company), many Japanese thought of him as the ōbantō of Japanese capitalism.[116] Nagai Yōnosuke sees still another historical parallel: "With its self-assertiveness, its strong native nationalism, its loyalist posture, . . . and its terrific 'workism,' MITI reminds us of the General Staff Office of the defunct army."[117] Whatever its roots, MITI's "spirit" has become legendary.

A part of the MITI perspective is impatience with the Anglo-American doctrine of economic competition. After the war MITI had to reconcile itself to the occupation-fostered market system in Japan, but it has always been hostile to American-style price competition and antitrust legislation. Sahashi likes to quote Schumpeter to the effect that the competition that really counts in capitalist systems is not measured by profit margins but by the development of new commodities, new technologies, new sources of supply, and new types of organizations.[118] MITI is highly competitive internationally, but it is often irritated by the disorderly competitive scramble among its domestic clients. As Robert Ozaki says, "Sometimes it is assumed [by MITI] that the adverse effects of private monopoly will not arise if the monopolists are Japanese."[119] During the 1970's many of these old MITI attitudes were modified by a new "internationalism." Nonetheless, Japanese commentators such as Kakuma have some reservations about the depth of the change; he calls the new MITI leadership the "nationalist international faction" and refers to the coming of the "age of the cosmopolitan nationalists."[120]

MITI men are powerful and outspoken, and the Japanese public enjoys reading about them. Several best-selling novels have been written about them, the best of which is Shiroyama Saburō's *The Summer of the Bureaucrats* (*Kanryō-tachi no natsu*) of 1975. English novelists sometimes choose bureaucrats as subjects (examples are Maugham's *Ashenden* or le Carré's *Smiley's People*), but economic bureaucrats in

America or Britain are rarely as interesting as spies or politicians. The opposite is true in Japan, where the power and influence of economic bureaucrats make fictional portrayals of their lives and struggles intriguing. In order to understand in greater depth why the Japanese find such people worth reading about in their newspapers and novels, we turn next to a history of the men and accomplishments of MITI.

THREE

The Rise of Industrial Policy

O LD TRADE and industry bureaucrats, looking back on their extraordinary history, like to note that the number 14 has figured prominently in their karma. The Ministry of Agriculture and Commerce (MAC; Nōshōmu-shō) was created in the fourteenth year of Meiji, or 1881; the Ministry of Commerce and Industry (MCI; Shōkō-shō) was created in the fourteenth year of Taishō, or 1925; and the organization of MCI into vertical bureaus, one for each strategic industry, was introduced in the fourteenth year of Shōwa, or 1939.

During December 1924, on the eve of the second of these landmark dates, three men sat working in the temporary quarters of MAC in the offices of the Japanese Chamber of Commerce and Industry in Ōtemachi, Tokyo. Their regular offices had been leveled by the earthquake of 1923. The highly political and bureaucratic task they were attending to, and even the fact that these three men were in charge of it, had as much to do with karma as with any policies or intentions of their own. They were dividing the old Ministry of Agriculture and Commerce into two new ministries—Agriculture and Forestry (Nōrin-shō) and Commerce and Industry. The three men were Shijō Takafusa (1876–1936), then vice-minister of agriculture and commerce; Yoshino Shinji (1888–1971), chief of the Documents Section (Bunsho-kachō); and Kishi Nobusuke (b. 1896), a young official in the Documents Section who had entered the ministry only four years earlier after graduating at the head of his class at Tokyo University's Law School.

These were three very different men, but each would have a significant impact on Japan, particularly through the influence he would have on his juniors. Shijō was one of Yoshino's most important patrons, Yoshino was one of Kishi's most important patrons, and Kishi was destined to become prime minister of Japan at the time of high-speed growth. Yoshino and Kishi together would establish Japan's first genuine industrial policy. The two younger men would also rise not just to the highest bureaucratic post in their service, vice-minister, but to the ministry's highest political post, minister of commerce and industry. But in 1924 none of them could have had the slightest suspicion of what was to come; all they were doing was arranging their rather untaxing bureaucratic lives to suit themselves—helping their friends, getting rid of people who irritated them, and taking advantage of a political change that did not affect them personally much at all.

The break-up of the Ministry of Agriculture and Commerce had been long in coming. Petitions calling for a separate agriculture ministry had been introduced in the Diet every year since 1918; and after the "rice riots" of the same year the issue had assumed major political significance. Equally important, with the emergence of the governments based on political parties that followed the passing of most of the Meiji oligarchs, genuine pressure groups were beginning to have a profound effect on Japanese governmental policy. Although in essence agricultural interests and their political allies were kicking commerce out of the Ministry of Agriculture and Commerce, the leaders of commercial administration were quite pleased to see this happen, particularly since they were in a position to execute the details of the split. The situation was somewhat comparable to the division in 1913 in the United States of the old Department of Commerce and Labor into two separate departments—at the insistence of the American Federation of Labor and not of business interests.[1]

The old Japanese ministry that was being divided had itself developed out of a basic change in Meiji economic policy that took place in 1880. After a decade of direct governmental investment in mines, railroads, arsenals, and factories, the Meiji leaders had had to confront the unpleasant fact that the new government of Japan could not afford to continue what it had been doing. The side effects of its policies were inflation, trade deficits, corruption, and looming bankruptcy. Liberal economists of the time such as Taguchi Ukichi, who wrote for the *Tōkyō keizai zasshi* (Tokyo economic journal), urged the government to control inflation by selling off its state enterprises and turn instead to the sponsorship of private capitalism.

Within the government the new minister of finance, Matsukata Masayoshi, agreed; and on November 5, 1880, he issued his famous "Outline Regulations for the Sale of Government-operated Factories."[2] Matsukata launched a deflationary policy quite comparable to that carried out seventy years later by Joseph Dodge and Ikeda Hayato, and with almost equally propitious results. As Arthur Tiedemann observes:

By all measures what came to be known as the Matsukata deflation accomplished its objectives. After 1881 interest rates, wages, and prices all fell. By 1882 imports were down 6 percent and exports up 33 percent compared with 1880; there was an export surplus of ¥8.3 million. The cumulative trade surplus for 1882–1885 amounted to ¥28.2 million. By 1885, the paper currency had been reduced to ¥118.5 million and the paper-silver ratio stood at 1.05 to 1.00. The following year, in the midst of the greatest export prosperity Japan had ever enjoyed, the country went on the silver standard.[3]

It must be understood that Matsukata's policy was not intended primarily as a new approach to economic development; it was instead a matter of hard necessity—of the pressing need to bring imports and exports under control and to keep the government solvent. In its "hyper-balancing of revenues and expenditures," the government did not touch military expenditures, these being considered essential to the maintenance of Japan's independence.[4] As an alternative to the state investment that was no longer possible, the government began helping private entrepreneurs to accumulate capital and to invest it in ways that seemed to promote Japan's needs for military security and economic development. The government sold them its pilot plants, provided them with exclusive licenses and other privileges, and often provided them with part of their capital funds. Japan had few other choices open to it at the time (it did not regain control over its own tariffs until July 1911), and although it neither understood nor believed in laissez faire capitalism, the government's policies seemed to reassure foreigners that Japan was becoming "modern" (that is, like them). The beneficiaries of this new policy were the big merchant houses of Mitsui, Mitsubishi, Sumitomo, Yasuda, Furukawa, Ōkura, and Asano, which later came to be known as the zaibatsu.

The relations that developed between the Meiji government and the private investors were not formal or official but, rather, personal and unofficial. They usually took the form of direct contacts between one or another of the oligarchs and an entrepreneur with access to him. Inoue Kaoru's services from within the government to Mitsui, for example, have been well documented.[5] Common clan origins and strategic marriages cemented many of these relations, and bribery and payoffs were not unknown. This working relationship between government and business needed a legal cover, however. In order to formalize and supervise the sale of government property, and also to unify all of the government's various economic activities, two of the Meiji oligarchs, Itō Hirobumi and Ōkuma Shigenobu, memorialized the throne on the desirability of a new economic ministry. This memorial was accepted and led to the creation on April 7, 1881, of the Ministry of Agriculture and Commerce.[6]

Attending to agriculture was certainly the most important activity of the new ministry. As Horie notes, Japan had one "God-sent" product in the form of raw silk, without which it might never have brought its trade deficit under control.[7] In addition to the supervision and promotion of agriculture, the new ministry was charged with the administration of all laws and orders relating to commerce, industry, technology, fishing, hunting, merchant shipping, inventions, trademarks, weights and measures, land reclamation, animal husbandry and veterinary affairs, forests, and the postal service. It combined functions that had been divided since the Restoration among the ministries of Finance, Civil Affairs, Industrial Affairs, and Home Affairs.

In 1885, with the success of the Matsukata reforms and the reorganization of the government into a cabinet system, MAC gave up its powers over shipping and the postal service to the new Ministry of Communications (Teishin-shō). However, with the abolition at the same time of the old Ministry of Industrial Affairs (Kōbu-shō), it assumed control over mining. Between 1885 and the end of the century MAC's internal structure underwent several changes that finally resulted in the configuration that would last with minor variations until its dissolution: a ministerial Secretariat, six internal bureaus—Agricultural Affairs (Nōmu Kyoku), Commercial Affairs (Shōmu Kyoku), Industrial Affairs (Kōmu Kyoku), Forestry (Sanrin Kyoku), Fisheries (Suisan Kyoku), and Mining (Kōzan Kyoku)—and one semidetached bureau, the Patent Bureau (Tokkyo Kyoku), with its own secretariat.

At the end of the century MAC acquired one more very important function, management of the government-owned-and-operated Yawata steel works. In 1896, during the ninth Imperial Diet, Prime Minister Itō Hirobumi and Minister Enomoto Takeaki of MAC successfully proposed a bill for the expenditure of about ¥4 million to build an iron and steel plant. First priority for its products was to go to armaments, but any surplus could be offered for general sale. It was built in Fukuoka prefecture at Yawata village, and thus was located both in the northern Kyushu coal fields and on the Japan Sea for easy access to iron ore from China. As a result of Japan's victory in the first Sino-Japanese War of 1894–95, iron ore from China was readily available, and it was of higher quality than that mined domestically. Production at Yawata began in the autumn of 1901 and immediately accounted for 53 percent of the nation's production of pig iron and 82 percent of its rolled steel. It had no serious domestic rivals until 1911 and 1912, when the privately owned Kobe Steel Company and Nippon Kōkan Company (Japan Steel Pipe) were founded.

MAC's sponsorship and operation of the Yawata works produced an identification between the ministry and big steel that has lasted to the present day. Long after the post–World War II Allied occupation had denationalized the steel industry, the Japanese public continued to believe that MITI officials had a soft spot in their hearts for the newly created "private" Yawata Steel Company. The press regularly suggested that Yawata officials had an unfair influence over the government, and went as far as to nickname MITI the "Tokyo Office of the Yawata Steel Company."[8] Certainly in 1970, at the time of the merger of the Yawata and Fuji steel companies into New Japan Steel—making it the world's largest steel producer and recalling the old nationalized company of 1934—no one in Japan thought MITI was either neutral or anything but pleased by the development. The trade and industry bureaucrats throughout this century have had a strong influence over Japan's steel industry, a relationship made all the more explicit by the Tokyo sales office of the Yawata works being located in the Ministry of Commerce and Industry building until 1934.

The creation of Yawata was the single most important achievement of MAC, but the inspiration came from the oligarchs and the military. The daily life of the ministry was always dominated by agricultural affairs. This was only natural since Japan was still predominantly an agricultural country. As late as 1914 agriculture accounted for 45.1 percent of the total national product and fishing for another 5.1 percent, while mining contributed 5.1 percent and manufacturing 44.5 percent. Manufacturing was still concentrated overwhelmingly in such light industries as textiles and foodstuffs; heavy industry—metals, machines, chemicals, and fuels—did not comprise more than half of all manufacturing until the 1933–37 period.[9]

The ministry's internal organization reflected these proportions. From before World War I newcomers to the ministry had informally divided themselves into an agricultural career path (*nōmu keitō*) and a commercial and industrial career path (*shōkō keitō*), although they often switched back and forth between each other's bureaus. The arrival after the turn of the century of the first graduates of Tokyo University Law School strengthened this separation. Technical agronomists had dominated the agricultural wing of the ministry from its early days, and law graduates felt at a disadvantage in competing with them in the agricultural career path. They therefore clustered in commercial and industrial administration.

There was not much work for them to do there, however. Before World War I commercial affairs and industrial affairs were always subordinate to the Agricultural Affairs Bureau, and they were regularly combined into one Commercial and Industrial Bureau (Shōkō Kyoku) as an economy measure. They were finally separated into two bureaus only in May 1919. The chief commercial function of MAC was supervising the insurance companies, the stock and commodity exchanges, and the warehousing business—all sectors of the economy that the commercial wing of the ministry would lose to other agencies by the time of the Pacific War. Industrial administration was almost nonexistent. Since the Matsukata reforms, and particularly after the creation of the Diet and the end of the 1894–95 war with China, the government's overall policy toward industry and foreign trade had become a more or less orthodox version of laissez faire. Even when MAC tried to take some initiative in the industrial arena, its ties with industrial leaders were weak, except for the personal relations between the oligarchs and the zaibatsu, and industrialists commonly ignored what government bureaucrats had to say.[10] In any case the biggest industries were the cotton textile firms of Osaka, and they were fiercely independent and suspicious of Tokyo.

When Yamamoto Tatsuo of the Mitsubishi zaibatsu became minister of MAC in 1913, he undertook to strengthen the commercial and industrial side of the administration. With a few notable exceptions, most of its officials still represented the lingering influence of Satsuma and Chōshū retainers in the state bureaucracy. The first vice-ministers from among government service examinees did not reach the top in any ministry until 1912. In retrospect Yamamoto's most important accomplishment was the recruiting of Yoshino Shinji. Yamamoto personally went to Tōdai and explained to the law faculty that he wanted some bright young law graduates for the Ministry of Agriculture and Commerce. As a result, the school's advisers steered Yoshino to MAC rather than to the more prestigious Home Affairs or Finance ministries, which he had expected to join. Yoshino recalled that when he entered the ministry in 1913 there were only three or four officials in commercial administration who had law degrees.[11]

Yamamoto was proud of Yoshino and took good care of him. Ten months after Yoshino had joined the ministry, Yamamoto delegated him as the resident Japanese representative to the San Francisco International Exposition of 1915. It was a superb opportunity for a young man to study abroad and to widen his horizons. Yoshino stayed in San Francisco for a year and a half, auditing courses in labor economics at Berkeley (he specifically recalls Professor Ira Cross), traveling around the country, and receiving an overseas salary of ¥245 per month compared with the ¥45 he would have been paid in Tokyo.

The efforts and the politics of people like Yamamoto were not particularly appreciated among the dominant agriculturalists within the ministry. Their orientation was physiocratic (*nōhonshugi*), and they felt a philosophical sympathy for the rural way of life, so they were not pleased by the rise of industrialism or by the growing influence of the zaibatsu. Soejima Sempachi, a commercial-track official who was nonetheless serving as chief of the Agricultural Policy Section at the time of the 1918 "rice riots," later charged that the whole Agricultural Affairs Bureau was sympathetic to the interests of landlords.[12] This was probably true, but it must be understood that agricultural bureaucrats also represented one wing of then current liberal opinion. To them the most serious social problem of the nation was rural poverty and tenancy, a problem to which they believed the government was insufficiently attentive, particularly in comparison to the privileges it extended to the zaibatsu.

This social consciousness of the agricultural bureaucrats is sometimes called "Ishiguroism," after the great elder statesman of agricultural administration, Ishiguro Tadaatsu (1884–1960). From 1919 to 1925 Ishiguro was chief of the Agricultural Policy Section, Agricultural Affairs Bureau, in MAC. He became vice-minister of agriculture in 1934 and minister of agriculture in the second Konoe (1940–41) and Suzuki (1945) cabinets. He was famous for recruiting social activists to his ministry (for example, the post–World War II socialist politician Wada Hiroo), and for donating a part of his salary during the 1930's to aid tenant farmers. During the period of World War I he and his followers imbued the ministry with a sense of mission to protect the small tenant farmer, and the Ministry of Agriculture and Forestry that resulted from the break-up of MAC was regarded as the most "progressive" in the interwar government.[13]

The dominance of the agricultural career path in MAC is also revealed by its personnel deployments. The ministry grew from 2,422 total employees in 1890 to 7,918 in 1920 and 8,362 at the time of the split, but of this final figure 5,879 went to the Ministry of Agriculture in 1925, and only 2,483 to MCI.[14]

World War I affected Japan's economy and economic bureaucracy in many significant ways. The war boom itself was extraordinary. In 1914 Japan's total exports and imports combined amounted to about ¥1.2

billion, but by 1919 this figure had grown to about ¥4.5 billion, excluding income from marine transportation and insurance premiums. During the period 1915–18 exports exceeded imports by about ¥1.3 billion, and the Bank of Japan used the profits from these years to pay off all of Japan's foreign debts, to purchase foreign bonds, and to increase the country's gold reserves. At the end of 1918 specie holdings reached ¥1.6 billion, about four times the figure for 1913. Some of Japan's established businessmen became rich overnight; Mitsui Trading Company, for example, reported paid-in capital of ¥20 million in February 1918, and of Y100 million a year later.[15] Many new firms were established, known at the time as *sensō narikin* (wartime nouveaux riches). The most famous of these was the new zaibatsu complex of Kaneko Naokichi, whose firms included Suzuki Trading, Kobe Steel, Harima Shipbuilding, Imperial Rayon (Teijin), Japan Flour Milling, Great Japan Celluloid, and Hōnen Refining.[16] The Japanese chemical industry started up during the war almost from scratch after exports from Germany, particularly textile dyes, were cut off.

The effect of the war boom on agriculture was equally profound but much less satisfactory. A significant rise in all price levels accompanied the growth of industry (see Table 7), but most important was the rise in demand for rice by the rapidly urbanizing industrial labor force. The government's policy at the outset of the boom was to allow prices to go up, hoping to increase production in that way. This was also what the politically influential landlords wanted. The landlords were organized into the Imperial Agricultural Association (Teikoku Nōkai), founded in 1910 as the successor to the Great Japan Agricultural Association (Dai Nihon Nōkai) of 1881, which began as a quasi-official organization for landlords and was oriented toward rural improvements.[17] During the war, however, the Teikoku Nōkai became more of a pressure group than an agrarian improvement society. Its interests were in rising prices for domestic rice and high tariffs on imports, which profited both landlords and their tenants.

The new industrialists, on the other hand, wanted prices to fall, both to relieve the pressure on them for wage hikes and to maintain industrial peace. Their organization was the Japan Industrial Club (Nihon Kōgyō Kurabu), which held a preliminary meeting in December 1915 and was formally established on March 10, 1917. Its first officers reflected the club's zaibatsu sponsorship: the chairman of the board was Dan Takuma of Mitsui; the chairman of the council was Toyokawa Ryōhei of Mitsubishi; and the managing directors were Nakajima Kumakichi of Furukawa and Gō Seinosuke, formerly of MAC and then chairman of the Tokyo Stock Exchange.

TABLE 7

Price Fluctuations, July 1914–March 1920

(July 1914 = 100)

Month	Index
July 1914	100
March 1919	267
June 1919	295
December 1919	381
March 1920	425

SOURCE: Fujiwara Akira et al., eds., *Kindai Nihonshi no kiso chishiki* (Basic knowledge of modern Japanese history), Tokyo, 1972, p. 278.

Both the agricultural and industrial groups attempted to influence the government directly and to shape policies in the Diet through their support of political parties. The landlords—led by their president, Matsudaira Kōsō, a descendant of the daimyo of Fukui prefecture, and their vice-president, Kuwata Kumazō, a member of the House of Peers—put their faith in the Seiyūkai party and in the upper house, where landlords with large holdings were entitled to seats because of the high taxes they paid. The industrialists were less vocal on the subject of rice prices, but they exercised their influence through their members who were appointed to the various cabinets as minister of agriculture and commerce. The most important of these men was Yamamoto Tatsuo of Mitsubishi, who served as minister in both the Yamamoto Gonnohyōe cabinet of 1913–14 and the Hara cabinet of 1918–21.

The issue of rice prices for city dwellers versus rice prices for farmers came to a head in 1918 when the combination of a bad harvest and the need to supply increased provisions to the armed forces for the Siberian Expedition led to a panic of rice speculation and profiteering. On September 1, 1917, the Terauchi government issued its famous Profiteering Control Ordinance (Bōri Torishimari Rei), which made crimes of both attempting to corner a market (*kaishime*) and holding goods off the market in anticipation of price rises (*urioshimi*). The result, however, was a chilling of all markets as producers held back goods until the uncertainty was over. Whether Mitsui Trading Company and Suzuki Trading Company were actually engaged in cornering the market, or whether they were importing rice from the colonies and evading the duties on it in order to sell it at the higher domestic prices, or whether Mitsui was primarily intent on driving Suzuki out of business are all relevant issues, but they need not be settled here.[18] The public's fears and suspicions were enough to cause the "rice riots." (The events of 1918 are similar to the panic of 1973–74 during the first "oil shock," when the economic bureaucracy again had to intervene to stop speculation in kerosene, toilet paper, soap powder, and other products.) Rice prices soared during 1918, and in July fishermen's wives in Toyama rioted over shortages. The panic spread to consumers elsewhere, and riots occurred through September in some five hundred different localities. The Terauchi cabinet was forced to resign in disgrace.

The new Hara cabinet, representing the Seiyūkai party, had to deal promptly with the matter. Hara made Yamamoto Tatsuo minister of agriculture and commerce for the second time, and Yamamoto pushed the Rice Law of 1920 through the Diet. It removed duties on imported rice and initiated a program for developing rice cultivation in the Japanese colonies of Taiwan and Korea. The law also established a system of price controls over rice that has persisted in one form or another to the present day. Yamamoto's policy thus secured food supplies at reasonable prices for Japan's growing industrial labor force, but in combination with the postwar recession of the entire economy that began in the spring of 1920, it also worsened the agricultural depression and tenant unrest that wracked Japan throughout the 1920's.[19]

These developments were a severe economic and political setback for the Teikoku Nōkai, the landlords' association, and it reacted in anger. What the association had previously requested it now demanded—a separate Ministry of Agriculture uncontaminated by commercial and industrial concerns and devoted exclusively to agricultural interests. The Hara government rejected these demands, but in 1923 the earthquake again focused government attention on relief of the cities of Tokyo and Yokohama, and again it seemed to farmers that the efforts undertaken on behalf of the cities were much more forthcoming than anything ever done for them. The following year a series of unusually propitious circumstances allowed the Teikoku Nōkai's petition to succeed.

Hara Kei, the first prime minister of Japan to head the government because he was president of the dominant political party in the lower house of the Diet, had been assassinated on November 4, 1921. His successor as president of the Seiyūkai party and as prime minister was Takahashi Korekiyo (1854–1936), one of the truly outstanding figures of Japan's modern economic and political history and not incidentally the first minister of commerce and industry. Born the illegitimate child of an artist and his 16-year-old maid, Takahashi was adopted by a lower-status samurai of the late Tokugawa Sendai *han*. The feudal han sent him to America in the late 1860's to study English, and in 1873, at the age of 19, he obtained a position in the new Meiji government. In 1886, at the age of 32, he became the first chief of the Patent Bureau in the new Ministry of Agriculture and Commerce, thus obtaining an intimate knowledge of the ministry he came to head in 1924. Three years after becoming a MAC bureau chief, he resigned to enter business, at which he was unusually successful. During the Russo-Japanese War he emerged as one of the key financiers of Japan, and by 1907 he was an appointed peer and a baron. In 1911 he became president of the Bank of Japan, and after that he went into politics.

In 1913 Takahashi became minister of finance in the same cabinet in which Yamamoto Tatsuo served as minister of agriculture and commerce. After the assassination of Hara in 1921, Takahashi briefly became prime minister (1921–22). However, antiparty forces were attempting to reestablish their supremacy, and they organized a series of nonparty bureaucratic governments. In order to resist this movement, Takahashi took the unusual step of resigning his title (he was a viscount by then) and his legal position as head of his family, thereby again becoming what of course he had been born—a commoner. He then stood for election to the House of Representatives in the district of the late Hara Kei in Iwate prefecture. After a difficult campaign he won. He and his colleagues forced the bureaucratic government of Kiyoura to resign, a government was formed based on a coalition of all the political parties, and in June 1924 Takahashi again accepted a ministerial portfolio, that of agriculture and commerce. It was as the last minister of MAC that Takahashi presided over the split. (After this term in office Takahashi went on to serve as minister of finance in four more cabinets, until he also was assassinated on February 26, 1936, in the abortive military coup d'etat.)[20]

When Takahashi took up the MAC post in 1924, he was known to favor the commercial side of the ministry. He held positive views about the need for governmental promotion of international trade and protection of Japan's growing industries (such as steel)—views that were anathema to the landlords and therefore to their association, the Teikoku Nōkai, which opposed imported food but at the same time wanted no duties on imported fertilizer. Because a coalition government was ruling at the time, and because Takahashi was still president of the Seiyūkai party, it was possible to act on the Teikoku Nōkai's petition for a separate agricultural ministry without the political divisions in the Diet that had frustrated action in the past.

On March 31, 1925, with Takahashi's backing, the government issued Imperial Ordinance Number 25 establishing a Ministry of Agriculture and Forestry and a Ministry of Commerce and Industry.

During late 1924, while the preparations for this event were taking place, Nakai Reisaku, class of 1903 and former chief of the Forestry Bureau, became vice-minister of MAC. Shijō Takafusa, class of 1904 and Takahashi's main internal ally, remained as chief of the Industrial Affairs Bureau.* Takahashi would have preferred Shijō as vice-minister, but he had no control over internal bureaucratic developments. Then an unusual opportunity developed.

Yoshino was out of the country during the spring and summer of 1924, when the party coalition government came to power. He had been sent to America and Europe to investigate the chemical industry and protective tariff policies. Yoshino was then chief of the Industrial Policy Section in the Industrial Affairs Bureau, having been appointed to that post at the youngest age in the history of MAC by his bureau chief, Shijō. Upon Yoshino's return, Shijō told him that the ministry was to be split. He also told him that Vice-Minister Nakai intended to appoint Yoshino chief of the Silk Section in the Agricultural Affairs Bureau but that Yoshino should turn down the job in order not to be trapped in agricultural administration when the division of personnel between the two new ministries took place.

In December 1924, however, Nakai was suddenly obliged to give up the vice-ministership in order to deal personally with a corruption scandal at the Yawata steel works.† Shijō, next in line in seniority to

---

*Shijō was chief of the Industrial Affairs Bureau of MAC from 1920 to 1924. He came from an aristocratic background. Born in Kyoto as an illegitimate son of the Nijō clan, he was adopted by Shijō Takahira, who sent him to Tōdai Law, where he graduated in 1904. One of his classmates was Yoshino Shinji's illustrious elder brother, Yoshino Sakuzō (1878–1933), a Tokyo University professor, *Asahi* journalist, and advocate of democratic government for Japan. After Shijō entered MAC, he became a personal aide to the former Satsuma samurai and Restoration politician, Ōura Kanetake, who was minister of MAC from 1908 to 1911. Ōura saw to Shijō's rapid rise in the bureaucracy, and by the 1920's, Shijō had caught the attention and won the respect of Takahashi Korekiyo.

†The incident that led to Nakai's giving up the vice-ministership and "sideslipping" (*yokosuberi*) to the post of chief of the steel works originated in the corruption scandals of 1917 and 1918. When the minister of justice's procurators began to investigate the Yawata operations, the chief of the steel works, who was also a MAC bureaucrat, committed suicide. In order to clean up the mess, a tough Home Ministry official was appointed to replace him, but he was forced to resign a few years later after having antagonized the entire staff and work force. During 1924 MAC decided internally to appoint Sakigawa Saishirō, then chief of the Mining Bureau, as a replacement. However, Sakigawa had earlier headed the politically sensitive Fukuoka Mine Inspectors Bureau, and in that post he had made enemies of the big coal mine operators in the area. They did not want him back at Yawata, and they appealed to Noda Utarō, vice-president of the

Nakai, thus became the last vice-minister of agriculture and commerce. He in turn promptly appointed Yoshino chief of the Documents Section, where all personnel matters are handled. Yoshino was assisted by a young official in his new section, Kishi Nobusuke, whom Yoshino was watching over and pushing ahead. According to Kishi's memoirs, Shijō and Yoshino sent all the stubborn and dull bureaucrats to the new agriculture ministry and kept in commerce the flexible and bright ones—although Kishi thought they had made a mistake in keeping the later vice-minister Takeuchi Kakichi.[21]

Shijō and Yoshino also arranged one other thing. The Agriculture Ministry moved to new quarters in Kasumigaseki, but Commerce retained and rebuilt on the property it had occupied since 1888. This was located in old Kobiki-chō ("the sawmill quarter") adjacent to the Kabuki theater and about midway between the Tsukiji fish market and Shimbashi station. Every MAC or MCI bureaucrat who has written his memoirs has recalled the actors, geisha, and "teahouses" in the neighborhood, and some of them have blamed their slow careers on too much *asobi* ("play") being readily available.[22] MCI remained in Kobiki-chō until Tōjō moved it as his new Ministry of Munitions to Kasumigaseki.

With the split into two ministries, the "old testament" days of trade and industrial administration (as MITI historians call it) came to an end. Shijō became the new vice-minister of commerce and industry, a post he held until April 1929, when he resigned and with the assistance of Takahashi entered the holding company of the Yasuda zaibatsu. He also took up the presidencies of the Yasuda Life Insurance Company and the Tokyo Fire Insurance Company (note that MAC-MCI was the governmental organ supervising the insurance business). As a descendant of the Nijō family he was also created a baronet, and he therefore assumed his seat in the House of Peers. Before leaving MCI, Shijō arranged for the promotion, on July 30, 1928, of Yoshino to Shijō's old position as chief of the Industrial Affairs Bureau. Three years after that Yoshino became vice-minister.

The internal organization of the new Ministry of Commerce and Industry perpetuated without change the commercial and industrial

---

Seiyūkai and Diet member from Fukuoka, who in turn protested to Takahashi, president of the Seiyūkai and minister of MAC. To settle the whole unpleasant affair, Takahashi asked Nakai to go to Yawata as head of the steel works, and he agreed. Nakai remained at Yawata until 1934, when he became the first president of the new Japan Steel Corporation, of which the Yawata works were the main component. Noda Utarō, who had intervened with Takahashi, succeeded him as minister of MCI (April to August 1925).

wing of the old MAC (see Appendix B). However, the economic environment in which the new ministry worked was changing rapidly. The "rice riots" were only the first signs of serious imbalances in the Japanese economy, both in its internal structure and in its relations with other economies. The more important sign was the postwar recession that began in the spring of 1920 and lasted throughout the 1920's until the world depression of 1930, when it got worse. The stock exchange index (1913 = 100) fell from 254.1 in February 1920 to 112.6 in September, and the total value of all exports and imports shrank from ¥4.5 billion in 1919 to ¥2 billion in 1920.[23] All sectors of the economy were hit hard, but the farming sector was hit the hardest. In the business and industrial sectors, the established zaibatsu banks and enterprises had greater financial resources than other enterprises, and their conglomerate structure dampened some of the shocks. The war-bred zaibatsu were hurt, but they were able to petition the government for special relief measures through their access to the politicians whom they financed. Small businessmen and tenant farmers were in serious trouble.

For MCI and the other economic bureaucracies the problems were conceptual. What was causing the recession to persist so long? Should anyone, including the government, do something about it? Why was the international balance of payments in chronic deficit? Why were corporate profits so low? What should be done? Numerous theories circulated. Japan was different from all other economies because of its "dual structure" (zaibatsu versus thousands of medium and smaller enterprises). Japan was experiencing an "overproduction crisis" because of the war boom. Japan was a victim of "destructive competition" because of the unrestricted growth in the numbers of banks and enterprises. And Japan was simply entering the "stage" of "monopoly capitalism" as foretold by the German Marxists.

The government did not have the answers to these questions, nor did it have a single policy. It did undertake ad hoc relief measures in response to each of the "panics" that were occurring regularly, spending money recklessly to bail out failing enterprises (for example, in the case of steel, it purchased private steel firms that had been started up during the war to meet the so-called steel famine and that now faced steeply declining demand).[24] The government's overall monetary policy was deflationary, but many of its particular policies fed the price inflation that was making many Japanese products uncompetitive on world markets.

The most notorious among these policies was the government's response to the catastrophic Kantō earthquake of September 1923. In order to avert immediate financial collapse at the time of the earthquake, the government ordered all banks closed for a month. When they reopened, the Bank of Japan instructed the banks to refinance all debts that had fallen due in the interim, with the Bank of Japan itself guaranteeing them against losses from these transactions. The government implemented this policy through "earthquake bills," of which it discounted a staggering ¥438 million. Included in this amount were many bad debts that had existed since the end-of-the-war recession. By the spring of 1927, some ¥231 million of these bills had been redeemed, but the outstanding balance of ¥207 million looked irrecoverable and also stood in the way of reconstructing the country's public finances on a sound basis. There was, however, considerable public sentiment against writing off this debt, which would amount to a major subsidy of big business while smaller firms and farmers were allowed to go bankrupt.[25]

In this general milieu, one person within MCI stands out as beginning to have some interesting ideas for reenergizing the economy. He was Yoshino Shinji. Yoshino's legal training at Tōdai had not taught him much about the economy, but after he returned from San Francisco in 1915, he had some experiences that gave him a more than purely bureaucratic perspective. The first was a period of duty as a transferee to the Home Ministry, during which he worked as a factory inspector in Kobe. There he discovered the world of medium and smaller enterprises (*chūshō kigyō*), which during the 1920's and 1930's Japanese defined as manufacturing enterprises with from 5 to 30 employees (small) and from 30 to 100 employees (medium).

His second useful experience came as an official in the Temporary Industrial Investigation Bureau (Rinji Sangyō Chōsa Kyoku) set up within MAC by the Terauchi government (February 1917) to study the effects of the war on the Japanese economy. The bureau was not intended to produce policy or take action, since the private sector led Japan's growth during World War I. But it was expected to compare Japan with other belligerent powers and to advise about possible social problems. Nothing ever came of the bureau's work, but Yoshino met there such famous figures as Kawai Eijirō (1891–1944) and Morito Tatsuo (b. 1888), both Tōdai economists who were working in MAC as consultants. Kawai, in particular, a man who later was to die in prison during World War II as an opponent of militarism from a non-Marxist socialist position, had a significant influence on Yoshino. In the bureau they wrote papers on such subjects as economic planning, stockpiling for emergencies, industrial finance, and American customs duties. As a result of these activities, Yoshino committed himself unequivocally to the industrial side of the ministry's commercial and industrial administration.[26]

During the early 1920's, while serving as a section chief in the Industrial Affairs Bureau, Yoshino became one of the first government officials to gain expert knowledge of the medium and smaller enterprises sector. He discovered that despite the strategic importance of the modern zaibatsu enterprises, medium and smaller factories employed the overwhelming majority of Japan's industrial workers. Even more important, the zaibatsu firms produced primarily for the domestic market, but the medium and smaller enterprises concentrated on production for export. With a few exceptions such as rayon, silk yarn, and cotton textiles, where large enterprises were also strong exporters, medium and smaller manufacturers of sundries such as bicycles, pottery, enamelware, canned goods, hats, silk textiles, and so forth were contributing from 50 to 65 percent of all of Japan's exports. And they were losing money doing it.[27]

Yoshino and his colleagues in MAC concluded that there were too many small firms, an overabundance of cheap labor, and inadequate channels and information for marketing; the result was that the small business sector was dumping goods overseas. The small export firm not only did not earn much foreign exchange, it was often not even meeting its costs. Moreover, the big zaibatsu trading companies, which monopolized the marketing of these products, were exploiting the medium and smaller enterprises by supplying raw materials at high prices and taking consignments of finished products at low prices.

During 1925 the new ministry sponsored and the Diet unanimously passed two new laws that were a first effort to alleviate these conditions, the Exporters Association Law and the Major Export Industries Association Law. In them we see in embryonic form major instruments of policy that the Japanese government has employed to the present day, notably the "recession" and "rationalization" cartels, as they were to be called in the MITI era.

The Exporters Association Law created export unions (*yushutsu kumiai*) in particular product lines among the medium and smaller enterprises. It authorized these associations to accept products for export on consignment from members, and to control quantities, qualities, and prices of export goods. The Major Export Industries Association Law attempted to end cutthroat competition among such enterprises. It established industrial unions (*kōgyō kumiai*), which differed from the export unions in being genuine cartels whose members agreed among themselves on the amounts each member could produce and sell.

There were several precedents for cartels in Japan. The Japan Paper Manufacturers Federation of 1880, the Japan Cotton Spinning Federation of 1882, and the Japan Fertilizer Manufacturers Federation of 1907 were the main trade associations with cartellike powers before World War I.[28] The Production Cooperatives Law of 1900 had authorized prefecturally supervised industrial unions (*sangyō kumiai*), but despite their name, these were actually agricultural cooperatives, not industrial manufacturers.[29] They were also hampered by the fact that in 1917 MAC, in an attempt to control the wartime prices of food and clothing, had prohibited them from agreeing on prices or wages. The primary functions of the early cartels were inspection and grading of products. The Japanese were not unfamiliar with cartels, but those authorized in 1925 were new in that they sought to organize a part of the whole economy, not just particular industries.

The 1925 laws did not work too well. The industrial unions were more popular than the export unions, because MCI subsidized the industrial unions from the outset but only began to finance the exporters after the world depression. There were also frequent clashes between the two. In order to get the laws passed in the Diet, MCI had to agree that membership would not be compulsory in either of the unions—although the ministry was given authority to order nonmembers to conform to some of the terms of cartel agreements among members.

During 1925 MCI was not a powerful ministry compared with Home Affairs, Foreign Affairs, or Finance, and it was all but unknown to the general public. Its efforts to aid medium and smaller enterprises were thus merely a first, and rather experimental, step toward industrial policy. Both its commercial and industrial activities during the mid-1920's were focused on trying to relieve Japan's balance of payments deficits by stimulating trade. Yoshino established a committee in the ministry to promote the use of nationally manufactured goods, and he sought budget authorization to station MCI trade representatives abroad. He also asked that the Trade Section in the Commercial Bureau be upgraded to a bureau. The Ministry of Foreign Affairs blocked the idea of overseas commercial attachés from MCI as an infringement on its territory, and the Finance Ministry approved an MCI Trade Bureau in 1927 but did not provide funds for it until 1930, when the world depression made it seem more important.[30] One of the leading historians of trade and industrial policy comments, "No one remembers working very hard in the early years of MCI." [31] Even Nakahashi Tokugorō, who became minister of MCI in April 1927 as part of the cabinet of General Tanaka Giichi, said on taking office, "As a government agency, MCI is not a place of exciting work." [32] But he was destined to help change that condition quite decisively.

Nakahashi became minister in the wake of the financial panic of 1927, which forced the resignation of the first Wakatsuki cabinet. This crisis was the culmination of all the panics that had afflicted the Japanese economy during the 1920's, and it constitutes the true dividing line between the "old testament" and the "new testament" of Japanese trade and industrial administration. It also marks the onset of the world depression for Japan—a period of economic stagnation and of radical attempts to find solutions to endemic problems that afflicted the rest of the world only three years later. On the significance of the 1927 panic, Nawa Taro observes, "MCI already existed as a body, but the financial panic brought it to life as an organization." [33]

One important, if deeply conservative, point of view concerning what to do about the recession of the 1920's is associated with the name of Inoue Junnosuke (1869–1932), a former official of the Yokohama Specie Bank, president of the Bank of Japan in 1919, and minister of finance in the Hamaguchi cabinet of 1929. (Like several other finance ministers of this era, he too was assassinated, on February 9, 1932, in the so-called Blood Brotherhood Incident, a fascist attack on the Japanese capitalist establishment.) Inoue's idea was that Japan should lift the "temporary" gold embargo that it and all other major countries had imposed at the outbreak of World War I. Japan had continued the embargo after the war because of its unfavorable balance of payments, and it was alone among major powers in not having returned to the gold standard. In Inoue's view this was the reason that efforts to revive exports had been unsuccessful. The situation was somewhat comparable to that in 1949, when Japan had to achieve a stable exchange rate for the yen in order to resume international trading, a goal that in turn required Japan to halt inflation and live within its means. In 1949 Dodge and Ikeda led the fierce deflation that was prerequisite to economic rebuilding.

In theory a nation in a situation like Japan's in the 1920's—one that imported more than it exported—would pay out gold to cover the balance. This outflow of gold, which had been prohibited during the 1920's, would raise the value of the domestic currency and thereby lower export prices. The effect would be highly deflationary, and would drive marginal firms out of business, but it would also thoroughly shake up an economy that was living off inflation and restore its international competitive capacity. This is what Inoue and the Minseitō party wanted to do.

Before any attempt to lift the gold embargo could be undertaken, however, the government had to get its own financial house in order, and this meant resolving the matter of the outstanding earthquake bills. During the 52nd Diet (December 1926 to March 1927), the Wakatsuki (Minseitō) government introduced two bills that would convert the outstanding earthquake bills into ten-year government bonds. The opposition parties complained bitterly that the government wanted to use the people's tax revenues to aid the capitalists, and during the course of a heated Diet debate the minister of finance accidentally revealed just how shaky the nation's entire banking structure really was. Runs began on banks, although they temporarily cooled after the Diet passed the bills on March 23.

The debate did not cool, however. It had revealed that two institutions, the Suzuki Trading Company and the government-owned Taiwan Bank, were in serious financial difficulties. Suzuki Shōten, the biggest of the wartime nouveaux riches, controlled some sixty companies, many of which were in the heavy and chemical industries and had been badly affected by the postwar recession. The China trade, in which Suzuki had invested heavily, had also stagnated due to anti-Japanese boycotts and the rising competitive ability of new Chinese firms. The Taiwan Bank had the mission of helping Japanese firms advance into China and Southeast Asia; it had lent Suzuki over ¥350 million, and it also held some ¥100 million in earthquake bills. Rumors spread that the real intent of the new laws was to save Suzuki and the Taiwan Bank, and when Suzuki's competitors, beginning with the Mitsui Bank, began withdrawing their deposits from the Taiwan Bank, the public run on all banks revived.

As a result of the panic, the Wakatsuki government fell, the Seiyūkai party came to power, some 37 banks went under, and the zaibatsu renewed their strength. Finally, the Suzuki zaibatsu collapsed, with Mitsui and Mitsubishi picking up the surviving firms. (One strong firm, Teijin, or Imperial Rayon, came back to haunt the government again in 1934, when a scandal erupted over the covert sale to high government officials of Teijin shares held by the minister of finance as collateral for the Taiwan Bank's debts.) Loans to medium and smaller enterprises became much harder to obtain, but access to capital for large zaibatsu enterprises was enhanced. Disastrous though it was, the 1927 panic produced one of the first "reforms" of the industrial structure in Japan: a large number of competing banks and enterprises were weeded out, and the economy's limited capital was concentrated in the strategic sectors. However, the way it was done and the enrichment of the zaibatsu in the process contributed to the radicalization of the whole society and brought forth demands that someone speak for the nation as a whole.[34]

In this climate of opinion, the new minister of commerce and industry, working with and on the inspiration of his chief of the Documents Section, Yoshino Shinji, undertook an initiative that is acknowledged to be the beginning of modern Japanese industrial policy. On May 23, 1927, Minister Nakahashi set up within MCI a Commerce and Industry Deliberation Council (Shōkō Shingikai). Its charter was to examine broadly what was ailing the Japanese economy and what the government ought to do about it. As a joint public-private forum, it is the direct antecedent of the 1950's-era Industrial Rationalization Council and its successor, the Industrial Structure Council—MITI's number one official channel to the business community. Nonbureaucratic members of the 1927 council included all the leading businessmen of the time. Among the most influential in the actual deliberations were Ōkōchi Masatoshi, who was both a Tōdai professor of engineering and a prominent private industrialist, and Nakajima Kumakichi of the Furukawa zaibatsu, who later became an important MCI minister.

The council achieved unprecedented results. It convinced MCI to strengthen its compilation of industrial statistics (this was Minister Nakahashi's pet project and his main contribution to the council), authorized some ¥30 million in loans to medium and smaller enterprises (a figure ten times larger than any previous loans), proposed for the first time the amalgamation of the Yawata steel works with private steel firms (an idea that came to pass in 1934), and underscored the need for improved trade intelligence and subsidies for export industries. The discussions also had their comic side. Both Kishi and Kogane Yoshiteru recall Okabe Nagakabe's objections to the introduction of the metric system in Japan as a way of standardizing industrial products. Okabe reflected the views of the House of Peers when he noted that the metric system was associated with the French Revolution and was therefore incompatible with the Japanese national spirit. Members of the council proposed shelving the issue until Okabe died. Since Okabe lived until 1970, twenty-five years beyond his term as minister of education in the wartime Tōjō cabinet, it would have meant a long wait.[35] As it turned out, Kogane managed to introduce the metric system in the late 1930's with the help of the army.

By far the most important achievement of the council was the introduction into Japan of the concept of "industrial rationalization" (*san-*

gyō gōrika). Since 1927 the concept has been in almost daily use by the economic bureaucracy. At first no one knew precisely what it meant, but it seemed admirably to sum up what the MCI bureaucrats thought was needed for Japan. Yoshino has written, "All we did with 'rationalization' was to hang out a signboard as a name for our activities, but having hung out the sign, we then had to find out what it meant." [36] The first government reference to the term seems to have been in one of Kishi's reports of 1926. He had been sent to Philadelphia as the Japanese representative to the 150th anniversary celebration of the United States, and he returned home via Europe. He reported on the Taylor and Ford movements in the United States for "scientific management" and "production lines," and on the promotion of trusts and cartels in Germany to improve industrial efficiency. No one paid much attention to Kishi's initial report, but with the onset of the depression "industrial rationalization" became a popular catch phrase in Japan for efforts to pull the country out of the slump. Within the ministry it became a rallying cry for the integration of industrial policy.

On July 2, 1929, the Minseitō returned to power, and Prime Minister Hamaguchi appointed Inoue Junnosuke minister of finance. Inoue proceeded to carry out his plan to lift the gold embargo, but he and other members of the government now linked the step to the industrial rationalization movement. The gold standard would tie Japan's prices to world prices, they said, and industrial rationalization would strengthen the nation's international competitive ability. Prime Minister Hamaguchi himself argued to the Commerce and Industry Deliberation Council during 1929 that "industrial rationalization is not just a matter of timely policy but must be a movement of all the people." [37]

On January 11, 1930, Inoue lifted the gold embargo. Whatever the theoretical merits of this policy, its timing was terrible. To pursue a deeply deflationary policy during the early months of the deepest depression the modern world has ever known could only make conditions worse. On December 13, 1931, the gold embargo was reimposed, and Japan turned to a homegrown version of Keynesian economics, pulling itself through the depression by means of governmental deficit spending on armaments. During 1930 and 1931, however, the depression was at its worst in Japan, and the other half of the Hamaguchi cabinet's economic policy, industrial rationalization, began to take on new meaning.

The Commerce and Industry Deliberation Council lasted from 1927 to July 5, 1930. On November 19, 1929, it set up as a kind of subcommittee an Industrial Rationalization Deliberation Council (Sangyō Gōrika Shingikai) within MCI. A month later this body produced a report on rationalization measures that were needed at once. Meanwhile, in response to the worldwide economic collapse, the cabinet on January 20, 1930, set up its own Emergency Industrial Deliberation Council (Rinji Sangyō Shingikai) with the prime minister as chairman and the minister of commerce and industry as vice-chairman. This supreme body lasted only a few months, but it took notice of the work on industrial rationalization within MCI and ordered the creation there of a Temporary Industrial Rationality Bureau (TIRB; Rinji Sangyō Gōri Kyoku) to formulate and carry out concrete measures of rationalization. This bureau came into being on June 2, 1930, as a semi-detached organ of MCI with the minister of commerce and industry himself serving concurrently as the bureau's director. The TIRB, which lasted until 1937, was also the brainchild of Yoshino Shinji; and it was so successful that he was chosen vice-minister a year later mainly on the strength of TIRB's performance.

Yoshino deliberately created the TIRB as a detached bureau headed by the minister in order to prevent internal ministerial rivalries from crippling its activities. He involved all of the ministry's bureau and section chiefs in it and gave it an unconventional internal structure. Instead of sections, it had only two large departments, the first headed by Kido Kōichi, who was concurrent chief of the Documents Section in the Secretariat, and the second headed by Yoshino, who was concurrent chief of the Industrial Affairs Bureau.

These departments drew up plans for the control of enterprises, implementation of scientific management principles, improvements in industrial financing, standardization of products, simplification of production processes, and subsidies to support the production and consumption of domestically manufactured goods. Continuing the precedent set by the Commerce and Industry Deliberation Council, Yoshino involved civilian industrial leaders in the active duties of the bureau, even to the extent of providing them with offices in the MCI building. Ōkōchi and Nakajima from the council continued as the TIRB's most important advisers, but representatives of all the zaibatsu as well as academics and journalists actively participated. They all proved extremely useful to the ministry in gaining acceptance for its ideas within the business community and in defending its proposed laws in the Diet—particularly the landmark Important Industries Control Law of 1931.

The Japanese term *gōrika*—literally "to make rational"—was not well understood at the time Yoshino chose it for his new bureau. He was worried about its implications and therefore deliberately named the bureau the Sangyō Gōri Kyoku instead of the wholly correct Sangyō Gōrika Kyoku. He explained that the "*ka*" worried him, since *ka-kyoku* means "old song," and he was afraid his critics and the opposition might turn this into a pun.[38] There certainly were critics. On the day before the bureau was scheduled to open, a workman scribbled the character "*fu*" in front of *gōri* on its new office signboard, thus transforming it into the "Industrial Irrationality Bureau."[39]

Leftists and antizaibatsu elements were skeptical about the rationalization movement. They sometimes referred to it as "Japanese-style rationalization," meaning wage cuts, reductions in the number of employees, and a stretching out of working hours.[40] There was also some international criticism to the effect that rationalization was a cover for "social dumping," a term of abuse that was especially applied to Japan at the time. During the early 1930's the International Labor Organization distinguished between what it called "commercial dumping"—an unfair business practice—and "social dumping"—a form of alleged exploitation of workers. Commercial dumping meant "an operation that consists in exporting goods at less than cost of production plus a fair profit, and at the same time, selling the same goods on the home market at a higher price than the cost of production plus a fair profit," whereas social dumping meant "the operation of providing the export of national products by decreasing their cost of production as the result of depressing conditions of labor in the undertakings which produce them or keeping those conditions at a low level if they are already at such a level."[41] The Japanese always resented the charge of social dumping, believing they were in fact trying to take the measures necessary to eliminate it.

The idea of industrial rationalization circulated widely in many countries during the 1920's and 1930's. Japan's specific conception of it originated as a poorly digested amalgam of then current American enthusiasms ("efficiency experts" and "time-and-motion studies"), concrete Japanese problems (particularly the fierce competition that existed among the large number of native firms and the consequent dumping of their products), and the influence of Soviet precedents such as the First Five Year Plan (1928–33) and the writings of the Hungarian economist and Soviet adviser Eugene Varga. With regard to Soviet influence, it should be remembered that during the 1920's socialist ideas had an impact on nonsocialist and even antisocialist groups and nations, particularly in the non-English-speaking industrialized countries. Later I shall draw attention to the specific link between Soviet and Japanese planning of the 1930's and 1940's in terms of its conceptual foundations. However, in 1930 by far the greatest influence on the Japanese theory of rationalization came from the Germans. Germany had been a powerful model for modern Japan ever since the Restoration, but in 1930 German precedents were introduced directly into the TIRB because of some unforeseen internal bureaucratic events. Such interaction between the demands of Japanese bureaucratic life and the policies that the Japanese government produced is a constant theme of this study.

During the year 1930 the ruling Minseitō government attempted to politicize MCI, much as the LDP would attempt to do to MITI some thirty years later. The industrial rationalization movement had made MCI an important center of policy, and the party clearly wanted to maneuver bureaucrats friendly to it into positions of leadership. The attempt ultimately failed, but it resulted in Yoshino Shinji's becoming vice-minister in 1931 and in Kishi Nobusuke's being sent to Germany to report back to the TIRB on the industrial rationalization movement there. The actual political incidents of 1930 are of slight importance in themselves, but they had consequences of lasting significance, among them the establishment of the so-called Yoshino-Kishi line in the ministry until 1936. Bureaucrats, like politicians, deal in power, and struggles for power are an inextricable part of bureaucratic life, regardless of what models organization theorists may have favored from Weber to the present.

Two Minseitō politicians served their party as MCI minister between 1929 and 1931—one a weak politician, Tawara Magoichi in the Hamaguchi cabinet (July 1929 to April 1931), and one a strong politician, Sakurauchi Yukio in the second Wakatsuki cabinet (April to December 1931). (On November 14, 1930, Prime Minister Hamaguchi Osachi was seriously wounded by a right-wing assassin. He remained in office and continued to serve as president of the Minseitō until April, when he and his cabinet resigned. He died August 26, 1931, of his wounds. Wakatsuki Reijirō, prime minister at the time of the financial panic in 1927, returned to power as president of the Minseitō after Hamaguchi's resignation.) Dominating both MCI ministers was the powerful Minseitō leader and minister of finance in both cabinets, Inoue Junnosuke. During 1930 Inoue became irritated by the growing influence of MCI in general, and of Yoshino Shinji in particular, because the activities of both impinged upon his own ministry's traditional bailiwick. He did not resist MCI directly. He served as a member of the Commerce and Industry Deliberation Council, and he supported industrial rationalization as the reverse side of his own policy of deflation through restoration of the international gold standard. But he wanted some changes made.

On July 2, 1930, a month after the creation of the TIRB, the vice-minister of MCI, Mitsui Yonematsu, resigned to take up positions as president of the Gōdō Fishing Company and of the Karafuto (Sakhalin) Mining Company. He had worked for many years in fishing and mining administration during the MAC and early MCI eras, but he had not intended to resign in 1930. Inoue and Tawara eased him out when he inquired about a shift to director of the Patent Bureau, since he was not fully in tune with Yoshino's TIRB and its policies. As Mitsui's replacement Inoue directed Minister Tawara to appoint Tajima Katsutarō, class of 1906, and Tawara did so—though with a considerable loss of face to himself personally.

Tajima was an unusual appointment. He had had no experience in any of the ministry's home office bureaus, having spent the later part of his career as head of the Fisheries Bureau during the MAC era, then as a transferee to the Tokyo metropolitan government, and most recently as chief of the Fukuoka Mine Inspectors Bureau. The last was the key to his appointment. Fukuoka was an important post since it exercised supervision over Japan's main coal fields, which supplied fuel to the Yawata steel works. The bureau chief there had to work closely with the powerful zaibatsu coal mine operators. Tajima had apparently developed something of a constituency in Fukuoka and was known to be ambitious to enter politics as a member of the Minseitō party. After his retirement as vice-minister in December 1931, he did join the Minseitō and was elected to the Diet as a member from Fukuoka for some three terms. Tajima's appointment in 1930 appeared to the bureaucracy and to the political world as an attempt by the Minseitō to take over the MCI. It was partly to overcome the rumors that Vice-Minister Tajima lacked the appropriate political independence for an Imperial bureaucrat that the succeeding Seiyūkai government ousted him and appointed Yoshino in his place. It was rumored that Takahashi Korekiyo himself had a hand in recommending Yoshino, even though Yoshino was only 43 years old and so had to be passed over nine of his seniors and three of his classmates.

During 1930, when Tajima was still vice-minister, Yoshino requested permission to go abroad to investigate the industrial rationalization movement in other countries. He was turned down on the grounds that Finance Minister Inoue thought it inopportune for the actual chief of the TIRB to be out of the country and therefore refused to pay for the trip. Yoshino countered with a proposal that his protégé, Kishi, go in his place—and this was readily approved for other bureaucratic reasons. On October 15, 1929, as part of the Minseitō's deflationary program, the Hamaguchi cabinet had ordered a 10 percent pay cut for all civil and military officials. The idea was very popular with the public, but it led to organized protests by the bureaucrats. Within MCI Kishi, then an assistant section chief in the Documents Section, led the opposition.

Kishi obtained about 50 signed letters of resignation from a few higher officials and from several noncareer officials. He threatened to present these to the minister if the pay cuts were not rescinded. Kishi's motives do not appear to have been primarily monetary; he was also concerned about the welfare of the noncareer employees and about the government's austerity measures as they applied to the military. During 1930 Yoshino and the minister worked out a compromise to paper over the dispute, and Yoshino used his first opportunity to get Kishi out of the country in order to let tempers cool. Kishi spent seven months (May–November 1930) in Berlin reporting on the industrial rationalization movement, and his reports directly influenced the path it took in Japan. One of Kishi's reports, that of July 13, 1930, was addressed to Kido Kōichi as one of the two department chiefs in the TIRB; it is of such interest in relation to the history of industrial policy that it was reprinted in *Chūō kōron* in September 1979, almost fifty years after it was written.[42]

Kishi said that German industrial rationalization, like the movement elsewhere, was devoted to technological innovation in industries, to the installation of the most up-to-date machines and equipment, and to generally increasing efficiency. What distinguished the German movement was its emphasis on government-sponsored trusts and cartels as the main means of implementing reforms. The Japanese translated this to mean that rationalization implied a lessening of economic competition, an approach that seemed plausible to them given the cutthroat competition and dumping of exports that existed in the medium and small enterprises sector.

In Japan rationalization came increasingly to emphasize that competition among enterprises should be replaced by "cooperation" (*kyō-chō*), and that the purpose of business activities should be the attempt to lower costs, not make profits. Yoshino himself has written,

Modern industries attained their present development primarily through free competition. However, various evils [of the capitalist order] are gradually becoming apparent. Holding to absolute freedom will not rescue the industrial world from its present disturbances. Industry needs a plan of comprehensive development and a measure of control. Concerning the idea of control, there are many complex explanations of it in terms of logical principles, but all one really needs to understand it is common sense.[43]

This view of economic competition has been characteristic of Japan's trade and industry bureaucrats from 1930 to at least the 1960's, and perhaps beyond. Sahashi Shigeru often made stronger statements when he was vice-minister about the evils of "excessive competition." One scholar of industrial policy concludes that around 1931 the term industrial rationalization in Japan became synonymous with the spirit of control as a substitute for the spirit of competition, which many people believed had caused the disasters of the 1920's and 1930's.[44] At the time of the TIRB's founding, the main question for policy-makers thus became Control by whom?

The first modern Japanese answer to this question was the Important Industries Control Law (Jūyō Sangyō Tōsei Hō, law no. 40, introduced in the Diet on February 25, 1931, passed April 1, 1931, and in effect from August 16, 1931). It was the most important product of the TIRB and the single most important piece of industrial legislation until the National General Mobilization Law of 1938 and the Important Industries Association Ordinance of 1941, which was based on the mobilization law. According to the 1931 law, control was to be exercised within an industry by the enterprises themselves—that is, the law legalized so-called self-control (*jishu tōsei*) in the form of treaty-like cartel agreements among enterprises to fix levels of production, establish prices, limit new entrants into an industry, and control marketing for a particular industry. The 1931 law took as its model the unions of medium and smaller enterprises of 1925; however, it strengthened government approval powers over such unions and extended them to big business.[45] The result, as Eleanor Hadley puts it, was a "cordial oligopoly" in the large-scale advanced sectors—as contrasted with the "cutthroat oligopoly" of the post–World War II period.[46]

The law was drafted in the Control Committee of the TIRB, where civilian and zaibatsu representation was strong, and the committee itself constitutes an early instance of the government's providing the auspices for private enterprises to help themselves, something it did often in the 1950's and 1960's. Within the committee, the term "control" (*tōsei*) generated a good deal of discussion. In retrospect one can see that the use of the term in the title of the law was probably unfortunate. Yoshino has often said that by "control" he and his colleagues meant the attempt to create "industrial order" and not bureaucratic supervision of industry. Although the MCI bureaucrats were aware that the army used the term in many different contexts, they specifically deny that their law had military implications or was influenced by the military in any way. Yoshino also argues that although the law authorized cartels, the purpose of the cartels was "order," not industrial profits, and that therefore the law was in the public's interest and not simply a way of making life easier for the zaibatsu.[47] Whatever he may have had in mind, however, the zaibatsu profited most from "control" and "industrial order."

The Important Industries Control Law was a relatively short statute of only ten articles. According to its terms, when two-thirds of the enterprises in a particular industry agreed to a cartel, MCI would examine its contents and, if it approved, then authorize (*ninka*) the cartel. The government could also change the terms or nullify the agreement. And it could force nonparticipants in the cartel agreement to abide by its terms if they did not do so voluntarily. As a result of an MCI-sponsored amendment to the law (introduced in the Diet during September 1932 and passed during 1933), the ministry obtained the powers to approve investments that would expand facilities by cartel members and to approve members' decisions to curtail production. Needless to say, all members of an industry were required to submit frequent reports on their investment plans and activities to the government. It is in this law that we find the origins of the government's licensing and approval authority and of the practice of "administrative guidance," which together became the heart of postwar industrial policy. To assuage skeptics in the Diet, the law had a five-year limitation written into it; on August 15, 1936, it was extended for another five years but it was superseded by the National General Mobilization Law before the second time period expired.

As a result of the law cartels were organized in some 26 designated "important industries," including silk thread, rayon, paper, cement, wheat flour, iron and steel, and coal. In industries suffering from excess capacity, such as cotton spinning, shipbuilding, and electrical machinery, it helped curtail competition and restore profitability. But Yoshino believes that the law did not actually work as he had intended it to. This was partly because only a month after it came into effect, the army seized all of Manchuria and the entire economy shifted to a war-preparatory footing. Even without this unforeseen development, however, the cartels seemed to work less in favor of "order" than in favor of strengthening and expanding the scope of zaibatsu operations (the *keiretsuka* of the economy, as the Japanese put it, or the structuring of the economy into conglomerates). In three industries, for example—petroleum, newsprint, and cement—MCI cartels promoted the interests of gasoline refiners over those of taxi companies, of the paper trusts over the newspapers, and of the cement industry over the lumber industry. All of the favored industries were areas of expanding zaibatsu strength.[48]

The zaibatsu had made it clear in the TIRB's Control Committee that they were less interested in cartels on the model of the industrial unions for medium and small enterprises than they were in easing competition through mergers and in the reduction of the number of competitors. Many mergers followed in the wake of the law: in May 1933 three companies merged to form Ōji Paper, in December the Sanwa Bank came into being as a result of a three-way merger, in January 1934 Yawata and five private companies united to become Japan Steel, in June Mitsubishi Heavy Industries appeared, and the following year Sumitomo Metals was created. Each of these cases fostered concentrations of economic power that came close to being monopolies rather than cartels. The zaibatsu believed that cartels did not allow for change and would prove unworkable over time. They would have preferred an individual industrial development law for each industry (for example, the Petroleum Industry Law of 1934 and the Automobile Manufacturing Law of 1936), that would also protect them from international competitors. As it turned out, this kind of law became more important than the original control law as the thirties progressed, but for reasons the zaibatsu did not foresee; the militarists wanted them, and even though they did not like working with the zaibatsu, they had no other choice.

At the time the control law was deliberated and enacted, Yoshino clearly stood for self-imposed control in industry and for government cooperation with private control agreements. However, the year 1931 ended up giving self-control a bad name, particularly insofar as it involved the zaibatsu, and this led to powerful demands for its opposite, namely, state control (*kokka tōsei*). The reason was the "dollar-buying" scandal. On September 21, 1931, England announced that it was leaving the gold standard because of the depression. This should have signaled the failure of Inoue's policy; Japan could not maintain the gold standard if its main trading competitor did not also abide by it. However, the Japanese gold embargo was not reimposed until three months later, and in the interim the zaibatsu banks engaged in an orgy of dollar buying, using yen they knew were soon to be devalued. Mitsui alone is said to have made $50 million in international currency transactions. The speculation ended in December with the return to power of the Seiyūkai (the last political party regime until after 1945) and Takahashi's reversal of Inoue's policy.

The effect on Japanese public opinion of the zaibatsu's dollar buying during the height of the depression was one of outrage. Many groups concluded that the zaibatsu were so irredeemably avaricious they were quite prepared to debase their own country's currency in the name of profits. Right-wingers assassinated Dan Takuma, the chief executive officer of Mitsui, and he was succeeded by the Harvard-educated Ikeda Seihin, who became MCI minister in 1938. After taking over at Mitsui, Ikeda carried out a public *tenkō* (conversion to patriotism) on behalf of his company. One important reason Ikeda took this action was that the military and some members of the economic bureaucracy were beginning to think in terms not of working with the zaibatsu in cartels but of dominating them—perhaps even nationalizing them—through the exercise of state power.

On December 21, 1931, as part of the Seiyūkai's housecleaning after taking over from the Minseitō, Yoshino Shinji was named vice-minister. He held the post until October 7, 1936. Although the TIRB had been associated with the Minseitō party, the Seiyūkai retained it because of the positive appeal of its ideology and because Yoshino, who was thought to have Seiyūkai sympathies even though he was publicly neutral, was now in charge of the ministry.

Within trade and industry circles the years 1931 to 1936 came to be known as the era of the Yoshino-Kishi line. This meant government promotion of heavy and chemical industrialization and a stress on industrial rationalization as the main objective of MCI policy. During his vice-ministership, Yoshino first promoted Kishi to the post of chief of the Industrial Policy Section (January 1932, the month after Yoshino took office), then chief of the Documents Section (December 1933), and finally chief of the Industrial Affairs Bureau (April 1935). Kishi was clearly on the "elite course," and he was expected to advance to the vice-ministership shortly after his mentor gave it up. Kishi did eventually become vice-minister, but a three-year Manchurian interlude intervened first. For although there was an orientation within the ministry that could be called a Yoshino-Kishi line, there were also differences between the two men. If Yoshino will always be identified with industrial "self-control," Kishi will always be identified with "state control" of industry.

The first phase of modern Japanese industrial policy seems remote from the postwar economic miracle, but it is, in fact, directly relevant to it for several reasons. During the 1920's Japan faced economic problems comparable in kind and in severity to those of the early 1950's: the need to restore competitive ability in international trade, the need to reorganize industry in order to achieve economies of scale and to take advantage of new technological developments, and the need to increase the productivity of the labor force. During the period from the creation of MCI to the passage of the Important Industries Control Law in 1931, the Japanese invented and experimented with the first of their three characteristic approaches to industrial policy, approaches that have remained in their repertoire to the present day. The first approach was the attempt to replace competition with self-control of an industry by the enterprises already established in it. The institutional form of this approach, state-licensed cartels, remains big business's preferred form of industrial policy down to the present day. Its major weakness, the tendency of cartelization to lead to zaibatsu domination and monopoly, was already fully visible by 1931; and this weakness in turn elicited demands for the opposite of self-control, namely, state control, that dominated the rest of the 1930's.

Another theme of this early period was the search for criteria of managerial and enterprise performance other than short-term profitability. Via the industrial rationalization movement, which began in the late 1920's but reached its full flowering only during the 1950's, the Japanese began self-consciously to think about how to build into enterprises and whole industries incentives to promote labor peace, job security, capital formation, increased productivity, and the development of new products. Although the earliest efforts at rationalization were largely frustrated by zaibatsu power and interests, a concern with rationalization—the attempt to gain a competitive edge through superior organization, labor peace, and cost cutting—is the most consistent and continuous feature of Japanese industrial policy throughout the Shōwa era. The greatest achievement of the early days of MCI was to begin seriously to forge a government-business relationship that was oriented to cooperation and development and that took the position of the whole Japanese economy vis-à-vis competitive foreign economies as its primary frame of reference.

The ideas and institutional innovations of this early period are not merely some "heritage" that had to be transmitted from one generation to the next. The generation that was to lead industrial policy during the 1950's and 1960's was already on the scene during the late 1920's and early 1930's. One of the most startling facts about the history of Japanese industrial policy is that the managers of the postwar economic "miracle" were the same people who inaugurated industrial policy in the late 1920's and administered it during the 1930's and 1940's. Unlike other nations defeated in World War II or torn by revolution in the wake of World War II, Japan did not experience a radical discontinuity in its civilian bureaucratic and economic elites. Men such as Yoshino Shinji, Kishi Nobusuke, Shiina Etsusaburō, Uemura

Kōgorō, and Inayama Yoshihiro were active in the formulation and execution of industrial policy before, during, and after the war. Equally important, all of MITI's vice-ministers during the 1950's entered the bureaucracy between 1929 and 1934. Thus, in studying the early origins of industrial policy, we are also studying the formative years of the officials who applied it with such seemingly miraculous effect during the 1950's. Not surprisingly, the institutions and policies first discussed in the Temporary Industrial Rationality Bureau bear more than a passing resemblance to the institutions and policies of the later period of high-speed growth.

This theme of historical continuity also draws attention to the fact that industrial policy is rooted in Japanese political rationality and conscious institutional innovation, and not primarily or exclusively in Japanese culture, vestiges of feudalism, insularity, frugality, the primacy of the social group over the individual, or any other special characteristic of Japanese society.

Economic crisis gave birth to industrial policy. The long recession following World War I, capped by the panic of 1927, led to the creation of MCI and to the first attempts at industrial policy, just as the need for economic recovery from World War II, capped by the deflation panic of 1949, led to the creation of MITI and to the renewal of industrial policy. All of the political and bureaucratic problems of the developmental state—including conflict between the bureaucracy and the central political authorities, and conflict among elements of the bureaucracy itself—appeared in this early period, just as they would reappear during the 1960's and 1970's. That the Japanese solved (or suppressed) these problems more effectively during the postwar period than during the 1930's is greater testimony to their ability to profit from experience than to any fundamental change in the situation they faced.

During the late 1920's the Japanese began to build new forms of state intervention in the economy, forms that differ in critical ways from those of either the command economy or the regulatory state. These initial efforts were soon overwhelmed by recurring crises—and contained unforeseen consequences that dismayed their inventors. As a result, the leaders of industrial policy were led to attempt a different approach, direct state control of the economy, that carried them to disaster. The bitterness of the era of the Yoshino-Kishi line was more than enough to warn those who managed both the state and private enterprise after the war that catastrophes could occur if they did not transcend both self-control and state control in favor of genuine public-private cooperation. Nonetheless, it should not be thought that these painful early experiences were wholly negative. The prototype of industrial policy did not fly well, and the improved model crashed, but the suitably modified production version of the 1950's amazed the world by its performance. From this perspective the early years of industrial policy were a period of indispensable gestation in the evolution and perfection of a genuine Japanese institutional invention, the industrial policy of the developmental state.

FOUR

Economic General Staff

D URING the period that Yoshino and his colleagues were dis-
covering rationalization and inching their way toward industrial policy, a different group of Japanese officials was taking up
parallel questions. They were military officers and civilian bureaucrats
working in military or cabinet-level agencies. Their concerns centered
on Japan's preparedness for war, particularly since Japan had not experienced the total mobilization during 1914–18 that had so deeply
influenced the general staffs of the Europeans. They were also concerned about the severe economic constraints that had appeared during Japan's last major war (with Russia during 1904–5), the economic
mobilization and growing industrial strength of the country's potential enemies (particularly Soviet Russia), and the emergence of problems in their planning for national security as it concerned primary
resources (particularly petroleum, but including other materials necessary for modern armaments).

These men were coming to believe that Japan needed an industrial
policy in order to ensure its military survival, not just to overcome the
depression. At an absolute minimum they wanted an "economic general staff" (*keizai sanbō honbu*) that would provide guidance for the
economy from the point of view of Japan's military needs and industrial and resource deficiencies. During the 1930's this stream of inspiration for industrial policy flowed into and merged with the civilian MCI stream, and both were transformed in the process.

The Japanese military's first thoughts about mobilizing the whole
private economy for war came during World War I. On April 17, 1918,
based on its understanding of Germany's mobilization effort and on
the actions of the United States after entering the war, the govern-

ment of Prime Minister (General) Terauchi enacted the Munitions Industries Mobilization Law (Gunju Kōgyō Dōin Hō). It was Japan's first
basic law relating to industrial control during wartime. It defined military supplies broadly and authorized the government after a declaration of war to supervise, use, or expropriate the industries producing
them. Most of its provisions were never enforced during World War I,
but it was still on the books in 1937, and it was implemented during
the early stages of the "China Incident" (the Diet asked for a distinction between a "state of war" and a "state of incident") before the National General Mobilization Law of 1938 replaced it.[1]

The 1918 law was virtually an afterthought of Japan's participation
in World War I. But in order to prepare for the possible need to implement the law, the government on May 31, 1918, set up a Munitions
Bureau (Gunju Kyoku) as a semidetached unit of the cabinet to prepare economic mobilization plans and to gather statistics on munitions industries. Its first chief, Hara Shōichirō of the navy, worked
hard at these tasks, but he found it almost impossible to get cooperation from the established ministries. On May 15, 1920, the government sought to lower the visibility of the bureau by merging it with
the cabinet's Statistical Bureau to create a new agency called the Census Board (Kokusei-in). This idea did not work any better than the
first one—the military officers and statisticians squabbled over turf—
and on November 30, 1922, with the military somewhat in disgrace
because of the Siberian expedition and with the government trying to
cut costs, the Census Board was abolished. The government transferred all the mobilization plans and accumulated statistics to MAC
and from it to MCI, where they greatly enhanced the resources of the
Secretariat's Statistical Section. Murase Naokai, the vice-minister of
MCI from 1936 to 1939 and a very important figure in our later discussions in this chapter, was working in the cabinet at the time the Census Board was abolished. He says that he recognized that these mobilization materials would be useful to his ministry in administering
industrial policy, and he implies that he had a hand in having them
transferred there.[2]

During the mid-1920's—the period of "Taishō democracy"—the
military was forced to drop its efforts to plan for economic mobilization, but by 1927 interest had revived. Many military officers had had
a chance to study and absorb the lessons of World War I, and they
were concerned about the growing economic might of Russia after
the consolidation of the Bolshevik revolution. During 1927 General
(then Major) Ishiwara Kanji, the chief economic architect of Manchukuo, wrote, "If national mobilization was taken to mean that the Japa-

nese home islands should attempt to mobilize vast quantities of men and munitions on the scale expended from 1914 to 1918 by France, for example, then the effort would certainly bankrupt Japan, no matter what the outcome."[3] The financial panic of April 1927 and the coming to power of a Seiyūkai government headed by a military officer, General Tanaka Giichi, afforded an opportunity to try again to set up an economic planning unit with a military outlook.

On May 26, 1927, the government established a Resources Bureau (Shigen Kyoku) as a semidetached organ of the cabinet. Because a heavy military presence in the old Munitions Bureau had led to conflicts with other ministries, this time the government toned down the military element, recruited bureaucrats from other ministries, and set up a joint public-private deliberation council to discuss resource questions. The staff of the Resources Bureau was small—only five people—but MCI sent to it one of its important young officials, Uemura Kōgorō, class of 1918, who was destined to become in May 1968 the president of Keidanren, the most influential post in the country for making policy for the business sector. Uemura spent the rest of his bureaucratic career working in the "economic general staff," where he rose to the position of vice-president of the Cabinet Planning Board in 1940. His position in the Resources Bureau was one of the earliest links between MCI and the military planners before the two were formally merged in 1943 in the Ministry of Munitions.[4]

The Resources Bureau of 1927 undertook the first measures of genuine economic planning in Japan. It pioneered the "materials mobilization plans" (to be discussed later in this chapter) that dominated the economic landscape after the outbreak of war with China. Its main achievement in the late 1920's, however, was to sponsor the Resources Investigation Law (Shigen Chōsa Hō, law number 53 of April 12, 1929), which required private enterprises to report to the government on their productive and financial capabilities. Since the Resources Bureau had no operating functions (lest it conflict with the territories of the established ministries), MCI was authorized to enforce the law by inspecting factories and mines to determine their resource potential. This was a significant development during peacetime. Interestingly enough, article 2 of this law refers to the need for "plans for the controlled operation" (*tōsei un'yō keikaku*) of enterprises, and this use of tōsei in a military economic statute is thought to be the origin of the term in the title of the Important Industries Control Law of 1931, even though Yoshino has denied that his law had a military purpose.[5]

If the financial panic of 1927 brought MCI to life as an organization, it was the invasion of Manchuria in September 1931 and the assassination of Prime Minister Inukai on May 15, 1932, that brought industrial policy to life as an element of military mobilization. The events of the succeeding few years in both Japan and Manchuria made even more insistent the need for an economic general staff, a coordinating organ that could unite military requirements with civilian capabilities and adjust both. After the militarist assault on Inukai the throne turned to a nonparty government of national unity under Admiral Saitō Makoto (1858–1936, assassinated in the military coup of February 26, 1936). Takahashi Korekiyo continued as minister of finance, and Nakajima Kumakichi (1873–1960) of the Furukawa zaibatsu (Furukawa Electric, Yokohama Rubber, Fuji Electric, and others), Yoshino's closest civilian associate in the TIRB, became minister of commerce and industry. Since this was a nonparty cabinet and Nakajima and Yoshino were good friends, the old practice of the vice-minister offering his resignation to a new minister was abandoned.

As we saw in the last chapter, Takahashi reimposed the gold embargo in December 1931, an action that advanced the government's intrusion into the private economy well beyond that of the cartels authorized by the Control Law. In order to make the embargo effective, the government also passed the Capital Flight Prevention Law (Shihon Tōhi Bōshi Hō, law number 17 of July 1, 1932); and when that proved to be ambiguous and therefore evadable, it passed the Foreign Exchange Control Law (Gaikoku Kawase Kanri Hō, law number 28 of March 29, 1933), which made all overseas transactions subject to the approval and licensing of the minister of finance. Although no one at the time could have imagined it, governmental control over the convertibility of yen lasted uninterruptedly until April 1, 1964, and over capital transfers until the capital liberalization policies of the late 1960's and early 1970's.

During 1932 Takahashi also launched his famous policy of deficit financing to overcome the depression (and thereby won the sobriquet that is now associated with his name, "the Keynes of Japan"). Military expenditures in the general account budget rose from 28 percent in 1930 to 43 percent in 1935, and the combined deficit of the years 1932 to 1936 reached an enormous ¥1.9 billion.[6] Takahashi's cutting the yen free from gold also produced a steep decline in the foreign exchange value of the yen. The rate against the U.S. dollar fell from ¥100 = $49 in 1931 to ¥100 = $19 in 1932, and the consequent lowering of prices of Japanese goods overseas fueled a tremendous surge of exports, particularly to South and Southeast Asia, that was loudly denounced abroad as Japanese "dumping." The Ministry of Finance covered the deficit through the issuance of bonds, which it sold to the Bank of Japan, and through some tapping of the trust fund accounts (the funds of small savers deposited in the Treasury through the postal savings system). A degree of inflation was expected, but Takahashi's theory was that a return to business prosperity would lead to a "natural" increase in government tax revenues sufficient to retire the debt. These methods were unorthodox for the time (the 1932 budget was the first unbalanced budget in Japan's modern history), and all the Finance Ministry officials under Takahashi were dubious.[7] But the policies seemed to work; Japan was well out of the depression before its international competitors had adopted similar policies (see Table 8).

During the autumn of 1935 the demand for goods began to outrun supply, and prices started to rise. Takahashi applied the brakes to military spending in order to control inflation and the balance of payments, but a section of the military revolted against what it took to be his civilian interference in the army's modernization efforts and assassinated him on February 26, 1936. Takahashi was once quoted to the effect that "it is much harder to nullify the results of an economic conquest than those of a military conquest," but this was a lesson that many more Japanese had to learn before they took it to heart after the Pacific War. His remark might well serve as an epitaph for his era—as well as a promise of the MITI era to come.[8]

Takahashi's successor gave the army a free hand to spend—which primarily meant to import needed resources—and within a year, well before the outbreak of war with China, Japan was facing a full-blown balance of payments and inflation crisis. The Tokyo wholesale price index (1934–36 = 100) jumped from 99.5 in January 1935 to 123.2 in January 1937—and then to 131.0 in April. Since the military had ruled out a tightening up of the economy by the Finance Ministry, the only other recourse was to economic controls and rationing. And the advent of rationing raised new demands that an "economic general staff" be empowered to plan for the whole economy. This economic general staff, in the form of the Cabinet Planning Board, came into being on October 23, 1937, under the added impetus of the China Incident.

Since the creation of the Resources Bureau in 1927, and especially after passage of the Important Industries Control Law in 1931, the military economists' primary efforts had been to enact individual laws in conjunction with MCI for particular strategic industries. The first industry law to be passed that had explicit military implications was the Petroleum Industry Law of March 28, 1934; it remains interesting to-

TABLE 8
Indices of the World Economic Crisis, 1930–1935
(1929 = 100)

Country	1930	1931	1932	1933	1934	1935
			Wholesale Prices			
Japan	82.3	69.6	77.2	88.5	90.2	92.5
United States	90.7	76.6	68.0	69.2	78.6	83.9
England	87.5	76.8	74.9	75.0	77.1	77.9
Germany	90.8	80.8	70.3	68.0	71.7	74.2
France	88.4	80.0	68.2	63.6	60.0	54.0
		Mining and Manufacturing Production				
Japan	94.8	91.6	97.8	113.2	128.7	141.8
United States	80.7	68.1	53.8	63.9	66.4	75.6
England	92.3	83.8	83.5	88.2	98.8	105.6
Germany	85.9	67.6	53.3	60.7	79.8	94.0
France	99.1	86.2	71.6	80.7	75.2	72.5

SOURCE: Arisawa Hiromi, ed., Shōwa keizai shi (Economic history of the Shōwa era), Tokyo, 1976, p. 52.

day as the direct ancestor and model for the Petroleum Industry Law of 1962. The 1934 law gave the government authority to license the business of importing and refining petroleum, and it required importers to stockpile at least a six months' supply of petroleum in Japan at all times. It also empowered the government to set quotas, fix prices, and make compulsory purchases of petroleum products.

An Imperial ordinance put MCI in charge of administering the law, and Yoshino, as vice-minister, set out to negotiate with Japan's foreign suppliers (chiefly the Standard Vacuum and Rising Sun oil companies). One of Stan-Vac's representatives in Japan recalls that in late 1934 Yoshino himself was not difficult to deal with or antiforeign, but that both of them had agreed it would be better to postpone their negotiations until after the current Diet session had ended in order to lessen possible military charges that MCI was bending to foreign coercion.[9] The result of the negotiations in 1934 was that the foreign suppliers more or less met the terms of the law in order to keep the Japanese business.

The Petroleum Law affected the ministry most directly by authorizing the creation of a Fuel Section in the Mining Bureau. Three years later, on June 9, 1937, this section became the Fuel Bureau (Nenryō Kyoku), an external agency of MCI charged with making fuel policy, developing new sources of petroleum, promoting the synthetic petroleum industry, and administering the Petroleum Industry Law. It was MCI's first industry-specific bureau—a pattern that the whole ministry would adopt in 1939—and it was the first bureau of MCI to which military officers on active duty were seconded.[10]

Meanwhile, during 1934 the first of two political events that were to lead to the creation of the economic general staff in its most fully developed form erupted on the political scene. This was the Teijin scandal that brought down the Saitō cabinet. The second incident was the military mutiny of February 1936 that dramatically increased military influence over the whole society. In January 1934, in a series of articles in his *Jiji shimpō* newspaper, the businessman and political polemicist Mutō Sanji charged that a group of ministers and higher officials were corruptly manipulating the stock of the Imperial Rayon Company (Teijin) for their own profit, and that Teijin shares held by the minister of finance since the bail out of the Taiwan Bank in 1927 had been secretly sold to them. It is unclear to this day whether Mutō sincerely believed what he wrote or whether his charges were part of a militarist plot to discredit the political parties and their capitalist supporters. The effect of his charges is not, however, in dispute; they contributed strongly to the belief that civilian politicians were hopelessly corrupt.[11]

Mutō himself was shot to death at North Kamakura station on March 9, 1934, by an unemployed worker. Two ministers—Nakajima of MCI and Hatoyama of education—along with a former vice-minister of finance and top business leaders were arrested and subjected to a sensational public trial that lasted from June 1935 to October 1937. All were ultimately acquitted. Three prominent businessmen who were arrested went on to hold positions as ministers in postwar cabinets (Kawai Yoshinari in the first Yoshida cabinet, Nagano Mamoru in the second Kishi cabinet, and Mitsuchi Chūzō in the Shidehara cabinet).

The role of Yoshino Shinji in the Teijin case deserves mention here. The interesting point is that he never said a word about the case even though many of the defendants were his close personal and professional associates—Nakajima as his minister and former TIRB colleague; Mitsuchi as a former counselor of the old MAC; Kawai as a former MAC bureaucrat (he resigned at the time of the rice riots); and Nagano as a director of the Tokyo Rice Exchange. Moreover, although the disposition of shares of stock put up as collateral by the Bank of Taiwan was the responsibility of the Finance Ministry's bank inspectors, the supervision of the stock exchanges was still under the jurisdiction of MCI. Yoshino did not have to know directly about the disposition of Teijin shares, but the manipulation of prices on the Tokyo and Osaka stock exchanges had to be of interest to MCI.

When Nakajima resigned as minister on February 9, 1934, he was succeeded for the remainder of the Saitō cabinet by Matsumoto Jōji, the famous legal scholar who later figured as an adviser on the constitution in 1946, and whose draft SCAP rejected in favor of its own. In 1934 Matsumoto favored vigorous prosecution of the Teijin defendants and made life difficult for Yoshino over the matter. Yoshino, however, never said a word on the subject of the Teijin case. He may have felt, along with many others at the time, that the case was a frame-up by the militarists and rightists to destroy "liberal" elements in politics. If so, his silence can be explained by the fact that it was extremely dangerous in the mid-1930's to contradict the nationalists on any subject. The Teijin case appears in retrospect to have been the equivalent in party politics of the Minobe case—the ouster of Minobe Tatsukichi from Tokyo University on charges of lèse majesté—in academic life.

After the Teijin incident the cabinet of Admiral Okada Keisuke (July 1934 to March 1936) sought to dispel the public's (and the military's) doubts about economic administration by establishing a Cabinet Deliberation Council (Naikaku Shingikai)—what the press called its "supplementary cabinet"—to advise it on economic policies. However, when the prime minister declared that his council was intended "to remove technical economic matters from political interference," the Seiyūkai vigorously opposed the council as a bureaucratic and militaristic device. Partly because of this Seiyūkai boycott, the president of the Minseitō and one of Japan's most accomplished political manipulators, Machida Chūji (1863–1946), entered the cabinet as MCI minister even though most party politicians shunned Okada's "non-party" government. Machida retained Yoshino as vice-minister for political reasons of his own, but in retrospect Yoshino believed that he should have resigned at the time. Okada's council was composed of fifteen members from among the "senior statesmen" (*jūshin*, the successors to the Meiji-era *genrō*), peers, political party leaders, and representatives of big business.

In order to service this brain trust, the Okada government also set up a Cabinet Research Bureau (Naikaku Chōsa Kyoku, established by Imperial ordinance 119 of May 11, 1935). This was not the older military-oriented Resources Bureau of 1927, also attached to the cabinet, but a new organ made up of bureaucrats detached on temporary duty from the main ministries to serve in this elite body. Two years later the Cabinet Planning Board—known at the time as the "economic general staff"—came into being by combining the Cabinet Research Bureau and the Resources Bureau.

In 1935 the Cabinet Research Bureau was the stronghold of the variously termed "new bureaucrats" (*shinkanryō*), "reform bureaucrats" (*kakushin kanryō*)—or, in Nakamura Takafusa's description, civilian bureaucrats who were attracted by Nazi ideology.[12] Ide and Ishida bluntly define the reform bureaucrats as "anti-liberal, anti-parties, nationalistic, pro-military, pro-fascist, and above all in favor of strengthening governmental control."[13] They were found in all ministries and rose to influence after the assassination of Inukai as part of the vigorous intrabureaucratic competition to fill the vacuum left by the political parties. By cooperating with the military, whether for ideological reasons or just because that was the way the wind was blowing, some bureaucrats rapidly advanced their own careers.

In old-line ministries such as Finance and Foreign Affairs, the mainstream of bureaucratic leadership tried to resist the growing influence of the military, but these ministries tended to lose power over the decade to the ministries that cooperated, such as MCI. Within MCI Yoshino was critical of the reform bureaucrats as "flatterers of the military," even though his protégé Kishi was a model reform bureaucrat and Yoshino himself was in good favor with the military because of his essentially technocratic political stance.[14] Yoshino also recognized that the admission of military officers on detached service into MCI, a practice he had authorized for the Fuel Bureau and several other new units, affected the ministry's personnel affairs. The militarists regularly used their political power to block promotions of young officials whom they considered insufficiently "reformist." Most of the officials working in industrial administration, as distinct from commercial administration, became reform bureaucrats to some extent, and this led to a factional alignment under Yoshino's successors and under Kishi that would affect the ministry for decades to come.

The military equivalent of the reform bureaucrats—the *kakushin bakuryō*, or "reform staff officers"—looked on the reform bureaucrats as possible civilian replacements for the old political party leaders, whom they held to be corrupt and to constitute prime obstacles to the building of a "national defense state" in Japan. In October 1934 the Army Ministry published an inflammatory pamphlet calling for national mobilization, opposition to "classes that live by unearned profit," and the expansion of production and trade under state control. To implement this program the army advocated that its cadres make alliances with "new bureaucrats," and the term thereby entered popular parlance.[15]

One important source of reform bureaucrats was officials who had served in Manchuria as transferees after the proclamation in March

1932 of the new state of Manchukuo. Since the army actually ran Manchukuo, those who were invited to work there had to be in sympathy with the military's ideas for the renovation of Japan itself. The MCI contingent that served in Manchuria is particularly important for postwar industrial policy because, as Shiina Etsusaburō wrote in 1976, Manchuria was "the great proving ground" for Japanese industry.[16] We shall identify them and describe their activities below.

Some important reform bureaucrats in MCI and in closely related economic bureaucracies were Kishi Nobusuke, Shiina Etsusaburō, Uemura Kōgorō, Kogane Yoshiteru (director of the Fuel Bureau in 1941 and a postwar Diet member), Hashii Makoto (who served in the postwar Economic Stabilization Board and then became president of Tokyo Gauge Company), Minobe Yōji (Minobe Tatsukichi's nephew, chief of the Munitions Ministry's Machinery Bureau and postwar vice-president of Japan Hydrogen Industries), Wada Hiroo (from the Agriculture Ministry and postwar minister of agriculture in the first Yoshida cabinet), Sakomizu Hisatsune (from the Finance Ministry and postwar director-general of the Economic Planning Agency and postal minister in the Ikeda cabinets), Aoki Kazuo (from the Finance Ministry, president of the Cabinet Planning Board, and postwar member of the House of Councillors of the Diet), and Hoshino Naoki (from the Finance Ministry, president of the Cabinet Planning Board, and postwar chairman of the Tōkyū hotel chain and the Diamond Publishing Company). Not surprisingly, a few of the reform bureaucrats turned out to be not rightists but left socialists and cryptocommunists; their presence on the "economic general staff" produced a major scandal in 1941, as we shall see later in this chapter.

Before the second Konoe cabinet was established in 1940, the mainstream factions in most ministries tried quietly to check the influence of the reform bureaucrats, whom they regarded as excessively ambitious. The promilitary bureaucrats therefore often sought transfers to Manchuria or to the cabinet-level bureaus of the economic general staff, where military influence was strong. In May 1935, when the Cabinet Research Bureau was set up, Minister Machida of MCI suggested that Yoshino take the post as first director of the bureau, but he did not insist when Yoshino refused.[17] Instead, the prime minister chose Yoshida Shigeru (1885–1954), who must be carefully distinguished from the Foreign Ministry bureaucrat of exactly the same name who became prime minister after the war. This Yoshida was a Home Ministry bureaucrat, a member of the ultranationalist Society for the Maintenance of the National Prestige (Kokuikai), and minister of munitions in the Koiso cabinet of 1944.

At the time of its establishment, Yoshida's Research Bureau brought together officials from the Army, Navy, Home, Finance, Commerce, Agriculture, and Communications ministries, plus two cabinet officials serving concurrently in the Resources Bureau.[18] MCI sent two officials, Hashii Makoto and Fujita Kuninosuke (from January 1934 to May 1935 chief of Department One of the TIRB and after the war first a member of the American-sponsored Securities and Exchange Commission and then a professor at Chūō University). Yoshida asked Kishi to join, but he had bigger fish to fry in MCI and in Manchuria and therefore declined. One of the two Agriculture Ministry officials at the Research Bureau was Wada Hiroo, a prominent leader of the left socialists in postwar politics.

The pronounced "new bureaucrat" coloration of both the deliberation council and the Research Bureau in the Okada cabinet produced strong denunciations by some political party and business leaders. The deliberation council soon became a dead letter and was quietly abolished when the government changed. The Research Bureau, however, persisted and became embroiled in one of the historic controversies of the early controlled-economy era. A plan like the Petroleum Industry Law of 1934 was sponsored by the Cabinet Research Bureau for the reorganization and state control of the electric power generating and distributing industry. In this instance, however, the owners of the companies resisted fiercely, and business leaders denounced the bureau for its advocacy of "bureaucratic fascism" and "state socialism."[19]

After two years of bitter debate in and out of the Diet, the bureaucrats finally achieved control over electricity through the Electric Power Control Law of 1938. They had wanted to nationalize the electric power industry, but they had to settle for public management and private ownership in order to get any law at all. Several revisions were needed, but when the law was fully implemented in September 1941, it forcibly merged 33 generating companies and 70 distributing companies into 9 public utilities under the control and supervision of the Electric Power Bureau of the Ministry of Communications. It was one of the most impressive reforms of "industrial structure" of the prewar period. The Electric Power Control Law is important to the history of MITI because the creation of the Ministry of Munitions in 1943 moved the Electric Power Bureau from the Ministry of Communications into MITI's line of descent. All nine companies created by the 1938 law exist today, except that they are now private utilities (Tokyo Electric Power is the world's largest privately owned utility), and all are still under the supervision and guidance of MITI.

If the Teijin case of 1934 marked the beginnings of the reform bureaucrats, the abortive military coup d'etat of 1936 transformed the political system and brought them into prominence. It also initiated the struggle between bureaucrats who favored state control of the economy and private industrialists who favored self-imposed control, a struggle that would last until the end of the Pacific War. Within MCI the military uprising alarmed many otherwise complacent bureaucrats; Yoshino acknowledges that in the wake of the incident he lost control of the ministry. Before the year was out he and Kishi would be fired. The military was riding high in the cabinet, but within the ministries some passive resistance to the militarists and their friends was developing. Business leaders also began to turn cautiously against the Yoshino-Kishi line, but they could not speak out openly because of the fear of assassination. However, in order to obtain the cooperation of industry, the military found that it had to compromise on whom it recommended for MCI minister and to tolerate ministers who came from or were acceptable to business.

One such compromise choice as minister of MCI was Ogawa Gōtarō (1876–1945), a former Kyoto University professor of economics and an elected member of the House of Representatives since 1917.* Ogawa made it known that he intended "to eliminate the control faction in MCI," and he had several reasons for wanting to do so. First, he was from Kansai and reflected the Osaka business world's hostility to the controlled economy. Second, he was worried about working with a vice-minister who had been in office for five years and who might try to upstage him. Third, as a leader of the Minseitō, he did not like Yoshino's Seiyūkai leanings or Kishi's ties with Chōshū political and industrial figures (for example, with Matsuoka Yōsuke, then president of the South Manchurian Railroad, foreign minister at the time of the Axis alliance, and the uncle of Satō Hiroko, the wife of Kishi's brother Eisaku). Finally, Ogawa evidently distrusted both Yo-

---

*Ogawa became MCI minister in the Hirota cabinet following the death after only a few weeks in office of Kawasaki Takukichi. Kawasaki had originally been selected as home minister, but the army vetoed him because he was one of Machida Chūji's lieutenants, and he went instead to MCI.

Interestingly enough, Ogawa died on April 1, 1945, in the torpedoing of the *Awa Maru* in the Taiwan Straits by a U.S. submarine. The *Awa Maru* was supposed to be carrying noncombatants and relief supplies for Allied prisoners of war, but some Americans believed that the Japanese were using the passage of the *Awa Maru* to return gold and important people to the home islands. About 2,045 passengers were killed. In April 1949 the *Awa* incident became a political issue when the Yoshida government abandoned efforts to obtain an indemnity from the United States because of U.S. aid to Japan's postwar reconstruction. Ogawa was, in fact, returning to Japan after serving as supreme adviser to the Burmese government.

shino and Kishi, but particularly Kishi because of his involvement in the protests against pay cuts a few years earlier.[20]

Ogawa offered Yoshino the presidency of the newly established Tōhoku (Northeast) Industrial Development Company, a Japanese version of the Tennessee Valley Authority for the development of a backward region. And Ogawa said to Kishi that the Kwantung Army had strongly requested Kishi's services in the Manchurian government (which was true). Yoshino contemplated refusing to resign on grounds that as an Imperial official he could not be dismissed, but he thought better of it. He realized that he had remained as vice-minister too long and was aware that junior officials in the ministry were holding meetings about the political situation from which he was excluded.[21] On Yoshino's birthday, September 17, 1936, he and Kishi jointly submitted their letters of resignation. Yoshino went to Tōhoku, where he had been born, and Kishi became the deputy director of the Industrial Department of the government of Manchukuo.

In strict accordance with custom Ogawa asked Yoshino to name his successor. Yoshino recommended Takeuchi Kakichi, class of 1915, and at the time director of the Patent Bureau. Takeuchi had never been popular with Kishi, who apparently believed that Takeuchi should have been sent to the Agriculture Ministry when MAC was divided in 1925. Nonetheless, Takeuchi served in many important, typically reform bureaucratic posts in MCI and elsewhere in the government: he was a department chief in the TIRB from 1930 to 1935, president of the Cabinet Planning Board from January to July 1940, and vice-minister of munitions from July 1944 to April 1945. In 1936 Ogawa appointed him vice-minister of commerce and industry but made clear that he distrusted him as a follower of the Yoshino-Kishi line. Under these circumstances Takeuchi resigned two months later, and after a short interval in Manchuria took up the post of director of the semidetached Fuel Bureau, where he felt much more comfortable. As his successor Ogawa selected Murase Naokai, an official much more to Ogawa's liking and the vice-minister who led MCI through the first years of the China war and through its total reorganization in 1939.

Murase Naokai (1890–1968) entered MAC from Tōdai Law in 1914. He had not had much experience in MAC or MCI, since from 1919 to 1933 he had worked as a transferee in the Cabinet Legislation Bureau (Hōsei Kyoku). This bureau was the most prestigious post for a prewar bureaucrat, and its directorship was the pinnacle of the Imperial service. By 1933 Murase had become a councillor in the bureau, and the only post still ahead of him was the director's. Because he was considered too junior for that, although he was regarded as an excellent legal technician, the bureau asked Yoshino to take him back as a bureau chief in MCI. Yoshino was glad to oblige, and in September 1933 he appointed Murase chief of the Commercial Affairs Bureau. Murase held that post until Yoshino's resignation.[22]

Murase thus had no experience in industrial administration or in the TIRB. He leaned toward the commercial wing of MCI, which was oriented to medium and smaller enterprises, the insurance business, the stock exchanges, and trade—and which reflected the business world's wary approach to the controlled economy. Murase's greatest achievement as chief of the Commercial Affairs Bureau was securing the passage in 1936 of the Commercial and Industrial Cooperatives Central Depository Law, the enabling legislation for the Shōkō Chūkin Bank. This was and is today the leading governmental financial organ devoted exclusively to support of medium and smaller enterprises. Murase became known as a champion of the small businessman, and after the Pacific War he served from February 1953 to February 1958 as chairman of the bank he had founded in 1936.*

While Murase was settling in at Kobiki-chō, Kishi was in Hsinking greeting old friends and colleagues. Kishi himself had been directly responsible for sending most of them there. During his service as Industrial Policy Section chief and as Documents Section chief (1932–35), Kishi had received many requests from the Kwantung Army for MCI officials to staff its new government of Manchukuo. This government was divided into a series of departments (*bu*) equivalent to the ministries in Japan, each with a Manchurian as director and a Japanese as deputy director. The General Affairs Agency (Sōmu-chō), whose director and deputy director were both Japanese, supervised the whole puppet structure. The army asked the ministries in Tokyo to send reform bureaucrats to serve temporarily in these "guidance" posts, and Kishi was only too willing to oblige. The first director of

---

*When Murase was forced from the vice-ministership in October 1939 by the "return of the Manchurians," Ikeda Seihin, the Mitsui leader and minister of MCI during the second half of 1938, arranged for his appointment as director of the Cabinet Legislation Bureau. He remained there until the appointment of the Tōjō cabinet, when he resigned from the government. On April 7, 1945, Prime Minister (Admiral) Suzuki Kantarō asked him to return as director of the Cabinet Legislation Bureau in order to assist in terminating the Pacific War. He stayed in the post until after the surrender. On August 28, 1946, the occupation authorities purged him, and on October 13, 1950, they depurged him. He became an adviser to MITI on March 1, 1953. After heading the Shōkō Chūkin Bank, a public corporation under MITI's control, he became president between 1961 and 1967 of the Japan Electronic Computer Company, one of MITI's main instruments for promoting the domestic computer industry.

the General Affairs Agency was Komai Tokuzō of the Kwantung Army's Special Affairs Department, but his successor was Hoshino Naoki of the Ministry of Finance. Kishi later served as Hoshino's deputy at the General Affairs Agency.

The first MCI official sent to Manchuria was Takahashi Kōjun, a former Documents Section chief, who went in June 1933 and became deputy director of the Industrial Department (Jitsugyō-bu, which changed its name during 1937 to Sangyō-bu). During the autumn of 1933 Takahashi returned to MCI to recruit more officials, and Kishi strongly recommended that he approach the young TIRB official, Shiina Etsusaburō (Kishi was Shiina's sempai by three years). This established a relationship between Kishi and Shiina that was as long lasting as that between Yoshino and Kishi. If the Yoshino-Kishi line prevailed in the ministry during the first half of the 1930's, the Kishi-Shiina line dominated it during the 1940's, 1950's, and well into the 1960's. Shiina served in the Industrial Department of Manchuria from 1933 to 1939. In addition, Kishi sent Okabe Kunio (chief of MITI's Trade Promotion Bureau in 1951 and, after retirement as a bureaucrat, the managing director of JETRO and a director of MITI's Electrical Resources Development Company). In his memoirs Yoshino refers to both Shiina and Okabe as members not of his faction but of "Kishi's faction." [23]

Others whom Kishi sent or Ogawa expelled to "the wilds of Manchuria" between 1933 and 1936 included Minobe Yōji (whose active duty at MCI lasted from 1926 to 1945), Kōda Noboru (1925 to 1943), and Shiseki Ihei (1930 to 1952, a member of the House of Representatives since May 1953, and one of MITI's key supporters in the Diet). However, the MCI official the army wanted all along was Kishi himself. His predecessor as deputy chief of the Industrial Department, Takahashi Kōjun, had not proved to be effective in the post, and in 1936 the army was insisting that Kishi come over to help get its faltering industrialization campaign underway. Thus, with an added push from Ogawa, Kishi went to Manchuria to replace Takahashi as deputy director of the Industrial Department.

The situation in Manchuria was changing significantly just at the time Kishi arrived. From 1933 to 1936 the army and the South Manchurian Railroad (SMRR) had attempted to apply a radical, state-controlled, antizaibatsu development plan, but they had failed due to a lack of capital and to amateur management of heavy and chemical industries. The reputation of the SMRR had suffered considerably as a result. By 1935 the Kwantung Army had begun to reconsider its earlier anticapitalist line and was now trying to create a much sounder and more realistic "five-year plan for Japanese and Manchurian in-dustry." The army's staff completed this plan in the summer of 1936 and presented it to the Japanese cabinet on May 29, 1937.[24]

There has been a good deal of controversy about Kishi's role in this plan. After the war the Prosecution Section of the International Mili-tary Tribunal for the Far East summoned Shiina some eight times to its offices at Ichigaya to ask him about Kishi's part in formulating the plan. His reply was that the plan was already completed when Kishi arrived and that Kishi had been invited to Hsinking primarily to su-pervise its implementation. Shiina was certainly the man to ask, since he had been conducting industrial surveys in Manchuria since 1933, and, according to Kishi, *he* was the central figure in drafting the 1936 plan. On another occasion, however, Kishi indicated that he had had a major input into the plan while serving in an advisory capacity in Tokyo.[25] Whatever the case, when Kishi arrived, he insisted that Chief of Staff Itagaki Seishirō of the Kwantung Army give him a free hand to implement the plan. Itagaki agreed, and army participation in Manchurian industrial affairs declined significantly.

The plan was extremely ambitious. It set targets of 5 million tons of pig iron, 3.5 million tons of steel ingots, 2 million tons of finished steel products, 38 million tons of coal, 2.6 million kilowatts of electric power, 400,000 tons of wood pulp, and so forth.[26] In order to carry out this plan, Kishi invited the leader of the Nissan zaibatsu, Ayukawa Gisuke, to come to Manchuria to manage it. Ayukawa was acceptable to the army because he represented a "new zaibatsu"—one of the concerns that had thrived as a result of the military expansion of the 1930's and that was made up of firms concentrated in comparatively high-technology industries—and because Ayukawa had many per-sonal ties to Kishi and Yoshino (Yoshino, in fact, eventually joined Ayukawa's Manchurian firm after he was dropped as minister of com-merce and industry in 1938). Also, Ayukawa's Nissan automobile firm was one of the two companies specially favored in the Automobile Manufacturing Industry Law of 1936 (discussed below). It was as a result of these plans and considerations that during the autumn of 1937 the Japan Industrial Corporation (Nissan) changed its name and incorporated in Manchukuo as the Manchurian Heavy Industries Corporation (Manshū Jūkōgyō K.K., abbreviated Mangyō) with Ayu-kawa Gisuke as president.

Ayukawa planned to raise some $250 million from United States sources. He believed that this, plus his own capital, would be enough to get started. As it turned out, the war with China erupted just as he arrived on the scene, and international financing never became available because of worldwide condemnation of Japan's conduct of the war. Nonetheless, Ayukawa worked at it for five years, setting up numerous satellite firms ("one company for one industry" was his and Kishi's model of industrial organization) and giving his staff of Japanese bureaucrats invaluable experience in industrial planning and operation.

Kishi subsequently wrote that in Manchuria he "imbibed the ideas of industrial guidance," and Shiina contends that the experience of economic planning in Manchuria was as important for the later "materials mobilization plans" and their postwar equivalents as the work of the Cabinet Resources Bureau. The biggest Manchurian undertakings were the dams for hydroelectric power generation on the Sungari and Yalu rivers and the extensive land reclamation projects. Mangyō built electrical transmission lines larger than any that had been constructed in Japan up to that time, and the Japanese aluminum industry, which requires large quantities of electric power, was first established in Manchuria.

The nucleus of the Manchurian power structure was known in Hsinking by the acronym "the two *ki*s and three *suke*s" (*ni-ki san-suke*), a phrase that referred on the political side to Hoshino Nao*ki* (chief of the General Affairs Agency), and Tōjō Hide*ki* (chief of the Kwantung Army's military police and after 1937 chief of staff of the Kwantung Army); and on the economic side to Kishi Nobu*suke* (deputy chief of the Industrial Department and subsequently deputy chief of the General Affairs Agency), Ayukawa Gi*suke* (president of Mangyō), and Matsuoka Yō*suke* (president of the SMRR). They all missed the political turmoil in Japan during the first years of the China Incident, but in 1939 and 1940 four of them returned to top positions in the Japanese government. Two of them, Tōjō and Kishi, went on to become prime ministers.

In Japan during this period the movement toward industrial control took the form primarily of industry-specific development laws. The second such law (after the Petroleum Industry Law of 1934) was the Automobile Manufacturing Industry Law (passed May 29, 1936, and in effect July 11). It required that manufacturers of cars and trucks in Japan be licensed (*kyoka*) by the government—hence the term *kyoka kaisha* (a licensed company) for the few firms left in this sector. The government supplied half the capital of the licensees, and taxes and import duties were eliminated for five years. Only two companies were licensed, Toyota and Nissan, and by 1939 the law had put foreign car manufacturers in Japan (Ford and General Motors) out of business, as it was intended to do. One of Kishi's last acts during

1936, while still serving as chief of the Industrial Affairs Bureau and before departing for Manchuria, was to draft this law. Kakuma notes laconically that although the law itself was rescinded during the occupation, its terms remained in effect until the late 1960's.[27]

The petroleum and automobile laws were the first of a series of laws designed to provide special governmental financing, taxes, and protective measures for individual industries, and the first that were defended in terms of national defense needs. Their importance cannot be overstated. They were resurrected during the 1950's and 1960's for different industries and for nonmilitary (but nonetheless national defense) objectives. They are a part of the prewar heritage most directly relevant to postwar industrial policy. Other laws passed during the late 1930's were the Artificial Petroleum Law (August 10, 1937), the Steel Industry Law (August 12, 1937), the Machine Tool Industry Law (March 30, 1938), the Aircraft Manufacturing Law (March 30, 1938), the Shipbuilding Industry Law (April 5, 1939), the Light Metals Manufacturing Industry Law (May 1, 1939), and the Important Machines Manufacturing Law (May 3, 1941).[28] These laws did much to promote the particular industries concerned, but politically they represented compromises between the state-control and the self-control persuasions. The business sector was still strong enough to withstand state and public pressure and to insist on private ownership and a large measure of private management, which is closer to the postwar pattern than some of the other measures enacted by the state-control group during the 1930's.

One area in which the military first caused a major problem and then supported a solution well ahead of its time was in the control of foreign trade. The military's competitors here were not private businessmen but other bureaucrats. After the assassination of the minister of finance in February 1936, the officials of the Finance Ministry more or less gave up trying to resist military demands for budget increases. One scholar notes that from the Konoe cabinet of 1937 to the outbreak of the Pacific War, no Finance Ministry personnel participated in key decisions.[29] As a result of this shoving aside of financial administrators, the budget jumped from ¥2.3 billion in 1936 to ¥3 billion in 1937, with all of the increase going for munitions. Companies supplying the military engaged in tremendous speculative importing of materials. In order to overcome the serious balance of payments deficits that resulted, the military demanded that foreign trade be put on a war footing. They wanted to promote industries that earned foreign exchange and to restrict all imports they deemed unnecessary. To do these things, the military advocated combining the trade functions of the Finance, Foreign Affairs, and Commerce ministries into a new trade ministry.

The Foreign Office opposed this plan, but MCI supported it. Terao Susumu, one of the leaders of MCI's Trade Bureau since its creation in May 1930, recalls that in 1937 they were searching for something like MITI—the first agency in Japan to combine industrial administration with the supervision of foreign trade.[30] The Foreign Ministry would not hear of it, however, and the idea had to be dropped. Instead, on July 14, 1937 (and wholly unrelated to the outbreak of war with China on July 7), MCI's Trade Bureau was elevated and transformed into a semidetached bureau with its own director-general and secretariat, and with military officers serving in it in policy-making roles. MCI's external Trade Bureau was the direct ancestor of the powerful Board of Trade (Bōeki-chō) of the occupation period, and MITI itself came into being in 1949 essentially as a merger of MCI and the Board of Trade.

In 1939 the army and MCI tried again for a trade ministry. This time every official of the Foreign Ministry's Trade Bureau handed in his resignation, and the foreign minister, Nomura Kichisaburō, threatened to bring down the cabinet with his own resignation if the idea was not dropped. The Abe cabinet ultimately fell over the issue anyway. The chief MCI official who worked to establish a trade ministry in 1939 was Ueno Kōshichi, MITI vice-minister from 1957 to 1960, and he remembers the entire episode with great frustration.[31] The Foreign Ministry and the trade and industry bureaucracy have fought unremittingly to the present day over the issue of who is to control foreign trade.

Although a trade ministry was not set up before the war, MCI became deeply involved in trade matters after the outbreak of the China Incident. When the China war expanded into the Pacific War, however, trade matters became concentrated almost exclusively in the new Greater East Asia Ministry, which absorbed the external Trade Bureau. The Greater East Asia Ministry was also violently opposed by the Foreign Ministry, and it was actually more of a colonial office for newly occupied areas than a foreign commerce bureaucracy. From 1942 until the creation of MITI, then, MCI had little to do with trade (although it retained its own small trade staff during 1942 and 1943 until the Ministry of Munitions wiped it out). In comparative terms, there is no question that MITI is a more effective industrial policy agency than MCI precisely because it combines control of trade and industry in one unit and plans for each in coordination with the other.

The cabinets that followed the army mutiny of 1936 were unpopular with almost everyone, either because military influence over them was strong or because they had to compromise with private business interests. This led first to calls for a government of national unity and then to its formation under the leadership of Prince Konoe on June 4, 1937. In view of the imbalance in international payments and the need for the military to import at least some of what it wanted, the selection of the minister of finance in the new government was a major issue. Konoe named Kaya Okinori, who was not a reformist but a fiscally conservative Finance Ministry bureaucrat. Kaya in turn recommended Yoshino to be minister of commerce and industry on grounds that he needed to be backed up by that ministry if he were going to bring army spending demands under control. As it turned out, the coming of war in China a month after the Konoe government came into being upset all of these plans. Nonetheless, Yoshino returned from his position in the northeast to become minister of the organization he had left as vice-minister only a few months earlier. He was the first MCI-bred bureaucrat to become minister of commerce and industry. Interestingly enough, Yoshino's and Kishi's careers are similar in that both were fired as vice-minister and then returned as minister in less than a year.

On June 4, 1937, the day the new cabinet was sworn in, Finance Minister Kaya and MCI Minister Yoshino issued their famous joint statement of "three fundamental principles" of economic policy: production must be expanded, the country must live within the limits set by the international balance of payments, and the government must control economic activities in order to achieve coordination between the first two principles.[32] The first principle was aimed at meeting military demands, the second was in response to the demands of business leaders, and the third put the whole country on notice that changes were needed in order to do what the military wanted and still avoid bankruptcy.

The intent behind the statement (to bring military spending under control) was clear enough in Japan, but it was misunderstood abroad as a declaration of aggression. American newspapers reported the Kaya-Yoshino statement as preparatory to a war with China, and in 1945 the International Military Tribunal for the Far East investigated Yoshino's radio speech on the three principles as possible evidence of his involvement in a war plot.[33] Yoshino and Kaya were in favor of expanded productive capacity, but they also stood for fiscal integrity and joint public-private management, principles that clearly distinguished them from their immediate predecessors.

When fighting broke out in China, the initial view of the cabinet was that the conflict should be minimized to the greatest extent possible. This attitude prevailed until approximately the time of the battle for Hsüchow, which fell to the Japanese on May 18, 1938. However, some wartime controls began to appear almost at once. In addition to reinvoking and strengthening the price control ordinance of 1918, the Konoe government obtained passage on September 10, 1937, of three new laws. The first of these legalized enforcement of the Munitions Industries Mobilization Law of 1918, even though no war had been declared. The second was the Emergency Funds Regulation Law (Rinji Shikin Chōsei Hō), which empowered the Ministry of Finance to direct public and private capital to munitions industries if it felt the normal flow of investment funds was too slow or inadequate. The full implications of this law were not spelled out at the time it was passed, but it inaugurated the Finance Ministry's administrative guidance of private banks, which has continued to the present day.

The third law is the most interesting. It was Yoshino's brainchild and probably his greatest accomplishment as minister. It bore the imposing title of Temporary Measures Law Relating to Exports, Imports, and Other Matters (Yushutsunyū-hin-tō ni kan suru Rinji Sochi ni kan suru Hōritsu, law number 92), and Yoshino and his associates have gleefully recounted how they chose this wording in order to confuse Diet members (specifically, through their use of legalese such as *kan suru* "relative to" twice in the title, and above all through their insertion of the suffix *tō* "et cetera") and how Yoshino dissembled and gave vague answers to questions in the Diet about the scope of the law.[34] Under the terms of this law of only eight articles, the government was authorized to restrict or prohibit the import or export of any commodity and to control the manufacture, distribution, transfer, and consumption of all imported raw materials. It meant, as Nakamura emphasizes, a grant of discretionary power to MCI to control *everything* if it so chose.[35] The 1937 trade law is the clearest precedent for the Foreign Exchange and Foreign Trade Control Law of 1949, which was MITI's single most powerful instrument for carrying out its industrial policy during the period of high-speed growth and into the present (the 1949 law was rewritten but still retained on the books during 1980).

Yoshino and MCI, who clearly had not thought through all the implications of this law, regarded it primarily as an emergency wartime measure. At the same time, however, other segments of the government were moving toward a planned and state-controlled economy. As MITI's semiofficial *History of Commercial and Industrial Policy* (*Shōkō seisaku shi*) notes, "In terms of wartime economic controls, the most important administrative change after the outbreak of the China Incident took place outside MCI; this was the establishment on October 23, 1937, of the Cabinet Planning Board (Kikaku-in)."[36]

On May 14, 1937, as a preparatory step toward planning and state control, the Hayashi cabinet had reorganized and strengthened the Cabinet Research Bureau of 1935 and renamed it the Cabinet Planning Agency (Kikaku-chō). When the Konoe government took office in the following month, it decided to merge the military research unit of 1927 (the Resources Bureau) and the Planning Agency into a new and very powerful organ that would, in theory, command and coordinate the activities of the various ministries. This was the Cabinet Planning Board (CPB). It brought together military officers, detached reform bureaucrats, planners from Manchuria, and (unwittingly) some of the leading Marxist economists of the time into what was hailed as the "economic general staff." It is directly relevant to the history of MITI for several reasons. First, many MCI officials worked there (or, alternatively, many former CPB officials entered MCI after the war). Second, it was merged in 1943 with MCI to create the Ministry of Munitions. And third, it is the precedent for the postwar Economic Stabilization Board and Economic Planning Agency, both of which MITI has either strongly influenced or dominated. Most important, the CPB's method of planning necessitated the reorganization of MCI into industry-specific bureaus, and these were perpetuated in MITI until 1973.

When first set up, the CPB was divided into six departments: general affairs, domestic plans, financial plans, industrial plans (Uemura Kōgorō was the first head of this department), communications plans, and research. In 1939, after the dismal failure of its first efforts at economic planning, the CPB was reorganized into a secretariat, first department (general policy for the expansion of national strength), second department (overall mobilization), third department (labor and civilian mobilization), fourth department ("materials mobilization plans" and "expansion of production plans"), fifth department (trade and finance), sixth department (transportation and communications), and seventh department (science and technology). It underwent several more minor changes in later years (the fourth department, for example, was merged with the second department). Prince Konoe named his old professor of law at Kyoto University, Taki Masao, to be the first president of the CPB, but subsequent presidents and vice-presidents were reform bureaucrats or military officers (see Table 9). The CPB's initial staff consisted of 116 career officials, technicians, and temporarily attached specialists.

TABLE 9
Leaders of the Cabinet Planning Board, October 23, 1937–October 31, 1943

Cabinet	President and vice-president of board	Remarks
First Konoe 10/37–1/39	Taki Masao	Postwar member of the House of Representatives of the Diet.
	Aoki Kazuo	Finance bureaucrat. Minister of finance, Abe cabinet. Ambassador to Nanking, 1940. Minister of greater East Asia, Tōjō cabinet. Postwar member of House of Councillors, Diet.
Hiranuma 1/39–8/39	Aoki Kazuo	See above.
	Takebe Rokuzō	Home ministry bureaucrat. Director, General Affairs Agency, Manchukuo, 1940–45. Prisoner in USSR, 1945–56.
Abe 8/39–1/40	Aoki Kazuo	Concurrently finance minister.
	Takebe Rokuzō	See above.
Yonai 1/40–7/40	Takeuchi Kakichi	MCI bureaucrat.
	Uemura Kōgorō	Postwar chairman, Fuji Television, Japan Airlines. President of Keidanren, 1968.
Second Konoe 7/40–4/41	Hoshino Naoki	Finance bureaucrat. Chief cabinet secretary, Tōjō cabinet.
	Obata Tadayoshi	Sumitomo zaibatsu.
Second Konoe 4/41–7/41	Suzuki Teiichi	Lt. General. Convicted class A war criminal. Released 1956.
	Miyamoto Takenosuke	Home ministry bureaucrat. Engineer.
Third Konoe 7/41–10/41	Suzuki Teiichi	See above.
	Abe Genki	Home ministry bureaucrat. Former chief, Special Higher Police. Lost election as LDP candidate for House of Councillors, 1956.
Tōjō 10/41–10/43	Suzuki Teiichi	See above.
	Abe Genki	See above.

NOTE: On December 6, 1940, in the second Konoe cabinet, the president of the CPB was given cabinet-level rank as a minister of state (kokumu daijin).

The most famous product of the CPB was the National General Mobilization Law (Kokka Sōdōin Hō, law number 55, introduced in the Diet on February 24, 1938, passed April 1, 1938, and put into effect May 5, 1938). It was more than an economic law. It was intended as a replacement for the munitions law of 1918, but it actually authorized the complete reorganization of the society along totalitarian lines. According to Murase, its drafter was Uemura Kōgorō.[37] Despite the law's scope, its 50 articles contain very few concrete rules or stipulations. All details of implementation were left to Imperial ordinances, which the bureaucracy could issue on its own initiative without reference to the Diet. The law, in fact, became a carte blanche for the executive branch to do anything that it and its various clients could agree on; its policies extended not just to industry and the economy but also to education, labor, finance, publishing, and virtually all social activities even remotely related to the war effort.[38]

The Diet vigorously debated the mobilization law. Leaders of the new zaibatsu approved it, even though they did not like controls, because it signaled more business for them. The old zaibatsu and independent business leaders raised numerous objections and demanded a say in the ordinances that would implement the law (this they received), but they were quieted during 1938 with assurances that the China Incident would end soon, or they were shouted down by military spokesmen in the Diet chambers. Some economic leaders seemed to imply that a façade of civilian control should be maintained in order to prolong friendly trading relations with the United States and Great Britain, to which the military agreed, and dividends on equity shares continued to be paid until virtually the end of the Pacific War, when the zaibatsu no longer objected to the nationalization of their destroyed factories. These zaibatsu ownership rights turned out to be virtually the only civilian rights that were respected throughout the wartime period.

More important than the mobilization law to an understanding of postwar industrial policy was the work of department four of the CPB, which was responsible for formulating the materials mobilization plans (*busshi dōin keikaku*, abbreviated *butsudō*).[39] Despite their being top secret (only during the 1960's were full details about them published), their influence on postwar economic management cannot be overstated. All analysts agree that the experience and methods of the wartime materials mobilization plans reappeared in the Temporary Materials Supply and Demand Control Law (Rinji Busshi Jukyū Chōsei Hō) of October 1946, which was MCI's basic control law during the occupation, and in the "foreign currency budgets" of 1950 to 1964, which were MITI's main instruments of control during the high-speed growth era. The plans also reflected the strong influence during the 1930's in Japan of Stalinist economics—particularly economic analysis in terms of the direct supply of commodities to industry rather than the attempt to reconcile supply and demand through prices and other market forces—and of the Soviet five-year plans as a means of rapid industrialization, regardless of their effects on consumption and welfare.[40]

The initial materials mobilization plan, not yet so named, took the form of a report dated November 9, 1937, from the president of the CPB to the prime minister estimating that there was a total of ¥470 million in currency reserves to pay for emergency military imports during the last quarter of 1937. The report also offered a budget for spending this amount. With the China Incident continuing to expand, Uemura's Industrial Plans Department set up a General Affairs Unit for Materials Mobilization Plans (Butsudō Sōmuhan) and charged it with designing a similar budget for the calendar year 1938. This was the first true materials mobilization plan. Prepared in two months, the plan took as its basic assumption that there would be an import capability of ¥3 billion for the year. It then calculated the military and civilian needs that this amount had to cover and specified the exact quantities of some 96 commodities that it authorized for import. The plan also calculated the supplies of each commodity that would be available from domestic production, from Manchuria and China, and from stockpiles. After approval by the cabinet on January 16, 1938, the plan was transmitted to MCI for implementation, using as a legal basis Yoshino's foreign trade law of September 1937. The CPB itself had no operational authority or capability.

By midyear the planners discovered that they had overestimated foreign exchange by about ¥600 million, and on June 23, 1938, they therefore issued a revised plan. Both the first and second plans of 1938 necessitated structural changes within MCI and also incorporated the first steps in the program to convert some industries, forcibly if necessary, to munitions production. This program affected primarily textile industries and medium and small enterprises (discussed in Chapter 5). The plan also led to the so-called link system (a system revived again for the same purposes during the mid-1950's) in which raw materials imports were authorized only for those civilian industries that manufactured goods for export and that earned more foreign exchange than they spent. The link system also caused a reorganization of the Trade Bureau into vertical departments for each market and commodity.

The 1939 plan was considerably more elaborate than the one for 1938. Calculated on the basis of quarters of the fiscal year rather than the whole calendar year, it covered about four hundred commodities grouped into ten master categories (steel, nonferrous metals, chemicals, and so forth), and it established an eightfold priority list for the distribution of raw materials:[41]

A   army munitions
B   navy munitions
C_1 military reserves (C_{1A} army and C_{1B} navy)
C_2 materials for the expansion of productive capacity
C_3 nonmilitary governmental requirements
C_{4i} materials for use in Manchuria and China
C_{4ro} materials for export goods
C_5 materials for the general population

Even though this plan was more carefully thought out than the first, several factors combined to make it go as haywire as its predecessor. Perhaps the most persistent problem was fighting between the control officers of A and B materials. They regularly interrupted conferences with accusations of plots, and this ultimately led to the military police's arresting some CPB military officers on charges of corruption. Other disputes often had to go to the cabinet for settlement. In addition, after the outbreak of war in Europe on September 1, 1939, the British embargoed exports from India, Canada, and Australia, which ruined all import forecasts; and the 1939 drought in western Japan and floods in Taiwan and China forced the government to allocate some 10 percent of its total import capability for food. Until then the planners had assumed that Japan was self-sufficient in food at least. The drought also cut hydroelectric power output and thus caused a decline in domestic production of munitions and export goods.[42]

Officials involved with the plans—such as Kaya Okinori (minister of finance during early 1938), Inaba Hidezō (arrested by the military police in the Cabinet Planning Board incident of 1941, discussed below, and a leading planner of Japan's postwar reconstruction), and Tanaka Shin'ichi (Inaba's successor as the highest-ranking civilian official in the General Affairs Unit)—have all written, in regard to the early years of materials mobilization planning, that their concepts and methods were primitive, that their statistical base was supplied by the industries they sought to control, and that competition between the military services for allocations made their lives almost intolerable.[43] Tanaka Shin'ichi divides the planning into two periods: 1938–40, during which the determining element in the plans was the amount of foreign currency reserves; and 1941–44, during which the determining element was marine transport capability. The leader of the General Affairs Unit during the first period was an army officer, and during the second period a naval officer.

Although there were many interesting technical problems of conceptualization and procedure in these plans, by far the most lasting influence they were to exercise on later Japanese industrial policy came from the experience gained by MCI in trying to implement them. On May 7, 1938, in order to deal with its new rationing function, MCI created a powerful external unit called the Temporary Materials Coordination Bureau (TMCB; Rinji Busshi Chōsei Kyoku, based on Imperial ordinance 324). The minister of commerce and industry was concurrently its director-general—to signify its importance—but its deputy director was actually in charge. Yoshino was still minister and therefore the first director, although he was dropped from the cabinet less than three weeks after the bureau was created. Its first deputy director and actual leader was Murase Naokai, who served at the same time as vice-minister of MCI.

The Fuel Bureau was the first unit in MCI to be devoted exclusively to a commodity, but the TMCB was the first unit to adopt the principle of vertical organizations classified by materials for its internal organization. The TMCB was divided into six departments and fourteen sections, ranging from department one, section one (in charge of steel and manganese), through department four, section nine (in charge of chemical textiles, paper, and pulp), to department six, section fourteen (in charge of import plans and funds to pay for imports). All commodities covered in the materials mobilization plan were assigned to one or another section, which then had to decide how to meet the targets and had to negotiate with other bureaus and with industries about terms, delivery dates, and so forth. The TMCB was heavily staffed with military officers, and all the civilian MCI officials who worked there became intimately familiar with the plan and with its authors in the Cabinet Planning Board.[44]

The TMCB did not work well. Among its many problems were conflicts of jurisdiction within MCI itself—particularly among the TMCB, the Trade Bureau, and the Fuel Bureau—and externally with the Ministry of Finance over the licensing of imports and the use of foreign exchange. The conflict with the Finance Ministry led in December

1941 to MCI's surrendering its long-standing control over the insurance business and over the stock and commodity exchanges in return for control over import and export licenses—a change that made MCI even more exclusively an industrial policy agency, and that established the link, seen again later in MITI, between industrial policy and trade. Conflicts also occurred between MCI officials and the military and between MCI officials and the Cabinet Planning Board. As a line organization, the ministry tried repeatedly to convince the staff of the CPB that drafting and executing a plan were two different things: zaibatsu firms were in competition with each other, skilled manpower was in short supply, capital availability was a problem, black markets were appearing, and the military regularly made direct deals on its own.

During the second half of 1938, the quality of life in Japan went rapidly downhill, and this, too, contributed to the TMCB's troubles. The revised materials mobilization plan halved imports for the civilian sector and drove innumerable medium and smaller enterprises out of business. By one estimate some 390,000 bankruptcies occurred during August 1938 alone.[45] During the same month the Home Ministry deployed what the public called the "economic police." This involved the stationing in all police offices of twelve or thirteen procurators and investigators who specialized in "economic crimes" and tried to control the black markets and maintain official prices. The TMCB thus became distinctly unpopular with the citizenry.

Perhaps the main reason the bureau did not work well was the persistent difference in political outlook that existed between MCI under Murase and the reform bureaucrats. Shiina says bluntly that both Murase and Takeuchi Kakichi, the TMCB's only deputy directors during its short existence, did not get along well with the military and sought to create their own factions as counters to those of the reform bureaucrats. Equally important, the zaibatsu and the party politicians in the Diet did not like the way they had been treated during the debate over the mobilization law, or the trend of events generally. They fixed their irritation particularly on the presence in the cabinet of two former bureaucrats in key economic positions, minister of finance and minister of commerce and industry. Their way of dealing with this problem was to ignore both Kaya and Yoshino and subtly to sabotage the controlled economy. Much of the control structure existed only on paper; the reality was that the bureaucracy had to negotiate every contract in order to get industry's cooperation.

In May 1938 Prime Minister Konoe sought to placate business interests by dropping Kaya and Yoshino from the cabinet and replacing them both with one man—Ikeda Seihin, a former Mitsui executive and an "elder" of the business world. Ikeda had retired from business following the military coup d'etat, and in 1938 he was serving as governor of the Bank of Japan. He was acceptable to the business community because of his background, and he was acceptable to the military because he was tolerant of economic controls as long as the business community dominated them. Konoe and his military advisers also hoped that a single leader serving concurrently as minister of both finance and MCI might mitigate the increasingly serious bureaucratic jurisdictional disputes between the two ministries.

Yoshino was infuriated by Ikeda's appointment. He realized why Ikeda might be politically preferable to an ex-bureaucrat, but he also believed that Ikeda would not carry out industrial policy faithfully, and that it was an insult to MCI to be put under a zaibatsu minister. Concerning his own future, Yoshino sought the advice of his sempai and long-time friend from MAC days, Itō Bunkichi, the illegitimate son of the genrō Itō Hirobumi and the son-in-law of former Prime Minister Katsura Tarō. Itō had left MAC in the early 1920's and taken a position in Ayukawa's Nissan zaibatsu. He now urged Yoshino to join his colleague Kishi in Manchuria and invited him to become an executive of the Ayukawa group. The Konoe cabinet recommended Yoshino as president of the new North China Development Company (while still minister Yoshino had drafted the law establishing the company, although the army sponsored it in the Diet), but the army vetoed him as insufficiently nationalistic to head an organization governing territory won by army blood.[46] Yoshino was probably lucky he did not get this job, as it very likely would have led to his arrest after the war as a war criminal—assuming, of course, that he would have survived the war. Forced to act on his own, Yoshino visited Hsinking, where Ayukawa instead appointed him as one of two vice-presidents (the other was a Manchurian) of Mangyō. Yoshino was frustrated in Manchuria by excessive army control and Ayukawa's lack of capital for big projects. While working there, he received an Imperial appointment to the House of Peers, and on November 10, 1940, he returned to Tokyo to take it up. He remained an adviser to Mangyō but was replaced as vice-president by Takasaki Tatsunosuke, then president of the Mangyō-affiliated Manchurian Airplane Company. Takasaki was later MITI minister in the second Kishi cabinet (1958–59), and he was the Japanese sponsor of the famous Liao-Takasaki agreement for unofficial Sino-Japanese trade during the 1960's.

During the Pacific War the Home Ministry appointed Yoshino governor of Aichi prefecture, and throughout 1944 he worked hard trying to cope with the bombing of Nagoya and with the death in his city of the chief Chinese puppet, Wang Ching-wei, who had been hospitalized there after an assassination attempt in China. Yoshino was purged but not tried during the occupation.

On April 24, 1953, Yoshino was elected to the House of Councillors from his native Miyagi prefecture. He had run on a platform of "economic independence" (from U.S. aid) and "rebuild Japan's economy." In the Diet he served as chairman of the upper house's Commerce and Industry Committee (where he was more of a problem for MITI than the ministry anticipated), and then as minister of transportation in the third Hatoyama cabinet (1955–56).

Yoshino never seemed to have any qualms about tapping the connections he had made during his bureaucratic service. Back in June 1934, while he was still vice-minister, he had helped Zen Keinosuke (1887–1951), Fujihara Ginjirō (1869–1960), and other business leaders to establish the Japan Mutual Life Insurance Company (Nihon Dantai Seimei Hoken Kai), a company promoted by the prewar predecessor of the Japan Federation of Employers' Associations (Nikkeiren) to provide life insurance at reasonable rates for industrial workers. (Zen was a school classmate of Yoshino's and a fellow MAC official from 1914 to 1926. He resigned to become the secretary and a director of the Japan Industrial Club. After the war he became the first director-general of the Economic Stabilization Board. Fujihara was the founder of the Mitsui-connected Ōji Paper Company and became MCI minister during the first half of 1940.)

In January 1952, following the death of Zen Keinosuke the previous November, Yoshino succeeded him as chairman of the Japan Mutual Life Insurance Company, a post he retained for the next thirteen years. Yoshino retired as a member of the Diet in May 1959 and devoted himself to service as president of Musashi College, a position he held concurrently with his other commitments from 1956 to 1965. He died May 9, 1971, at the age of 84. Kishi Nobusuke delivered the eulogy at his funeral.

During 1938, in Tokyo, the new MCI minister Ikeda and vice-minister Murase got along fine. They liked each other, and both saw the world in essentially the same (commercial) terms; they shared the belief that economic control should mean self-imposed control by civilian industrial leaders themselves. Ikeda led the fight in the government to prevent the state-control view from prevailing—Shiroyama calls him the leader of the "status quo faction"—and he established the precedent of businessmen serving in the cabinet in order to restrain the military, one that his successors Fujihara Ginjirō and Kobayashi Ichizō continued.[47]

During late 1938 Ikeda clashed violently with Home Minister (Admiral) Suetsugu Nobumasa over the attempts to enforce articles 6 (labor control) and 11 (limitation on dividends and forced loans) of the mobilization law. Suetsugu took the view that if the government were going to control the people, it should also control the capitalists. Ikeda was not completely successful in preventing this, but as Tiedemann remarks, "In the future, control over capital would become tighter, but Ikeda had set the pattern for making the controls on the business community the lightest of all in the war economy."[48] A result of his battle was that Ikeda was forced to leave the cabinet, and in January 1939 the Konoe government resigned in favor of the Hiranuma government, which was conservative but not necessarily pro–state control.

In order to eliminate the defects in the TMCB system and also to make MCI conform more closely in its overall operation to the mission it had been given by the economic general staff, Murase totally reorganized the Ministry of Commerce and Industry during early 1939. Despite his lack of sympathy with the controlled economy, Murase's reform was ironically the single most important structural change of MCI in the direction of greater control until the creation of MITI. Maeda Yasuyuki argues that Murase's vertical bureaus organized according to industry were the most valuable legacy of the war years; and former MITI Vice-Minister Kumagai Yoshifumi (1968–69) holds that industrial policy itself is synonymous with the industrial bureaus; without them a ministry would not be close enough to industry to exercise real guidance or control and could achieve no more than general economic policy.[49] MITI's *History of Commercial and Industrial Policy* says that after the reform MCI had already become a ministry of munitions, although it did not receive that name officially for four more years.[50]

Murase abolished the Temporary Materials Coordination Bureau, the Commercial Affairs Bureau, the Control Bureau (successor after May 1, 1937, to the Temporary Industrial Rationality Bureau), and several other units. He combined their functions into one powerful coordinating and policy-making organization, the General Affairs Bureau (Sōmu Kyoku), which is the origin of the contemporary MITI Secretariat. In addition, Murase took the specialized sections of the Industrial Affairs and Mining bureaus and made each of them into separate bureaus (see Appendix B). The result was not yet the internal structure of MITI—still needed were the Enterprises Bureau (created in 1942), the functions of the CPB, and absolute control over trade—but MCI after 1939 was much closer in form and orientation to the industrial policy apparatus of the high-speed growth era than was MCI from 1925 to 1939.

The thanks that Murase received for these efforts from his political superiors was to be fired. During the autumn of 1939 a series of issues came to a head that caused a major realignment of MCI personnel. First, it was becoming apparent that materials mobilization planning alone was not going to overcome Japan's industrial weaknesses, which were being exposed daily in the China war. On January 17, 1939, in recognition of this fact, the new cabinet adopted a "General Outline Plan for the Expansion of Productive Capacity" (Seisanryoku kakujū keikaku yōkō), which had been prepared in the CPB on the basis of ideas first advanced by the Manchurian planners in 1936. The result was a detailed four-year proposal for the promotion of some fifteen industries in Japan, Manchuria, and China. They were steel, coal, light metals, nonferrous metals, petroleum and petroleum substitutes, soda and industrial salts, ammonium sulfate, pulp, gold mining (to earn foreign exchange), machine tools, rolling stock, ships, automobiles, wool, and electric power. The problem with the plan was how to implement it: was it to be through industrial self-control, public-private cooperation, or state control? These issues were debated throughout 1939 and ultimately led in 1940 to the Economic New Structure—part of the Japanese version of Hitler's New Order.

Second, the outbreak of war in Europe vastly complicated Japan's import arrangements. In order to force imports from the still unconquered territories in East Asia, Japan began to advance the idea of the Greater East Asian Coprosperity Sphere; to attain their goal they undertook direct negotiations with, for example, the Dutch in the Netherlands East Indies for petroleum shipments. The development of the so-called yen trading bloc also put pressure on the rest of the nation's trade relations, because Japanese exports to Manchuria and China no longer earned foreign exchange. The government demanded that exports to hard currency areas be expanded, and prices began to explode as shortages worsened. On October 18, 1939, the government issued its famous Price Control Ordinance, based on article 19 of the mobilization law, which fixed all prices, wages, rents, and similar economic indices at the level that had existed a month earlier—hence the nickname "September 18 stop ordinance." However, all this did was eliminate the last traces of realism in the price structure and reinforce tendencies toward budgeting in terms of commodities and barter deals. It also led to the black markets and black prices that persisted throughout the Pacific War.

Third, Japan's poorly informed diplomacy had led to the unpleasant surprise of the Molotov-Ribbentrop agreement. Since the Japanese had thought that they were allied with Germany against Soviet Russia, this inexplicable turn of events led the government to resign. Two days before the outbreak of war in Europe a new cabinet was formed. Godō Takuo (1877–1956)—a doctor of engineering, a former ordnance vice admiral, a recent head of the Shōwa steel works in Manchuria, a connection of the Asano zaibatsu through the marriage of his daughter, and a supporter of medium and smaller enterprises as an active director of the industrial unions association—became minister of both agriculture and commerce. Godō first told Murase that he wanted him to remain as vice-minister, but less than a month later he shamefacedly had to say that the army had asked for Murase's resignation in order to bring back Kishi from Manchuria. The problems of the bogged-down war in China, the need for industrial expansion, and the rapidly changing world scene had combined to generate a clamor inside and outside the ministry for the return of the Manchurians. Tōjō was already serving as vice-minister of the army, and Hoshino and Matsuoka did not come back until the following year. But Kishi paid quick heed to the call and became vice-minister of MCI on October 19, 1939.

Kishi had to proceed cautiously. He was one of the best-known reform bureaucrats, and the business community was still determined to keep MCI under its own control. Its method was to withhold support of the government unless a business figure were named MCI minister. In January 1940, following another change of cabinet, the business community replaced the technocratic Admiral Godō with a real businessman, Fujihara Ginjirō; and seven months later, when the Manchurians really began to take over the second Konoe government (Tōjō as army minister, Hoshino as CPB president, and Matsuoka as foreign minister), the business leaders asked for and got Kobayashi Ichizō (1873–1957).

Kobayashi was the founder of the Hanshin Electric Railroad Company (the Osaka to Kobe express), the Takarazuka girls operatic troupe, the Takarazuka and Nichigeki theaters in Tokyo, the Tōhō Motion Picture Company, and many other enterprises. After the war he served in the Shidehara cabinet as a planner of economic reconstruction. His clash with Vice-Minister Kishi was the greatest confrontation within the ministry before that of 1963, when the politicians appointed Imai Zen'ei as vice-minister in place of the MITI bureaucrats' choice of Sahashi Shigeru. Kobayashi was not a compromise business candidate like Ikeda Seihin or Admiral Godō (that is, acceptable to both sides); he was a famous entrepreneur who made no bones about the fact that he did not like state control, reform bureaucrats, or Kishi. Ikeda had recommended his appointment in order to maintain peace with the business community, but it was clear from the outset that MCI was not big enough to hold both Kobayashi and Kishi. One of them had to go.[51]

Before Kobayashi arrived on the scene, Kishi had been able to overturn many of Murase's personnel appointments, although he retained his new structure. In December 1939 Kishi made his most important personnel move: he installed his Manchurian colleague and "junior," Shiina Etsusaburō, as director of the pivotal General Affairs Bureau.

Shiina then proceeded to bring into the bureau the brightest, most ambitious, control-oriented minds he could find within the ministry. They all subsequently became leaders of industrial policy during the era of high-speed growth, and most of them went on to become MITI vice-ministers. Among those working as section chiefs or officials in the General Affairs Bureau under Shiina were Yamamoto Takayuki (chief of the Production Expansion Section and later MITI's first vice-minister), Hirai Tomisaburō (chief of the Materials Coordination Section and MITI vice-minister from 1953 to 1955), Ueno Kōshichi (a section chief in the General Affairs Bureau after Shiina became vice-minister in 1941 and MITI vice-minister from 1957 to 1960), Tamaki Keizō (also a section chief in the General Affairs Bureau in 1941 and MITI vice-minister during 1952–53), Yoshida Teijirō (a section chief while Shiina was bureau chief and postwar deputy director of the Coal Agency), Ishihara Takeo (a deputy section chief in 1940 and MITI vice-minister from 1955 to 1957), and Tokunaga Hisatsugu (an official in the General Affairs Bureau under Shiina and MITI vice-minister from 1960 to 1961).

This was the beginning of the Kishi-Shiina line. It was perpetuated after the war, while Kishi was in prison and Shiina was purged, by Toyoda Masataka (the first head of the Enterprises Bureau in 1942 and Shiina's successor as vice-minister in 1945) and Matsuda Tarō (a section chief during 1940 in the vertical bureaus and in 1949 the last MCI vice-minister). Matsuda Tarō was the official in charge of the creation of MITI.

In July 1940 Japan was a troubled place. The China war was dragging on with no end in sight, the allies had begun to boycott Japanese goods, and Germany and Italy were offering an alliance (the Axis pact was signed September 27, 1940). To deal with this situation the throne turned once again to Prince Konoe, as it had earlier when others had been unable to restore stability in the wake of the army mutiny. Konoe's most important action in the realm of industrial policy was to sponsor the Economic New Structure. This was a sweeping proposal for the nationalization of industries, the operation of factories by bureaucrats, and the rapid expansion of production. Ryū Shintarō (1900– 67), a member of Prince Konoe's brain trust, the Shōwa Research Association, provided the first outline of this quintessentially reform bureaucratic scheme. His book, *The Reorganization of the Japanese Economy* (*Nihon keizai no saihensei*), was published in 1939 by *Chūō kōron* and very widely read. Its anticapitalist and even Marxist orientation was hardly disguised at all, and Ryū only avoided intimidation by the police because of his elite connections.[52]

Among Ryū's friends and readers were some of the officials of the CPB, and they gave his ideas concrete form in a CPB report of September 13, 1940, entitled "General Plan for the Establishment of the Economic New Structure." Its immediate authors were the "star" reform bureaucrats of the Cabinet Planning Board, Colonel Akinaga Tsukizō, Minobe Yōji (who had recently returned from Manchuria to the CPB rather than to MCI), and Sakomizu Hisatsune. They called for the seminationalization (*kōkyōka*, literally "to make public") of private enterprises, the creation of industrial control organs that incorporated the then popular Nazi "leadership principle" (*hyūrā genri*, or *Führerprinzip*), the "reform of the Commercial Code in order to separate ownership of capital in enterprises from management functions and to establish the public character of industrial management," and strict limitations on profits.[53] The whole report was infused with a sense of outrage that the capitalists were still making a profit while one war was going on and a bigger one was clearly coming.

The business community did not take this lying down but responded with a business leaders' offensive. The businessmen charged, on the one hand, that Ryū Shintarō was a communist—the preferred term at the time was "red" (*aka*)—and that the Konoe brain trust and the Cabinet Planning Board were also infiltrated with reds—which came close to saying that the army itself was promoting Bolshevik policies. The business spokesmen also argued that the separation of management and ownership and the reduction of interest and profits would only worsen the already critical shortage of capital. Some seven private economic organizations, led by the Industrial Club, sent written statements of protest to the cabinet. The business community would tolerate self-regulation in order to expand production and further the war effort, but they wanted no part of the economic side of the New Order. The government and the business community deadlocked over the issue.

Between September 12 and October 22, 1940, MCI Minister Kobayashi was out of the country leading a delegation; it included Chairman Mukai Tadaharu of the Mitsui Trading Company and other business leaders and had gone to Batavia, Netherlands East Indies, to negotiate shipments of oil to Japan. The Japanese had been invited by the major oil companies, with the full knowledge of their governments, in an attempt to appease Japan and stave off an attack on the N.E.I., which at the time seemed imminent.[54] While Kobayashi was gone, Prime Minister Konoe ordered each ministry to draw up plans for the implementation of the Economic New Structure. At MCI Kishi was in charge, and in consultation with his old associate from Manchuria, President Hoshino of the CPB, he produced a draft that conformed closely to the September 13 CPB general plan.

When Kobayashi returned and saw Kishi's proposal, he denounced Kishi and his plan in a speech to the Industrial Club, calling the proposal a reflection of "red thinking," a fatal charge in the prevailing political climate. Others recalled Kishi's actions at the time of the protest over the pay cut a decade earlier and contended that he had always been "a little red."[55] Unable to counter these charges, since he *was* advocating a Japanese version of national socialism, Kishi had to resign on January 4, 1941.

Kishi was only the biggest casualty of the businessmen's offensive. Beginning on January 17 and continuing through April 1941, the police took into custody some seventeen civilian officials of the CPB and charged them with violations of the Peace Preservation Law. All were held in prison for three years before being released on bail. Their trials were finally held during 1944 and 1945, and all but one were found not guilty. This so-called Cabinet Planning Board incident has never been fully explained. Some hold the view that it was a frame-up by the business community and that the police had no more evidence against those arrested than that they had been known to read works by Lenin and Kautsky and sing communist songs.[56] One of the most important among those arrested, Inaba Hidezō (then working in the materials mobilization planning unit), has two theories: the first is that the army on its own wanted to get rid of officials in the CPB who were accurately if pessimistically reporting to the cabinet that Japan did not have the material means to wage war successfully against Great Britain and the United States; and the second is that the incident was a rather unimportant purge of mildly Marxist bureaucrats by the Thought Police.[57]

The most widely held opinion is that Kobayashi was right—there were reds in the Cabinet Planning Board. This view is based on the list of those arrested and their postwar careers. The list includes Wada Hiroo, a postwar left socialist and the subject of an uproar in 1946 when Yoshida named him agriculture minister; Sata Tadataka, a left socialist and leader of the Economic Stabilization Board under the Katayama government in 1947; Katsumata Seiichi, a Socialist Party Diet member and leading theorist of the left socialist faction; and Masaki Chifuyu, a postwar socialist mayor of Kamakura. Many of these men had entered the Cabinet Research Board (and, from there, the CPB) through backgrounds in agricultural administration or, at least in Inaba's case, as staff members of the old Harmony Society (Kyōchō Kai), an organization set up in 1919 after the rice riots by the Industrial Club to promote cooperation and friendly relations between labor and management.[58] As Inaba says, most of them were not communists but "humanists" attracted to vaguely socialist programs. Nonetheless, they were definitely to the left of most reform bureaucrats.

Kobayashi himself became a casualty of the Cabinet Planning Board incident. During early 1941 CPB elements tried to get even with him by attacking his personal fortune and accusing him of income tax evasion. In order to try to end the whole affair, Konoe and Home Minister Hiranuma, who represented a kind of conservatism that was lukewarm about national socialism, arranged for a balanced purge: on April 4, 1941, both MCI Minister Kobayashi and CPB President Hoshino were forced to resign. Given the problems they had encountered, Konoe and Hiranuma decided that they had better look for military officers as replacements. Lieutenant General Suzuki Teiichi became president of the CPB and headed it for the rest of its existence. Looking for a similar type to head MCI, Konoe first chose Admiral Toyoda Teijirō, a former vice-minister of the navy and son-in-law of a Mitsubishi director. However, Toyoda shortly left, first to become foreign minister and then to be president of Japan Steel (he returned as minister of munitions under the Suzuki cabinet at the end of the war). Konoe therefore selected another admiral, Sakonji Seizō, a former chief of naval staff and the head of the North Sakhalin Petroleum Company (a Mitsui affiliate), and he headed MCI until the Tōjō government was established.

The stand-off over policy between the government and the business community still had to be resolved. MCI therefore came up with a compromise that retained many CPB ideas but that more than met the business community's objections. Instead of going to the Diet with a new law, as the CPB wanted to do, MCI proposed amending the mobilization law and then implementing industrial control through Imperial ordinances. This would avoid any further public debate on the subject. The result was the Important Industries Association Ordinance (Jūyō Sangyō Dantai Rei, Imperial ordinance 831 of August 30, 1941). It created control organs for each industry but assigned the management functions originally sought by the bureaucrats to civilian industrial leaders. All enterprises in an industry became members of a "control association" (*tōseikai*), which was a special legal entity comparable to a government-authorized cartel; control associations were empowered to allocate materials, set production targets, and distribute products of the member firms. This approach was very similar to Yoshino's in the Important Industries Control Law of 1931. Business had won a major point: the president of each control association was invariably the chief executive officer of the largest enterprise in an industry, and as a result the control associations were utterly dominated by the zaibatsu.[59]

As relations with the United States deteriorated, the throne in October 1941 turned to General Tōjō and asked him to form a government. He chose as minister of commerce and industry his colleague and friend from Manchurian days, Kishi; and Kishi in turn cleansed his old ministry of people who had not supported him against Kobayashi. Kishi also appointed Shiina as vice-minister. Some of the strains within the ministry were revealed by a unique event. Higashi Eiji, the first head of the General Affairs Bureau in 1939 and director of the Fuel Bureau when the Tōjō cabinet was installed, resigned in protest. According to Shiroyama, Higashi sought to protest the recklessness of the movement toward war; as the official responsible for the supply of petroleum, he knew that the war would inevitably be lost.[60]

Although the "control bureaucrats" finally came to power, they did not change Japanese industrial policy significantly. They were always hampered by the structure of industrial control that they had inherited. As T. A. Bisson noted from the perspective of 1945, during the Pacific War Japan operated essentially a private enterprise economy with surprisingly little governmental interference.[61] One result is pointed out by Mark Peattie: "The myriad of controls, under which

Japan fought first the China War and then the Pacific War, provided no overall coordination, but rather left the prosecution of these conflicts scattered among various and competing agencies. At the same time, Japan's economy, subjected to conflicting pressures from business and military leadership, remained partly free and partly controlled. Such a system could hardly be called totalitarian and in any event was ultimately disastrous for Japan's war effort."[62]

There were two major ironies in this situation. First, despite Tōjō's and Kishi's best efforts to achieve state economic control while they were in office, state control was actually realized in Japan only under the Allied occupation, when SCAP in effect transferred the powers of the control associations to the government. Second, although the prewar and wartime system of divided control *was* disastrous for Japan's war effort, when a similar pattern reemerged after the occupation, it proved optimal for Japan's peaceful industrial expansion. The 1930's and the war had demonstrated to all who were involved with postwar industrial policy that neither state control nor self-control alone was adequate to achieve cooperation and coordination. What was needed was an amalgam of the two.

As we have noted earlier, the most striking structural characteristic of the capitalist developmental state is an implicit political division of labor between the tasks of ruling and the tasks of reigning. The politicians reign and the bureaucrats rule. This should not be thought of as a cynical comment on modern government or a counsel of despair concerning the realities of democracy. Both sides have important functions to perform. The politicians provide the space for bureaucrats to rule by holding off special interest claimants who might deflect the state from its main developmental priorities, and they legitimate and ratify the decisions taken by bureaucrats. The bureaucrats in turn formulate developmental policies, draft and administer the laws needed to implement the policies, and make midcourse adjustments as problems arise. This general pattern of the democratic developmental state, which we shall consider further in Chapter 9, did not really appear in Japan until after the creation of the Liberal Democratic Party in 1955. But the 1930's were important to its creation both in fostering the rise of the economic bureaucracy—or the "economic general staff" to name its true function—and in revealing that although it could and did rule, it could not reign.

The disarray that developed during the 1930's in the system of government inherited from the Meiji era provided the opportunity for the rise of the economic bureaucracy, and the political problems of the time called it forth. Through the direct and terrorist actions of the military and the ultranationalists, men in uniform took over the government. They co-opted the legitimacy of the Imperial institution and largely neutralized the influence of its managers, and they also weakened and nearly discredited the elected politicians of the Diet. But they could not destroy the interests the politicians represented—primarily those of the zaibatsu—and the zaibatsu undertook, in self-defense, to enter the government and represent themselves: they stopped working through politicians. Moreover, the military had neither the capacity nor the leadership ability to formulate and administer the "second-stage industrialization" (that is, capital-intensive industrialization, in contrast to the labor-intensive industrialization of the Meiji period) that its aggressive empire-building plans necessitated.

It was in this context that MCI transformed itself from a lowly commercial bureaucracy whose primary task was to represent the interests of capital in the government into a task-oriented planning, allocating, and managing agency for heavy and chemical industrialization. Its officials learned how to introduce new, advanced-technology industries, first in Manchuria and then in Japan itself, and they also learned that they could not accomplish much of anything unless they worked in conjunction with the zaibatsu. Throughout the 1930's MCI was torn by its political alliances. On the one hand, it rose in power vis-à-vis its better established rivals such as the Finance and Foreign Affairs ministries by cooperating with the military and the reform bureaucrats. On the other hand, it also fought against military arrogance and interference in its development plans and kept its ties to the zaibatsu, which were the only sources of capital and managerial ability for second-stage industrialization. The economic bureaucrats never resolved these problems in the politics of the government-business relationship until the true capitalist developmental state came into being after the war.

The main contributions of the 1930's to the postwar economic "miracle" were to create and install in the government an economic general staff, and to demonstrate to the satisfaction of all parties concerned that such an agency could not be effective until the political problems of determining who was to reign were resolved. Once installed, the economic general staff never relinquished its new powers or retreated from its mission; Japan would never again return to the laissez faire policies of the first thirty years of the twentieth century. But, equally important, the economic general staff could not really unleash the developmental forces of the society until the defeat of 1945 had broken the hold of the military completely and had tipped the balance of power decisively away from the zaibatsu and in favor of the bureau-crats. Just as World War I had led European nations to assign to the state new tasks of economic mobilization and development—and to remove these tasks from the agendas of parliaments—so the crises and wars of the 1930's led to the same thing in Japan. But it took the catastrophe of the Pacific War to supply the political prerequisites of the developmental state. By the 1950's Takahashi Korekiyo's observation that "it is much harder to nullify the results of an economic conquest than those of a military conquest" had become not uncommon wisdom but simple common sense.

FIVE

From the Ministry of Munitions to MITI

A S JAPAN entered the Pacific War, the Ministry of Commerce and Industry could look back on a decade of considerable accomplishment in terms of planned industrial expansion. Between 1930 and 1940 Japan's mining and manufacturing production had more than doubled, and, equally important, the composition of manufacturing had changed drastically from light industries (primarily textiles) to heavy industries (metals, machines, and chemicals). In 1930 heavy industries accounted for approximately 35 percent of all manufacturing, but by 1940 this proportion had grown to 63 percent. Another way to visualize this shift of industrial structure is to look at the top ten companies in terms of their capital assets in 1929 and 1940 (see Table 10). Whereas at the end of the 1920's three of Japan's ten largest enterprises were textile companies, a decade later only one was. Interestingly enough, the top ten of 1940 bear a much greater resemblance to the top ten of 1972 than they do to the top ten of 1929 (Japan Steel, Mitsubishi Heavy Industries, Hitachi, and Tōshiba were ranked first, second, fourth, and eighth respectively in both 1940 and 1972, whereas only Mitsubishi was even on the list in 1929).

Not much further expansion of total output occurred during the Pacific War, but the shift from textiles and food products to mining, nonferrous metals, and machines continued and accelerated. The war caused a change of industrial structure almost as profound as Japan's original industrialization, and it decimated Japan's medium and smaller enterprises as well as its previously dominant textile industry. The immediate cause of this shift was the enterprise readjustment (kigyō seibi) movement, a set of government policies that came to be so heartily disliked by the public that after the war even the phrase was dropped from the lexicon of trade and industry bureaucrats, although they of course invented new euphemisms for the same thing. The wartime shift of industrial structure was emphatically not a by-product of the working of market forces but was, instead, the invention and the responsibility of MCI. The ministry's pursuit of enterprise readjustment led in 1942 to the creation of the Enterprises Bureau (Kigyō Kyoku), which still exists today under the title of Industrial Policy Bureau, to be the control center for both the ministry and the Japanese industrial world.

Writing at the end of the war, Jerome B. Cohen concluded, "All the evidence indicates . . . that the major [Japanese] reliance for the wartime economic effort, as it was conceived at the outbreak of war, was to be placed upon a further shift in resources from nonwar to war uses rather than upon a lifting of the whole level of output."[1] Similarly, the authors of MITI's authoritative *History of Commercial and Industrial Policy* comment that the second Productivity Expansion Plan, written by the CPB and approved by the cabinet on May 8, 1942, was

TABLE 10

The Top Ten Japanese Mining and Manufacturing Corporations, 1929–1972

Name[a]	Total capital in yen	Remarks
	I. 1929 (Thousands)	
1. Kawasaki Shipbuilding (14)	239,848	Est. 1896. Today Kawasaki Heavy Industries.
2. Fuji Paper (—)	159,642	Est. 1887. Merged with Ōji Paper 1933.
3. Ōji Paper	154,228	Est. 1873. Today Jūjō Paper (63), Ōji Paper (69), and Honshū Paper (88).
4. Kanegafuchi Textiles (47)	145,989	Est. 1887. Today Kanebō, Ltd.
5. Karafuto Industries (—)	117,353	Est. 1913. Merged with Ōji Paper 1933.
6. Dai Nippon Textiles (55)	116,398	Est. 1889. Today Unitika, Ltd.
7. Mitsubishi Shipbuilding (2)	112,341	Est. 1917. Today Mitsubishi Heavy Industries.
8. Mitsui Mining (74)	111,827	Est. 1911. Today Mitsui Mining and Mitsui Metal Industries.
9. Tōyō Textiles (48)	111,490	Est. 1914. Today Tōyōbō, Ltd.
10. Taiwan Sugar (—)	109,539	Est. 1900.

TABLE 10 (*cont.*)

Name[a]	Total capital in yen	Remarks
	II. 1940 (Thousands)	
1. Japan Steel (1)	1,242,321	Est. 1934. Today New Japan Steel.
2. Mitsubishi Heavy Industries (2)	969,491	
3. Ōji Paper	562,088	
4. Hitachi Seisakusho (4)	552,515	Est. 1920. Today Hitachi, Ltd.
5. Japan Mining (30)	547,892	Est. 1912.
6. Japan Nitrogenous Fertilizer (—)	540,344	Est. 1906. Postwar Chisso, Ltd.
7. Kanegafuchi Textiles	434,716	
8. Tokyo Shibaura Electric (Tōshiba) (8)	414,761	Est. 1904.
9. Mitsubishi Mining (53)	407,555	Est. 1918.
10. Sumitomo Metals (7)	380,200	Est. 1915.
	III. 1972 (Millions)	
1. New Japan Steel	2,113,335	
2. Mitsubishi Heavy Industries	1,648,235	
3. Nippon Kōkan (Steel Pipe)	1,162,308	Est. 1912.
4. Hitachi, Ltd.	1,036,178	
5. Ishikawajima-Harima	982,021	Est. 1889.
6. Nissan Motors	949,029	Est. 1933.
7. Sumitomo Metals	930,197	
8. Tōshiba, Ltd.	852,999	
9. Kawasaki Steel	843,838	Est. 1950.
10. Kobe Steel	683,629	Est. 1911.

SOURCE: History of Industrial Policy Research Institute, *Waga kuni daikigyō no keisei hatten katei* (The formation and development of big business in our country), Tokyo, 1976, pp. 26, 38, 56.
[a]Numbers in parentheses are the rank in 1972 of those corporations still in existence in that year.

oriented solely to the maximum use of existing facilities rather than to investment in new installations.[2]

Although Cohen and the Japanese analysts are critical of this policy, it is hard to imagine what alternatives were available to MCI, given the fact that Japan had already entered the war, thereby endangering its most vital imports, before the industrial implications of a long war with the United States had dawned on the military. It is of no great relevance to postwar industrial policy to recall that the Japanese government did not begin to mobilize fully for World War II until after the battle of Midway and the American landings on Guadalcanal (August 1942), but it is of considerable relevance that when the government took action, its policies injected economic bureaucrats much more intimately into the affairs of individual enterprises than they had ever been before. Botched though it surely was, the wartime enterprise readjustment movement lies at the beginning of the path that leads to the Industrial Rationalization Council of the 1950's and to the Industrial Structure Council of the 1960's and 1970's.

As early as 1937 Professor Arisawa Hiromi, who in 1975 was one of the leaders of the Industrial Structure Council, had argued against the prevailing wisdom that medium and smaller enterprises were essential to Japan's export capability. Citing the work of the economist and Cabinet Planning Board official Minoguchi Tokijirō, Arisawa contended that, contrary to MCI policy, fostering and protecting smaller enterprises was a mistake because they were of only incidental importance to Japan's long-term export prospects, although he did acknowledge that they provided work for a large proportion of Japan's labor force.[3] He would have preferred to see all of these small factories organized into large productive units, or at least made subcontractors of large enterprises—an idea that the zaibatsu found quite congenial. One important legacy of the enterprise readjustment movement is today's pattern of extensive subcontracting between large, well-financed final assemblers and innumerable small, poorly financed machine shops.[4]

The problem of converting and closing small enterprises emerged concretely as a result of the failure of the first materials mobilization plan in mid-1938. The Cabinet Planning Board scrapped its original plan in part because it discovered that much of the country's imported materiel was being used not by large enterprises for creating munitions or exports but by medium and smaller enterprises that manufactured for domestic consumption. The CPB's revised plan radically cut imports for these types of businesses, which drove a large number of them into bankruptcy but also raised for the government the question of what to do with the workers who had been forced out of work. In September 1938 MCI took its first steps to come to grips with the problem by creating the Tengyō Taisaku Bu (Industrial Conversion Policy Department).

The idea behind the department was that through a combination of subsidies and governmental pressure, the depressed medium and smaller enterprises could be shifted to production of munitions, production for export, or production of import substitutes. Officials of the department also used techniques learned in the rationalization movement to promote joint management and enterprise mergers for large numbers of firms. The workers who could not be easily reorganized were encouraged and paid to emigrate to Manchuria and China. The Unemployment Policy Department of the new Welfare Ministry also sponsored such emigration in order to help prevent social unrest among the unemployed.

In the reorganization of MCI on June 16, 1939, the Industrial Conversion Policy Department was renamed and continued as the Promotion Department (Shinkō Bu). It is not clear who thought of the term "promotion" or what was meant by it, but the "promotion department" was perpetuated in the MITI era as a component of the Medium and Smaller Enterprises Agency, created on August 2, 1948. MITI historians see in the reorganization of 1939 a fundamental change of function for the ministry; until then commercial and industrial policy had been carried out without reference to the scale of enterprises, but after 1939 policy was explicitly committed to the nurturing of large-scale enterprises.[5] This function seems to underlie the meaning of "promotion"—namely, the promotion of the expansion of small businesses into larger ones.

The movement to convert small businesses to a war footing began slowly during late 1938 as an ad hoc response to the stretching out of the China Incident. The government did not agree on a basic policy for the Promotion Department until January 12, 1941, when MCI announced its "General Plan for the Conversion and Closing of Medium and Smaller Enterprises." Two years later the government would need to apply the policy to all enterprises, not just medium and smaller firms.

The first half of 1942 was a period of great euphoria for Japan's industrial planners. The 1942 materials mobilization plan was the most optimistic of all of them, and the Cabinet Planning Board even relaxed regulations over the use of petroleum, now that Dutch East Indies supplies were in Japanese hands. Shortly after the fall of Singapore the military expressed its appreciation to the economic bureaucrats for their efforts by supplying the CPB and MCI with large numbers of commemorative rubber balls made of Malayan rubber for distribution to the *shōkokumin* (children of the rising generation).[6] Kishi Nobusuke, at age 46 the youngest minister in Japan's modern history, was immensely popular with the public and received extravagant praise in the press, both for himself and for his ministry.

Still, Kishi had problems. The control associations for each industry were not working well. The theory behind them—a compromise forced on the state-control bureaucrats because of the resistance of the business community—was the integration of the public and private sectors (*kanmin ittai*).[7] The reality, however, was the perpetuation of the privately controlled cartels of the 1931 Important Industries Control Law, which the zaibatsu dominated. Hadley characterizes the control associations as "cartels with a bit of government thrown in."[8] The government's power over them was more or less limited to the issuing of licenses. The control associations themselves were busy making good profits, distributing market shares in ways that favored the zaibatsu leaders, and making side deals with the military, regardless of what MCI or the CPB said or did. Moreover, the military often undercut bureaucratic efforts at control by keeping critical materials out of channels and in its own arsenals because of interservice rivalries and military distrust of the cartels' civilian leadership.

Most analysts have blamed the zaibatsu for the "spinelessness" of the control associations, but blame should be shared by the ministries. All of the economic ministries fought endless battles of jurisdiction over the designation of an industry as "important" and over influence in its control associations. The first control association, and the model for all the others, came under MCI jurisdiction; this was the Steel Control Association, created April 26, 1941, with President Hirao Hachisaburō of Japan Steel as the association's president—or Führer, as the reform bureaucrats liked to call him. However, the steel control association was not so much an MCI invention as an MCI discovery; it had been formed by the steelmakers themselves following the American embargo on selling scrap iron to Japan, and it was little more than a renamed Japan Steel Federation (Nihon Tekkō Rengōkai), the trade association of the industry. Between April 1941 and January 1942 MCI and the Communications Ministry fought over the setting up of a control association for the machine sector, and MCI and the Agriculture Ministry fought over the fertilizer sector. Both of these disputes had to go to the cabinet for settlement. It was only in August 1942 that some 21 control associations covering production and distribution for 15 industries finally came into operation.

The ministries also fought a rearguard action against giving the control associations real authority. Kishi finally broke bureaucratic resistance over this issue by demanding that in return for governmental enforcement powers the control associations appoint full-time presidents, and not just accept, ex officio, the chief executive of the largest enterprise in an industry. This resulted in the Transfer of Administrative Authority Law (number 15 of February 18, 1942) and the Transfer of Administrative Authority Ordinance of January 21, 1943, which made the directors of the control associations quasi-governmental officials and gave the force of law to their orders. Hirao resigned as president of Japan Steel and of the Steel Control Association, and he was replaced in both capacities by Admiral Toyoda (MCI minister from April to July 1941). But in most other control associations the zaibatsu simply arranged for an acceptable figure as president, while they retained true control.

Legally speaking, the control associations were joint public-private corporations modeled after the so-called national policy companies (*kokusaku kaisha*) such as Japan Steel or the South Manchurian Railroad—or after the "licensed companies" such as Nissan and Toyota. Since the disputes between the self-control and state-control groups had made the mixed public-private corporation an acceptable compromise to both sides, the idea occurred to the frustrated MCI bureaucrats that they might get around the control associations and still not draw the wrath of the business community if they created true public corporations with all capital subscribed by the government and the board of directors appointed by a ministry. Thus was born the *eidan* (an abbreviation of *keiei zaidan*, or "management foundation"). The eidan were not necessarily oriented toward war, and one of them still exists today—the Teito Rapid Transit Authority (Teito Kōsokudo Kōtsū Eidan), which was created in 1941 as the public segment of the Tokyo subway system; they all came into being as bureaucratic devices to bring a sector of the economy under official control while avoiding the weaknesses and zaibatsu domination of the control associations.

The eidan of greatest interest to us in this work was the Industrial Facilities Corporation (Sangyō Setsubi Eidan), created by law on November 25, 1941, with Fujihara Ginjirō, ex-MCI minister and founder of the Ōji Paper Company, as president. It was authorized to purchase or lease idle factories—particularly factories that had been idled by orders of MCI's Promotion Department—and to convert them to munitions production. Funds for these objectives came from corporate bonds, which the eidan could issue up to five times its total capital, with the government guaranteeing the redemption and payment of interest on the bonds. The Industrial Facilities Corporation was, in effect, the operating arm of the Promotion Department for the positive implementation of the enterprise readjustment movement.[9]

Several months passed before the corporation could begin operations; bonds had to be sold, a staff gathered, and clear policies formulated by MCI for its operations. Meanwhile, the war outlook worsened. The battle for Midway was fought in June 1942, and in August American forces began landing on Guadalcanal. One official MITI history notes laconically, "Japan's true wartime economy began only after Guadalcanal." [10] In order to prepare for what he feared was coming and in order to get around the stumbling block of the control associations in a future emergency, Kishi arranged for two Imperial ordinances to be issued, neither of which he could fully implement for more than a year. They did not make a great contribution to the war effort, but their influence can still be felt in Japan in terms of the postwar industrial structure. The first was the Enterprise Licensing Ordinance (Kigyō Kyoka Rei, number 1084 of December 11, 1941), which made it illegal to open a new business without a government license; the second and more important was the Enterprise Readjustment Ordinance (Kigyō Seibi Rei, number 503 of May 13, 1942), which gave the government legal authority to order any enterprise whatever to convert to munitions production.

Kishi and Shiina next concluded that they needed a new control apparatus within MCI to administer the Enterprise Readjustment Ordinance and to supervise the work of the Industrial Facilities Corporation. On June 17, 1942, they created the new Enterprises Bureau, placed it immediately after the General Affairs Bureau in the ministry's internal chain of command, and designated it as the policy center for all industrial reorganization and production-increase activities. The Enterprises Bureau absorbed the existing Promotion Department and the Financial Section of the General Affairs Bureau. It was made responsible for the supply of capital, the internal organization, the management practices, and the efficiency of all Japanese enterprises. Its duties included supervising the Industrial Facilities Corporation, dealing with all questions concerning medium and smaller enterprises, and inspecting and controlling company financial and accounting affairs. The bureau was divided into four sections—Facilities (Setsubi-ka), Commercial Policy (Shōsei-ka), Industrial Policy (Kōsei-ka), and Finance (Shikin-ka)—and it was given authority over all other bureaus in the ministry in order to insure that its programs were executed. The first director was Toyoda Masataka, Shiina's successor as vice-minister after the war and a member of the Diet from 1953 to 1968.

During the second half of 1942 and into 1943 the Enterprises Bureau used its various policy instruments—the two ordinances, the corporation, and virtually unlimited financial powers—to convert one industrial sector after another to war production. Toyoda later recalled that he traveled around the country to explain the new policies and was surprised to find he was none too popular.[11] The industry hardest hit was textiles. Following Enterprises Bureau directives, the Textiles and Machinery bureaus forced the reduction of installed spindles from 12,165,000 in 1937 to only 2,150,000 in February 1946, a decline of 82 percent.[12] Some of this reduction was caused by war damage, but by far the largest proportion came from the conversion of textile mills to airplane and airplane parts production. In 1937 Japan had some 271 textile mills, but only 44 still existed in February 1946. Prior to the war there had been 23 cotton-spinning companies in operation, but forced amalgamations had reduced this number to 10 by the end of the war.

The full force of the movement hit in 1943. On June 1 the cabinet adopted its "Basic Policy for Enterprise Readjustment to Enlarge Fighting Strength" (Senryoku Zōkyō Kigyō Seibi Kihon Yōkō).[13] This directive divided all enterprises into three categories: the so-called peace industries (textiles, metals, chemicals), munitions industries (aircraft, steel, coal, light metals, and shipbuilding), and daily necessity industries. It ordered that the first category be converted into the second category, and that the third category be abolished. The policy also sought to strengthen the munitions industries by designating all war-related medium and smaller enterprises as belonging to two groupings: "cooperating factories," most of which became subsidiaries (*kogaisha*, literally, "child companies"), that is, permanent subcontractors of large enterprises; and "group-use factories." The effect was greatly to increase the industrial concentration in zaibatsu hands (the aspect of the program that is most often noticed), but it also produced a significant shift of the industrial structure toward heavy and chemical industries.

The Japanese public paid a heavy price for this shift in industrial structure. Jerome B. Cohen argues that "the Japanese consumer was hit harder by war than civilians in any other major belligerent country for which data is available."[14] Tanaka Shin'ichi, who was in charge of drafting the materials mobilization plans in the CPB, acknowledges that during 1943 consumer goods virtually disappeared from the economy; and Maeda Yasuyuki notes ruefully that Japan's "peace industries" were destroyed by their own government before a single American bomb had fallen.[15] Still, the effort was not enough. Japan had taken eighteen months after the outbreak of war to try to forge the economic institutions necessary to wage the war. By the time the war production apparatus was in place, the tide of war was beginning to run strongly against Japan. It was against this background that, in late 1943, Kishi and Tōjō took their final step to achieve full state control of the economy. They converted MCI into the Ministry of Munitions.

Writing as an Allied analyst of the Japanese economy during World War II, T. A. Bisson perceived the existence of "a chronic behind-the-scenes political crisis throughout 1943," and he was quite right to do so.[16] The crisis had at least three aspects. First, Tōjō and Kishi were seeking to centralize authority over war production, but the business community was resisting this movement, and MCI was being pulled in both directions. Second, the Cabinet Planning Board and MCI were engaged in almost daily shouting matches over priorities and deliveries, in part because the CPB was writing plans for the empire as a whole, including the occupied areas (which were under military control), but MCI had jurisdiction only over Japan proper. And third, interservice rivalries were tending to nullify all efforts at expanded production, particularly production of fighter aircraft, which had become the highest priority for the battles to be fought in Japanese home waters.

In March 1943, in response to the Tōjō cabinet's assertion of greater control powers and to the enterprise readjustment movement, the business community and its supporters in the Diet had demanded and won a much larger voice at the top of the government concerning war production policies. This led on March 17, 1943, to the creation of a Cabinet Advisers Council, the businessmen on which wanted above all to supervise the comparatively young MCI minister, Kishi. These businessmen were not unpatriotic or opposed to the war effort, but they remained suspicious of the dictatorial tendencies of Tōjō and Kishi and of their known antizaibatsu sentiments. From Kishi's point of view the creation of the council was a personal insult; it recalled forcefully to him the clashes of the 1930's between the reform bureaucrats and such MCI ministers as Ikeda Seihin, Fujihara Ginjirō (who became a member of the 1943 council and ultimately Kishi's successor), and Kobayashi Ichizō. The council of 1943 also signified that neither the state-control nor the self-control group had ever seen its views totally prevail as a result of those earlier battles.

Members of the council included Admiral Toyoda, president of the Iron and Steel Control Association; Ōkōchi Masatoshi, one of Yoshino's civilian colleagues in the old Rationality Bureau and president of the Industrial Machinery Control Association; Fujihara, head of the Industrial Facilities Corporation and personally affiliated with Mitsui;

Yūki Toyotarō, president of the Bank of Japan and affiliated with the Yasuda zaibatsu; Gōko Kiyoshi, former president of Mitsubishi Heavy Industries; Yamashita Kamesaburō, former president of the Yamashita Steamship Company; and Suzuki Chūji, president of the Shōwa Denkō Company and president of the Light Metals Industry Control Association.[17]

Although these men were attached to the cabinet primarily to look after zaibatsu interests, they were quickly educated by Kishi about the problems of the control associations. One sample of Kishi's position is available from a Tokyo radio broadcast of June 23, 1943:

At a time when the readjustment of industries is being carried out on a large scale, there are still entrepreneurs living on their unearned incomes. Concerning this, the minister of commerce and industry, Kishi, . . . emphasized the necessity of maintaining a strict control over various industries, causing a profound sensation among the leaders of industrial circles. . . . The minister of commerce and industry has been kept busy preparing a concrete plan in order to make the control companies function as national policy companies. . . . The directors of the companies, although they are regarded as the responsible authorities, are still remaining as they were before.[18]

Of all the members of the council, the one Kishi feared and resented most—because of his long association with MCI and his insider's knowledge—was Fujihara. In fact, on November 17, 1943, after the founding of the Munitions Ministry on November 1, Fujihara was secretly appointed a state minister without portfolio—the same rank as Kishi—and placed within the ministry to oversee his activities. Nonetheless, the evidence indicates that Fujihara was every bit as alarmed as Kishi by the ineffectiveness of the control associations at a time when the war was entering its most dangerous phase for Japan. After several inspection trips Fujihara reported to the council that there was no real shortage of coal, only inefficiency and negligence by the mine operators, and that aircraft production was stymied not by a shortage of aluminum—only 55 percent of the aluminum available was being used for airplanes—but by the intense competition for and hoarding of materials by the army and navy.[19]

Kishi devised two answers to these various problems: the enactment of a new law to enhance governmental supervision over the control associations, and a total reorganization of the government's economic bureaucracies. On October 31, 1943, an extraordinary session of the Diet passed the Munitions Companies Law (Gunju Kaisha Hō, number 108), which sought to establish once and for all the principle contained in the old Konoe New Structure Movement of 1940—namely, the separation of management from ownership. It authorized the stationing of governmental officials called "munitions supervisors" in each factory and made these officials, rather than the industrywide control associations, responsible for seeing that targets were fulfilled and rules followed.

As it turned out, this law came too late to make much difference to the war effort. It merely added another layer of officialdom on top of the control associations, which still allocated materials and distributed products on an industrywide basis. The Munitions Companies Law was the last serious effort of the state-control group before the Allied occupation, and it remained a compromise; with the cabinet council looking on and the Diet increasingly dubious about Tōjō's leadership, Kishi could not go beyond the basic parameters of the capitalist system. The government continued to pay dividends to owners and guarantee their costs of production until June 1945, when the zaibatsu were only too happy to see the government buy out and nationalize their ruined munitions plants.[20]

The Munitions Companies Law was not an important precedent for postwar industrial policy (although the law of 1948 authorizing state control of the coal industry has strong similarities to it). The reorganization of the economic ministries, however, had lasting consequences. In essence the government abolished the Cabinet Planning Board and four old ministries—Commerce and Industry, Agriculture and Forestry, Communications, and Railroads—and replaced them with three new ministries—Munitions (Gunju-shō), Agriculture and Commerce (Nōshō-shō), and Transport and Communications (Un'yu Tsūshin-shō). Concrete plans for this reorganization were drafted on the MCI side by Yamamoto Takayuki, the first MITI vice-minister in 1949; on the CPB side they were drafted by Tanaka Shin'ichi, deputy director of MITI's Enterprises Bureau after 1949, and Morisaki Hisatoshi, director of MITI's Heavy Industries Bureau in 1964.

The new Munitions Ministry (MM) was the brightest star in the firmament. The CPB and MCI's General Affairs Bureau were united into a single new agency for both planning and execution; it was called the General Mobilization Bureau (Sōdōin Kyoku), with Shiina Etsusaburō as director. MCI's old bureaus for Steel, Machinery, Light Metals, Nonferrous Metals, Chemicals, and Fuel, plus the now defunct Communications Ministry's Electric Power Bureau, went to Munitions. MCI's old bureaus for Textiles, Daily Life Commodities, and Prices went to the new version of the old Ministry of Agriculture and Commerce. MCI's Enterprises Bureau continued on in MM as the Enterprises Readjustment Headquarters (Kigyō Seibi Honbu), although it did not have many enterprises left to convert to war production. The few remaining functions of MCI in the area of international trade were transferred to the Greater East Asia Ministry. MM also established nine regional Munitions Supervision Departments (Gunju Kanri Bu), which are the concrete origins of the contemporary MITI regional bureaus. Finally, the factory inspectors of the Army-Navy Aviation Headquarters were integrated into a new Aircraft Ordnance General Bureau within MM under Lieutenant General Endō Saburō.

From the perspective of 1945 Allied intelligence, Bisson thought that this structure plus the Munitions Companies Law had "largely rectified" the chaotic situation that had prevailed in Japan's war economy during 1942 and 1943. He was, however, astonished that MCI—"this old-line standby of the business interests"—and not the military, as had been supposed in Washington, had been responsible for creating the new ministry.[21] The MCI officials who went to MM, a contingent that included all of MITI's later industrial faction, were much less sanguine about their prospects for success. Even Shiina, despite his own Manchurian background, later complained bitterly about having to work with arrogant military officers; and many able officials, such as Ueno Kōshichi (MITI vice-minister from 1957 to 1960), found their effectiveness reduced because of clashes with military officers.[22] One of the first things the former MCI men did when the war was over was to kick out the military officers while retaining the ministry's expanded jurisdiction.

The chief significance of MM for later industrial policy is that MITI managed to retain all of the functions—including electric power, airplane manufacture, and industrial planning—that had first been brought together in MM. The experience of working as factory supervisors was also important for later MITI cadres. And for some the Munitions Ministry would have a great personal meaning: two MITI vice-ministers, Sahashi (1964–66) and Morozumi (1971–73), met and married women who served in MM's Women's Volunteer Corps. Perhaps also worth mentioning, Prime Minister Tōjō evicted the prestigious Board of Audit (Kaikei Kensa-in) from its offices in Kasumigaseki and moved his new MM there from the old MCI headquarters near the Kabuki theater. As a result of the war, the industrial policy bureaucrats finally made it to the Tokyo equivalent of Whitehall, never again to leave.

At the level of top leadership some arrangements were made for MM that would soon have serious political consequences. After November 1, 1943, Tōjō served concurrently as prime minister, minister of the army, chief of the General Staff, and minister of munitions. He took on MM not simply as a gesture to give it more prestige, even though he never exercised any personal administrative control over the ministry. It was instead, as Ōkōchi Shigeo stresses, a final attempt to overcome the structural disunity of the Japanese government that had been imposed on it by the Meiji Constitution. Tōjō was attempting to achieve elementary coordination of his government by assuming a one-man dictatorship, despite the fact that he could never achieve control over the navy.[23] But in order to make Kishi effective, although Tōjō was the formal minister, Tōjō had to adopt an expedient that ultimately made his own political problems worse. He appointed Kishi both vice-minister of munitions and state minister with cabinet rank (*gunju jikan kokumu daijin*), thus making him the de facto head of MM.

Kishi himself has commented on this strange arrangement, as have numerous outside observers. Kishi says that he told Tōjō that as vice-minister he would have to obey Tōjō as his minister and superior, but that as minister of state he did not have to obey him because they would both have equivalent ranks. Tōjō certainly understood this point, but he appointed Kishi state minister anyway in order to give him sufficient authority to command the generals and admirals who would be working in Kishi's ministry. Tōjō remarked to Kishi that military men are trained to take orders according to the number of stars a person wears; a vice-minister has only two stars, but a minister has three.[24] Kishi's becoming minister and vice-minister simultaneously set up and conditioned his clash with Tōjō less than a year later. This clash was of much greater significance historically than Kishi's earlier ones (over the pay cuts and with ministers Ogawa and Kobayashi), and it contributed one of Kishi's nicknames, the "quarreler" (*kenka*), and added to his reputation as a man of principle.[25]

Trouble between Tōjō and Kishi began almost at once. The secret appointment of Fujihara as Kishi's watchdog barely three weeks after the new ministry had been launched caused Kishi to tender his resignation. He argued that it was hard enough to run MM with two ministers; three was impossible. Tōjō refused to accept his resignation, accused Kishi of being irresponsible, and said that Fujihara was necessary to keep the zaibatsu quiet. However, six months later, in July 1944, Tōjō asked for Kishi's resignation, and this time Kishi refused to give it, citing his independent responsibility as a minister to the throne. This impasse could not be resolved, and the Tōjō government fell.

The ostensible cause of the resignation of the Tōjō cabinet was the American capture of Saipan. Kishi forthrightly expressed his opinion that Japan had no chance of winning after Saipan and should therefore sue for peace. Tōjō was enraged. The word "defeat" was all but taboo in the Japan of 1944, and Tōjō accused Kishi of meddling with the military's prerogative of supreme command. This was an extremely dangerous charge for Kishi. Tōjō exercised effective control over the military police (*kempeitai*)—he was a former Kempei commander in the Kwantung Army—and he had caused several political figures to meet their deaths at the hands of the military police for disagreeing with him (for example, Nakano Seigō, 1886–1943, a member of the Diet since 1920).

Kishi nonetheless stood his ground. The inner reality was that powerful figures in the Diet and the Imperial Household agreed with Kishi and wanted to be rid of Tōjō. Some of these men were Kido Kōichi (in the palace); Funada Naka (in the Diet); Ino Hiroya (an old MAC associate of Kishi's and one whom Kishi wished had gone to MCI instead of Agriculture in 1925; he served from 1941 to 1943 in the Tōjō cabinet as agriculture minister); and Fujiyama Aiichirō (a prominent businessman and adviser to the navy who plotted with the admirals against Tōjō after the Saipan disaster). It appears that Tōjō did not dare move against Kishi because he feared Kishi's numerous but unseen supporters. Incidentally, after Kishi became prime minister in 1957, he named Fujiyama minister of foreign affairs in his first cabinet and Ino minister of justice in his second.

The cabinet of General Koiso, who succeeded Tōjō, was transitional. The "watchdog" Fujihara moved up to become minister of munitions, and he appointed Kishi's old bureaucratic competitor, Takeuchi Kakichi (one of Murase Naokai's associates), as vice-minister. Fujihara only lasted six months. He resigned at the end of 1944 because of "ill health" (he was 75 years old but lived on until 1960); the real reason, however, was that a Mitsubishi-Sumitomo coalition forced him out because they were worried that a Mitsui-affiliated minister might threaten their own interests. As a replacement the prime minister chose a neutral figure—the old Home Ministry bureaucrat and first director of the Cabinet Research Bureau back in 1935, Yoshida Shigeru.*

In the spring of 1945 the fall of Iwo Jima, the invasion of Okinawa, and the great March 10 air raid on Tokyo precipitated the resignation of the Koiso cabinet. The new government of Admiral Suzuki was charged to bring the war to an end, which it did. For his munitions minister, Suzuki chose a fellow admiral, the ubiquitous Toyoda Teijirō, who was then working as head of the Iron and Steel Control

---

*Again it should be remembered that this is not the Yoshida Shigeru who became prime minister after the war.

Association. Toyoda, in turn, appointed Shiina Etsusaburō as vice-minister, the same position Shiina had held in MCI before it became MM. It was Shiina who actually presided over his ministry's end-of-the-war arrangements, and in retrospect he must be given credit for taking quick action at a time of major confusion.

On August 15, 1945, the nation heard the *gyokuon hōsō*—the Emperor's broadcast announcing the surrender. Two days later the Suzuki cabinet resigned and was replaced by the transitional government of Prince Higashikuni. Nakajima Chikuhei, the famous aircraft industrialist, was asked to hold the portfolio for MM, which ironically put Nakajima back in nominal control of the aircraft plants that had been taken from him and nationalized only the previous June. Shiina, however, continued to run the ministry. Only ten days after the fighting stopped and barely a day before the first Allied troops arrived at Atsugi air base to prepare the way for General MacArthur, Shiina told several of his younger colleagues that he had an important assignment for them, one that they must complete overnight. They were to recreate MCI before the occupation began.

Yamamoto Takayuki, MITI's first vice-minister in 1949, has said that the overnight rebirth of MCI was ordered because all the civilian bureaucrats in MM feared that the Allies would fire or arrest anyone connected with munitions. Shiina has indicated that he also had personal reasons for wanting to put some distance between the MCI contingent and the military officers in MM, and that he recognized the necessity for getting rid of the Munitions Ministry before the Americans did so. According to various accounts, those involved in the resurrection were Yamamoto, Ueno Kōshichi, Tokunaga Hisatsugu, and Hirai Tomisaburō, all of whom became MITI vice-ministers during the 1950's.[26] Thus, by Imperial ordinance 486 of August 26, 1945, the Ministry of Munitions and the Ministry of Agriculture and Commerce disappeared, and in their places were reinstalled the old MCI and the old Ministry of Agriculture and Forestry.

Shortly after the establishment of SCAP headquarters, Allied investigators discovered the end-of-the-war juggling of ministries, but they did not attempt to do anything about it because the changes had been in the direction the Allies wanted the Japanese to go anyway. One of the official, although nameless, American historians of the occupation merely noted, "Bureaucrats were aware that their presurrender cooperation with militarists and zaibatsu interests constituted a threat to their continued hegemony. In the weeks before the occupation began officially, personnel records were destroyed, wholesale shifts of higher officials were made, and initial steps were taken to divorce administration from some of the most obvious features of aggressive imperialism."[27]

Since SCAP had decided on an indirect occupation, which left the Japanese government intact even if taking orders from SCAP, the Allies did not demand a reform of all ministries, only those that had been closely connected with the military or the police (one was the Home Ministry), which the occupation ordered abolished. SCAP intended to deal on an individual basis with those bureaucrats whom it held responsible for the war—through the purge rather than through structural change. But as we saw in Chapter 2, recent Japanese estimates put the number of MCI officials who were actually purged at only 42; and according to SCAP's own figures, it investigated 69 MCI officials but removed from office only 10.[28] Thus Shiina's last-minute ploy worked quite well; the trade and industry bureaucracy maintained its continuity despite the crisis of defeat.

The accounts of what happened during the four years from mid-1945 to mid-1949 in the realm of economic and industrial policy—whether by SCAP officials or Japanese—often differ so markedly as to make it appear that each side is talking about a different country. SCAP began the occupation by declaring that the Japanese had brought about their own economic difficulties and that the Allies therefore took no responsibility for maintaining any particular level of living in Japan. However, the Americans quickly discovered that if they stuck to this position—given the collapse of all Japanese international trade—they would merely ensure a communist revolution in Japan and not a "democratically reoriented" country.[29] The Americans therefore began state-controlled trade and demanded that the Japanese government impose economic controls. As it turned out, the prewar and wartime victories of the zaibatsu over the state-control bureaucrats proved to be the zaibatsu's undoing. SCAP declared that the zaibatsu had been responsible for the war economy, banned any further private cartels, and ordered government officials to exercise the powers previously reserved for the control associations. MCI officials of the "Kishi-Shiina line" were only too happy to oblige; after their struggles of the previous fifteen years, it suddenly seemed as if they had arrived in the bureaucratic promised land.

Similarly, with regard to emergency economic rehabilitation measures or positive economic reforms, the Japanese and the Americans often seemed purposely to misunderstand each other. Yoshida Shigeru (1878–1967), the great ex-bureaucrat prime minister who presided over Japan's rise from the ashes, once commented, "The occupation, with all the power and authority behind its operation, was hampered by its lack of knowledge of the people it had come to govern, and even more so, perhaps, by its generally happy ignorance of the amount of requisite knowledge it lacked."*

Thus SCAP would sometimes approve of MCI proposals that the Americans thought were temporary expedients but that ended up lasting until well into the 1960's (foreign exchange budgets, for example). As for SCAP's policies calling for zaibatsu dissolution, the officials of MCI's old Enterprises Bureau—now called the Readjustment Department (Seiri Bu)—administered this program with enthusiasm. But when it came to economic deconcentration generally, toward which the breakup of the zaibatsu was only a means and not an end, the industrial bureaucrats quickly discovered that there were divisions within SCAP and took advantage of them. Eleanor Hadley, herself a SCAP trustbuster, explains:

Inasmuch as in the United States commercial banks are not permitted to have industrial and trading subsidiaries or affiliates, the American vocabulary and way of thinking is to regard commercial banking as quite separate from industry and commerce. . . . The Economic and Scientific Section of [SCAP] Headquarters . . . was set up with an Antitrust and Cartel Division and a Finance Division, which was a mistake. . . . The result of the actual arrangement was that the Antitrust and Cartel Division claimed jurisdiction in antitrust matters over the banks, but the staff of the Finance Division insisted that the banks were entirely theirs (and their responsibility included no antitrust assignment!).[31]

After the occupation the old zaibatsu were recreated on the basis of their banks rather than their former family holding companies. This was a much more rational and effective arrangement, but it is certain that this was not exactly what SCAP had in mind. In fact, in 1975, with no apparent sense of irony, the Japanese government awarded its Second Class Order of the Sacred Treasure to Tristan E. Beplat, who had recently retired as a senior vice-president of the Manufacturers Hanover Trust Company of New York. As the *Japan Times* explained, Beplat was "an American banker who the government said

---

*See *The Yoshida Memoirs*, p. 128. However, Yoshida himself was not above attempting to fool SCAP officials. "The original GHQ plan, as handed to us," Yoshida writes, "called for the purging of 'standing directors' as well as others occupying top positions. This was translated into Japanese by our side as 'managing directors.' Strictly speaking, however, a 'standing director' could be interpreted as one who functioned regularly in a company, which would have included most ordinary directors. We held to our interpretation that 'standing directors' were, in fact, managing directors, and by so doing were able to save many ordinary directors who might otherwise have been so classified from the purge. Which shows that upon occasion mistranslations serve their turn." *Ibid.*, pp. 155–56. The issue here is the translation of the difficult terms *senmu torishimariyaku* (executive director), *jōmu torishimariyaku* (managing director), and *torishimariyaku* (director).[30]

had made a vital contribution to Japan's postwar economic recovery. . . . He was in charge of occupation policy toward Japanese banking from 1945 to 1948. . . . Many financial leaders, including [then] Deputy Prime Minister Fukuda Takeo, credit him with preventing the breakup of Japanese banks and insurance companies in the postwar dismemberment of zaibatsu companies in Japan."[32] Without wishing to detract from Beplat's award in any manner, one may suggest that from the Japanese, and especially from MCI's point of view, there was a degree of *menjū fukuhai* (following a superior's orders to his face while reversing them in the belly) at work during those immediate postwar years.

Sometimes Japanese officials genuinely did not understand what SCAP wanted them to do. For example, with regard to the Antimonopoly Law (number 54 of April 14, 1947), Morozumi Yoshihiko, who 25 years later became vice-minister of MITI, recalls his painful efforts during the occupation to translate article by article into legal Japanese the draft of the Antimonopoly Law that General MacArthur's headquarters had sent over to MCI for enactment. "It seems laughable today," he writes, "but then we didn't really know what they were talking about."[33] When Morozumi showed his draft to his "senior," Murase Naokai, then chief of the Cabinet Legislation Bureau, Murase asked him what something he had translated meant and he was forced, much to his embarrassment, to reply that he did not know. Murase got the drift of the law only by looking at the original English text. Needless to say, the Antimonopoly Law was not something the Japanese were able to avoid or evade. As we shall see in the next two chapters, MITI spent the succeeding 30 years struggling to get around Morozumi's handiwork. The tension that developed between MITI on the one hand and the Fair Trade Commission (created by the law) on the other undoubtedly made a contribution to the favorable climate in which high-speed growth took place. This tension, unintended by either SCAP or MCI, may have been one of the occupation's greatest contributions to the economic "miracle."

Although SCAP's accounts are virtually silent on the subject, the Japanese characterize the first four years of the occupation by reference to two great debates over Japan's economic reconstruction and by one overwhelming fact—the rise of the state as the central actor in the economy. The first of the two controversies was over whether reconstruction should give priority to expanding production (the *seisan fukkō setsu*, or the theory of reconstruction through production) or to price stabilization and control of inflation (the *tsūka kaikaku setsu*, or the theory of currency reform).[34] The second controversy concerned what type of economy Japan should rebuild—one oriented to light industries and Japan's comparative advantage of a large, still cheap labor force, or one oriented to heavy and chemical industries with their greater value-added potential (that is, the greater value of the products produced after the cost of materials, taxes, and depreciation have been subtracted).

The emphasis on production rather than stabilization and on heavy industry rather than light industry usually prevailed, but the advocates of the opposite positions were not necessarily wrong. They made their contribution during the "Dodge Line" (1949–50) and the Korean War (1950–53), when the advocates of production and of heavy industries had to come to grips with controlling inflation and with Japan's dependence on international trade. It was then that MITI was born and that both sides of the occupation controversies were synthesized to form the high-growth system.

The rise of state power and its role in reconstruction dominated all of the controversies. The historian Hata Ikuhiko states flatly that "never has the Japanese bureaucracy exercised greater authority than it did during the occupation"; and the MITI Journalists' Club refers to the occupation as MCI's "golden era"—the period in which it exercised total control of the economy.[35] The government's assumption of all functions previously shared with the private sector, its recreation of the "economic general staff" and the materials mobilization plans under new names but in much stronger forms, and its enactment of legislation that made the National General Mobilization Law pale by comparison led to an enormous growth of the bureaucracy. During 1948 and 1949 MCI came to control the third largest share of the general account budget (only the Prime Minister's office and the Ministry of Finance had larger shares); and when MITI was founded in 1949, it had a total of 21,199 employees, as compared with 13,891 in 1974 to serve an infinitely larger and more complex economy.

The growth of the public sector caused an intensification of the bureaucratic struggles for jurisdiction on which a ministry's security and even its existence depended. The Finance Ministry and the Bank of Japan fought tooth and nail over control of the banks, a struggle that Finance eventually won. Ichimada Naoto was president of the Bank of Japan and an advocate of both the currency reform theory and light industries; had he instead of Ikeda Hayato accepted Prime Minister Yoshida's offer to become minister of finance in 1949, the economic history of postwar Japan would surely have been very different from what it was.[36] But the struggle of greatest interest to this study occurred between the Ministry of Foreign Affairs and MCI. With all of

Japan's foreign legations closed, there existed during the occupation a vast surplus of diplomats who had to be given work in the government. They were, moreover, of all officials the most adept at the English language, and this gave them a great advantage in dealing with SCAP.

Most important in this struggle was the fact that the key politician of the postwar years, Prime Minister Yoshida, was an ex–Foreign Office official. Yoshida has always acknowledged that he did not know much about and was more or less uninterested in economics, but he had quite firm views on certain other matters about which he knew a great deal. Two such issues concerned Japan's wartime controlled economy and the economic bureaucrats who had cooperated with the military. He deeply disliked both of them. According to many accounts, Yoshida "could not distinguish an MCI official from an insect"; and he was determined to put reliable Foreign Office men over what he regarded as the dangerously national socialist MCI bureaucrats.[37] MCI had to move nimbly in order to survive at all, since its greatest danger came not from SCAP but from its own country's political leader and from some of his official colleagues. As we shall see, MITI did not escape fully from Foreign Ministry influence until 1956.

In these important bureaucratic struggles, SCAP was not so much "supreme" as a major player on a national chessboard, sometimes the queen but more often merely a pawn. Yoshida on occasion manipulated the purge apparatus to get rid of a politician who had crossed him. And MCI men took full advantage of the proclivities of some of SCAP's "new dealers" toward a "planned economy," much to Yoshida's irritation. The coming to power in 1947 of Japan's only socialist government, something that SCAP was very enthusiastic about, was a godsend for MCI—not because MCI advocated socialism but because socialism afforded it a plausible cover for its own industrial policies and because the socialist government put Yoshida out of power for eighteen months.[38] These are matters to which we shall return. The first four years of the occupation were a period of immense complexity, extremely rapid social change, and for the Japanese people a bitter struggle for survival—the time of the "prison of hunger," as they spoke of it then. But out of it came a summing up of the experiences of the prewar, wartime, and occupation industrial policies that allowed the government during the next decade to lead the country to prosperity.

The initial postwar problem, and the one that conditioned all the others to come, was inflation. If we take the price level of August 1945 to be 100, then the level rose to 346.8 in September, to 584.9 in December, and to 1184.5 the following March.[39] Several factors caused this inflation, including mustering-out payments to the Japanese armed forces, but the most important was the continuation and even acceleration of government disbursements for wartime contracts, war production loans, munitions companies guarantees and indemnities, and various other obligations the government had assumed under wartime laws and ordinances. One of these was payments for factories that had been seized and converted to munitions production by the Industrial Facilities Corporation. In mid-1946, when SCAP's order to the government to default on its wartime obligations was finally carried out, the Industrial Facilities Corporation still owed the cotton textile industry some ¥12 billion for factories it had taken over. Before SCAP stopped the payments, the government had literally flooded the economy with money. The *Mainichi* estimates that in a little over three months after the surrender, the government paid out some ¥26.6 billion, a truly colossal sum amounting to about one-third of the total amount Japan had spent for military purposes between September 1937 and August 1945.[40]

During 1946 these disbursements led to one of the first big clashes between SCAP and the Japanese over economic policy. Ishibashi Tanzan, minister of finance in the first Yoshida cabinet (May 1946 to May 1947), was a strong advocate of increased production; he boldly argued that "the current economic crisis is not one of inflation but rather of a surplus of unused labor and production facilities. The only way to get out of it is to increase production."[41] For this purpose Ishibashi was prepared to throw money at industry through war claims payments and price support subsidies and to deal with the resultant inflation merely by issuing "new yen" whenever necessary. SCAP profoundly disagreed; in its view price stabilization had to take precedence over any efforts to restore production. Ishibashi's position reflected the war-bred theories of many industrial bureaucrats who believed that what counted was materials, labor, and output—not prices and money; SCAP's views were closer to those of Governor Ichimada of the Bank of Japan, who was also a confidant of such senior SCAP officials as General Courtney Whitney.[42]

During November 1945 SCAP issued direct orders to the Japanese government to stop paying off war claims. Ishibashi stalled as long as possible, fearing that the government's suspension of payments would ruin many banks, dry up industry's working capital, and bring what production there was to a halt. This is rather close to what actually happened during the autumn of 1946: the government stopped its subsidies, inflation accelerated rather than being brought under control, and production dropped precipitously. It was under these circumstances that the Japanese government began to take its own initiatives to revive the economy.

On June 25, 1946, the cabinet finally ended wartime compensation payments, but a month later it took the first steps to restore them under new names. The government set up the Reconstruction Finance Committee (Fukkō Kin'yū Iinkai), with Ishibashi as chairman, to prepare the way for the Reconstruction Finance Bank (RFB), created on January 24, 1947. It was one of a set of institutions that the Japanese created after the war to try to pull themselves out of the postwar economic collapse and to restore production to prewar levels regardless of the fierce inflation it generated.[43] SCAP derided these institutions as perpetuations of the old cozy relationship between government and business, and the specific acts of Ambassador Joseph Dodge in 1949, which came to be known as the "Dodge Line," were to terminate all further RFB lending and to order the government to balance its budget. Nonetheless, key Japanese leaders contend that the so-called priority production system of 1947 actually worked in that it restored the production of commodities such as coal and steel to levels close to those of the prewar period. The priority production system is significant because it and its institutions were clearly based on prewar and wartime precedents and because, except for the fiscal innovations made in 1949 and 1950 to control inflation, it was the prototype of the high-growth system that MITI and other ministries were to forge during the 1950's.

The specific institutions of the priority production system, in addition to the RFB, were the Coal Agency, the Economic Stabilization Board, the fifteen *kōdan* (public corporations for rationing of materials and products; they were modeled after the wholly governmental *eidan* rather than the zaibatsu-dominated control associations), and the Temporary Materials Supply and Demand Control Law (Rinji Busshi Jukyū Chōsei Hō, number 32 of September 30, 1946) that empowered these institutions to control all commodities.

At the end of the war coal production all but collapsed, plunging Japan into an acute energy crisis. Output fell from better than 4 million tons per month during the war to only 554,000 tons per month in November 1945. The reason was SCAP's immediate repatriation of about 9,000 Chinese and 145,000 Korean miners, many of whom Kishi had imported as virtual slave laborers when he was MCI minister. On December 6, 1945, on cabinet orders, the new MCI transformed its old Fuel Bureau into an enlarged semi-detached agency, the Coal Agency (Sekitan Chō). Destined to become one of the biggest units of the economic bureaucracy, it got off to a slow start. SCAP purged its first two directors, one a former president of the South Manchurian Railroad and the other a representative of the Yasukawa zaibatsu, and tried to purge its deputy director, Okamatsu Seitarō, who escaped only because his superiors pleaded that he was indispensable to economic recovery (he went on to become MCI vice-minister during 1947 and 1948). The Coal Agency's immediate task was to transfer Japanese miners from metal mines to coal mines and to arrange through the Agriculture Ministry and SCAP to have them supplied with larger food rations than had been given to the Korean and Chinese miners during the war or to the public at large after the war. "Food for coal" thus became Japan's first postwar industrial policy.[44]

The new system did not work well. After their governmental subsidies were cut off, the mine operators had difficulty in meeting payrolls. Insufficient coal was being produced to meet both industrial and civilian needs, and the costs of production skyrocketed—not least because of the virulence of the new labor movement among the miners. The Planning Office of the MCI Secretariat worked throughout 1946 on policies to overcome these conditions. The chief of the Planning Office was Tokunaga Hisatsugu (a future MITI vice-minister), and assisting him were Takashima Setsuo (a chief of the Heavy Industries Bureau during the 1960's), Morozumi Yoshihiko, and others. They drafted the Temporary Materials Supply and Demand Control Law of September 1946 and proposed the revival of the materials mobilization plans—renamed "materials supply and demand plans"—to guarantee shipments of coal to the industrial and transportation sectors rather than to civilians for consumption.[45] What they really needed, however, was an institution comparable to the old Cabinet Planning Board or MM's General Mobilization Bureau, an organ that could not only draft further plans but also administer the new control law.

As early as February 15, 1946, the cabinet had called for an "emergency economic policy headquarters" to deal with the coal and food shortages, inflation, the conversion of old yen into new yen, the freezing of credit funds, and new taxes. SCAP also recognized the need for something like this, but before it would give its approval, it insisted that the new agency be ranked above the existing ministries in order to try to end the frequent jurisdictional struggles. SCAP also wanted it to recruit its leadership from civilian rather than bureaucratic sources. SCAP's conditions naturally prevailed, but they insured that the new organization would start life rather anemically, since the established ministries were hostile to it and boycotted it as a threat to their territories.

The new organization, called the Economic Stabilization Board (ESB; Keizai Antei Honbu), came into being on August 12, 1946. It was the successor institution to the old CPB and the predecessor of the contemporary Economic Planning Agency. Like both of them, it was a planning and coordinating organ, not an operating unit; MCI was charged with executing its plans. Some of the staff of the new board was drawn from old CPB cadres—notably from among those who had been arrested as "reds" in the Cabinet Planning Board incident of 1941, since they now qualified as civilians. According to its charter, the ESB president was the prime minister, but its actual director was a civilian appointee with cabinet rank.

The Yoshida government had a hard time finding the first ESB director-general. Yoshida offered the job to Arisawa Hiromi, a Tōdai economics professor who had been fired from the university in 1938 for antimilitarist sentiments, but he turned it down, although he agreed to become a personal adviser to Yoshida on economic policy. Yoshida next approached Takahashi Masao, another academic economist and an adviser to SCAP's Economic and Scientific Section, but he too refused. Yoshida then gave up on professors and offered the job to Yanagida Seijirō, vice-governor of the Bank of Japan (and later president of Japan Air Lines), but SCAP purged him before he could take office. Finally, Yoshida settled on Zen Keinosuke, an ex-bureaucrat of MAC and MCI, a member of the House of Peers, and the man whom Yoshino had helped in the early 1930's to found the Japan Mutual Life Insurance Company. The problem was that no one knew what the ESB was supposed to do, and until that was clarified, the ministries and their clients looked on it as a pure SCAP invention.[46]

During the autumn of 1946, when the subsidies finally ground to a halt, the economy virtually collapsed. Yamamoto Takayuki and Tokunaga Hisatsugu of MCI, together with Inaba Hidezō of the ESB, put forward their famous thesis of a "March crisis"—their prediction that by March of 1947 the Japanese economy would no longer be producing anything due to an exhaustion of stockpiles, a lack of imports, and an acute coal shortage. On November 5, 1946, in order to forestall this, Prime Minister Yoshida established a personal brain trust known as the "Coal Committee" to tell him what to do. Its chairman was Arisawa Hiromi, and its members included Inaba Hidezō (formerly of the CPB), Ōkita Saburō (foreign minister in the Ōhira cabinet of 1979–80), Tsuru Shigeto (Harvard-trained economist and author in

Directors of the Economic Stabilization Board August 1946–August 1952

Director and tenure	Remarks
Zen Keinosuke, 8/46–1/47	Former MAC-MCI bureaucrat.
Ishibashi Tanzan, 1/47–3/47	Concurrently finance minister.
Takase Sōtarō, 3/47–5/47	President, Tokyo Commercial University. MITI minister, 1950.
Wada Hiroo, 6/47–3/48	Former agriculture bureaucrat. Arrested in Cabinet Planning Board incident, 1941.
Kurusu Takeo, 3/48–10/48	Arrested in Shōwa Denkō scandal, 10/48.
Izumiyama Sanroku, 10/48–12/48	Former Mitsui Bank official.
Shūtō Hideo, 12/48–2/49	Former agriculture bureaucrat. Former director, Department Four, Cabinet Planning Board (1942).
Aoki Takayoshi, 2/49–6/50	Former professor (economics), Nihon University.
Shūtō Hideo, 6/50–8/52	See above.

1947 of Japan's first *Economic White Paper*), Satō Naokuni (of MCI), Ōshima Kan'ichi (of the Finance Ministry), and several staff aides such as Kojima Keizō (formerly of the CPB and at the time working in MCI's Coal Agency). This group invented "priority production" (*keisha seisan*). On January 31, 1947, in a cabinet reshuffle, Ishibashi Tanzan was asked to take on the post of director of the ESB in addition to serving as minister of finance, and he made priority production the central objective of the ESB (for a list of the ESB leaders, see Table 11).

Priority production was a scheme to concentrate all of the economy's assets in a few strategic sectors, regardless of the effects this might have on civilian consumption or inflation. In this respect it was quite similar to the revised materials mobilization plan of 1938. The Arisawa committee had recognized that the first objective had to be to increase coal production. Calculating from the 1946 production figure of 22.8 million tons, the committee had set a goal of 30 million tons for 1947. In order to try to achieve this, it had suggested that the coal industry get first priority on RFB loans and subsidies. Allocation of coal was an equally serious problem. Before the war 60 percent of coal output had been used by industry and only 40 percent for transportation, electricity generation, and other so-called civilian uses, but in 1946 these proportions were reversed. Demand for nonindustrial use had become so great that there was no possibility of reviving industry unless coal production was increased. The committee therefore earmarked 16 million of its targeted 30 million tons for industry, and the

ESB was authorized to implement the Supply and Demand Law to achieve this distribution. Because the coal industry was a big steel user and steel production was itself dependent on coal, the committee designated steel as a second priority industry. It finally added fertilizer, which also uses coal, in order to try to expand food production.

Priority production was put into effect during the spring of 1947. Under Ishibashi's leadership and SCAP's orders that all ministerial planning functions be transferred to it, the ESB came to life. By May it had grown from a unit with 5 bureaus and 316 employees into a virtually new unit with a secretariat, 10 bureaus, 48 sections, and over 2,000 employees. MCI supplied the largest number of these new recruits. At the same time, the Diet enacted one law after another setting up the government corporations (kōdan) that under ESB orders purchased all major commodities from their producers at high prices and sold them to consumers at low prices, covering the difference with price subsidies from the general account budget. Table 12 summarizes the government's payments of subsidies and indemnities through the 1940's. It reveals that between 1946 and 1949 some 20 to 30 percent of all expenditures from the general account budget went to industry to cover operating costs and priority production.

SCAP liked the new economic institutions and the fact that the ESB had finally achieved authority (the Americans assumed that the real inspiration for the ESB was a comparable bureau they had set up in 1943 to supervise their own war economy), but SCAP still did not like the indifference to inflation of ESB Director Ishibashi.[47] It therefore purged him. Several observers on the scene at the time have suggested that Yoshida got rid of Ishibashi as a political rival by suggesting his name to General Whitney as an appropriate purgee, even though Ishibashi's prewar and wartime career as president of the *Oriental Economist* Publishing Company (Tōyō Keizai Shimpōsha) had much less to do with the war effort than Yoshida's own activities. Whatever the case, Yoshida and Ishibashi became political enemies. Ishibashi did not return to the government until December 1954, when he became MITI minister in the Hatoyama cabinet and proceeded to dismantle the restraints placed on the ministry by Yoshida's Foreign Office appointments.[48]

Shortly after Ishibashi's purge, the first Yoshida government fell and was replaced by the socialist cabinet of Katayama Tetsu. The Katayama cabinet continued and accelerated priority production, even though it no longer used that term since SCAP did not like it. The year from mid-1947 to mid-1948 was the high tide of priority production, during which the ESB, MCI, the Coal Agency, the kōdan, and

TABLE 12

Government Payments of Price Subsidies and Indemnities, 1940–1952

(Million yen)

Year	Total general account budget expenditures		Price subsidies (*kakaku chōsei hi*)		Indemnities for losses (*sonshitsu hoshō hi*)	
1940	5,856	(100%)	17	(0.3%)	60	(1.0%)
1941	7,929	(100)	95	(1.2)	55	(0.7)
1942	8,271	(100)	305	(3.7)	240	(2.9)
1943	12,491	(100)	510	(4.1)	265	(2.1)
1944	19,872	(100)	1,266	(6.4)	567	(2.8)
1946	115,207	(100)	3,731	(3.2)	22,661	(20.0)
1947	205,841	(100)	28,178	(13.7)	8,566	(4.2)
1948	461,974	(100)	93,118	(20.2)	16,632	(3.6)
1949	699,448	(100)	179,284	(25.6)	31,838	(4.6)
1950	633,259	(100)	60,162	(9.5)	7,830	(1.2)
1951	749,836	(100)	26,975	(3.6)	9,560	(1.3)
1952	873,942	(100)	40,308	(4.6)	8,183	(0.9)

SOURCE: Nakamura Takafusa, "Sengo no sangyō seisaku" (Postwar industrial policy), in Niida Hiroshi and Ono Akira, eds., *Nihon no sangyō soshiki* (Japan's industrial organization), Tokyo, 1969, p. 309.

the RFB dominated the lives of all Japanese. The strong grip of the government over the economy also led to a "black mist" (*kuroi kiri*) of corruption charges that culminated in the Shōwa Denkō case of 1948—alleged corrupt appropriations of RFB funds for the Shōwa Denkō Company—and the arrest of ESB Director Kurusu Takeo and others. Thus the irony that SCAP's transfer of all economic powers to the government (instead of leaving some of them in the hands of civilians as was done during the war) heightened public mistrust of the government.

In economic affairs the Katayama cabinet is known above all for two initiatives, both failures, that through their negative influence moved the discussion of economic policy to a new plane a year later. The first was the attempt to end inflation through wage and price controls. The priority production scheme was proving to be very hard on ordinary citizens since it subsidized producers but ruined households through inflation, rigged prices, and shortages.

It was the incoming director of the ESB in the Katayama cabinet, Wada Hiroo, who announced a new price system that was supposed to overcome these problems and guarantee a subsistence livelihood. He set prices at 65 times the 1934–36 level and wages at 27.8 times the same level, calculated on the basis of his theory that a worker's productivity had fallen to a half or a third of what it had been before the war. He also set up a guaranteed minimum wage oriented to the official price of rice, and he predicted that by November 1947 a family should be able to survive on it without going into debt or resorting to the black market. As it turned out, inflation persisted and Wada was ruined when, on October 11, 1947, the press made a sensation out of the discovery that a judge of the Tokyo District Court, Yamaguchi Yoshitada, had starved to death while trying to live on the official ration. Judge Yamaguchi left a diary stating that "even bad laws are the law, and I am pledged to defend the law." He had refused to buy black market rice.[49] However, the longer-range consequence of Wada's abortive attempt to control inflation was a much greater degree of agreement among economic planners that priority production had to be wedded in some way to control of the sources of inflation.

The second important but unsuccessful Katayama initiative was a proposal to nationalize the coal industry, an idea borrowed from the British Labour Party's policies of September 1946. Hirai Tomisaburō of MCI enthusiastically drafted a state control law for the government, but it met with intense hostility in the Diet, despite MacArthur's endorsement of the plan. Mizutani Chōzaburō, MCI minister in the socialist cabinet, attempted to gain publicity for the measure by having himself photographed in a coal mine wielding a pickax and wearing only a loincloth, and he was thereafter always known as the "loincloth minister" (*fundoshi daijin*). After innumerable disruptions and fist fights in the Diet, the heavily modified Law for the Temporary State Management of the Coal Industry (Rinji Sekitan Kōgyō Kanri Hō, number 209 of December 20, 1947, implemented on April 1, 1948) came into being. It had a three-year time limit and covered some 56 ex-zaibatsu mines. Its only concrete result was to cause a reorganization and vast expansion of the Coal Agency, which by 1950 employed some 12,000 officials. The law did not, however, serve to increase coal production beyond what the priority production system had already achieved, and it was abrogated prematurely on May 2, 1950, unlamented as the last formal effort of MCI or MITI to separate management from ownership and turn management over to the state.[50]

There can be no question that priority production achieved results. Coal production for 1947 was 29.3 million tons, or 97.7 percent of the target of 30 million tons, and production was raised during 1948 to 34,790,000 tons, or about 60 percent of the highest levels ever before achieved. The increased availability of raw materials and energy influenced all other designated industries. The ESB defended priority production in its first *Economic White Paper* (July 22, 1947) with the theory that "a twofold increase in coal production leads to a fourfold increase in general manufacturing." Kudō Shōshirō, deputy chairman of the

RFB, has written, "The size of the RFB loans was foolhardy, but by the time the Dodge Line was promulgated, Japan's industrial facilities had been 80 percent restored." Moreover, according to Ikeda Hayato the RFB saw all but 2.9 percent of its loans repaid, although the RFB's successor, the Development Bank, puts the RFB's recovery rate at only 25 percent on plant and equipment loans and 78 percent on operating subsidies. Whatever the case, Ikeda concludes, "It is not right to deny the significant role that the RFB played in the recovery of Japan's postwar economy. . . . Loans were effective to a considerable degree. It is fair to say that the RFB accomplished its purposes." [51] Although no Japanese official doubts that the RFB inflation inflicted enormous hardships on the people and that it ultimately had to be stopped, priority production had an important effect on later bureaucratic attitudes as a precedent for bolder rather than more cautious, fiscally responsible courses of action. It also intensified the nationalistic attitudes of MITI officials, since the policy had been executed in the teeth of SCAP's disapproval. [52]

There can also be no question that the actual institutions of priority production—the RFB, the Supply and Demand Control Law, the ESB, and the Coal Agency—were recreations of Japan's wartime state apparatus for the economy. RFB financing was copied directly from the wartime policies of the Ministry of Finance and the Bank of Japan. The Supply and Demand Law was, if anything, stronger than any wartime law, since it gave the state control over all commodities, not just over trade. The ESB duplicated the CPB's functions and techniques, and employed many of its personnel. And the Coal Agency was the old Fuel Bureau, reborn without its seconded military officers. The creation of the ESB and the enactment of the Supply and Demand Law also forced the reorganization of MCI on November 9, 1946, into vertical bureaus for each industry, just as the creation of the CPB and its materials mobilization planning had done in 1939. As Jerome Cohen noted at the end of his study of the wartime economy, "The wartime control system with its vestiges of cartel domination was abolished, but the substitute allocation system had a very familiar appearance." [53]

The obvious flaw in priority production was its effect on inflation, but an equally serious problem was the fact that it was carried out in the hothouse atmosphere of a blockaded economy. As the indices of economic activity for 1949 and 1950 indicate (see Table 13), great progress had been made toward the restoration of prewar levels—except in one area, foreign trade. The raw materials of Japanese industry, particularly raw cotton for the textile industry, plus petroleum and

TABLE 13

Indices of Economic Activity, 1949 and 1950

(1934–36 = 100)

Category	1949	1950
Real national income	82	97
Mining and manufacturing	72	94
Agriculture, forestry, fishing	97	100
Exports (including SCAP purchases)	15	35
Imports	30	39
Private plant and equipment investment	70	82
Per capita real national income	69	80

SOURCE: Japan Development Bank, *Nihon kaihatsu ginkō 10-nen shi* (A ten-year history of the Japan Development Bank), Tokyo, 1963, p. 18.

food, were being supplied by the United States. In 1949 Joseph Dodge contended that U.S. aid was one of the two "stilts" on which Japan's rigged economy rested; the other was RFB financing. According to SCAP, "The realization of a self-supporting status [for Japan] by 1953 requires a 700 percent increase in the volume of exports over 1948 with no more than a 120 percent increase in the volume of imports." [54] In 1949 Japanese exports were running at about $500 million per annum and imports at $900 million, with the difference being covered by disbursements from the U.S. Treasury.

According to the terms of the Potsdam Declaration, which Japan had accepted at its surrender, SCAP exercised complete control over all exports or imports of goods and services, as well as all foreign exchange and financial transactions. The little Japanese foreign trade that SCAP allowed was conducted government to government until September 1947, when private foreigners were first allowed to participate. Private Japanese could not engage in international commerce until December 1949.

On October 9, 1945, SCAP had directed the Japanese government to create a single governmental agency to account for and distribute the goods that SCAP itself imported into Japan and to receive and transfer to SCAP products manufactured by the Japanese for export. This order led to the creation of the Board of Trade (BOT; Bōeki Chō, established by Imperial ordinance 703 of December 13, 1945) as an external bureau of MCI. [55]

The BOT was an unusual institution. The fact that it was even tenuously attached to MCI rather than to the Foreign Ministry—which SCAP would have preferred, since U.S. practice is to give the Department of State final authority over American trade—was due to some fast action by Shiina and his successor as vice-minister after October 12, 1945, Toyoda Masataka. When MCI was recreated in August 1945, Shiina had thoughtfully set up a Trade Section (Kōeki-ka) in the Commercial Bureau, even though it did not have anything to do. Its head was Matsuo Taiichirō, class of 1934 and one of the few MCI foreign trade specialists. During the Pacific War he worked as chief of the Import Section in the Greater East Asia Ministry, and in September 1956 he became the first genuine MITI bureaucrat to head the International Trade Bureau after the ministry finally freed itself of dominance by Foreign Office transferees. After retirement in 1960 Matsuo headed the New York office of the Marubeni Trading Company, and during the 1970's he became president of Marubeni. Arguing that MCI already had the nucleus of the organization SCAP wanted, Toyoda barely managed to beat back the claims of the Foreign Ministry. He also recalled years later that this MCI victory had occurred early in the occupation, before SCAP knew the lay of the land very well.[56]

Even though the BOT was attached to MCI, the ministry had very little influence over it. BOT staff members from MCI were heavily outnumbered by Foreign Office officials who spoke English—an indispensable requirement, since the BOT's main business was with SCAP—and who needed assignments during the period when Japan had no other foreign relations. Until April 1947 the BOT conducted its domestic business through some 78 "semigovernmental" trade associations of exporters and importers. These associations were straight postwar continuations of the old control associations, although under new names; when SCAP realized what was going on, it banned any further use of the cartels. They were then replaced by four fully governmental corporations (kōdan), one each for minerals and industrial products, textiles, raw materials, and foodstuffs (see the Foreign Trade Public Corporations Law, number 58 of April 14, 1947). The BOT also controlled the Foreign Trade Fund, which concentrated all U.S. aid receipts and foreign exchange earned from exports into a single account to be used to buy strategic imports.

During 1947 and 1948, when the priority production system was in full operation, the ESB set basic trade policy and drew up a foreign exchange budget; the BOT in turn kept the accounts for the fund and supervised the kōdan, whose fixed capital was supplied by the government and whose working capital was obtained by loans from the BOT's Foreign Trade Fund. The kōdan actually purchased goods for export from domestic producers and sold them to the BOT, and they received consignments of SCAP imports from the BOT, which they in turn sold to consumers. Before April 1949 SCAP and the BOT also subsidized these transactions by maintaining an exchange rate between the dollar and the yen of US$1 = ¥130 for imports and US$1 = ¥330 (or ¥500, depending on the product) for exports.[57] Imports were sold in Japan at prices fixed in accordance with the ESB's supply-and-demand plans.

During the autumn of 1948 both SCAP and the Japanese recognized that they had to make some fundamental changes in the priority production system and in the state trading operations of the BOT. On October 15, 1948, the Ashida cabinet resigned—the prime minister himself had been arrested in the Shōwa Denkō scandal over the misuse of RFB funds—and Yoshida returned to power. SCAP was now determined to stop the so-called RFB inflation, for two reasons in particular. First, beginning in July 1948, in order to increase Japanese imports and thereby try to rehabilitate the economy, SCAP had started to draw on two new accounts of U.S.-appropriated aid funds—the so-called GARIOA and EROA ("Government Appropriations for Relief in Occupied Areas" and "Economic Rehabilitation of Occupied Areas")—and it could not afford to see these politically sensitive funds consumed by the fires of inflation. Second, in December 1948 Washington unequivocally ordered SCAP to make the quick attainment of Japanese economic self-sufficiency its primary objective. In order to do this, trade had to be increased, which in turn required the establishment of a fixed commercial exchange rate for the yen, and this could not be accomplished without halting inflation. The world was changing: the Cold War had begun, the communist revolution in China was nearing its denouement, and the United States now saw Japan as a strategic territory of critical importance to its own security and not just as an object for political reform policies that had grown out of the ideological confrontations of World War II.

On the Japanese side a group of planners within the ESB led by Inaba Hidezō drafted a five-year plan for Japan's economic reconstruction. It called for investment in heavy and chemical industries as the best way to increase the value of exports and to end price subsidies. Yoshida eventually disowned this plan, not because he disagreed with its contents (it is very similar to the plans MITI actually implemented during the 1950's) but because he believed that planning was synonymous with socialism.[58] Influenced by his own background and several of his closest associates, Yoshida felt that the best medicine for the Japanese economy would be to open it up to the world economy and to the discipline of international competition.

The most important of Yoshida's advisers during this period was Shirasu Jirō (b. 1902). A graduate of England's Cambridge University,

Shirasu was the son-in-law of Kabayama Aisuke, the titled (count), American-educated Satsuma clansman of Yoshida's father-in-law, Makino Nobuaki. Makino in turn was the second son of the Meiji oligarch Ōkubo Toshimichi and, like Kabayama, also a graduate of an American university. Yoshida and Shirasu had become friends during the 1930's in London, where Yoshida was serving as Japanese ambassador and Shirasu was the manager of the English branch of the Imperial Fisheries Corporation. Linked by family background, education, and overseas experience, Yoshida and Shirasu continued their affiliation after the war. Yoshida appointed Shirasu first as deputy director of the bureau for liaison with SCAP and then as deputy director of the ESB in his first cabinet. Shirasu also participated in many important negotiations, including those with General Whitney over the new constitution and, as a consultant, in those conducted by the Japanese delegation at the San Francisco Peace Conference. On December 1, 1948, Yoshida appointed Shirasu director-general of the Board of Trade.

On December 19, three weeks after Shirasu took over at the BOT, General MacArthur transmitted to the Japanese government his nine-point Economic Stabilization Plan. This called for a balanced budget, strengthened tax collection, limitations on RFB loans, improved controls over foreign trade and U.S. aid, increased production, and several other reforms that were intended to bring Japan back into international commerce but that would also impose very harsh conditions on the Japanese people until the exports started to flow. The immediate objective of the plan was to establish a fixed exchange rate. MacArthur made it clear that concrete policies to implement the nine principles were the responsibility of the Japanese government, but he added that the United States was sending an adviser to assist the government in its efforts and to monitor its progress. This adviser was the Detroit banker and former financial consultant to General Lucius D. Clay in Germany, Joseph Morrell Dodge (1890–1964).

Dodge arrived in February 1949 and, working with Yoshida's new minister of finance, Ikeda Hayato, he compelled the government to write an overbalanced budget. On April 25 he also established the official exchange rate of US$1 = ¥360 that was to last until 1971. He authorized the creation of the Japanese Export-Import Bank and the Japan Development Bank, and he supervised a host of other critical decisions that affected the Japanese economy for years to come. Dodge's most important achievement was the sudden, drastic curtailment of inflation through a draconian reduction of demand—what Maeda has called "rationalization through unemployment" (*kubikiri gōrika*). Dodge once and for all ended the debate over increased production versus control of inflation by choosing the second. His policies are properly compared with the Matsukata deflation of the 1880's and with Inoue Junnosuke's deflationary lifting of the gold embargo in 1930. Moreover, just as Inoue's deflation was overcome by the war profits of the Manchurian Incident, so Dodge's deflation was overcome by the war profits of the Korean War beginning in 1950.

While these great events were taking place, and almost unnoticed by Dodge or any other SCAP official, the Japanese contributed to the nine-point stabilization plan a reform of their own—one that probably had as great an impact on the Japanese and world economies as any of Dodge's measures. They abolished MCI and the BOT and combined their former functions into a new ministry called the Ministry of International Trade and Industry. Shirasu Jirō was the prime mover behind this development.[59] In retrospect it is clear that the merging of MCI and the BOT—or, more precisely, the turning of the BOT into an internal bureau of MCI and giving it a prime position in the ministry's chain of command—was a brilliant idea. But that it was Shirasu Jirō who had the idea and he and Yoshida who supervised its execution produced some of the most anxious days that the men of the "Kishi-Shiina line" had ever known in their bureaucratic lives.

Yoshida and Shirasu were genuinely committed to SCAP's program for the restoration of Japanese international trade, but they also were motivated by political and bureaucratic interests of their own in pushing the reform. As noted earlier, Yoshida had a deep aversion to MCI and to its close association with the controlled wartime economy and the military. Shirasu shared these views, and in addition he wanted to clean up what he claimed were corrupt practices in the BOT that he had discovered after taking office as director.[60] Yoshida planned to elevate both the Ministry of Finance (under his protégé Ikeda) and his own Ministry of Foreign Affairs to positions of greater influence in economic administration vis-à-vis MCI, and Yoshida as well as Shirasu believed that trusted Foreign Office people would be better at export promotion than the industrial policy bureaucrats. Thus, Shirasu's original idea was not so much to merge the BOT and MCI as it was to place a restaffed BOT inside MCI in order to reform it and keep it under control.

MCI officials were aware of these intentions of Yoshida and Shirasu, and they did what they could to forestall the worst. On February 2, 1949, they sent a comparatively young MCI official, Nagayama Tokio (class of 1935), to the BOT as chief of the Trade Section in the General Affairs Bureau; he was to keep tabs on Shirasu's plans. Unfortunately for MCI, this turned out to be one of the most abortive maneuvers its leaders ever undertook. Shirasu turned Nagayama around and made him one of his own lieutenants. Nagayama then returned to MITI, where he was dubbed "Emperor Nagayama," to become the first head of the MITI Secretariat (1949–53) and the official in charge of personnel appointments (the case of "Emperor Nagayama" is discussed further in Chapter 6).

Another thing the MCI officials did was to write the MITI Establishment Law (number 102, introduced in the Diet on April 22, 1949, passed on May 24, and implemented on May 25). In this law MCI tried to accommodate itself to the new order by putting the prefix "international trade" (*tsūshō*) in front of the name of each of its policy-making and industrial bureaus, the result being a series of odd-sounding titles like International Trade Enterprises Bureau (Tsūshō Kigyō Kyoku), and so forth. They also grouped all of the bureaus in charge of energy problems into one separate external bureau, the Resources Agency (Shigen Chō), to downplay their importance. The Resources Agency was abolished in 1952 in the sweeping restructuring of MITI that followed the end of the occupation, but it was re-established in 1973, when energy policy once again became salient, as the Natural Resources and Energy Agency (Shigen Enerugī Chō). All of these internal MITI arrangements were intended to reorient it away from MCI's emphasis on internal control and priority production and toward international trade and the promotion of exports; they also had the secondary purpose of trying to smuggle as much of the old MCI as possible past Shirasu's and Yoshida's scrutiny. (MITI's initial internal organization is detailed in Appendix B).

During early 1949 rumors circulated that Shirasu himself intended to become MITI's first vice-minister. This was the moment of truth for the old MCI. Its last vice-minister, Matsuda Tarō, undertook to negotiate personally with Shirasu to try to prevent this from happening. He succeeded through a compromise in which it was agreed that Matsuda would resign, that Nagayama would take over the Secretariat even though there were men senior to him in the ministry, and that the directors of the new International Trade Bureau (ITB; the old BOT reborn within MITI) would come from the Foreign Ministry—in return for all of which MCI could name one of its own people as vice-minister (Matsuda named Yamamoto Takayuki, a "Kishi-Shiina line" official). As it turned out, the first four ITB directors were, in fact, very distinguished diplomats—namely, Takeuchi Ryūji, later ambassador to West Germany, who served from May to December, 1949;

Ōda Takio, later ambassador to Indonesia, who served from December 1949 to June 1951; Ushiba Nobuhiko, later ambassador to the United States (1970–73) and in 1977 "minister of external economic relations" to deal with the U.S.-Japan trade crisis, who served from June 1951 to July 1954; and Itagaki Osamu, later ambassador to the Republic of China (Taiwan), who served from July 1954 to September 1956. It was against this backdrop of strong Foreign Office coloration that MITI came into being and Yamamoto began trying to rebuild the Kishi-Shiina line from within. Nonetheless, from the third Yoshida cabinet of February 1949 to the fall of the fifth Yoshida cabinet in December 1954, the prime minister named eight different people as MITI minister, only two of whom had any political clout at all (Ikeda, briefly, and Aichi Kiichi at the very end). This was, of course, Yoshida's way of showing that he still regarded MITI as of no political importance.

As for Shirasu, after failing to be appointed ambassador to the United States, which he had wanted, he left politics and in May 1951 became president of the Tōhoku Electric Power Company. He and Yoshida had had a parting of the ways. In 1974, for the first time in many years, Shirasu's name was again mentioned in the press. The *Japan Times* reported on August 19 that as the director of the exclusive Karuizawa Golf Club and chairman of its course committee, he refused to allow former American ambassador Robert Ingersoll to play a round on a weekend, even though Ingersoll presented a letter of introduction from Prime Minister Tanaka Kakuei. The rules of the Karuizawa Club prohibit visitors from playing on weekends, and Shirasu stuck to the rules. In order to become a member of the club, one must own a villa in Karuizawa.

The last minister of MCI and the first minister of MITI, Inagaki Heitarō (an industrialist from the old Furukawa zaibatsu, the president of Yokohama Rubber, and a member of the House of Councillors), made a speech at the time of MITI's inauguration. He pledged the new ministry to international trade and export promotion—or "trade number one–ism" (*tsūshō daiichi-shugi*) as he put it.[61] Inagaki added, however, that an increase in production, the rationalization of enterprises, and the raising of the technical level of industry were all prerequisite to an expansion of trade. He entrusted these vital tasks to the Enterprises Bureau, the only internal bureau he mentioned by name. The old MCI cadres found this very satisfactory. For almost a decade they had not paid much attention to trade and certainly not to export promotion. But the new ministry seemed to offer great opportunities for their skills, and industrial guidance in the name of trade promotion seemed like a better and more secure basis for their existence than war production or postwar rationing. The future was looking brighter.

During 1949 SCAP began a policy of transferring some of its own controlling and supervisory powers to the Japanese government in anticipation of the coming peace treaty. On February 2, 1949, the occupation delegated to the Japanese government all control over foreign exchange accruing from international trade, and it ordered the creation of a Foreign Exchange Control Board to supervise the investment of these funds in industries that were essential to Japan's economic recovery. To complete the transfer of authority, SCAP encouraged the Japanese government to pass the Foreign Exchange and Foreign Trade Control Law (number 228 of December 1, 1949).[62] Among other things, this law required that any citizen who acquired foreign exchange through trade must turn it over to a government account, and the Foreign Exchange Control Board was put in charge of how these funds would be used. Until the end of the occupation the ESB drew up periodic foreign exchange budgets to spend the foreign exchange thus concentrated, but on August 1, 1952, both the ESB and the Foreign Exchange Control Board were abolished. Their powers to enact and supervise the foreign exchange budget were transferred to the newly created Budget Section of MITI's International Trade Bureau. At the same time the powers of the ESB's old Foreign Capital Committee to supervise all imports of technology and all joint ventures were transferred to the Industrial Finance Section of the Enterprises Bureau.[63] When these changes were made, MITI came to possess weapons of industrial management and control that rivaled anything its predecessors had ever known during the prewar and wartime periods.

SCAP believed that the Foreign Exchange and Foreign Trade Control Law of December 1949 was merely temporary. As it wrote in one of its official histories:

This broad enabling act authorized the Government to maintain a unified system of control over foreign exchange and foreign trade transactions only to the extent necessary to safeguard the balance of international payments, and in effect transferred to the Government certain responsibilities which had been exercised by SCAP since the beginning of the occupation. The restrictions in the law were to be gradually relaxed by cabinet orders and ministerial ordinances as the need for them subsided.[64]

Far from being "gradually relaxed," the law persisted for the next thirty years and was still on the books during 1980; it was the single most important instrument of industrial guidance and control that MITI ever possessed. As Leon Hollerman put it from the perspective of 1979, "In liquidating the occupation by 'handing back' operational control to the Japanese, SCAP naively presided not only over the transfer of its own authority but also over the institutionalization of the most restrictive foreign trade and foreign exchange control system ever devised by a major free nation." [65] In the next chapter we shall turn to what the officials of MITI did with these and other new powers.

Virtually all Japanese regard the defeat of 1945 as the most important watershed in modern Japanese history since the Meiji Restoration of 1868. However, from the point of view of the history of industrial policy, I believe that the 1940's are one continuous era: the period of the high tide of state control. Beginning with the policies of the Tōjō government and continuing with their acceleration by SCAP, the Japanese state came to dominate virtually all economic decisions, from those of zaibatsu enterprises to those of individual households. Tōjō and his associates intended this outcome but were unable to achieve it completely; the Allied reformers did not intend it but promoted it anyway, first out of their commitment to making the government more responsible, and subsequently out of their commitment to Japanese economic recovery and growth as part of the renewed global resistance to totalitarianism. The prime political beneficiaries of these developments were the economic bureaucrats; the ultimate economic beneficiaries were the Japanese people.

The longer-range significance of the achievement of state control, however, was to reveal its weaknesses. The fundamental political problem of the state-guided high-growth system is that of the relationship between the state bureaucracy and privately owned businesses. If this relationship is overbalanced in favor of one side or the other, it will result in either the loss of the benefits of competition or the dilution of the state's priorities. State control refers to the attempt to separate management from ownership and to put management under state supervision. Whereas big business typically prefers self-imposed control, economic bureaucrats typically prefer state control. During the 1940's, when state control was achieved, its weaknesses— the growth of bureaucracy, irresponsible management, corruption, and lowered efficiency—were also fully manifested. The result was that just as the deficiencies of self-control under the Important Industries Control Law of 1931 led to the movement toward state control, the deficiencies of state control under the Ministry of Munitions and the postwar MCI led to the government-business relationship of the high-growth era—that is, to genuine public-private cooperation.

True state control did not last long after 1949. Its primary contribution to the later high-growth system was the irreversible establishment of the economic general staff at the heart of all Japanese economic policy-making and administration. In the years after the occupation the economic bureaucracy began by degrees to share its powers with big business, consulting it on all important issues, providing state incentives for industrial rationalization, and blurring the distinctions between the state and the private sector by insinuating numerous ex-bureaucrats into the board rooms of the economically strategic industries.

This trend toward genuine public-private cooperation grew out of a combination of the effects of war destruction and the reforms of the occupation. The old zaibatsu were weakened vis-à-vis the state-control bureaucrats by the physical depletion of their capital assets and by the occupation's goal of deconcentrating the economy. At the same time the new constitution and other reforms such as the fostering of the labor movement made state control politically impossible except as a short-term expedient. The economic bureaucrats might rule on the basis of their intrinsic talents, but they could never reign openly under Japan's new democratic system. Thus, both government and industry recognized the need for a political division of labor—one that would both advance the positive development program and forestall disruptions of it by the newly enfranchised groups in the society.

The resulting Japanese political system of the 1950's and 1960's bore some resemblance to the "corporatism" that Charles Maier believes emerged in interwar continental Europe. He writes:

The key to consensus or mere civic peace was either forcible suppression or constant brokerage. Any major organized interest could disrupt a modern economy or imperil social order, hence had to be silenced by duress or granted a minimum of demands. The need for brokerage switched the fulcrum of decision making from the legislature as such to the ministries or new bureaucracies. During the war, ministries of munitions had developed into economic planning agencies. . . . They coopted private business in this task, sharing public powers to increase the scope of regulation. Although wartime controls were not retained, the 1920s did not simply revert to the degree of market freedom prevailing before 1914. . . . A defining characteristic of the corporatist system . . . was the blurring of the distinction between political and economic power. Clout in the market place—especially the potential to paralyze an industrial economy—made for political influence. Consequently, economic bargaining became too crucial to be left to the private market, and state agencies stepped in as active mediators.[66]

The causes of post–World War II Japanese-style "corporatism" were similar, but its priorities were different, and the state played a role that went beyond mediation. The Japanese well understood the potential in their situation for disruption and civil strife as new groups in the society tested and adapted the Allied-installed democratic system. It is astonishing how easily foreign admirers of the tranquility of Japanese society during the 1970's forget the strikes, riots, demonstrations, and sabotage that marked the period 1949–61. But more important than the need to mediate among the demands of interest groups was the need, recognized by all Japanese, to escape from the economic misery and dependence on foreign assistance that the events of the 1940's had produced. Capital was in short supply, the new technology needed was to be found only overseas, costs were too high, the country imported more than it sold abroad, and the ability to compete internationally was as yet only a dream. Under these circumstances, the role of the state was never questioned. In circumstances quite different from either the 1930's or the 1940's, the economic general staff, enjoying more power than under self-control but less than under state control, was finally given a chance to try to make Japan a wealthy nation.

SIX

The Institutions of High-Speed Growth

N O O N E observing the Japanese economy from the vantage point of Dodge's "stabilization panic" of 1949–50 could have imagined either the high-speed growth that was to occur between 1955 and 1961 or the "golden sixties" that lay beyond. The years of the Dodge Line and the Korean War were characterized by constant confusion, high hopes alternating with deep despair, political and bureaucratic contention among numerous power centers, and governmental expediency in the face of one crisis after another. The Japanese had to adjust successively to the virtual strangulation of their economy under Dodge's draconian antiinflation measures, to the Korean War boom, to fundamental changes in United States foreign policy, to the deep post–Korean War recession, and to the discovery of their own balance-of-payments business cycle. They also had to come to terms with the institutions the occupation had left behind and with the attitudes of their own bureaucrats and industrialists toward these institutions.

During the period 1949 to 1954 the Japanese forged the institutions of their high-growth system. In 1954, with the passing of the Yoshida government and other political developments, MITI put the system into effect. To understand the Japanese economic performance of the late 1950's, it is necessary to appreciate that when all the various institutions of the Korean War era were put together and operated by an "economic general staff," they constituted a system—although no single institution was ever created with the emerging system in mind. As Nakamura Takafusa has argued, the agencies of 1955–61 for forcing investment from a poor, capital-starved society resulted from the combination of two complicated sets of circumstances—the persistence of wartime and occupation controls until very late in the postwar era, and the tremendous strengthening of competition that was an unintended consequence of the emergency measures for industrial financing adopted by the government during the "stabilization panic."[1]

Some of the elements of what became MITI's high-growth system derived from the government's selection of industries for "nurturing," perfection of measures to commercialize the products of these chosen industries, and development of means for regulating the cutthroat competition that the first two sets of policies generated. The tools in the hands of the economic bureaucrats included control over all foreign exchange and imports of technology, which gave them the power to choose industries for development; the ability to dispense preferential financing, tax breaks, and protection from foreign competition, which gave them the power to lower the costs of the chosen industries; and the authority to order the creation of cartels and bank-based industrial conglomerates (a new and rationalized version of the zaibatsu, now made totally dependent on government largesse), which gave them the power to supervise competition. This high-growth system was one of the most rational and productive industrial policies ever devised by any government, but its essential rationality was not perceived until after it had already started producing results unprecedented for Japan or any other industrialized economy.

The system began to be forged during the Dodge Line. Dodge's policies certainly ended inflation, but at the cost of almost shattering what little economic recovery had been achieved through priority production. The cutting off of government price subsidies and loans to industry from the Reconstruction Finance Bank (RFB) eliminated the main sources of capital in the system, and there simply were no alternative sources to fill the void, either from the internal savings of enterprises or from the new capital market that SCAP was trying to foster. Equally important, when governmental aid to designated sectors of priority production stopped and SCAP began to promote export industries, there was a radical reallocation of what little private capital was available. Funds for coal and electric power development declined drastically, while funds for the reestablished textile industry shot up.[2] SCAP was pleased by this development, since textiles earned foreign exchange, but Japanese bureaucrats saw an energy crisis looming. And even the policy of export promotion was seriously undermined by the devaluation on September 18, 1949, of the British pound. The pound was cut by 30.5 percent in terms of U.S. dollars, its value dropping from $4.03 to $2.80, a step that caused some 30 other countries also to devalue their currencies. Japan, which had just pegged its own currency at ¥360 to $1, suddenly found that its products were overpriced in its principal export markets. During the winter of 1949–50 the Japanese people faced some of the harshest economic conditions they had seen since the war ended, and the threat of revolution came perilously close.[3]

On June 25, 1950, warfare erupted on the Korean peninsula, and the United States intervened. This development ended the "stabilization panic" quantitatively, if not qualitatively. In addition to the American foreign aid that had sustained the Japanese economy since stabilization began, the United States now began to place extensive orders with Japanese firms for ammunition, trucks, uniforms, communications equipment, and other products needed for the war effort. The Americans also started to buy fertilizers and consumer goods destined for South and Southeast Asian noncommunist countries as part of the American foreign aid effort. For example, between July 1950 and February 1951 the U.S. armed forces and the U.S. Economic Cooperation Administration placed orders with Japanese firms for some 7,079 trucks worth nearly $13 million; this was the key to the revival of the Japanese automotive industry.[4] The Enterprises Bureau of MITI supervised these "special procurements" (*tokuju*) to ensure that the foreign exchange thus gained was used for investment in basic industries. For a while the "special procurements boom," as it was called, provided a false sense of euphoria and a feeling that the hard times were over. Special procurements plus the expenditures of U.S. troops and their dependents constituted 37 percent of all foreign exchange receipts in 1952–53, and they still contributed 11 percent in 1959–60.[5]

This windfall, however, created major internal financial difficulties. Japanese firms could not obtain investment capital fast enough to retool to meet the orders that the Americans were placing, and their working capital was insufficient to keep them in business if even a few of their contracts involved delays in payment of six months or more. The Japanese economic bureaucrats debated among themselves about what emergency measures to take to rectify this situation, and the outcome of this debate had a profound significance for the economy of later years and for governmental economic policy. It led to the two-tiered structure of government-guaranteed "city bank" overloaning and newly created government-owned "banks of last resort." These latter institutions, particularly the Japan Development Bank (Nihon Kaihatsu Ginkō, abbreviated Kaigin), came to possess—and still retain today—tremendous indicative powers over the whole economy as a result of their decisions to make or refuse "policy loans."

TABLE 14

Governors of the Bank of Japan, 1945–1975

Governor and tenure	Background
Shibusawa Keizō, 3/44–10/45	Yokohama Specie Bank; Dai Ichi Bank.
Araki Eikichi, 10/45–6/46	Bank of Japan; purged; depurged, 1950.
Ichimada Naoto, 6/46–12/54	Bank of Japan; later minister of finance in the Hatoyama and Kishi cabinets.
Araki Eikichi, 12/54–11/56	See above.
Yamagiwa Masamichi, 11/56–12/64	Ex-vice-minister of finance; Export-Import Bank.
Usami Makoto, 12/64–12/69	Mitsubishi Bank.
Sasaki Tadashi, 12/69–12/74	Bank of Japan.
Morinaga Teiichiro, 12/74–12/79	Ex-vice-minister of finance; Export-Import Bank.

The two great antagonists in this industrial finance debate were Ikeda Hayato (1899–1965), former vice-minister of finance and minister of finance in the third Yoshida cabinet (February 1949 to October 1952), and Ichimada Naoto (b. 1893), governor of the Bank of Japan from June 1946 to December 1954.* Their conflict was based as much on political and bureaucratic differences as it was on genuine differences over policy. As it turned out, Ikeda emerged victorious and his ministry asserted its dominance over the Bank of Japan (particularly after November 1956, when for the first time in 29 years the ministry named one of its own officials governor of the bank; see Table 14). But Ichimada made his own important contribution to Japan's economic future, despite the bad press he has received from MITI officials because of his opposition to heavy industrialization. During the Dodge Line and Korean War periods, Ikeda and Ichimada each invented one tier of the two-tiered Japanese system of industrial financing—a wonderful instrument on which MITI would become a virtuoso player.

Ikeda was not precisely an inflationist in the mold of Ishibashi Tan-

---

*In order to follow Ikeda's activities, the following dates should be kept in mind. While serving as minister of finance in the third Yoshida cabinet, Ikeda also held the concurrent post of minister of MITI from February to April, 1950. Yoshida then named him MITI minister in his fourth cabinet, but he was forced to resign after only a month in office (Oct.–Nov. 1952) because of his "slip of the tongue" in the Diet (discussed below). Between 1952 and 1956 he held various Liberal Party posts, including that of secretary-general. From December 1956 to July 1957 he returned to the cabinet as minister of finance. His last cabinet post (June 1959 to July 1960) before becoming prime minister was again as minister of MITI. References to Ikeda's "own" ministry of course refer to the Ministry of Finance, in which he served as a bureaucrat from 1925 to 1948.

zan, but he was also not a typical fiscal conservative of the Finance Ministry. During the late 1950's he fought as hard against his own ministry to get his ideas of "positive finance" accepted as he had earlier against the deflationists of the central bank.[6] He believed that the government was the only available source of capital for industry, and he was a supporter of the activities of such governmental financial institutions as the Industrial Bank before and during the war and the RFB during the occupation. Although his name is associated with so-called low-posture politics because, as prime minister after Kishi and in the wake of the 1960 security treaty riots, he shifted the focus of government from politics to economics, he was very outspoken in internal debate.[7] On November 27, 1952, in a famous incident, Ikeda was forced to resign as MITI minister and accept a temporary setback in his political career because he had said too candidly in the Diet, "It makes no difference to me if five or ten small businessmen are forced to commit suicide" as a result of the heavy industrialization efforts.[8] Ikeda must be recorded as the single most important individual architect of the Japanese economic miracle.

Ichimada held almost directly contrary financial views. He had served in Germany before the war and was personally acquainted with the German inflation, so he strongly agreed with SCAP's opposition to Ishibashi's inflationary policies of 1947. Throughout the occupation, with most senior zaibatsu executives purged and the commercial banks virtually the only institutions left unscathed, Ichimada wielded enormous powers over the banks and their borrowers through his decisions on how much the Bank of Japan would let them borrow. After Dodge launched his deflation and the "stabilization panic" hit, Ichimada—now known to the press as "Pope Ichimada"—came to exercise life-or-death powers over businesses. Partly as a result of his German experiences and partly because most of the inflationists were concentrated in the Finance Ministry, Ichimada came to stand for a deflationary, balanced-budget fiscal policy and for a mildly expansionist monetary policy. During the capital shortage Ichimada upped the tempo of government loans to city banks (the twelve national banks to which the Bank of Japan extends loan privileges), who in turn distributed the funds to the industrialists who were clamoring for money to expand their facilities. He never went as fast as Ikeda and MITI would have liked, but he started the process of central bank "overloaning" that led to the nexus between the city banks and industry that persists to the present day. In the process he virtually insured that SCAP's proposal for a capital market for industrial financing (a stock exchange) would remain stillborn for at least twenty years.

After only a few years of the Bank of Japan's monetary expansion, the Japanese industrial system took on one of its most distinctive characteristics—the pattern of dependencies in which a group of enterprises borrows from a bank well beyond the individual companies' capacity to repay, or often beyond their net worth, and the bank in turn overborrows from the Bank of Japan. Since the central bank is the ultimate guarantor of the system, it gains complete and detailed control over the policies and lending decisions of its dependent "private" banks. This so-called indirect financing formula (*kansetsu kin'yū hōshiki*) is really only indirect in appearance. As Itō explains, "Unlike prewar enterprise which was founded on the basis of its own capital, postwar enterprise has been dependent on loans from commercial banks for about 70–80 percent of its capital; and in the final analysis these loans are provided on credit from the Bank of Japan, Japan's central bank."[9] The opposite side of this coin, of course, is a relatively slight dependence on equity. "In 1935," writes Broadbridge, "68 percent of industrial funds raised, apart from reserves and depreciation, were derived from sales of stock; in 1963, the figure had fallen to 10 percent."[10] At least in terms of its financing and ownership structure, Japan was a more capitalist country in the 1930's and 1940's than it was in the 1950's or 1960's.

Ichimada himself appears to have been reluctant to see the system of overloaning expand as far as it did. He regularly declared that the limits of central bank underwriting had been reached, and that a capital crisis was imminent.[11] Also, in order to protect himself and his bank, he became increasingly dependent on guidelines supplied by MITI's Enterprises Bureau on the amounts of capital various industries would need for a given period, and above all on the industries that other branches of the government were protecting and promoting.[12] If the Bank of Japan or the city banks had ever ventured very far from MITI's guidelines and taken on support of an undesignated industry, the risks not just to a particular bank but to the whole system would have become intolerable.

Although it was born of the capital shortage that accompanied the Dodge Line (and is not, as some writers contend, an element of Japanese culture itself), the system of bank overloans was also attractive to Ikeda and his MITI colleagues.[13] It revealed such possibilities of control over and coordination of their highly limited resources that they took steps to continue and institutionalize the system. As Ikeda noted in 1952, dividends on equity shares are paid from corporate profits after taxes, whereas interest on bank loans is deductible for tax purposes. It was thus less expensive for an enterprise to borrow the

funds it needed from a bank—assuming that it could get them at all—
than to try to raise money through issuing new shares.[14] Since the tax
system inherited from the occupation was under the control of the Finance Ministry, it was an easy step—along with many others to be
discussed below—to insure that these tax advantages were perpetuated and enlarged. And since the bureaucratic proponents of heavy
industrialization saw merits in Ichimada's system, it was continued
long after the crisis it was intended to meet had disappeared. A capital market slowly developed in Japan and came to play an increasingly
important role in industrial finance, but it did not even begin to rival
bank lending as a source of capital until the 1970's.

One advantage of the overloaning system was that managers were
not pressured by stockholders, which meant that they could ignore
short-term profitability as a measure of their own performance and
could concentrate instead on such things as foreign market penetra-
tion, quality control, and long-term product development. This became a considerable advantage when Japanese managers began to
compete seriously with American firms, since short-term profitability
and the payment of dividends were the keys to the availability of capital for American enterprises (not to mention also being the keys to an
American manager's longevity in his job). Another advantage was the
ease and precision with which the government could employ monetary controls alone to expand or contract the tempo of economic activity in response to international balance of payments constraints. A
less desirable feature of the dependence on borrowing was that it left
Japanese companies with so little paid-in capital that they were easy
targets for foreign purchase. However, this state of affairs only increased civilian demands for the protection of the Japanese economy,
which the bureaucrats wanted to pursue anyway on nationalistic
grounds. The resultant community of interests reinforced both sides.

Of all the consequences of Ichimada's system, certainly the most
important was the fostering of bank keiretsu (conglomerate groups)
as successors to the zaibatsu, since without them the Japanese economy might not have enjoyed the high degrees of competition that
prevailed in its otherwise government-dominated big business sector.
By the 1960's, as we shall see in the next chapter, many MITI officials
had begun to doubt the value of this feature—but it must be said that
MITI bureaucrats, none of whom had ever experienced an open economic system until the 1960's, have consistently undervalued the role
of competition in the structure they created.

Since the time of the stabilization panic, which had made enterprises dependent on banks for their capital, each enterprise had tried

to develop a close working relationship with a particular bank; it did not necessarily get all the money it needed or preferential terms from its primary bank, but it did get the one thing it could not do without—access to capital in the first place because it was an established customer. The banks in turn became dependent upon the financial health of their heavily indebted priority industries and therefore took responsibility for them. The resulting cooperative arrangements looked very much like the old German banking groups, such as those of the Deutsche or Dresdner banks, with cross-shareholding between banks and affiliated industries (such shareholding is illegal in the United States).* The difference from the German pattern was that the Japanese government exercised much greater control over the "financial lineages" (*kin'yū keiretsu*), as they came to be called, than the German government ever did over its bank groups and syndicates. The "big six" among the Japanese conglomerates that came into being during the 1950's were those based on the Fuji, Sanwa, Dai Ichi, Mitsui, Mitsubishi, and Sumitomo banks. The Fuji Bank, for example, established financial ties with the old Yasuda zaibatsu, the old Asano zaibatsu (which contributed the Fuji group's steel company, Nippon Kōkan), and Ayukawa Gisuke's old Nissan companies—and after 1955 with its own trading company, Marubeni-Iida, formed by the merger of Marubeni and Takashimaya-Iida.

A typical Japanese group includes a big bank, several industrial firms, and a general trading company. The bank plays the critical role during expanding business conditions by supplying capital to the members, and the trading company plays the critical role during contracting business conditions by importing raw materials on credit and fiercely promoting exports of products that cannot be sold domestically. SCAP broke up the old zaibatsu trading companies, but as soon as the occupation was over, MITI busily rebuilt them. Mitsui Bussan and Mitsubishi Shōji were dissolved on November 30, 1947, and their liquidation completed on August 31, 1950. The largest and most successful Mitsui offshoots were the Dai Ichi, Sanshin, and Kyokutō trading companies, while the leading Mitsubishi splinters were the Tōzai, Fuji, and Tōyō trading companies. By the end of 1952, the successor Mitsubishi companies had already recombined, but Mitsui took until the end of 1955 to come back together.[15]

*Ralf Dahrendorf's observation is to the point: "One of the decisive differences between industrialization in Germany and in the Anglo-Saxon countries lies in the role of banks, which themselves combined into mammoth financial empires at an early stage, carried by their credits and investments a considerable part of the weight of German industrialization, and at the same time facilitated the rapid growth of large industrial units." *Society and Democracy in Germany* (Garden City, N.Y.: Doubleday, 1967), p. 37.

MITI helped rebuild the trading companies by issuing laws that authorized tax write-offs for the costs of opening foreign branches and for contingency funds against bad debt trade contracts, and as early as 1953 the ministry's powerful Industrial Rationalization Council (discussed below) called for the "keiretsu-ization" of trading companies and manufacturers. This meant, in practice, that MITI would assign an enterprise to a trading company if it did not already have an affiliation. Through its licensing powers and ability to supply preferential financing, MITI ultimately winnowed about 2,800 trading companies that existed after the occupation down to around 20 big ones, each serving a bank keiretsu or a cartel of smaller producers.[16] The bank groups were the successors to the old zaibatsu, and they came into being for the same reason that the old zaibatsu had been fostered in the Meiji era—to concentrate scarce capital on key developmental projects. However, they differed from the old zaibatsu in that their internal organization was much more businesslike than the old family-centered empires, and they competed with each other much more vigorously.

This competition was ultimately caused by the nature of the banks' assets. As Abegglen and Rapp observe, "The financial risks associated with high debt levels are very much reduced in Japan by the fact that the central bank stands implicit guarantor of the debt positions of major Japanese companies."[17] It was this elimination of risk that above everything else made competition mandatory. And the risks for bank managers were even further reduced by powerful Finance Ministry controls over all interest rates and dividend rates, over the scope of a bank's operations, and over permission to open new branches, which meant that a banker really had only one thing to concentrate on—competition for the expansion of a bank's share of loans and depositors. Under these conditions city banks did everything in their power to discover and come to the aid of growth industries and growth enterprises. Most important, each bank group had to have its entry in each new industry fostered by MITI or face being frozen out of the truly riskless sectors.

The result of these pressures and incentives was the famous "one set–ism" of high-growth Japan, a term meaning that each bank group acquired or created within it a full complement of companies covering all the government-designated growth industries, regardless of whether it made business sense to do so. This competition became the bane of MITI's existence during the 1960's, when, for example, the ministry fostered four petrochemical companies but soon found that five more were building their own complexes as fast and on as big a scale as the chosen leaders. Overproduction was inevitable, but this was not as serious a danger from the point of view of any one particular group (since MITI would have to organize a cartel to allocate market shares) as not being in on an important government-guaranteed industry at all.

Controlled though the Japanese economy surely was, Ichimada's modest efforts to expand the supply of capital during the dark days of 1950 thus led to much fiercer competition among big businesses than is common in other open economies dominated by oligopolies. Even the government's purely indicative "plans" of 1955 and after (discussed below) fed the competitive fires by revealing the industries that the government planned to commercialize over the coming term—that is, those in which the risks would be close to nil unless Japan itself went under. It is not at all surprising, therefore, or a reflection on the competence of government planners (as some scholars seem to think), that the targets for the designated priority sectors in all EPA plans have invariably been wildly overfulfilled.[18]

The second tier of the industrial finance system, the government banks created by Ikeda, came into being to supplement the city banks at the point where the Bank of Japan had to place ultimate limits on how much it could lend. Shortly after the outbreak of the Korean War, Ichimada declared that the overloans had in fact reached their limits.[19] It would never have been possible, in any case, for the city banks alone to have supplied all the capital needed for the rehabilitation of Japan, particularly during the early period of capital shortage and particularly for the nonexporting but key infrastructure sectors of coal, steel, and electric power. These were the industries that the RFB had served, and Ikeda clearly recognized the need to create a replacement for it. His problem was that the Government Section of SCAP and Dodge both derided the RFB as the cause of hyperinflation, and some SCAP purists remained hostile to anything that smacked of the "national policy companies" of the prewar and wartime eras. The RFB's primary weakness was that a good portion of its funds had come straight out of the general account budget; Dodge had eliminated that source through his absolute requirement that Japan maintain balanced and even overbalanced budgets. What other sources of capital for a new bank were there?

There were two sources, primarily. The first was U.S. "counterpart funds" (*mikaeri shikin*)—the yen proceeds from the sale in Japan of U.S. aid products; since Dodge's arrival, these proceeds had been carefully segregated into a special account rather than being combined with all foreign receipts, as was the case during the first half of the occupation. The second source of capital was the funds from the government-operated postal savings system, which were held in trust accounts by the Ministry of Finance. The postal savings system for small savers had existed since the Meiji era, and it had experienced a checkered career of alleged scandals and misuse by the government for various political ventures; for example, the Terauchi government in 1917 and 1918 had used the people's savings to redeem the notorious Nishihara loans to China. During the occupation SCAP had restricted government use of the postal savings accounts primarily to collateral for local bonds, but with the ending of inflation the accounts began to grow quite large as savers turned to the post offices rather than the private banks, which they did not fully trust. Ikeda wanted to open up the use of these funds to support the reindustrialization effort, and he wanted to see the counterpart monies spent for vital projects that the banks could not cover. He thus set out to negotiate these proposals with Dodge.

Ikeda first proposed an export bank, and this idea went down much easier with the Americans than his second one—a new version of the RFB. The lack of adequate banking facilities to handle longer-term loans than were commercially available for the export of capital goods was having a retarding effect on trade, and SCAP therefore readily agreed to the creation of the Export Bank of Japan (law number 268 of December 15, 1950). The bank was established on December 28, 1950, and opened for business on February 1, 1951. The initial capital of ¥15 billion came from U.S. aid counterpart funds and from general account budget appropriations. The prime minister appointed the bank's president, and the Ministry of Finance supervised the bank. In April 1952, when the occupation ended, the government renamed it the Export-Import Bank of Japan and gave it the additional task of lending Japanese importers the funds they needed for advance payments for commodity imports approved by MITI. By 1958 the Export-Import Bank's capital account had risen to ¥38.8 billion, and its total loans outstanding amounted to ¥60.3 billion.

During the 1950's the largest proportion of Export-Import Bank loans went for exports, but not all of these truly left the country. A favored category of loans was for what MITI dubbed "plant" (*puranto*) exports, except that the term "plant" in Japanese had come to have a special bureaucratic meaning. Shimamura Takehisa of MITI's Machinery Bureau (MITI 1938 to 1965, and after retirement a senior executive of Furukawa Electric) defined the word—since there were so few actual exports of complete factories in the early period—to mean any export contract worth more than ¥10 million and with a delay in payment of six months or more. Most "plant exports" in the mid-1950's were actually ships, and a good many of them were only exported for a day. They were then resold back to Japanese shipping companies, the whole transaction having been subsidized by the Export-Import Bank. During the recession of 1954, as we shall see later in this chapter, MITI came up with an even more ambitious scheme for paying for ship "exports"—it linked their manufacture and sale to the extremely lucrative sugar and banana importing business.[20] The age was one of quite inventive ad hoc arrangements.

Of the six government banks established between 1949 and 1953 (plus two more that continued undisturbed from the prewar era), the most important for industrial policy was the Japan Development Bank (JDB), created by law number 108 of March 31, 1951.* Despite Ikeda's pleas to Dodge that the JDB be allowed to borrow from the postal savings accounts, Dodge refused. During 1951 Dodge authorized disbursements from the savings trusts for specific government projects, but because of SCAP's hostility to the JDB, the funds could not be assigned to cover such an RFB-like operation. SCAP provided all of the JDB's initial capital of ¥10 billion from counterpart funds, and it allowed the bank to be established only on condition that it would not be permitted to issue debentures, borrow funds, or grant loans to cover an enterprise's operating costs. Old occupation hands were still very wary of reigniting inflation. According to SCAP historians, the JDB "was to provide long-term equipment loans to private enterprise when the commercial banks were not in a position to assume the risks involved."[21]

Within a year of its creation the JDB became one of MITI's most important instruments of industrial policy. The bank itself had been put under the Ministry of Finance's administrative jurisdiction, but MITI exercised a predominant policy-making influence because it was given the duty of screening all loan applications and making annual estimates—to be transmitted to the bank's board of directors—of the shortfall between available and needed capital. For example, for fiscal 1952 the Enterprises Bureau calculated that investments in the steel industry would require ¥42 billion, of which the steel firms could generate or borrow from their banks ¥31.5 billion, and that coal

---

*The eight government banks existing at the end of 1953 were the Central Cooperative Bank for Agriculture and Forestry (1926), the Bank for Commerce and Industrial Cooperatives (1936), the People's Finance Corporation (1949), the Housing Loan Corporation (1950), the Export-Import Bank (1950), the Japan Development Bank (1951), the Agriculture, Forestry, and Fishery Finance Corporation (1953), and the Smaller Business Finance Corporation (1953). See Chalmers Johnson, *Japan's Public Policy Companies* (Washington, D.C.: American Enterprise Institute, 1978).

would need ¥40 billion, of which ¥27 billion could be raised from civilian sources. The rest was to be provided by the JDB.[22] In addition to these inputs to the bank, MITI also placed some of its important retired "seniors" on the JDB's board, beginning with Matsuda Tarō, the last MCI vice-minister and a member of the JDB board from August 1952 to June 1957 (Matsuda was succeeded by Yoshioka Chiyozō, MITI 1934 to 1957, and Yoshioka was succeeded by Imai Hiroshi, MITI 1937 to 1962).[23]

Almost as soon as the occupation ended, the government amended the JDB's charter (law number 224 of July 1, 1952) giving it authority to issue its own bonds and lifting the loan ceilings that SCAP had imposed. At the same time the Ministry of Finance modified all of the statutes covering the postal savings accounts, combining them into one large investment pool named the Fiscal Investment and Loan Plan (FILP; Zaisei Tōyūshi Keikaku). This "second" or "investment" budget was constructed annually by officials of the Ministry of Finance and of the Industrial Capital Section of MITI's Enterprises Bureau. From 1953 on it became the single most important financial instrument for Japan's economic development.

In order to keep FILP healthy and to ensure that people kept depositing their savings in the post office, the Ministry of Finance made the interest on the first ¥3 million (circa $15,000) that an individual deposited tax exempt and authorized highly competitive interest rates. The system became a rousing success, so much so that during 1980 the total amount of postal savings was estimated at nearly ¥55 trillion (four times the assets of the Bank of America, the world's largest commercial bank); this compares to ¥31 trillion in personal deposits with all city banks and ¥30 trillion in personal deposits with regional banks. (During the 1970's the postal savings system was to become the major means of tax evasion in Japan, since an individual saver could open as many ¥3 million savings accounts as there were post offices in the country, and the Postal Ministry claimed that it was simply unable to monitor the numbers of the accounts involved. To compound the problem, postmasters routinely recommended to savers whose accounts threatened to exceed ¥3 million that they open an account at another post office.)[24] When FILP was created, the Development Bank was authorized to borrow from its funds, and then to make loans to industrial customers who had been approved by MITI.

From 1953 to 1961 the direct supply of capital by the government to industry (as distinct from its indirect supply via overloans) ranged from 38 percent to 19 percent (see Table 15). The JDB itself contributed 22 percent in 1953 and only 5 percent in 1961, but even as the size of its loans declined relative to the expansion of city-bank funding, the bank retained its power to "guide" capital through the indicative effect of its decisions to support or not support a new industry. A JDB loan, regardless of its size, became MITI's seal of approval on an enterprise, and the company that had received a JDB loan could easily raise whatever else it needed from private resources.[25]

Much more important than the figures for all industry during the period 1953–55 are the figures on the JDB's contributions to MITI's designated strategic industries—electric power, ships, coal, and steel. Some 83 percent of JDB financing in this period went to these four industries, accounting for 23.1 percent of all investment in electric power, 33.6 percent in shipbuilding, 29.8 percent in coal mining, and 10.6 percent in new steel plants.[26]

The enormous weight of government investment is the inspiration behind the most common expression employed by Japanese academics to characterize their own economy—namely, "state monopoly capitalism" (*kokka dokusen shihon-shugi*)—even though the Marxist flavor of this concept is more of a tribute to academic fashion in Japan than it is to any genuine Marxist idea. Professor Endō explains that he means by the term the activities of the state to supply capital or other funds to industry on terms not available from the private sector and for specific, state-determined policy objectives. In his view FILP is the most typical institution of state monopoly capitalism, a configuration that he believes originated in Japan during the great depression, and that has continued uninterruptedly to the present time.[27]

Although they would be unlikely to employ so ideologically loaded a concept and would certainly reject the Marxist implication that as state officials they worked for some propertied "class," the officials of MITI's Enterprises Bureau would have to admit that Endō has accurately described the functions of FILP. From 1953 on FILP has always been from a third to a half the size of the general account budget and has ranged from a low of 3.3 percent (1956) to a high of 6.3 percent (1972) of GNP. Until 1973 it was totally controlled by the economic bureaucrats and was not subject to the scrutiny or approval of the Diet. As Boltho says, it was "the main means of circumventing the rigid balanced-budget principles laid down after the war."[28]

During the period that Ichimada and Ikeda were erecting this two-tiered financial structure, MITI was busy putting its own house in order and preparing to lead the operational side of the developmental effort. When MITI came into being in May 1949, it still faced three more years of occupation and five more years of hostility from Prime Minister Yoshida. The most important organ of the ministry in these

TABLE 15

Sources of Industrial Capital, 1953–1961

(Hundred million yen)

	1953	1954	1955	1956	1957	1958	1959	1960	1961
Private financial organs:									
Banks only	1,945	1,592	1,767	3,387	3,559	4,125	4,808	6,427	7,053
	(49%)	(42%)	(40%)	(49%)	(44%)	(44%)	(42%)	(42%)	(39%)
All other organs	511	969	1,289	1,913	2,351	3,029	4,132	5,849	7,286
	(13)	(25)	(29)	(28)	(29)	(32)	(36)	(39)	(40)
SUBTOTAL	2,456	2,531	3,056	5,300	5,910	7,154	8,940	12,276	14,339
	(62)	(66)	(69)	(77)	(74)	(76)	(77)	(81)	(80)
Public financial organs:									
Japan Development Bank	871	575	464	448	632	589	681	650	862
	(22)	(15)	(11)	(7)	(8)	(6)	(6)	(4)	(5)
All other government banks	415	455	559	716	930	1,009	1,338	1,555	1,850
	(11)	(12)	(13)	(10)	(12)	(11)	(12)	(10)	(10)
Special accounts	195	274	341	431	569	716	587	651	986
	(5)	(7)	(8)	(6)	(7)	(8)	(5)	(4)	(6)
SUBTOTAL	1,481	1,303	1,364	1,595	2,131	2,314	2,606	2,856	3,697
	(38)	(34)	(31)	(23)	(27)	(24)	(23)	(19)	(20)
TOTAL	3,937	3,835	4,420	6,896	8,040	9,468	11,547	15,132	18,036
	(100)	(100)	(100)	(100)	(100)	(100)	(100)	(100)	(100)

SOURCE: Endō Shōkichi, Zaisei tōyūshi (Fiscal investment and loan funds), Tokyo, 1966, p. 149.

early years was the International Trade Bureau, the successor to the old Board of Trade. But the fact that the bureau's chief and most of its senior officials were diplomats marking time until foreign relations were restored inevitably meant that the bureau was known as a "branch store of the Foreign Office" (*Gaimu-shō no demise*)—and was deeply resented as such by the veterans of the Kishi-Shiina era. This was also MITI's "dark age," when the position of chief secretary was occupied by Nagayama Tokio, who had been placed in office by Yoshida's personal adviser, Shirasu Jirō.[29]

The first order of business for the new vice-minister, Yamamoto Takayuki, was to try to restore the morale of the industrial policy bureaucrats and to deal with the factional problems created by Nagayama's presence. Two situations aided him in these endeavors: Dodge's balanced budget policy had dictated a major reduction in the numbers of government officials, and SCAP after the outbreak of the Korean War had turned its purge directives against communists, who as a practical matter were primarily trade union leaders. MITI possessed a very vigorous union—Zenshōkō (All Commerce and Industry Workers' Union), an affiliate of the radical Kankōrō (Federation of Government and Public Workers' Unions)—that regularly took actions that provided suitable pretexts for letting people go. For example, in April 1950 Zenshōkō blocked the car and later barricaded the office of Takase Sōtarō (the former president and great "senior" of the Tokyo University of Commerce, renamed Hitotsubashi University in May 1949), who had just come to MITI as minister while serving concurrently as minister of education.[30]

On the basis of direct orders from the cabinet to cut the size of the bureaucracy, Yamamoto used incidents such as this to fire about 10,000 officials between 1949 and 1951. The staff of MITI's internal bureaus fell from 13,822 in 1949 to 3,257 in 1952.[31] This was surely one of the most salutary consequences of Dodge's deflation; MITI became a much leaner and more cohesive organization than the postwar MCI had ever been.

On the factional front Yamamoto appointed Ishihara Takeo as chief of the Enterprises Bureau, Tokunaga Hisatsugu as chief of the Mining Bureau, Hirai Tomisaburō as chief of the Trade Promotion Bureau, and Tamaki Keizō as chief of the Machinery Bureau. All were experienced cadres from the Kishi-Shiina era and all became vice-ministers during the 1950's. When Yamamoto resigned in March 1952, he passed on the vice-ministership to Tamaki. Nagayama, meanwhile, named most of the other bureau and section chiefs; and one of his notable successes was to remove Sahashi Shigeru, a rising young "control bureaucrat" and later vice-minister, from the critically important post of chief of the Cotton Textiles Section in the Textiles Bureau (which he held from December 1948 to August 1951) to a mere outpost as chief of the General Affairs Department of the Sendai regional bureau (August 1951 to August 1952).

During the period of rapid unionization in the early years of the occupation, Sahashi had been elected the first chairman of Zenshōkō, and although he was not a communist, this put him in an exposed position when the "red purge" began. In the course of the Dodge Line reduction in force, members of Zenshōkō one day seized Chief Secretary Nagayama and subjected him to a kangaroo court. Although he was no longer a union leader, Section Chief Sahashi was summoned to mediate the dispute. In his typically outspoken manner (of which we shall have several examples in the next chapter), Sahashi ended the incident by loudly haranguing the workers that they would not save their jobs by pressuring a fool such as Nagayama. Shortly thereafter Sahashi found himself on a train heading northeast.[32]

The objections to Nagayama were not just that he was serving as an agent of Yoshida and Shirasu but also that as chief secretary he had jumped over several other officials in the seniority hierarchy. It was during this period of poverty and firings that seniority became entrenched in all Japanese organizations as a vital source of job security. Nagayama's use of his political connections was thus seen as a potential threat to everyone. He was not, however, easy to dislodge. Tamaki, as vice-minister, worked on the problem, and he gained the support of his minister, Ikeda. When Ikeda had to resign after his "slip of the tongue" in the Diet about his not caring if a few small businessmen were driven to suicide, he advised his successor, Ogasawara Sankurō, that Nagayama must go. At this same time Nagayama's position was weakened because his mentor, Shirasu, publicly criticized Prime Minister Yoshida and promptly lost his own influence.

In January 1953 Ogasawara and Tamaki succeeded in moving Nagayama out of the secretaryship and made him chief of the Tokyo regional bureau (they replaced him as secretary with Ishihara Takeo, who became vice-minister two years later). Nagayama remained in his new post until July of the following year, when he returned to headquarters as chief of the Textiles Bureau. He finally resigned as a bureaucrat in December 1955, and sought to use his contacts developed in the Tokyo and Textiles positions—among the best places to build political support—to run for the upper house of the Diet. However, he was unsuccessful at the polls and therefore made a normal amakudari to the presidency of the Shōwa Oil Company (a Shell affiliate) and a directorship at Mitsubishi Yuka (petrochemicals).[33] Over the years since his retirement Nagayama has become a respected "senior" in the oil-refining business, but the age of "Emperor Nagayama" is still remembered within ministry circles as one of the three most divisive periods in the ministry's history (the other two were Kishi's appointment as minister in 1941 and Sahashi's rejection as vice-minister in 1963).

In addition to these personnel and factional problems, the early years of the ministry saw the first steps taken toward the formulation of the high-growth policy. The International Trade Bureau was the busiest place in MITI, but it spent most of its time processing import and export applications and consulting with SCAP instead of thinking about where the Japanese economy should be going. Within a few years it had been completely outclassed by the Enterprises Bureau as the center of planning and policy-making. During 1949 the Enterprises Bureau worked quietly—its name is scarcely mentioned in the SCAP archives—but with great effectiveness. On September 13, 1949, the cabinet adopted the Enterprises Bureau's "Policy Concerning Industrial Rationalization" (Sangyō Gōrika ni kan suru Ken), which must be regarded as one of the most crucial, if least acknowledged, milestones of the Dodge Line and of postwar Japanese industrial policy.[34]

This document contains the seeds of the Japan Development Bank, the Foreign Capital Law of 1950, the attacks on the Antimonopoly Law, the reform of the tax system to favor industrial growth, and the creation in December 1949 of the Industrial Rationalization Council (Sangyō Gōrika Shingikai). One of the most concrete results of the cabinet's policy decision was the passage two years later of the Enterprises Rationalization Promotion Law (Kigyō Gōrika Sokushin Hō, number 5 of March 14, 1952), the first of at least 58 separate industrial policy statutes enacted between 1952 and 1965 under MITI's sponsorship.[35] During the 1950's the work of the Enterprises Bureau and its Rationalization Council became as important for the country's economy as Yoshino's Temporary Industrial Rationality Bureau and Commerce and Industry Deliberation Council had been twenty years earlier. The paternity of the 1949 ideas also clearly goes back to the MCI initiatives formulated at the beginning of the great depression.

The leaders of the Enterprises Bureau during the waning years of the occupation were its bureau chief, Ishihara Takeo; its deputy chiefs, Tanaka Shin'ichi (who was in charge of the materials mobilization plans in the old Cabinet Planning Board) and Iwatake Teruhiko (who after retirement was on the board of Kobe Steel); and its section chiefs, Imai Hiroshi (who was subsequently on the board of the JDB) and Hizume Nobuaki (who was later executive director of Daimaru Department Stores). Their chief policy-making organization was the Industrial Rationalization Council. Composed originally of 45 committees and 81 subcommittees covering every industry in the country and bringing together several hundred business executives and academic specialists centered around Ishikawa Ichirō of Keidanren and Arisawa Hiromi of Tōdai, it was the main means of liaison between the government and the business community. Its committees went over and modified government proposals ranging from the rationalization of the steel industry to the possibilities of earning foreign exchange through the export of Japanese motion pictures.[36]

Perhaps the council's least known but later most applauded activities were in the areas of the reform of management, the institutionalization of the lifetime employment system, and the raising of the productivity of the Japanese industrial worker. Noda Nobuo, a former Mitsubishi executive and chairman of the council's Management Committee, has always contended that the committee got its ideas for quality control and the measurement of productivity from the United States—even though, ironically, during the 1970's the Japanese began to export some of these same ideas back to the United States.[37]

The Management Committee borrowed speakers on industrial management from SCAP and the U.S. Air Force, many of whom it sent around the country to lecture to managers and newspaper reporters; and it was so impressed by the ideas concerning statistics and industrial engineering of the American professor W. E. Deming that it named a prize after him. The "Deming Prize" for quality control, established by the Union of Japanese Scientists and Engineers and the newspaper *Nihon keizai*, was first awarded in 1951 to the Shōwa Denkō Company, Yawata Steel, and Tanabe Pharmaceuticals. Deming became a popular lecturer for his close friend Ishikawa Ichirō, who was then president of Keidanren, head of the Industrial Rationalization Council, chairman of the Shōwa Denkō Company, and a champion of industrial standards and the certification of products by independent testing institutions.[38]

Excited by the American concept of "scientific management," the Industrial Rationalization Council churned out publications and sponsored speakers, leading during the mid-1950's to what was called the "business administration boom" (*keiei būmu*) and to making bestsellers of books such as Peter F. Drucker's *The Practice of Management* (published in 1954 and translated into Japanese in 1956). Equally significant (particularly for those who contend that the contemporary

Japanese employment system derives from traditional practices), the Council's Labor Subcommittee met some 22 times during 1951 alone to produce standards for the wage system and promotion system, for the organization of work sites and measures to avoid strikes, and for employee training programs; these were subsequently recommended to all Japanese firms. The Industrial Rationalization Council had no legal authority to force its proposals on a particular enterprise, but it should be recalled that the council's sponsor, MITI, could and did cut off the access to foreign exchange of any firm that it felt was wasting valuable resources. Not surprisingly, the Council's educational programs were well attended and their suggestions widely adopted.[39]

After setting up the Council, the Enterprises Bureau's next big initiative was the enactment of the Foreign Capital Law (Gaishi Hō, number 163 of May 10, 1950). The Foreign Exchange and Foreign Trade Control Law of 1949 had already given the government the power to concentrate all foreign exchange earned from exports (by law such foreign exchange had to be sold to a foreign exchange bank within ten days of its acquisition), and this power made possible the control of imports through the use of a foreign exchange budget. MITI made every effort to suppress imports of finished goods, particularly those that competed with domestic products, but it urgently sought imports of modern technology and machinery. The problem was to keep the price down and to "untie the package" in which such foreign technology normally came wrapped—to separate the foreign technology from its foreign ownership, patent rights, know-how agreements, proposals for joint ventures, capital participation, voting rights, and foreign managers on boards of directors.

The Foreign Capital Law dealt with this problem. It established a Foreign Investment Committee and stipulated that foreign investors wanting to license technology, acquire stock, share patents, or enter into any kind of contract that provided them with assets in Japan had first to be licensed (kyoka) by the committee. (At the end of the occupation, the powers of this committee were transferred to the Enterprises Bureau). SCAP approved the law in order to guarantee the availability of foreign exchange for license payments, but the Japanese were more interested in restricting the import of foreign technology to those cases deemed necessary for the development of Japanese industries. As SCAP wrote, "Restrictive provisions of the law were to be relaxed and eliminated as the need for them subsided."[40] But restrictions did not even begin to be relaxed until 1968, long after Japan's balance of payments constraints had been overcome.[41]

The next big accomplishment of the Enterprises Bureau was the Enterprises Rationalization Promotion Law of 1952, on which it had spent some two years in planning, consultation, and political preparation. Its actual drafters were Ishihara and Hizume. MITI refers to it as a "completely epoch-making law." [42] Its complex provisions can be reduced to three basic points: first, it provided direct governmental subsidies for the experimental installation and trial operation of new machines and equipment, plus rapid amortization and exemption from local taxes of all investments in research and development; second, it authorized certain industries (to be designated by the cabinet) to depreciate the costs of installing modern equipment by 50 percent during the first year; and third, it committed the central and local governments to building ports, highways, railroads, electric power grids, gas mains, and industrial parks at public expense and made them available to approved industries. [43]

The last provision was perhaps the most important because it drastically reduced production costs. It began the extensive efforts by MITI and the Ministry of Construction over the next two decades not just to build the infrastructure for industry but to rationalize it as completely as possible. The idea behind the provision was the recognition that since Japan's industries had to import most of their raw materials and to export their products, factories and port facilities should be completely integrated. The prewar Japanese steel industry had worked out the rule of thumb that it had to transport six tons of raw materials in order to produce one ton of steel. [44] MITI planned to change that by dredging harbors, building factories at dockside, and locating intermediate processors next to final manufacturers. One of the most famous products of this policy is the Keiyō industrial belt and petrochemical *kombinato*, which was built in Chiba prefecture on land entirely reclaimed from Tokyo Bay. The Kawasaki Steel Company alone, which in 1953 fired the first blast furnace of its new, integrated facility (pig iron to rolled steel; at the time, the world's most modern), received some 3 million square meters of free land from Chiba prefecture. Ichimada, the banks, and Kawasaki's biggest competitors (Yawata, Fuji, and Nippon Kōkan) all derided the Kawasaki effort at the time as beyond Japan's capabilities and needs—something MITI has never let them forget in view of its unexampled success. [45]

Despite MITI's own early successes with the Development Bank, the Foreign Capital Law, and the Rationalization Council and Law, Japan was still some remove from a true high-growth system. Throughout the 1950 to 1954 period economic fluctuations buffeted the country. These fluctuations were caused, first, by the Korean truce negotiations and truce and, second, by balance of payments problems, since

TABLE 16
Japan's Business Cycle, 1950–1974

Popular name	Period	Duration
Dōran būmu (Korean War boom)	6/50–6/51	13 months
Kyūsen handō (Truce recession)	7/51–10/51	4 months
Shōhi keiki (consumption boom)	11/51–1/54	27 months
Nijūku-nen fukyō (the 1954 recession)	2/54–11/54	10 months
Jimmu keiki (boom unprecedented since the emperor Jimmu)	12/54–6/57	31 months
Nabezoko fukyō (bottom-of-the-pot recession)	7/57–6/58	12 months
Iwato keiki (boom unprecedented since the time of the sun goddess Amaterasu)	7/58–12/61	42 months
Sanjūshichi-nen fukyō (the 1962 recession)	1/62–10/62	10 months
Kōkyōkan-naki hanei (prosperity without a sense of boom)	11/62–10/64	24 months
Yonjū-nen fukyō (the 1965 recession) (also called the Kōzō-teki fukyō, the structural recession)	11/64–10/65	12 months
Izanagi keiki (boom unprecedented since the god Izanagi joined with Izanami to create the islands of Japan)	11/65–6/70	56 months
Yonjūgo yonjūroku-nen fukyō (the 1970–71 recession)	7/70–12/71	18 months
Ijō infure no jiki (period of unusual inflation)	1/72–1/74	25 months
Sekiyu shokku igo (after the Oil Shock)	2/74–	

SOURCE: Togai Yoshio, "Sengo Nihon no kigyō keiei" (Postwar Japanese enterprise management), in Kobayashi Masaaki et al., eds., *Nihon keieishi o manabu* (The study of Japanese enterprise management), Tokyo, 1976, 3: 2.

imports outran exports whenever the people's economic conditions improved even slightly (see Table 16). The recessions of 1951 and 1954 caused numerous bankruptcies (the largest was that of Amagasaki Steel, which was absorbed by Kobe Steel), and manufacturers turned increasingly to the government for direction. The government, however, was divided. To the extent that Yoshida had an economic strategy at all, it was to ally Japan with the United States as closely as possible. MITI officials did not necessarily disagree with this approach, but their nationalism prompted them to plan to compete with the United States as well as rely on it. Moreover, some of them wanted to try to restore Japan's traditional China trade, which Yoshida and the Americans resolutely opposed. Most important, MITI stood for a shift of industrial structure from light to heavy industries, which neither Ichimada nor most consumers thought made economic sense.

On April 28, 1952, the San Francisco peace treaty restoring Japan's independence came into effect. On May 29, 1952, thanks to U.S. sponsorship, Japan was admitted to the International Monetary Fund and the International Bank for Reconstruction and Development (the "World Bank"); and on August 12, 1955, Japan joined the General Agreement on Tariffs and Trade (GATT). However, at the time both Japan's IMF and GATT memberships were in the special category reserved for poor countries. On September 15, 1953, Japan also concluded a basic commercial treaty with the United States. Some of these affiliations did not go down well in Japan—particularly Yoshida's plan to "introduce foreign capital" via loans from the World Bank, which irritated many nationalists and led to shouts of "national dishonor" in the Diet.[46] Yoshida pushed the loan agreements through anyway; in the autumn of 1953 the World Bank made its first loan of $40.2 million to the Kansai, Chūbu, and Kyushu Electric Power companies to build thermal generating plants. In later years the steel companies also borrowed from the World Bank. MITI was delighted with these loans, but it also saw in the political controversy surrounding them a potent reason to continue with its own approach to rapid economic development.

Once the occupation had ended, the Yoshida government ordered a general review of the executive branch and of all laws and ordinances inherited from the SCAP era. Among other things Yoshida himself wanted to abolish the Economic Stabilization Board as a symbol of the controlled economy, but MITI, which sent by far the largest number of officials to it, liked it. In order to save it, Hirai Tomisaburō of MITI bypassed Yoshida to obtain the Liberal Party's agreement to transform the ESB into a smaller (only 399 officials) organ for economic analysis and forecasting.[47] Thus, on August 1, 1952, the powerful ESB ("whose name alone would stop a child's crying") became the Economic Deliberation Agency (EDA; Keizai Shingi Chō), a "think tank" with no operational duties at all. On July 20, 1955, after Yoshida had left the scene, its name was changed to Economic Planning Agency (EPA; Keizai Kikaku Chō).

MITI continued to regard the EDA/EPA as its own "branch store"—it appointed the agency's vice-minister, the chief of its Coordination Bureau, and numerous other key posts. Moreover, in 1952 the substantive powers of the old ESB were all transferred to MITI. The International Trade Bureau (ITB) took over preparation and administration of the foreign exchange budget, and the Enterprises Bureau began to screen all foreign investment proposals. These developments transformed the ITB; its offices on the third floor of the old MITI office building became known as the "Toranomon Ginza" because of the hundreds of importers gathered there daily to seek licenses. Journalistic observers of MITI have also concluded that this was the ministry's most corrupt period. Officials of the ITB received numerous presents and invitations to mahjong sessions (at which they never seemed to lose money); and some trading companies employed attractive female negotiators to deal with the ITB.[48] It has been alleged that officials even sold copies of the "secret" foreign exchange budget for large sums, it being of great value to importers in calculating how much of each commodity would be approved.[49] These conditions were the natural concomitants of tightly controlled trade, but they did not do anything for the ITB's reputation.

MITI used the opportunity of Yoshida's postoccupation review to reorganize itself totally. The Secretariat rewrote the MITI Establishment Law, and the new law, number 275, was passed on July 31, 1952. It eliminated the old prefix tsūshō (international trade) from the names of the industrial bureaus; combined the ITB and the Trade Promotion Bureau into one large unit; and abolished SCAP's Public Utilities Commission, which had been attached to the prime minister's office. In its place there was set up in MITI a Public Utilities Bureau, the direct successor of the old Electric Power Bureau that the Ministry of Munitions had acquired when it was established in 1943. The sections of the Enterprises Bureau were also expanded to accommodate the planning and control functions of the defunct ESB. MITI thus took on the form that it would retain throughout the high-speed growth period and down to the reform of 1973 (see Appendix B).

During the crucial years 1952–53 MITI undertook some other initiatives that set it on a collision course with a famous SCAP-created institution, the Fair Trade Commission (FTC; Kōsei Torihiki Iinkai), guardian and administrator of the so-called economic constitution, the Antimonopoly Law. The Antimonopoly Law, which is formally called the Law Relating to the Prohibition of Private Monopoly and to Methods of Preserving Fair Trade (Shiteki Dokusen no Kinshi oyobi Kōsei Torihiki no Kakuho ni kan suru Hōritsu, number 54 of April 14, 1947) had a checkered career even before the occupation ended. SCAP defended it on the grounds that "with the exception of the Unfair Competition Law of 1934, which primarily dealt with imitating and palming off one's goods as those of another, Japanese legislation did not embody any rules against unfair trade practices generally and did not recognize any concept of free, competitive enterprise as being in the public interest"; but SCAP also acknowledged that "many civil servants in various departments of the Government exhibited a strong lack of sympathy or support for the antitrust program."[50]

As originally drafted, the law prohibited collusive activities among entrepreneurs to set prices, restrict the volume of production or sales, divide markets or customers among themselves, limit the construction or expansion of facilities, or refuse to share new technologies or methods of production. Article 9 of the law—as famous in its own right as article 9 of the constitution, which outlaws the use of armed force—banned holding companies, and this article has survived intact to the present day. Holding companies in fact do not exist in the postwar Japanese economy; the zaibatsu were rebuilt on another basis entirely—that of the banking keiretsu discussed above. The law also created the Fair Trade Commission, composed of seven members who are appointed by the prime minister with the consent of the House of Representatives for five-year terms.

Modifications to the law began almost as soon as it had been passed. SCAP discovered that firms could evade the law by creating "trade associations" as noncommercial unions or foundations (*kumiai, shadan,* or *zaidan*) under the terms of the Civil Code. Because of this, SCAP ordered the Japanese government to enact the Trade Associations Law (number 191 of July 29, 1948), which required any association of two or more businessmen to register with the FTC within thirty days of its establishment. MITI had this law abolished in 1953.

Another problem was that ever since Yoshino's industrial unions law of 1925, medium and smaller enterprises had depended on their cartels to remain in business without resorting to dumping. SCAP agreed that they needed some special help, but rather than authorize their cartels as exceptions to the Antimonopoly Law (AML), it sponsored the creation on August 1, 1948, of the Medium and Smaller Enterprises Agency (MSEA) as an external agency first of MCI and subsequently of MITI. This organ was supposed to gather, analyze, and freely distribute information on the procurement of materials, marketing possibilities, business methods, and so forth—in effect, to act as a cartel headquarters for the small business sector. The first director of the MSEA, Ninagawa Torazō (former dean of economics at Kyoto University), fought vigorously with both SCAP and the Yoshida government to get more powers and a secure budget for his unit; he particularly wanted governmental financing for small businesses.

After SCAP pressured the government to do as Ninagawa asked (law number 108 of April 24, 1950, amending the MITI Establishment Law), he resigned and was elected mayor of Kyoto, a city with many medium and smaller enterprises. Backed by the socialists and communists, Ninagawa served from 1950 to 1978 as mayor of Kyoto, where he became a persistent thorn in the side of the national conservative establishment. MITI was never very enthusiastic about the MSEA, but it had no choice other than to support it because of the political clout the small-business sector wields. Moreover, some MITI officials discovered that the directorship of the MSEA was an excellent place from which to build support for their own postretirement political careers. MITI's attitude toward the MSEA has consequently remained ambivalent over the years; it is today an integral, if nonmainstream, unit of the ministry.

By far the most serious problem with the original Antimonopoly Law was its ban on agreements that provided for the exclusive use of technologies or know-how. SCAP historians have rather lamely acknowledged after the fact that "such a proposal represented advanced antitrust thinking."[51] In fact, the stipulation was so advanced it did not exist in the United States, where know-how and trade secrets can be legally protected under the laws of the various states, not to mention the constitutional protection of patent rights (art. I.8.8). The original AML seemed to ban exclusive patent licensing agreements, which stopped in their tracks all Japanese efforts to import technology.

SCAP does not appear to have realized how long the issue of industrial property rights had been a bone of contention between Japanese and foreign firms. The problem went back at least to the Firestone Rubber Company's suit of 1933 against Japan's Bridgestone Rubber Company, founded in 1931, because of the similarity in their names (Bridgestone won the case when its founder, Ishibashi Shōjirō, demonstrated that "bridgestone" was a literal translation of his family name). In 1949 these issues were still highly salient because the government had extended all prewar patents issued to foreigners (Japanese patents normally run for 15 years, American patents for 17 years), and because the du Pont Company was just then charging Toray Textiles with infringing on its patent for Nylon 6 (this was settled out of court, and du Pont and Toray became partners).[52]

Under the AML many foreign companies concluded not just that they could not protect their know-how and trade secrets in Japan (Japanese law had never provided protection against "breach of trust" with regard to know-how), but that even patent-licensing agreements would not be honored. Most refused to sell their patents until the law was clarified. Thus, to promote economic recovery, SCAP authorized the first formal amendment to the AML itself (law number 214 of June 18, 1949), which liberalized the provisions covering patent and exclusive agent contracts and allowed foreign corporations to acquire stock

in Japanese firms. This amendment of course also spurred MITI to enact the Foreign Capital Law in order to give the Japanese government
control over who licensed what patents and how much they paid for
them in royalties.

These various challenges to and changes in the AML were all preliminary to MITI's actions of 1952. As noted in the preceding chapter,
from 1946 on MCI, the ESB, and their subsidiary public corporations
(kōdan) exercised absolute control over all commodities in the domestic economy under the terms of the Temporary Materials Supply and
Demand Control Law. This law—approved by SCAP as an emergency
replacement for the wartime National General Mobilization Law—
was due to expire on April 1, 1948; but SCAP extended it for two more
years because of the continuing shortages and consequent need for
rationing. In 1950, when the government wanted to extend it again,
SCAP balked: "To SCAP this proposal looked very much like a bid by
the Government to continue the controls system as a government institution instead of ending it."[53] However, SCAP finally went along
with a one-year extension because the Japanese feared that abandoning the materials supply-and-demand plans would destabilize the
economy. During April, 1951, the effects of the "truce recession" that
followed the beginning of negotiations in Korea were just being felt,
so SCAP extended the law for yet another year. But SCAP and Yoshida were both determined to let it lapse on April 1, 1952.

MITI has often contended that its acquiescence in the expiration of
the Temporary Materials Supply and Demand Control Law demonstrated that it is a more liberal and less control-oriented ministry than
either Finance or Agriculture, whose control laws (over the banks and
rice production) have never ended.[54] Professor Maeda, on the other
hand, believes that the expiration of the Supply and Demand Law
merely ushered in a "second control era" based on MITI's use of the
foreign exchange budgets to carry out its policies, a phase that lasted
until 1964.[55]

Whatever one thinks about this issue, the fact that the law was
coming to an end in the spring of 1952 had a major unsettling effect
on several industries, particularly those in which there were many
firms, strong competition, and damage due to the decline in American procurements. Under these circumstances MITI took its first totally independent action as a new ministry. On February 25, 1952, it
informally advised ten big cotton spinners to reduce production by 40
percent, and the ministry assigned quotas to each individual firm.
To enterprises that rejected this "administrative guidance," MITI
mentioned (again verbally and informally) that foreign currency al-

locations for their next month's supply of raw cotton might not be available. This was the first postwar instance of a famous Japanese institution, the MITI *kankoku sōtan* (advice to limit production), and of the inevitable government-organized cartel that followed in its wake. Similar kankoku sōtan were issued in March and May for rubber and steel. The FTC said that MITI's actions were illegal, but the ministry replied that the Antimonopoly Law did not cover informal advice from the government, and it persisted in its policies.

Thus was the issue joined. As soon as the occupation ended in April, MITI introduced in the Diet two laws—the Special Measures Law for the Stabilization of Designated Medium and Smaller Enterprises (number 294 of August 1, 1952) and the Exports Transactions Law (number 299 of August 5, 1952)—both of which authorized MITI to create cartels among small businesses as exceptions to the Antimonopoly Law. They were the precedent for many such laws to come—and for the revision of the AML itself in 1953, the first such revision by an independent Japanese government.

Throughout 1953 both the Steel Federation and the Federation of Economic Organizations petitioned the Diet (some say they also bribed Diet members) to permit cartels for businesses in recession or businesses trying to implement rationalization plans. MITI's position, according to its annual reports, was that it respected the intent of the original AML but had found that in practice it led to the excessive fragmentation of industries and stood in the way of capital accumulation in order to enhance international competitiveness. In its proposed amendment to the AML, MITI asked for the power to approve "cooperative behavior" (*kyōdō kōi*, the new euphemism for cartel) to limit production and sales for depressed industries and to lower costs and promote exports for industries undergoing rationalization. Such "cooperative behavior" was to include the sharing of technologies, the limiting of product lines, the joint use of warehouses for raw materials and finished products, and joint consultations on investment plans. On September 1, 1953, the Diet amended the AML (law number 259) to permit so-called depression and rationalization cartels, and it also abolished SCAP's Trade Associations Law. The Tokyo correspondent for the *New York Times* wrote that "hardly a vestige now remains of the anti-trust measures forced upon the Japanese during the occupation of General of the Army Douglas MacArthur."[56]

In the years that followed MITI kept up the pressure on the FTC and the AML, although neither ever did disappear completely. In 1955 MITI amended the Exports Transactions Law (now called the Export-Import Transactions Law, number 121 of August 2) to make the cartels compulsory for all small exporters and to strengthen the general trading companies. During that same year it also abolished the occupation-era Law Prohibiting Excess Concentrations of Economic Power. During 1956 the ministry began its sponsorship of a long series of "industry laws" that provided for exceptions to the AML—including, for example, the Textile Industry Equipment Special Measures Law (number 130 of June 5, 1956), the Machinery Industry Promotion Special Measures Law (number 154 of June 15, 1956), and the Electronics Industry Promotion Special Measures Law (number 171 of June 11, 1957). And in June 1958 MITI caused the FTC to approve its plan for a "public sales system" (*kōkai hambai seido*) for the steel industry—an ingenious system of price rigging invented by the old MCI cadre Inayama Yoshihiro, then a director of Yawata Steel, and Sahashi Shigeru, then the deputy director of the Heavy Industries Bureau.[57] It seemed to some that the FTC would approve anything short of piracy if MITI said it was necessary for Japan's rapid economic growth.

In fact, MITI judged the time was ripe to get rid of the AML altogether. From October 1957 to February 1958 the Enterprises Bureau sponsored a cabinet-level deliberation council on the future status of the AML. Professor Nakayama Ichirō chaired it. The council stated in its final report that "the stipulations of the AML do not necessarily conform to the proper operation of our country's economy," and that "the public interest is not best served by the legal maintenance of a free competitive order." The council recommended a new law that would allow for the "coordination of investment" and that would encourage mergers to overcome "excessive competition" among the banking keiretsu.

The new law was introduced in the Diet in October 1958, but it "got lost" in the turmoil surrounding the Kishi government's attempts to revise the police duties law. The following year, according to MITI, interest in abandoning the AML "fell asleep under the pleasant clouds of the Iwato boom."[58] After that the situation began to change subtly. The FTC did not regain its earlier powers, but it stopped losing what powers it had left. Until about 1958 the country was united in its belief that MITI's measures were necessary to regain national economic independence. After that time divisions over the issue began to appear. Most of MITI's subsequent innovations were based on administrative guidance—for example, the coordination of investment that was implemented after the failure of Sahashi's Special Measures Law for the Promotion of Designated Industries (discussed in the next chapter). The FTC continued in existence and finally, during February 1974, it brought its first ever formal complaint against a restraint of trade (discussed in Chapter 8).

Antitrust legislation is a controversial subject. Western theory asserts that it is an indispensable tool of industrial policy in order to maintain competition. Former MITI Vice-Minister Sahashi Shigeru has argued, on the other hand, that Japan's industrial policy, which is hostile to antitrust legislation, has produced higher levels of both competition and growth than the economies of Japan's Western critics.[59] From the point of view of the history of MITI, the major significance of the 1953 reform of the AML was that it almost completed MITI's ensemble of industrial-policy tools. The ministry now had under its control foreign exchange, foreign capital, cartels, banking keiretsu, industrial location, and direct government finance, plus the whole range of activities of the Industrial Rationalization Council. It was almost ready to put the high-growth system into operation, but it still needed some innovations on the tax front and political backing for its particular point of view. It was the harsh recession of 1954 following the Korean War that provided the opportunity to acquire both. As Kakuma has observed, the recession following the special procurements boom was as important as the Korean War itself to Japan's economic development; its influence has too long been unrecognized.[60]

During the four years that followed the outbreak of the Korean War in June 1950, the United States pumped some $2.37 billion worth of special procurements into the Japanese economy. This factor, plus the effects of the rationalization campaigns in putting people back to work and of the euphoria that followed the end of the occupation, led to a major consumption and investment boom throughout 1952 and into 1953. Imports of consumer goods and industrial machines skyrocketed. By the end of 1953 Japan was showing a deficit of $260 million in its balance of payments, and the prospects for 1954 looked even worse. Inventories had grown very large, but export sales were sluggish because of the comparatively high prices of Japanese goods and the slowdown in the growth of international trade following the Korean War. The Ministry of Finance and the Bank of Japan had no choice but to tighten credit and cut governmental expenditures, including disbursements from FILP and loans from the Development Bank. Their squeeze on credits and imports caused the recession.

At MITI Minister Okano Kiyohide (May 1953 to January 1954) ordered the International Trade Bureau to cut the foreign currency quotas for the import of food, chemicals, medicine, and textiles from over $8 million during the period April to September 1952, to $4 million for April–September 1953. In October 1953 he abolished the quota for these imports altogether, which immediately caused the closing of hundreds of stores in the Tokyo area dealing in consumer goods and led to the reappearance of black markets. Under these circumstances many bureaucratic organizations began to think about how to overcome Japan's dependence on U.S. special procurements, and even Prime Minister Yoshida had to recognize that his piecemeal approach to the economy was not working.

The first important plan came from the Economic Deliberation Agency, where MITI Minister Okano (a former president of the Sanwa Bank) was serving concurrently as director-general and Hirai Tomisaburō of MITI was working as his deputy director (May 1951 to November 1953). Known both unofficially as the "Okano Plan" (Okano kōsō) and by its formal title of "On Making Our Economy Independent" (Waga kuni keizai no jiritsu ni tsuite), the plan outlined a new effort to expand exports. However, in order to do this Okano and Hirai called not just for more rationalization campaigns but also for efforts to restore economic ties with Southeast Asia, a rationalization of the tax system, and a vigorous program to develop import-substitution industries.

The Okano Plan also reflected the view within MITI that the only way to break out of Japan's inevitable balance of payments constraints was through "heavy and chemical industrialization," by which was meant the building of an industrial structure whose export products would have a much higher income elasticity of demand than Japan's traditional light industries. Income elasticity of demand refers to the ratio of the percentage change in the quantity of a product demanded to the percentage change in the income of a group of purchasers. Okano and Hirai were among the first to recognize that as a people's income goes up their demand for food and textiles changes very little but their demand for products such as appliances and automobiles increases proportionally. Their conclusion, even though it flew in the face of Japan's so-called comparative advantages (chiefly a large, cheap labor supply), was that these products were what Japan should be manufacturing if it ever hoped to break out of its dependent position.[61]

Prime Minister Yoshida rejected the Okano Plan out of hand, not because of its contents but because it was an instance of "planning," which he felt was appropriate only for socialist countries. Okano left the government, and Hirai returned to MITI as vice-minister (November 1953 to November 1955). But during 1954, as the recession continued and worsened, the ideas of the Okano Plan reappeared in many forms and places. Yoshida was beginning to lose his grip on the Liberal Party, and the man he chose to succeed Okano, Aichi Kiichi, was both an old associate of Ikeda's in the Ministry of Finance (he was Banking Bureau director during the period of zaibatsu dissolution) and a much more influential politician than Okano had been.

On September 6, 1954, Aichi and others in the government led the cabinet into adopting a "Comprehensive Policy for Economic Expansion" (Keizai Kakudai Sōgō Seisaku Yōgō), and this in turn provided MITI, later the same month, with the authority to issue its own fundamental statement of strategy, entitled "Outline of the New International Trade and Industry Policy" (Shin Tsūshō Sangyō Seisaku Taikō).[62] Both of these documents were upgraded versions of the Okano Plan. Finally, in December the Yoshida government fell from power, and Yoshida's rival, Hatoyama Ichirō, became prime minister. He in turn brought Ishibashi Tanzan back into the government as minister of MITI. The ministry's days of political oblivion were over; from now on the minister of MITI would be one of the most powerful men in the government—his position one of the three indispensable stepping stones to the prime ministership itself (the other two are Finance and Foreign Affairs).

Hirai has testified that Ishibashi contributed the final theoretical formulation that all other planners had been missing. Ishibashi pointed out that the key to exports was, of course, the lowering of costs, and the key to that was enlarging production to effect economies of scale. But to enlarge production, Japanese manufacturers needed more customers. And where were they to be found? In the huge potential market of Japan itself. The Japanese people had suffered from economic stringency for at least two decades; they were ready to buy anything offered to them at prices they could afford. Ishibashi's idea was that MITI should promote *both* exports and domestic sales. When problems in the international balance of payments arose, the government could curtail domestic demand and promote exports; when the problems of paying for imported raw materials eased, the focus should be on enlarging sales at home. If this could be achieved, Japan's factories could keep operating throughout all phases of the business cycle. In Hirai's words, Ishibashi "combined export promotion and high-speed growth into a coherent theory."[63]

These ideas were very congenial to Ikeda Hayato. As a protégé of Yoshida's, he did not receive a post in the Hatoyama cabinets, which were transitional between the old Yoshida order and the new Liberal Democratic Party regime; the LDP was created on November 15, 1955. But in the succeeding cabinets of Ishibashi and Kishi, Ikeda served as minister of finance and proceeded to execute Ishibashi's ideas with a vengeance. Through his famous ¥100 billion cut in the income tax of December 1956, Ikeda put money back in the hands of consumers and industrialists as it had never been done before and began the positive stimulation of a domestic market fully half the size of that of the United States. As one contemporary Japanese analyst has put it, "the only industries in which we have seen export increases induce a production increment—instead of the other way round—are transistor radios and perhaps cameras. We do not regard these industries as very soundly based because demand for them, especially transistors, may be saturated too soon. Export increases of all our other products have been induced mainly by expansion for the domestic market."[64] Thus it was thanks to Ishibashi and Ikeda that the high-growth system, fed by both a domestic "consumer revolution" and a new apparatus for export promotion, was finally underway.

MITI's policy statement of September 1954 led to several new institutions on the export promotion front. One was the Supreme Export Council (Saikō Yushutsu Kaigi), composed of the prime minister; the ministers of MITI, finance, and agriculture; the governor of the Bank of Japan; the president of the Export-Import Bank; and several business leaders. Its highly public function was to set export targets for the coming year and to publicize at the highest level of government the need to promote exports by all possible means. This cabinet-level council did not, of course, make its own calculations of targets. Instead, it assigned this task to the new Economic Planning Agency (a renamed and reorganized Economic Deliberation Agency). The chief task of the EPA was the writing of "plans" that would indicate to government and business alike the goals that the nation should be striving to achieve during a given term. Needless to say, the new EPA remained as bound to MITI as its predecessors had been, although during the 1960's it attempted (unsuccessfully) to assert some independence from its powerful patron. Table 17 summarizes the EPA's first three long-range plans for the economy as a whole.[65]

Another new institution was the Japan External Trade Organization (JETRO), an international commercial intelligence service set up to overcome the problem of what Hirai called "blind trade." By "blind trade" he and others meant that during the mid-1950's Japanese manufacturers were operating without detailed information on what they should be producing for various foreign markets. They also lacked agents abroad to help them keep close tabs on changes in tariff rates and specifications for products, as well as to assist in publicizing and marketing new Japanese products. JETRO was set up to do these

TABLE 17

Plans of the Economic Planning Agency, 1955–1960

Item	I Five-year plan for economic independence	II New long- term economic plan	III National income- doubling plan
Date of plan	12/1955	12/1957	12/1960
Cabinet	Hatoyama	Kishi	Ikeda
Plan period	1956–60	1958–62	1961–70
Planned growth rate	5.0%	6.5%	7.2%
Realized growth rate	9.1%	10.1%	10.4%[a]

[a]Rate for 1961–67.

things. By 1975 it operated some 24 trade centers and 54 reporting offices in 55 different countries.

During the 1950's there were actually three JETROs. The first was set up in 1951 in Osaka on the initiative of the mayor, Akama Bunzō (an old MCI cadre, 1925–47), and Sugi Michisuke, chairman of the Osaka Chamber of Commerce and Industry. Kansai industrialists and the individual prefectures put up the money for this early organization, and MITI merely approved its activities. In 1954 MITI took it over, provided more national funds for it, and greatly expanded its operations. Finally, in 1958, in recognition of the fact that national funding now heavily outweighed that of the prefectures and that MITI wanted to bring it more securely under the ministry's control, JETRO was transformed into a public corporation with all of its capital coming from the central government (Japan External Trade Organization Law, number 95, of April 26, 1958). From 1951 on MITI also began providing key executive personnel for JETRO, notably its managing director (from 1951 to 1954 he was Okabe Kunio, the recently retired director of MITI's Trade Promotion Bureau; and from 1954 to 1965, Nagamura Teiichi, who had ended his MITI career as vice-minister of the EDA). Virtually all of JETRO's overseas personnel are MITI transferees.[66]

Except during its earliest days, when it was the brainchild of Osaka business leaders, JETRO has always been an operating arm of MITI. However, its post-1958 legal status as a public corporation rather than as an agency of the government has sometimes gotten it into trouble in the United States. During the late 1950's JETRO set up in Washington an organization wholly staffed by Americans called the United States–Japan Trade Council but failed to register it under the Foreign Agents Registration Act of 1938. As a result of this oversight, in 1976 the U.S. Department of Justice sued the Trade Council for civil fraud, charging that 90 percent of its funds actually came from MITI via the New York office of JETRO. The Council settled out of court. It also agreed to file as a foreign agent and to identify its publications as coming from Japanese government sources. The issue in this case was not JETRO's lobbying efforts on behalf of Japanese interests but possible American confusion over just whom, exactly, JETRO represented.[67]

One of the more innovative aspects of the early JETRO was its funding. During the 1954 recession MITI raised the money for it from the import of bananas. Under the system of foreign exchange quotas, licenses to import bananas and sugar had become the most valuable in the country; supplies of both commodities were in such short supply that any amounts that could be brought to market commanded exorbitant prices. In the case of bananas, the government charged importers a tax on their profits and turned the proceeds over to JETRO. The organization's funds grew from slightly under ¥3 million in 1954 to over ¥100 million in 1955, all because of bananas. This scheme was similar to the sugar-link system for subsidizing ship exports. Between 1953 and 1955 MITI would issue import licenses for sugar to trading companies—which were then selling Cuban sugar in Japan at from two to ten times the import price—only if they had allied themselves with a shipbuilder and could submit an export certificate showing that they had used 5 percent of their profits to subsidize ship exports. For the two years it was in effect, the sugar-link system supplied some ¥10 billion to the shipbuilding industry. It ultimately had to be stopped because too many other industries wanted subsidies from the sugar and banana fees and because the IMF frowned on the practice.[68]

The sugar and banana links were only two of the more spectacular tax breaks that Ministry of Finance and Enterprises Bureau officials invented in this era to aid industries and to help commercialize particular products. Nakamura Takafusa argues that tax exemptions replaced direct subsidies as early as 1951 as the main means by which the government pursued its industrial policy.[69] And it is certainly true that after Dodge cut off subsidies created through price differentials and RFB loans, MITI's Enterprises Bureau moved decisively into the tax field in search of alternatives.

The main obstacle to its work was the lingering influence of SCAP's special tax mission, which Prof. Carl S. Shoup of Columbia University had headed, and which included such experts as Jerome B. Cohen of the City College of New York. In the spring of 1949 the Shoup mission accompanied Dodge to Japan, and it delivered its report in September. The Ministry of Finance held the mission in high regard, and its advice on the proper system of national and local taxes in Japan still carried great weight during the period 1950 to 1955. In essence, Shoup had called for a simplification of the tax system that would aggregate all types of income of a taxpayer (whether an individual or a "juridical person") and eliminate to the greatest degree possible the special tax benefits that were contained in the Taxation Special Measures Law (Sozei Tokubetsu Sochi Hō, number 15 of 1946) and its numerous amendments.

Some of Shoup's proposals, such as a locally controlled value-added tax, were simply too advanced for the time; businessmen were outraged at the thought that they might have to pay a tax even when operating at a deficit, and it was quietly abandoned. But Shoup's ideas were not necessarily hostile to the use of the tax system to stimulate the economy. For example, his advocacy of a revaluation of assets in the light of Japan's inflation as a way to enhance the capitalization of enterprises met with a very favorable response and resulted in the passage of the Capital Assets Revaluation Law (Shisan Saihyōka Hō, number 110 of April 1950). This statute literally created capital where none had existed before by a (downward) reassessment of industrial assets for tax purposes, a process that was conducted some three different times between 1950 and 1955.

But the main problem with the Shoup system was its hostility to the preferential treatment of strategic industries. Ikeda felt that Japan had to go in this direction—although of course it meant an increasingly inequitable distribution of tax burdens throughout the society—and many of his Finance Ministry colleagues followed his lead because they preferred tax exemptions to subsidies on practical grounds. As Yoshikuni Jirō (former director of the National Tax Agency and vice-minister of finance) has put it, taxes are better than subsidies, even though they are the same thing in theory, because a tax advantage is valuable only after an enterprise has done what the government wants it to do, whereas a subsidy is paid prior to performance and sometimes does not produce any improvement in performance.[70] Another reason to prefer tax breaks to subsidies is their lower political salience—a feature of some value to Japanese bureaucrats during the 1950's in light of the Shōwa Denkō and other scandals associated with the early occupation era.*

---

*Randall Bartlett's comments are apropos: "Specific tax breaks offered to particular firms and industries act, in effect, like governmental subsidies to these agents. Rather than directly taking money from other segments of society and redistributing it to these firms through the budget process, these tax concessions merely leave them with greater financial resources (and lower costs). The resources which finance this subsidy are essentially the higher taxes paid by other agents. Because the use of taxes elimi-

Beginning in 1951 the Ministry of Finance, in consultation with the Enterprises Bureau of MITI and the Industrial Rationalization Council, proceeded very slowly with annual revisions of the old Taxation Special Measures Law, which resulted by the end of the decade in the complete dismantling of the Shoup system. Among the ministry's actions were the exclusion of up to 50 percent of a firm's income earned from exports (this was raised to 80 percent by the tax revision of 1955), rapid depreciation of designated investments for industrial rationalization, exclusion of strategic machinery from import duties, deductions for royalties paid for foreign technology, and many others. A "deliberation council" controlled by the Ministry of Finance supervised and approved these annual revisions. In 1959 this council, renamed the Tax System Deliberation Council (Zeisei Chōsa Kai), became a permanent organ of the prime minister's office. It, and not the cabinet or the Diet (which normally only rubber-stamps its recommendations), makes annual revisions in the tax system in the light of changing needs and economic conditions. The minister of finance chooses the council's members, and its proceedings are not open to the public. After the creation of the LDP the council became the Finance Ministry's main tool for attempting to prevent the party from politicizing the tax system.[71]

Among the more creative of the special tax measures invented during the 1950's were the "reserve funds" set up to assist developing industries. These came in two types, *hikiatekin*, which are normal, accepted reserves of the sort found in most nations' corporation tax laws, and *jumbikin*, which the Ministry of Finance describes candidly as "those reserves which may not be duly justified by generally accepted accounting principles."[72] Both types of reserves can be excluded from taxable profits. The best-known of the hikiatekin is that used for lump-sum payments to employees when they retire. This reserve fund was authorized in 1952 following an incident in which an automobile repair facility run by the U.S. military at the Yokosuka naval base was closed down and all the employees fired without receiving any retirement allowance. In order to prevent a recurrence of the turmoil that surrounded the case, the government authorized re-

---

nates the necessity of actual government-to-producer payments and because it eliminates the necessity of annual review of the wisdom of such action, it is more desirable than a direct subsidy from the producers' point of view. It is also easier for the government to establish since the low visibility of the action will have less of a detrimental effect on consumers' perceived utility streams than would a more visible, direct subsidy." *Economic Foundations of Political Power* (New York: Free Press, 1973), p. 109.

tirement reserves for all companies as well as for enterprises run by the U.S. forces.[73]

The jumbikin are much more imaginative. They provide for tax deferment, not tax exemption, but used creatively they can effectively free a company of all taxes during a given year (as, for example, they did for Toray Industries, the big nylon manufacturer, during the early 1950's).[74] Various jumbikin include the price fluctuations reserve fund (*kakaku hendō jumbikin*, 1952), the water shortage reserve fund (*kassui jumbikin*, 1952), the breach-of-contract reserve fund (*iyaku sonshitsu hoshō jumbikin*, 1952), and the abnormal hazards reserve fund (*ijō kiken jumbikin*, 1953). By the 1970's reserve funds of the jumbikin variety had been authorized for bad debts, losses on goods returned unsold, bonuses, special repairs, warranties, overseas market development, overseas investment losses, losses incurred in the free trade zone of Okinawa, pollution control, specified railway construction projects, the construction of atomic power generating facilities, reforestation projects, losses due to stock transactions, repurchase of electronic computers (for computer manufacturing and sales companies), and guarantees of the quality of computer programs (for software manufacturers).[75] Most of these jumbikin had time limits on them, except that the 1957 tax revision lifted such limits on reserve funds for export losses.[76]

Other comparable business tax benefits include special deductions from taxable profits for foreign sales of patents and know-how (55 percent); foreign sales of copyrights, except royalties from the showing of movies (20 percent); and payments for planning and consultation services in overseas construction projects (20 percent). The Enterprises Bureau of MITI has always been particularly ingenious on the tax front. In 1964, for example, when Japan had to end its tax deductions for income from exports because of its changed status in GATT, the Enterprises Bureau came up with a new scheme to reward exporters. It replaced export income deductions with changes in the way a company calculates its depreciation based on its previous export performance. The new system allowed a firm to augment its normal depreciation allowance during a given period by multiplying it by the previous periods' export transactions, divided by the previous periods' gross receipts, times 0.8.[77] Tsuruta estimates that for the period 1950 to 1970, the net loss of taxes to the treasury because of enterprise tax benefits of all kinds was nearly ¥3.1 trillion, or a 20 percent cut in the corporate tax rate (30.2 percent for the period 1955–59).[78]

Another area of innovative tax policy was the elimination of excises on targeted products in order to make them easier for consumers to buy (and for producers to sell). The Ministry of Finance credits itself with nurturing the Sony Corporation through its formative years because it lifted commodity taxes on transistor radios for the first two years after their market appearance and because it levied taxes on television receivers only in two-year stages as mass production brought down their prices (taxes went up as prices, calculated in terms of the price per inch of picture tubes, went down).[79] These government policies led to the Japanese phenomenon of all households buying the same goods during a particular period—for example, the "three sacred treasures" (television, washing machine, and refrigerator) of the early sixties, and the "three c's" (car, cooler, and color TV) of the late sixties. Annual reductions in the individual income tax rate in proportion to the growth of the economy, plus selective elimination of excises, thus fueled a made-in-Kasumigaseki "consumer revolution."

In its fully elaborated form, the late 1950's MITI system of nurturing (ikusei) a new industry (for example, petrochemicals) included the following types of measures: First, an investigation was made and a basic policy statement was drafted within the ministry on the need for the industry and on its prospects—an example is the Petrochemical Industry Nurturing Policy adopted by a MITI ministerial conference on July 11, 1955. Second, foreign currency allocations were authorized by MITI and funding was provided for the industry by the Development Bank. Third, licenses were granted for the import of foreign technology (every item of petrochemical technology was obtained on license from abroad). Fourth, the nascent industry was designated as "strategic" in order to give it special and accelerated depreciation on its investments. Fifth, it was provided with improved land on which to build its installations, either free of charge or at nominal cost. (In August 1955, MITI Minister Ishibashi approved the sale of the old military fuel facilities at Yokkaichi, Iwakuni, and Tokuyama to four newly created petrochemical companies despite howls in the Diet from two old military officers, Tsuji Masanobu and Hoshina Zenshirō, in protest against the government's selling to the zaibatsu installations built with military blood). Sixth, the industry was given key tax breaks—in the case of petrochemicals, exemption from customs duties on imported catalytic agents and special machinery, the refund of duties collected on refined petroleum products used as raw materials for petrochemicals, and special laws exempting certain users from gasoline taxes. Seventh, MITI created an "administrative guidance cartel" to regulate competition and coordinate in-

TABLE 18

Growth Rates, 1955–1965

(percent change over previous year)

Year	Real Gross National Product	Civilian plant and equipment investment
1955	8.8	−3.2
1956	7.3	39.0
1957	7.4	25.1
1958	5.6	−4.7
1959	8.9	16.9
1960	13.4	40.9
1961	14.4	36.8
1962	7.0	3.4
1963	10.4	5.3
1964	13.2	20.0
1965	5.1	−6.4

SOURCE: Arisawa Hiromi, ed., *Shōwa keizai shi* (Economic history of the Shōwa era), Tokyo, 1976, p. 371.

vestment among the firms in the industry—in this case, the "Petrochemical Cooperation Discussion Group," established by MITI on December 19, 1964.[80]

There could, of course, be variations on this pattern. Some new industries, such as electronics, were created under a new "temporary measures law"; and if the business was simply too risky or expensive for private enterprise to undertake, a joint public-private corporation might be created—for example, the Japan Synthetic Rubber Corporation, established by law number 150 of June 1, 1957. During approximately the first half of the 1950's, MITI concentrated on steel, electric power, ship-building, and chemical fertilizers. It then fed into the economy, as it deemed them ready for commercialization, synthetic textiles (basic MITI policy adopted in April 1953), plastics (June 1955), petrochemicals (July 1955), automobiles (law of June 1956), electronics (law of June 1957), and so forth.

The results were impressive. The 1956 edition of the EPA's *Economic White Paper* included the famous line "We are no longer living in the days of postwar reconstruction," and the 1961 edition said, "Investment invites more investment."[81] Between the appearance of these two catch phrases, the Japanese economy experienced an average annual industrial investment rate of better than 25 percent, and of over 35 percent during three years (see Table 18). At the end of January 1961 the Enterprises Bureau estimated that the 1,500 "important" companies that reported to it had plant and equipment investment plans worth ¥1.795 trillion, a 30.3 percent increase over the ¥1.377 trillion of fiscal 1960, which was itself a 59.5 percent increase over the ¥863.4 billion of fiscal 1959. The Bureau planned to cool this down to a mere 20.4 percent (¥1.658 trillion) for 1961.[82] One of the big events of the period was the 1961 "Machine Industry ¥3 Trillion Annual Production Memorial Congress," held at Harumi Pier in Tokyo with the Emperor in attendance. According to the sponsor of the Congress, Heavy Industries Bureau Chief Sahashi, the industry had already broken through the ¥4 trillion mark by the time the congress opened.[83]

Not everything was perfect, however. Alarm bells had started ringing in Washington and Western European capitals, and MITI officials dared not ask for whom they were ringing. In the autumn of 1959 the IMF met in Washington, and in December GATT held its general conference in Tokyo. Both gatherings resounded with demands that Japan move at once to free convertibility of its currency and open its domestic market to foreign products. MITI officials knew that their high-growth system would not work with large numbers of foreigners participating in it, and they were worried about the kind of "invasion of American capital" that appeared to have taken place in Europe. Perhaps most important, they were concerned about what role they could play in a "liberalized" economy. They did not have too much time to think about it. On June 24, 1960, as its last official act before resigning, the Kishi cabinet, beleaguered by some 300,000 demonstrators surrounding the Diet building during the security treaty riots, adopted a "Plan for the Liberalization of Trade and Exchange."[84] By mid-July Kishi was gone, Ikeda had become prime minister, and the age of "liberalization" had dawned.

Reflecting on the critical attributes of the postwar high-growth economies, Alfred Chandler concludes, "The German and Japanese miracles were based on improved institutional arrangements and cheap oil."[85] It is the first of these two causes that is of interest to us here, since the second was available to any nation that was clever enough to exploit it, not just to Japan and Germany. Chandler defines institutional arrangements as formal and informal, explicit and implicit social structures "developed to coordinate activities within large formal organizations such as corporations, governmental bodies, and universities and to link those organizations to one another." This comment is refreshingly different from the numerous explanations of Japanese achievements (or failures) in terms of nature, environment, culture, or other ineluctable forces. It contributes to a long overdue demystification of the Japanese high-growth system. That system, it seems to me, resulted from three things: a popular consensus favoring economic priorities, one that was dictated by the harsh conditions of the 1940's and by Japan's situational imperatives; an organizational inheritance from the first 25 years of the Shōwa era; and conscious institutional manipulation starting from the Dodge Line and Korean War periods. All of these political and institutional alignments were aimed at national mobilization to achieve high-speed economic growth, and that is precisely what they brought about.

Japan's priorities are not hard to fathom. As was discussed in the previous chapter, the Pacific War had already imposed on the Japanese some of the harshest conditions endured by the civilian population of any belligerent nation, and the postwar inflation merely exacerbated these conditions. In addition to providing ample incentive to economic mobilization, the misery of the 1940's also provided one other structural support; it made all Japanese equally poor. The high-speed growth of the 1950's was therefore not socially divisive in the sense of benefiting one group or class at the expense of another. Those who gained from the egalitarianism of the 1950's were the Japanese born in the 1960's: the part of the profits of high-speed growth that was distributed was portioned out more or less equitably, and a large proportion was not distributed at all but reinvested. Strongly bolstering the priorities of the Japanese themselves, the United States encouraged Japan to regain its economic strength and did everything an ally could do to help.

The organizational heritage of the Shōwa era is somewhat more complicated. I am thinking of such social supports for public-private cooperation as the experience of failure of both self-imposed and state control, the convergence of views about the nature of economic management among bureaucrats and entrepreneurs as a result of common or very similar educational experiences (for instance, at Tōdai law school), and an extensive cross-penetration of elites as a result of the recruitment of politicians and managers from among the ranks of former government officials. These features of Japanese society are not purely cultural givens, although they would be hard to duplicate in other societies since they reflect what Japan was able to salvage from the rubble of the early Shōwa era. A nation that wished to adopt them might have to reexperience Japan's modern history. The famous Japanese "consensus" appeared only during the 1950's; it did not yet exist during the 1930's and 1940's, which suggests that it was based on changes in historical circumstances and political consciousness and not on unique social values.

The "improved institutional arrangements" have already been discussed in this chapter. In addition to the two-tiered banking system, FILP, an elaborate trade promotion apparatus, high levels of competition among the bank groups, total control of foreign exchange, total screening of foreign capital, and a tax system that made Japan a businessman's paradise, there were all the other institutional arrangements mentioned in Chapter 1. These include a work force made docile by enterprise unionism, extensive subcontracting, "lifetime" employment, massive internal migration from farms to factories, freedom of managers from interference in their programs by corporate stockholders, a system of forced savings due to weak or nonexistent welfare commitments (further powered by government incentives to save through the postal system, which fed its accumulation of funds directly into Ministry of Finance accounts), and many other examples of ad hoc harnessing of seemingly unrelated social institutions to the high-growth system. And it should not be forgotten that the government actively promoted and popularized these innovations through such public-private forums as the Industrial Rationalization Council.

The most important "improved institutional arrangement" of them all was MITI. It has no precise counterpart in any other advanced industrial democracy to play its role as "pilot agency" or "economic general staff." Ironically, its effectiveness was improved by the loss of its absolute powers of state control following the expiration in 1952 of the Temporary Materials Supply and Demand Control Law. MITI did not lose all controls—it still exercised complete control over foreign trade and the introduction of foreign technology—but after 1952 it had to learn to employ indirect, market-conforming methods of intervention in the economy. This differentiated it from both the Ministry of Finance and the Ministry of Agriculture and Forestry, and promoted a form of true public-private cooperation in the industrial sector that preserved the advantages of both self-control and state control while mitigating their disadvantages.

The period 1952 to 1961 was the ministry's golden age. Using FILP, the Development Bank, the Industrial Rationalization Council, and several other powerful institutions, the Enterprises Bureau single-mindedly turned the Japanese industrial structure from light, labor-intensive industries to steel, ships, and automobiles, of which Japan is today the world's leading producer. To find comparable achievements by governmental bureaucracies in other nations, one would have to look to cases like the wartime Manhattan Project in the United States, or to NASA's sending a manned rocket to the moon. Although it is obvious that MITI could not have accomplished what it did without a mobilized people, without innovation and competition in the private sector, nor without the supplementary programs of other agencies of the government, it is equally true that the developmental effort itself required management. This is what MITI supplied.

In 1945, amid the ruins of Osaka, a group of businessmen lamented to an American observer that the militarists had "started the war twenty years too soon."[86] Although the figure should probably be more like forty years than twenty, it is nonetheless true that from about 1941 to 1961 the Japanese economy remained on a war footing. The goal changed from military to economic victory, but the Japanese people could not have worked harder, saved more, or innovated more ruthlessly if they had actually been engaged in a war for national survival, as in fact they were. And just as a nation mobilized for war needs a military general staff, so a nation mobilized for economic development needs an economic general staff. The men of MCI, MM, and MITI had been preparing to play this role since the late 1920's. During the 1950's the trumpet finally sounded.

SEVEN

Administrative Guidance

S AHASHI SHIGERU was born April 5, 1913, in Toki city, Gifu prefecture, a small ceramics center about an hour and a half by train
from Nagoya. He came from a family of modest means (for some
60 years his father operated a small photographic studio near Toki station), and the fact that he ultimately graduated from the Law School
of Tokyo University reflects the considerable openness to talent, regardless of financial capability, of the educational system before the
war. Sahashi attended Tōkai Junior High School in Nagoya, commut-
ing daily on the 5:00 a.m. train; after passing the entrance examination to the Eighth Higher School (Hachikō), in Nagoya—comparable
to an American liberal arts college—he received the support of his father in attending the famous prep school, despite the economic difficulties the family faced in helping him. From Hachikō he went on to
Tōdai, where he graduated in the class of 1937. Sahashi failed in an
attempt during his junior year to pass the Higher-level Public Officials
Examination, but he succeeded as a senior. Because of his lack of connections, he applied to all the ministries. He was accepted by both
Finance and MCI, and he chose Commerce and Industry on the
grounds that even if the country went socialist (as seemed possible
during the depression), MCI would have a role to play.[1]

Four months after Sahashi joined the ministry, Japan was at war
with China, and four months after that Sahashi was drafted and dis-
patched to the central China front. Most graduates of the Imperial
universities in this period were found unfit for military service on
physical grounds, but Sahashi always had a strong constitution and
passed the exam easily. As a Tōdai graduate he experienced a good
deal of physical abuse in the army, but the experience seemed to have
hardened him—he participated in the battle for Wuhan—and to have

contributed to his growing self-confidence. He completed his military service and returned to MCI during the same month that Kishi took over as minister (October 1941). He notes in his autobiography that during his absence the ministry had been completely transformed: the old Industrial Affairs Bureau he had joined in 1937 had been replaced by half-a-dozen industry-specific vertical bureaus, each of them devoted to fostering and controlling its industry for war production. He worked throughout the war in various MCI and Munitions Ministry bureaus until November 1946, when he received his first appointment as a section chief (see Appendix C).

Sahashi Shigeru was destined to become the best-known and certainly the most controversial of MITI's vice-ministers. His background, outlook, and personality all contributed to his reputation as an "exceptional bureaucrat" (*ishoku kanryō*), a "samurai among samurai," an "official who uses force" (*gebaruto kanryō*), the "monster Sahashi" (*kaijin Sachan*) in the press's amused term, the undisputed leader of the "nationalist faction" within MITI, and, in Suzuki Yukio's words, the leading "industrial nationalist" of his time.[2] As chief of the Enterprises Bureau and later as vice-minister, he presided over the ministry's initial response to economic liberalization, and his policies laid the groundwork for the extremely rapid industrial growth of the late 1960's. Through his actions and his strongly enunciated opinions he set off a series of explosions that sent shock waves not only through the worlds of bureaucracy, industry, and finance, but also through the world of politics. His career offers what is probably the best Japanese example of the inseparability of bureaucratic interests and substantive issues of policy when the state dominates administration of the economy.

As one measure of his influence, Sahashi and his era have been made the subjects of at least three popular novels—one of which (by Shiroyama Saburō) Sahashi liked and one of which (by Akaboshi Jun, the pseudonym of Nawa Tarō of the *Asahi shimbun*) deeply irritated him; all of them reflect the public's fascination with his spirited, "high posture" defense of MITI's handling of the economy. Among his many achievements, intentional and inadvertent, he institutionalized "administrative guidance" (*gyōsei shidō*) as MITI's main means of implementing industrial policy after it lost its control over foreign exchange; and the internationalization of the ministry that followed in the wake of his vice-ministership was as much a reaction to him personally as to the policies he espoused.*

---

*The novels are Shiroyama's *Kanryō-tachi no natsu* (The summer of the bureaucrats; 1975), Akaboshi's *Shōsetsu Tsūsan-shō* (A MITI novel; 1971), and Akimoto Hideo's work

Sahashi spent virtually all of his career in the various industrial bureaus—textiles, coal, and heavy industries—where he was also to spend the four critical years 1957 to 1961. As we saw in the last chapter, in 1951 he clashed with Chief Secretary Nagayama and was exiled to Sendai. Upon his return to the home office, he worked as chief of the Coal Policy Section just as the initial rationalization policies were being undertaken to try to save some of Japan's domestic energy production in the face of imported (and at the time highly price-competitive) petroleum. Because of his successful work in coal, the great senior of coal administration and then vice-minister, Hirai Tomisaburō, named Sahashi chief of the sensitive Secretarial Section (Hisho-ka), which was the office in charge of all hiring and personnel assignments for the ministry and also the MITI equivalent of MCI's Documents Section (Bunsho-ka), which Yoshino and Kishi had used so effectively to establish the Yoshino-Kishi line.

Sahashi served longer in charge of personnel than any other postwar official. During his three years in the Secretariat he undertook many important initiatives: he was the first to employ women as career officers in the ministry, he shifted people about on the basis of their capabilities rather than strict seniority (which bothered some of his colleagues), and he eliminated the last vestiges of Nagayama's influence. Most important, he devoted himself to perpetuating the so-called Kishi-Shiina approach (heavy industrialization) to policy-making within the ministry. Through careful and timely transfers of both his seniors and his juniors, he set up the line of descent for the vice-ministership from Ishihara Takeo to Ueno Kōshichi to Tokunaga Hisatsugu to Matsuo Kinzō—and, so he hoped, to Sahashi Shigeru. The key to this strategy was making the post of chief of the Enterprises Bureau the last stop before the vice-ministership, which ap-

---

of the same name, *Shōsetsu Tsūsan-shō* (1975). Akimoto's novel first appeared serially in the popular weekly magazine *Shūkan bunshun*. Both Akaboshi and Akimoto use the real names of people in their books, and Akaboshi's is not really a novel (the word "novel" appears to have been added to try to inhibit attacks on it). All three cover the same ground—the reaction to liberalization, the Sahashi-Imai fight for the vice-ministership, Sahashi's clash with Sumitomo Metals, the involvement of politicians in the personnel affairs of the bureaucracy, and so forth—and Akaboshi's differs only in having come first. For a concordance to the names in Shiroyama, see *Kankai*, November 1975, pp. 130–31; to cite a few examples, Kazagoshi in the novel is Sahashi, Sudō Keisaku is Prime Minister Satō Eisaku, and Minister Kuki ("nine devils") is Miki Takeo, MITI minister from June 1965 to December 1966. Sahashi expressed his dislike of Akaboshi's book to me in an interview in Tokyo, September 5, 1974; and Ōjimi Yoshihisa, vice-minister in 1971, has written that he was appalled that the novel should have been published while he was in office (*Tsūsan jyānaru*, May 24, 1975, p. 44). For Sahashi's elliptical praise of Shiroyama's book, see *ibid.*, p. 38.

peared to have been achieved in July 1961 when Matsuo Kinzō moved from the Enterprises Bureau to the top job and Sahashi moved to the Enterprises Bureau.

In the course of arranging things in this way, Sahashi developed within the ministry two groups, one made up of his close associates and one of men who were more distant from him—they were not yet explicit factions but rather different career specializations within trade and industrial administration. The group closest to him comprised the industrial-policy specialists from the Enterprises Bureau and the industry-specific bureaus; the more distant group was made up of officials who had served overseas in embassy or JETRO postings or who worked in international trade positions within the ministry. Sahashi once described himself as "weak in foreign languages" and as a "domestic-use-only bureaucrat," descriptions that would also apply to most of the people he favored.[3] Sahashi's personnel administration was not particularly controversial during the 1950's; it became so only in retrospect, with the onset of liberalization and MITI's response to it. The people whom Sahashi advanced and who in turn helped him were all acknowledged to be the leaders of heavy and chemical industrialization, at the time the basic policy that was widely supported throughout the ministry.

Just before Ishihara Takeo retired as vice-minister in June 1957, he asked Sahashi what post he would like in the ministry in return for his long and effective service as personnel officer. Sahashi chose deputy director of the Heavy Industries Bureau, which was just then at the peak of its influence and also the most old-fashioned bureau in the ministry. The Heavy Industries Bureau had jurisdiction over both the nurturing and the export sales of steel, machine tools, general machinery, automobiles, electronics, heavy electrical equipment, rolling stock, and aviation products—and over the industries that turned them out. Machines in general were beginning to occupy a commanding share of Japan's high-value-added exports, and its enterprises were also among the leading investors in all domestic industry. The Heavy Industries Bureau was at the cutting edge of the Kishi-Shiina line (and, it should also be noted, Kishi was prime minister from 1957 to 1960, Shiina MITI minister from 1960 to 1961). Sahashi had chosen well.

Among his many duties Sahashi had to deal with the steel industry. One of his first achievements was setting up a price maintenance cartel for steel in 1958 and getting it approved by the Fair Trade Commission. This type of work was not difficult for a MITI officer. Steel had been a government enterprise for half of the twentieth century, and most of the people Sahashi dealt with were either his ministerial seniors or industrialists he had known since his wartime work in the Iron and Steel Section of the Munitions Ministry. They included Ojima Arakazu, Kishi's successor as vice-minister in 1941 and subsequently president of Yawata Steel, one of the two successor companies to Japan Steel after SCAP had broken it up; Inayama Yoshihiro, who had entered MCI in 1927 as an official at the then state-owned Yawata works and who in 1962 followed Ojima as president of Yawata Steel; Nagano Shigeo, president of Fuji Steel, the other successor of old Japan Steel, and a man who had worked with Sahashi in the wartime Iron and Steel Control Association; Fujii Heigo, a Yawata vice-president and a man who came to Sahashi's aid in his clash a few years later with the non-state-oriented Sumitomo Metals Company; and Hirai Tomisaburō, a Yawata director and the vice-minister who had appointed Sahashi to the Secretarial Section in 1954. Ojima would soon be playing a key role in MITI's affairs as head of the new Industrial Structure Investigation Council, the ministry's blue-ribbon committee for thinking of ways to counter the effects of liberalization. Sahashi's relations with the Yawata and Fuji steel companies were cordial—so cordial that when he was vice-minister, leaders of Sumitomo Metals would charge that MITI had become the "Kasumigaseki office of Yawata Steel."[4]

Not so cordial were Sahashi's relations with the International Business Machines Corporation. The IBM case did, however, afford him one of his first opportunities to appear as a samurai warding off the "invasion of American capital." MITI already had various policies intended to exclude foreign enterprises from the Japanese domestic market—informal rules such as not allowing foreigners more than a 50 percent share in a joint venture, restricting the number and voting rights of foreigners on the boards of directors of Japanese firms, stopping foreigners from buying Japanese firms without the firm's consent—and, ultimately, excluding all foreign participation in the Japanese economy without MITI's permission. In a sensational case of the late 1950's, the Heavy Industries Bureau had done everything in its power to obstruct a proposed joint venture between Singer Sewing Machines of the United States and Pine Sewing Machines of Japan. Singer, the prewar leader, was attempting to recapture its old markets, but MITI was fostering a domestic sewing-machine industry, and so it slapped production limitations on the Singer-Pine collaboration.[5] IBM, however, posed special problems. Since it had organized itself in Japan as a yen-based company, MITI's controls over the use or repatriation of foreign exchange did not apply. More important, IBM held all the basic patents on computer technology, which effectively blocked the development of a Japanese computer industry.

Sahashi wanted IBM's patents and made no bones about it. In as forthright a manner as possible, he made his position clear to IBM-Japan: "We will take every measure possible to obstruct the success of your business unless you license IBM patents to Japanese firms and charge them no more than a 5 percent royalty."[6] In one of his negotiating sessions, Sahashi proudly recalls, he said that "we do not have an inferiority complex toward you; we only need time and money to compete effectively."[7] IBM ultimately had to come to terms. It sold its patents and accepted MITI's administrative guidance over the number of computers it could market domestically as conditions for manufacturing in Japan. Since IBM leased its machines rather than selling them outright, in 1961 Sahashi responded by setting up a semiofficial Japan Electronic Computer Company, financed by the Development Bank, to buy hardware from domestic producers and lease it to customers. To ensure MITI's control, he appointed the old MCI senior, Murase Naokai, president of the leasing company.

Sahashi's vigorous industrial xenophobia made him quite popular with many industrialists, but in another realm of his official activities—relations with the political world—he was not nearly so clever or perceptive an operator as he had been vis-à-vis IBM. Ever since the creation in 1955 of the Liberal Democratic Party, politicians slowly had been rising in power as rivals to the bureaucrats, although the bureaucrats were not fully attuned to what was happening. First the military bureaucrats and then the economic bureaucrats had dominated Japanese government from 1932 to at least 1955. From around 1960, however, a milieu comparable to the one that Yoshino Shinji had worked in during the 1920's began to reappear; the new politicians were much more dependent on the bureaucracy than they had been in the earlier period, but on the other hand they had much stronger constitutional powers than before. The bureaucrats were lulled because after Ishibashi's untimely resignation in 1957 because of illness, his successors as prime minister had all been famous ex-bureaucrats—Kishi, Ikeda, and Satō.* However, even Ikeda and Satō had to pay attention to the political process; they were not merely for-

---

*Some Japanese political analysts lament the control from 1957 to 1972 of the prime ministership by former bureaucrats. They comment rather wanly that if only Ishibashi had worn an overcoat on the February day in 1957 when he attended an outdoor celebration at his alma mater, Waseda University, the political history of postwar Japan might have been quite different. See *Yomiuri shimbun*, Political Department, *Sōri daijin* (The prime minister), rev. ed. (Tokyo: Yomiuri Shimbun Sha, 1972), p. 80.

mer bureaucrats but had also become very skilled politicians. This is something Sahashi did not understand.

The LDP was quite prepared to leave basic policy-making to the bureaucracy, but when bureaucrats began to try to use politicians in their own intrabureaucratic struggles, they had to be prepared to provide a quid pro quo. For example, while still director of the Heavy Industries Bureau, Sahashi had a brilliant idea for the promotion of exports of Japanese machines—he would send a ship outfitted as a floating industrial exposition to call at American and European ports. For this purpose he first used a converted cargo vessel, but he really wanted a new ship, to be constructed at government expense and specifically designed as an oceangoing trade fair. Officials of the Budget Bureau were not convinced that the new ship was needed. In order to bring some pressure on his budgetary colleagues to change their minds, Sahashi sought the assistance of Ōno Bamboku (1890–1964), a powerful LDP faction leader, strong man of the "party-men's factions" (as distinct from the ex-bureaucrats' factions) in the Diet, and a fellow native of Gifu prefecture. Ōno came through, Sahashi got his ship, and everyone agreed that it was a splendid idea. (Ironically enough, seventeen years later the Japanese loaned the ship, the *Sakura Maru* or *Cherry Blossom*, to the United States so that it could bring *its* products to show off in Japanese ports.)[8] Sahashi made only one mistake; he forgot to thank Ōno. A few years later, after Sahashi had tried this ploy with a few other politicians (some of them Ōno's rivals), Ōno got even—and Ikeda could not help Sahashi since Ikeda had political problems of his own. The *Sakura Maru* was very effective as a kind of waterborne JETRO, but it came back to haunt Sahashi in 1963 when he sought the vice-ministership.[9]

While Sahashi was thus engaged in the Heavy Industries Bureau, a fellow member of the class of 1937, Imai Zen'ei, was busy dealing with the prime issue of the time: What should be the country's response to demands from international organizations and from Japan's allies that it liberalize its controls over the economy? Imai had had a career in MITI very different from Sahashi's. Born in Niigata on October 5, 1913, he—like Sahashi—graduated from Tōdai Law, although he came to Tokyo University via the more elite First Higher School (Ichikō) in Tokyo. During the war he worked on the materials mobilization plans, which was good preparation for his occupation-era assignments in the Coal Agency and the Economic Stabilization Board (see Appendix C). Many leaders of the ministry had identified Imai as one of the most capable officials from the class of 1937 well before Sahashi gained prominence. After the creation of MITI Imai worked primarily in international trade administration, and he served in the Japanese Embassy in Washington for the first year after it reopened. He and Sahashi served in the Secretariat at the same time, but in different sections, and Imai received his first assignment as a bureau chief two years before Sahashi got his. It was as chief of the Textiles Bureau from August 1958 to February 1961 that Imai had to confront the liberalization problem.

There is no question that MITI, as a bureaucracy, feared that liberalization might eliminate its raison d'etre, and for this reason, if no other, it sought to obtain new control powers. However, MITI officials, as economic administrators, were also deeply worried about structural flaws in the system they had created—what they sometimes called its *hizumi*, or "distortions"—and about the likelihood that liberalization would heighten these "distortions." Nationalism played a part in their concerns—the possibility that a fully "opened" Japanese economy would be swamped by larger, much better capitalized foreign enterprises—but even without the pressures to liberalize, they knew that they would have to do something about the superficially risk-free overinvestment the system was generating. The rise of "excess competition," as it was called, coincided with the appearance of liberalization as a policy problem, and the issues involved in dealing with the one greatly influenced the response to the other. The textile industry provided one of the worst examples of overinvestment and excess competition.

Imai's term as chief textiles administrator was one of deepening crisis. The system of foreign exchange budgets was still in full operation, but Imai recognized that he needed still more controls in order to prevent recurring overproduction in the unruly cotton textile industry. "The abuses that accompanied the allocation system for raw cotton," he has recalled, "were simply extraordinary. I advocated replacing the system with a Raw Cotton Import Public Corporation [Menka Yu'nyū Kōdan], but the industry violently opposed this idea. The fundamental problem of the allocation system was that it encouraged excess investment in production facilities and led to overcapacity. We needed allocation authority over investment, not just over raw materials."[10] The big spinners—Teijin, Toray, Kanebō, and Unitika—were hard enough to control, since they often fell back on the old Osaka tradition of resisting governmental intervention in their affairs; but the smaller manufacturers were even worse. They had borrowed from their banks and invested in their equipment with the full expectation that they would receive government-guaranteed allotments of imported raw cotton; the menace of liberalization brought down on the government and the Diet a blizzard of protest from the industry.

During the late 1950's imports of raw cotton and wool took over 20 percent of the foreign exchange budget, a figure higher than that for crude oil during the 1970's. This situation had to change. Moreover, the United States was starting to object to the flood of "dollar blouses" from Japan, and on November 16, 1960, President Eisenhower promulgated his "defense of the dollar" policy, which the Kennedy administration continued. It reduced dollar payments by U.S. forces stationed overseas, put priority on the purchase of American products for U.S. foreign aid programs, and called for negotiations between the U.S. and Japan over limitations on exports of cotton textiles.

As a first step in dealing with these problems, in October 1958 Imai convened a meeting of an informal government-industry discussion group called the Textiles Overall Countermeasures Committee (Sen'i Sōgō Taisaku Kondankai). The key figure on the committee was Horie Shigeo, then president of the Bank of Tokyo (the postwar successor to the Yokohama Specie Bank and the country's main foreign exchange institution). Other members included Ōya Shinzō, former MCI minister and the president of Teijin; Nakayama Sohei from the Industrial Bank of Japan; Inaba Hidezō, formerly of the Cabinet Planning Board and in 1958 a leading economic commentator; and other leaders of the textile industry.

Horie spoke often to the group about the moves toward full currency convertibility among the European nations (achieved in December 1958) and of the creation of the European Common Market. He was well informed on the recent shift by Germany and England to "article 8 status" in the IMF, which required an end to restrictions on payments for current transactions and on the convertibility of currency held by nonresidents; and he said that Japan as a nation that had to trade to live could not lag far behind its trading partners and competitors. Upon becoming MITI minister in June 1959, Ikeda attended the committee meetings, where he was quoted as saying, "Mr. Horie knows what he's talking about in terms of global trends." [11]

In December 1959, on the basis of the committee's deliberations and Imai's recommendation, Ikeda took his first liberalization decision: he freed raw cotton and wool imports from all governmental restrictions. This was a powerful precedent. In January 1960 the government established a Cabinet Council on the Advancement of Trade Liberalization (Bōeki Jiyūka Sokushin Kakuryō Kaigi) to prepare liberalization plans for other industries, and this in turn led on March 8, 1960, to a great debate at a MITI ministerial conference called to discuss liberalization. According to the report of Komatsu Yūgorō, Matsuo Taiichirō, then director of the International Trade Bureau, was alone in speaking in favor of the policy. Imai did not have to speak; he was already identified with liberalization—a hero to some and a near traitor to others.[12] He had, however, clearly won the trust and confidence of the MITI minister, who was soon to become prime minister.

Imai himself has noted that liberalization was as much a political and administrative problem as an economic one. He favored it because of his personal dislike for the controlled economy, a dislike that grew out of the occupation. But he also saw liberalization as an opportunity to move Japan toward an industrial structure with fewer enterprises overall, but with more, proportionately, in high-technology industries, and in this his position and Sahashi's coincided. Within the ministry as a whole, however, young officials thought that liberalization would mean the end of their jobs, senior officials in the vertical bureaus were worried about the structural weaknesses of their industries, and politicians feared for their reelection. Ikeda persisted nonetheless. In June the outgoing Kishi cabinet adopted Ikeda's trade liberalization plan, which set the goal of an economy that would be 80 percent liberalized within three years.

The figure of 80 percent was to be calculated according to the commodities and products listed on the Brussels Customs Schedule. On this basis, the rate of import liberalization, which in April 1956 stood at 22 percent, had been raised by April 1960 to 41 percent. The plan's 80 percent liberalization was to be attained by fiscal 1963, the initial target for 1961 being set at 62 percent. The mere publication of these figures set off a complicated process of jockeying by each industry (and its MITI bureau) to have the lifting of its controls scheduled late rather than early. Shiroyama suggests in his novel that Ikeda actually began with cotton and wool because these industries were heavy contributors to his political rivals, although Imai never mentions this as a consideration.[13]

It is hard to recapture today the crisis atmosphere that existed in Japanese industrial circles during 1961. The press prattled on endlessly about "the second coming of the black ships," "the defenselessness of the Japanese islands in the face of attack from huge foreign capitalist powers," and "the readying of the Japanese economy for a bloodstained battle between national capital and foreign capital."[14] Sahashi himself invoked the name of the National General Mobilization Law of 1938 and said that Japan again required a "national general mobilization" in order to create an economic system that could withstand the rigors of international competition.[15] As it turned out, the crisis was considerably overstated—from 1960 to 1965 exports more than doubled on a customs-clearance basis (from $4 billion to $8.7 billion), suggesting the existence of substantial international competitive strength in the economy. Nonetheless, the sense of crisis was real, and it may well have helped to motivate the economy's export performance.

The Ikeda government took many measures intended to relieve the widespread anxiety. In 1960 it created the Asian Economic Research Institute as a government organ concerned with the study of markets in underdeveloped countries, and in 1961 it set up the Overseas Economic Cooperation Fund to disburse foreign aid. Both agencies were promoted abroad as evidence of Japan's expanding contributions to allied foreign aid efforts, but domestically they were justified as export promotion agencies, since the aid Japan gave would be tied to purchases of Japanese plants and equipment. During 1960 the government also revised tariff rates and schedules to offer greater protection to liberalized industries, and it expanded the capital of the Export-Import Bank in order to finance more exports.

The most famous of the government's calmatives was Ikeda's Income-doubling Plan, formally adopted by the cabinet on December 27, 1960. The plan itself was wildly overfulfilled, and its chief importance in retrospect was the psychological effect it had in creating optimism about the future to counterbalance the pessimism about liberalization coming from the press and MITI. The Income-doubling Plan did, however, have one important bureaucratic consequence. Ikeda had assigned to the Economic Planning Agency the task of drafting the plan, and the publicity surrounding the EPA's efforts gave its so-called agency economists—that is, career officials of the EPA rather than transferees from MITI or Finance—a chance to try to break free of MITI's dominance. The EPA sought to name one of its own officials, the prominent economist and future foreign minister Ōkita Saburō, to be vice-minister of the agency, rather than accept another senior MITI official. MITI successfully beat back this attempt, but in the process it had to make the EPA post a terminal position in the MITI chain of command; a MITI official sent to the EPA as vice-minister could no longer return to the ministry. As we shall see, this was important because it gave Sahashi the chance to eliminate two final rivals in his quest for the MITI vice-ministership by seeing to it that the MITI minister appointed them EPA vice-minister, where they would be out of the running for the big prize.

The most important bureaucratic response to liberalization was

MITI's invention of the concept of "industrial structure" and the creation on April 1, 1961, of the Industrial Structure Investigation Council (Sangyō Kōzō Chōsa Kai). The concept was simply a shorthand term for comparisons of Japanese industries with those of North America and Western Europe in terms of their capitalization, export ratios, concentration, economies of scale, and other indicators of international competitive ability. Once such comparisons had been made, the concept was further used to assert that Japanese industries were fully capable of competing in the international commercial arena—but not as they were presently structured. The number of enterprises competing in each industry had to be reduced, the few that were to remain had to be enlarged, and the preemptive investment and excess productive capacity that the keiretsu system had generated had to be brought under control. Industrial structure became the key intellectual defense for the devices Sahashi later promoted as vice-minister—mergers and investment-coordination cartels in important industries.[16]

The Investigation Council perfected and legitimized the concept. Led by Ojima Arakazu, former MCI vice-minister and president of Yawata Steel, the council brought together all the top leaders of Japanese industry; and it produced one of the most searching analyses of any economy ever undertaken by a government.[17] When the council's charter expired in 1964, it was merged with the old Industrial Rationalization Council of 1949; and it continues to the present as MITI's main official channel for administrative guidance of industry, the Industrial Structure Council (Sangyō Kōzō Shingikai).

The original Industrial Structure Investigation Council was an outstanding example of MITI's employment of an ostensibly civilian commission to popularize and provide authority for its policies. The actual work of the council was done by MITI; the Enterprises Bureau was charged with writing reports and recommendations on such topics as industrial finance, labor, technology, and international economics, while the new Industrial Structure Investigation Office, which was attached to the Secretariat, investigated individual industries. The head of the office was Ōjimi Yoshihisa, the author of Ikeda's 1960 liberalization plan and himself a future MITI vice-minister.

The 50 members of the council strongly reflected MITI's "old boy" networks. In addition to its chairman, Ojima Arakazu, the membership included Ishihara Takeo, executive director of the Tokyo Electric Power Company; Ueno Kōshichi, executive director of the Kansai Electric Power Company; and Tokunaga Hisatsugu, executive director of Fuji Steel—all of them recently retired MITI vice-ministers—plus such old stalwarts from MCI, MM, and the Cabinet Planning Board as Uemura Kōgorō, Inaba Hidezō, Kitano Shigeo, Inayama Yoshihiro, and several other former officials. The key subunit of the council, its Industrial Order Committee (Sangyō Taisei Bukai), where Sahashi worked out his ideas for a new comprehensive control law, had only seven members. They included an ex-Agriculture bureaucrat, the president of the Development Bank, an *Asahi* editor, the executive director of Keidanren, the president of a private economic research institute, and a former MITI vice-minister (Tokunaga); the committee's chairman was the ubiquitous Arisawa Hiromi, the inventor of priority production during the occupation, a leader of the Industrial Rationalization Council, an authority on the coal industry, and MITI's most important academic adviser.

During July 1961 Satō Eisaku succeeded Shiina Etsusaburō as MITI minister, and Sahashi Shigeru succeeded Matsuo Kinzō (who became vice-minister) as director of the Enterprises Bureau. When this occurred Imai Zen'ei was working in the difficult job of chief of the International Trade Bureau, where in conjunction with the MITI-controlled Coordination Bureau of the EPA he actually decided on the liberalization schedules for various industries. A year later, during July 1962, Imai was transferred to what was normally a preretirement position, director of the Patent Agency. Sahashi thus was left as the last major figure from the class of 1937 with an outstanding record in the mainstream of the ministry, industrial policy.

He still had one obstacle in his path to the vice-ministership, however. Matsuo Kinzō, the incumbent vice-minister, was from the class of 1934; but there were within the ministry two outstanding officials, one each from the classes of 1935 and 1936, who might be expected to take precedence over a member of the class of 1937. One of them, Koide Eiichi (1935), was out of the running because he was vice-minister of the EPA, the post that had been made a preretirement slot after the agency's economists' attempted coup. The other, Ōbori Hiromu (1936), former chief of the Mining and Public Utilities bureaus and the current director of the Medium and Smaller Enterprises Agency, was Sahashi's problem. To get him out of the way, Matsuo and Sahashi suggested to Minister Satō that he appoint Ōbori as vice-minister of the EPA when Koide made his amakudari.

Despite protests from Koide, Ōbori himself, many other officials in the ministry, and even Chief Cabinet Secretary Ōhira Masayoshi (a future prime-minister and himself no stranger to bureaucratic infighting from his years in the Ministry of Finance), Satō went ahead with

Ōbori's appointment to the EPA. The path ahead now seemed clear for Sahashi, but the involvement of powerful politicians in the internal affairs of the ministry would, like the *Sakura Maru* affair, come at a price for both the ministry and Sahashi. Satō's motives were to try to secure MITI as a base of operations for his own political drive to succeed Ikeda as prime minister—much as Ikeda himself had done with Finance and Kōno Ichirō with Agriculture. Moreover, rumors had circulated that Sahashi was thinking of running for the Diet after his own retirement, and Satō wanted to make sure that if elected he would join the Satō faction—a point not lost on two other faction leaders, Ikeda and Ōno Bamboku.[18]

Meanwhile, Sahashi's great achievement as chief of the Enterprises Bureau was the conception and advocacy of the Special Measures Law for the Promotion of Designated Industries (Tokutei Sangyō Shinkō Rinji Sochi Hōan, cabinet submission number 151 of 1963). This bill ultimately died in the Diet because it became simply too controversial for any politician to touch, but the debate over it crystalized all the key issues that had surfaced in the Japanese economy after postwar reconstruction, and it paved the way for the informal implementation of the bill's provisions during the late 1960's through administrative guidance. The Special Measures Law was without question the single most important piece of proposed economic legislation since the early years of the occupation.[19] Its genesis, the furor surrounding it, and its final demise involved liberalization policy, jurisdictional disputes between MITI and the Ministry of Finance, the Antimonopoly Law, a debate over "excess competition" in the Japanese economy, factional politics in the LDP, and a battle inside MITI over the vice-ministership—in short, the whole range of issues that go to make up Japanese industrial policy.

The basic problem addressed by the Special Measures Law was not liberalization itself, although the foreign demands for liberalization provided an excellent cover to avoid saying too publicly what the problem really was. Sahashi was less enthusiastic about liberalization than Imai, but he too recognized that it was an inevitable—even a desirable—development if Japan was to continue to expand its overseas markets and economic growth. The basic problem was virtually the same as that confronted by Yoshino Shinji during the late 1920's and early 1930's—too many protected enterprises in too many small factories engaged in too vigorous and economically unproductive competition. Liberalization was going to expose this situation to international commercial pressure, which would thoroughly disrupt the Japanese economy, possibly see a good part of it pass into foreign ownership, and very likely leave MITI without any continuing function.[20]

For Sahashi the essence of the problem was to find some way to bring the financial and investment decisions of enterprises into the framework of control and nurturing (ikusei) that MITI had developed. The Ministry of Finance (which controlled the banks) and the Fair Trade Commission (which administered the Antimonopoly Law) were sure to object to any encroachment on their territory. And the intervening decades notwithstanding, the answer to these structural problems seemed, mutatis mutandis, to be the same one Yoshino and Kishi had discovered during the 1930's—cartels, enforced mergers, pressure on medium and smaller enterprises, converting some businesses to other lines of activity, something like the old "enterprise readjustment" movement but under a different name. Sahashi's new terms for these old activities were public-private cooperation (*kanmin kyōchō*); consolidation of the industrial order (*sangyō taisei seibi*); and structural finance (*taisei kin'yū*), meaning government loans and tax breaks to encourage mergers.

A much more difficult problem was how to do it. The old debates between state control and laissez faire were still quite familiar to the seniors of the industrial world, and they were agreed that they did not like state control. In order to try to deal with such objections, Takashima Setsuo, Sahashi's deputy director of the Enterprises Bureau (June 1962 to October 1963), published a skillfully argued article in the May 1963 issue of the journal *Keizai hyōron* (Economic review). He patiently dissected the weaknesses of "bureaucratic control"—he did not find many, but he acknowledged that people did not like it. And he discussed "self-coordination"—"It does not achieve the results desired by the people." And then he introduced MITI's proposed resolution of the dichotomy, "administration by inducement." In Takashima's view, although this leaves to the government the determination of the direction industry is to take, it avoids the worst problems of policy implementation.[21] As a practical matter, administration by inducement came to mean committees of cooperating bureaucrats, industrialists, and financiers that would set investment rates, promote mergers, discourage new firms from entering given industries, and in general try to build an industrial structure on a par with those of the United States and West Germany, the two prime external reference economies.

To draft a law encompassing these goals and methods, Sahashi brought together in the Enterprises Bureau an extremely talented group of MITI officers. Shortly after taking over as bureau chief, he sent a personal letter to Morozumi Yoshihiko, who was then working in the Japanese Embassy in Paris (June 1956 to August 1961), telling him that liberalization was inevitable, that a new industrial policy to deal with it was mandatory, and asking him to join the Enterprises Bureau. Morozumi represented a new breed of officer in the ministry, men who combined overseas service, primarily in continental Europe rather than in the Anglo-American countries, with industrial policy expertise. Many of them, including Morozumi, became vice-ministers during the 1970's. They were the authorities within the ministry on the Common Market, on the so-called invasion of Europe by American capital, and on such ideas for industrial development as the French concept of *économie concertée*, or what the Japanese call the "mixed economy" (*kongō keizai*).* In addition to Morozumi, MITI men with this sort of experience included Hayashi Shintarō (director of the JETRO office in Hamburg, 1961–65), Komatsu Yūgorō (Japanese Embassy, Bonn, 1960–65), and Masuda Minoru (Japanese Embassy, Brussels, 1962–66).[22] Before Sahashi's downfall, these officers were strong supporters of his proposed law, but during the late 1960's they shifted to the so-called international faction.

Morozumi was a major author of the Special Measures Law, contributing to it his experience gained in General de Gaulle's Paris, his fear of "American capital," and his knowledge of French precedents for what Sahashi wanted to do in Japan. On August 25, 1961, Sahashi named him chief of the First Enterprises Section in the Enterprises Bureau. Other participants in the drafting of the law were Takashima, the bureau's deputy director; Miyake Yukio, chief of the Industrial Fi-

---

* According to Stephen S. Cohen, "The *économie concertée* is a partnership of big business, the state and, in theory though not in practice, the trade unions. The managers of big business and the managers of the state run the modern core of a nation's economy—mostly the oligopoly sectors. Positive cooperation—not conflict, as in a market ideology—is its motor. The state is not a silent partner; it is an initiating, active partner. It intervenes in every aspect of economic affairs, encouraging, teaching, sometimes even threatening. Its purpose is to promote economic modernization: greater efficiency, greater productivity, greater expansion. The partnership works for the general interest; and it works outside the traditional political arena. Parliament and the constellation of institutions that surrounds parliament are not necessary for the smooth functioning of the system. . . . The *économie concertée* is the new higher civil servants' favorite model of economic and social organization. It is fundamentally an attitude of cooperation between the stewards of the state and the managers of big business." *Modern Capitalist Planning: The French Model* (Cambridge, Mass.: Harvard University Press, 1969), pp. 51–52. Former MITI Vice-Minister Ōjimi Yoshihisa states bluntly that "the Special Measures Law was actually an attempt to introduce the French *économie concertée* into Japan." Ōjimi Yoshihisa and Uchida Tadao, "Nihon no kanryō gyōsei to kanmin kyōchō taisei" (Japan's bureaucratic administration and the public-private cooperative system), *Gendai keizai*, September 1972, p. 30.

nance Section and a protégé of Sahashi's; and two younger officers, Konaga Keiichi (who later served as Prime Minister Tanaka's assistant and was the actual author of Tanaka's *Plan for the Reform of the Japanese Archipelago*) and Uchida Genkō (an engineer who had played an active role in fostering the automobile industry).[23]

The Enterprises Bureau first entitled its brainchild the Draft Law of Special Measures for Strengthening the International Competitive Ability of Designated Industries. It was the cabinet that changed its name. Article 1 spelled out the law's objectives: to promote the sound development of the national economy by raising the international competitive ability of designated industries in order to counter the effects of liberalization. Article 2 designated the first three industries—special steels, automobiles, and petrochemicals—and authorized the designation of others by cabinet order after consultation with the Industrial Structure Investigation Council. Articles 3 and 4 incorporated the public-private cooperation formula, which Sahashi held to be the very heart of the whole law.[24] These articles authorized three-way committees (*kondankai*), composed of representatives of government, industry, and finance, which were to establish and carry out "promotion standards" for each particular industry. It is perhaps worth noting that the Japanese word kondankai (discussion group, or committee) implies more than its English equivalents. *Kenkyūsha's New Japanese-English Dictionary* (4th ed.) gives for kondankai the Italian word *conversazione*, "a verbal agreement between two or more parties," which suggests something less than a contract but considerably more than a "conversation."

Articles 5 and 6 required managers of designated industries to cooperate in raising the competitive ability of their firms, said that banks had to "give heed to" loan requests from designated industries, and ordered government banks to assist them. Articles 7 and 8 provided for "structural financing" for designated industries, various tax exemptions to be specified by cabinet orders, and reductions in the corporate income tax. Article 9 legalized "cooperative behavior" by enterprises in a designated industry and specifically exempted such behavior from the purview of the Antimonopoly Law. Articles 10, 11, 12, and 13 were given over to legal technicalities. Like most Japanese statutes, the Special Measures Law was comparatively short.[25]

Disclosure of the contents of the law in the Industrial Structure Investigation Council immediately set off three major controversies. The first was the old favorite of self-coordination versus public-private cooperation. Much in the tradition of Kobayashi Ichizō at the time of Prince Konoe's New Structure Movement, Ishizaka Taizō, the venerable head of Keidanren, let it be known that he favored self-imposed control. He went on to say that "all the government has to do is watch for fires and thieves. It can leave the rest of work up to civilians"; but he also believed that "opponents of foreign investment are like grown men wearing diapers, refusing to leave their mothers' breasts."[26] Although Keidanren refused to support the bill, Sahashi did gain the support of its rival organization, the Japan Committee for Economic Development (Keizai Dōyūkai).

The second controversy concerned the law's stipulation that banks and bankers be included in the various "discussion groups." Leaders of the banking community concluded, accurately, that this was a direct attack on their keiretsu; and the Ministry of Finance responded with indignation to this intrusion into its territory by MITI. Usami Makoto, president of the Mitsubishi Bank and then chairman of the National Banking Association (Zenkoku Ginkō Kyōkai), refused to have anything to do with the Special Measures Law.

The third controversy was generated by the Fair Trade Commission and its belief that Sahashi was trying to get rid of the Antimonopoly Law once and for all. On December 5, 1962, Sahashi opened negotiations with the FTC concerning the purposes of the law, the threat posed by liberalization to Japan's economy, and the need for cartels. After some six meetings Sahashi seemed to have made some headway with the commission, and on February 1, 1963, the ministry published the law. Nevertheless, after the matter went to the cabinet, Ikeda still had to order the FTC to cooperate.

Sahashi's main backing in these disputes came from the Industrial Structure Investigation Council. The Industrial Order Committee (headed by Professor Arisawa), which Sahashi had consulted on every step he took, was his main bastion of strength, but during October 1962 the Industrial Finance Committee (Sangyō Kin'yū Bukai) also contributed its support. Headed by Nakayama Sohei of the Industrial Bank, and with only four other members (former MITI Vice-Minister Ueno, the president of a paper company, a newspaper executive, and the president of the Export-Import Bank), the committee concluded that adding banks to the discussion groups was an excellent idea and long overdue.

Given the general furor, the politicians had no choice but to step in and try to resolve these numerous issues. On February 14, 1963, Prime Minister Ikeda ordered all the economic ministers in the cabinet to meet with him on a regular basis until the law's future was decided. Hardly a week after this group went to work, the Kansai Branch of Keidanren expressed its formal opposition to MITI's proposed evisceration of the Antimonopoly Law (as we shall see, there was more to this opposition from Osaka than met the eye). When the ministers finally acted, they changed the name of the law to the more innocuous Special Measures Law for the Promotion of Designated Industries, put a five-year limit on it, altered the ways in which industries could be designated, and strengthened the participation of the minister of finance in the law's administration. With these changes the LDP's Political Affairs Research Council (where former Finance Ministry bureaucrats were very strong) signed on over the objections of the Banking Bureau, and on March 22, 1963, the party gave its final approval. On the same day the cabinet formally voted to sponsor the bill, and on March 25 it was introduced in the House of Representatives and referred to the Commerce and Industry Committee.

As expected, the opposition parties denounced the law as a return of bureaucratic control, the press personalized it as a "save MITI" bill, pundits referred to it as the "charge of the Sahashi brigade," and orators droned on about the demise of the "economic constitution." Sahashi spent hours answering questions in the Diet, but his problem was not with the opposition. He soon discovered that the cabinet, the LDP, and even his own minister had quietly decided not to make a fight. The Special Measures Law became known as "sponsorless legislation," meaning that the establishment had abandoned it. The bill was never defeated; it simply never came to a vote. The government introduced it in the 43rd (December 24, 1962, to July 6, 1963), the 44th (October 15 to October 23, 1963), and the 46th (December 23, 1963, to June 26, 1964) sessions of the Diet, but after having done that, LDP party leaders never lifted a finger to bring it to the floor for a vote. Officially MITI explained the law's failure as due to "misunderstandings, [bureaucratic] sectionalism, and political tricks," and called its demise a "bitter setback." [27] But there were many in the ministry who understood what had happened. Opposition from the banking community and the Kansai business community was serious, but more serious was the fact that Sahashi himself had become an issue.

Several incidents had occurred during Sahashi's tenure as director of the Enterprises Bureau to irritate the business community in general and the business community of Osaka in particular, even when Sahashi's policies were proven sound. The best-known incident concerned the Maruzen Oil Company, whose head office is located in Osaka. Founded in 1933, Maruzen was part of the Sanwa Bank's keiretsu (also based in Osaka); it was and is a domestically owned refining and distribution company, but it had a long-term tie-up with Union Oil Company of California, which was a prime supplier of its crude oil. In the wake of the closing of the Suez Canal in 1956, Maruzen's president, Wada Kanji, had signed long-term shipping contracts that during the recession of 1962 turned unfavorable and threatened the company's financial viability. President Wada proposed accepting a very large loan from Union Oil to keep his company afloat, and he applied to MITI for approval of the loan under the terms of the Foreign Capital Law.

Sahashi turned him down cold, arguing that the company's own mismanagement had caused its problems, and that the introduction of foreign capital in an industry already thoroughly dominated by foreign companies was contrary to the national interest. Wada was not without political influence, which he began to mobilize to put pressure on MITI, but this pressure only caused Sahashi to become more combative. However, in the end Sahashi agreed to organize a five-man committee to try to salvage the Maruzen Oil Company. Chaired by Uemura Kōgorō, it recommended that Wada retire and that MITI negotiate the terms of the loan directly with Union Oil in order to ensure that Union did not gain control of the company. MITI accepted these recommendations: Sahashi struck a deal with Union, Miyamori Kazuo of the Sanwa Bank replaced Wada as Maruzen's new president, and the company was successfully rebuilt. But several Osaka legislators made speeches in the Diet accusing "the bureaucrat Sahashi" of throwing their local business leader Wada out into the streets.[28]

Meanwhile, on July 18, 1962, Satō Eisaku resigned as MITI minister, and Prime Minister Ikeda appointed Fukuda Hajime to replace him. Fukuda was a classic politician of the party-men's factions, a former war correspondent (Singapore) and chief of the political department of the Dōmei News Agency, a five-times-elected member of the House of Representatives from Fukui prefecture—and a stalwart of the Ōno faction. Ikeda named him on the recommendation of Ōno, whose support he needed to hold off the political challenges coming from both Satō and Kōno Ichirō. Fukuda was exactly the type of man whom the elite bureaucrats of MITI would—and did—deride as a "small-time politician," but he will never be forgotten within the ministry as the cause of the "Fukuda typhoon" of July 1963.

During June 1963 Vice-Minister Matsuo Kinzō was preparing for his amakudari as director (later vice-president) of Nippon Kōkan. He recommended to Minister Fukuda that Sahashi be named as his successor—a change of command that had been long and carefully planned. However, on July 1, 1963, Fukuda was involved in a wideranging discussion with a group of journalists, during which one of them said, "Various personnel matters are pending within MITI.

Could you tell us about them?" "Certainly," replied Fukuda. "Since MITI is an agency that serves the public, the fact that Sahashi has gotten a bad reputation with industry makes him unsuitable. I think that Imai would be good. I intend to appoint him as the next vice-minister." [29]

The ensuing explosion within MITI has become legendary. All work stopped. Just as at the time of the military mutiny in 1936, officials met in groups according to their entering classes to caucus on this unprecedented development. Some were quoted in the next day's newspapers as asking, "How is it that a party-politician minister, who knows nothing about the traditions of our glorious MITI, can pick a vice-minister we don't like?" The press club commented sardonically that the bureaucratic *amai seikatsu* (*la dolce vita*) at MITI had come to an end. And the public was confused: it thought that the minister always chose his own top subordinates, at MITI and at other ministries. Some cooler heads remarked, "Of course the minister technically has the final say in personnel matters. Both Sahashi and Imai are OK, and except for the fact that Sahashi has developed a faction within the ministry, neither can change MITI as a whole." Thus was born the "Sahashi faction"—and its opposite number, the "international faction," which would take over the ministry in 1966. The press coverage of the "Fukuda typhoon" effectively diverted attention from the Special Measures Law in the Diet and raised enough questions about its author to cause it to become "sponsorless legislation."

The reasons for Fukuda's action are not hard to find. First, as a party politician in a party increasingly dominated by former bureaucrats, Fukuda wanted to put the bureaucrats in their place. He was often quoted as saying, "It is sheer arrogance that some bureaucrats want to usurp the authority of politicians." Second, both the Maruzen affair and the Special Measures Law had made the business world nervous about a restoration of bureaucratic controls over the economy. Fukuda's action reassured business leaders on this score, since Imai was not only a champion of liberalization but had also won the trust of the prime minister and was the son-in-law of Yamazaki Taneji, president of the Yamazaki Securities Company. Third, LDP insiders believed that there was a link between Satō Eisaku and Sahashi, and this was something Fukuda's faction leader, Ōno Bamboku, wanted severed.

The MITI elders were called in to try to control the damage. Outgoing Vice-Minister Matsuo advised Sahashi to keep his mouth shut while they worked out a solution. Sahashi made it clear that even though he and Imai were both from the class of 1937, he would not resign as custom would normally have dictated. The result was a ceremonial meeting, presided over by the great senior Shiina Etsusaburō, in which it was decided that Imai would become vice-minister, Sahashi would take Imai's old job at the Patent Agency, Imai would hold the top spot for only a year (he actually stuck it out for 15 months), and Sahashi would succeed him. Sahashi has written that this affair was his most unpleasant experience in 30 years of government service, and one can believe him. Nonetheless, he did have the satisfaction of seeing his ideas for the economy accepted and implemented, even if he and his law were none too popular.[30]

Throughout this period foreign pressure on Japan to speed up liberalization increased in intensity. At the first Joint Meeting of Economic Ministers of Japan and the United States at the end of 1961, the Americans asked for a faster pace of liberalization than the 80 percent Ikeda had promised; and in September 1962 the IMF recommended a level of 95 percent (the IMF and Japan compromised on 90 percent). Then, on February 20, 1963, the IMF Board of Directors met, rejected Japan's stated reasons for not having shifted to article 8 status, and insisted on a pace of liberalization greater than 90 percent. Japan really had no choice if it intended to continue to participate in international trade. It therefore gave notice that it would formally become an article 8 nation on April 1, 1964, and would simultaneously stop rationing foreign exchange through MITI-controlled budgets.

Pressure from GATT also developed. Before the British would sign a basic treaty of commerce and navigation with Japan, they insisted that Japan accept article 14 of GATT (no governmental subsidies of exports); and Japan's acceptance of IMF article 8 was tantamount to adhering to GATT's article 11 (no trade controls because of balance of payments deficiencies). Therefore, with its ratification on April 4, 1963, of the Anglo-Japanese treaty, Japan notified GATT that within a year it would shift to article 11 status. During July 1963 Japan also applied for membership in the Organization for Economic Cooperation and Development (the first Asian nation to do so), and it was admitted on April 29, 1964—but with some seventeen temporary reservations to the OECD's code of behavior for members. Nonetheless, membership in the OECD meant that Japan was committed not only to trade liberalization but also to the removal of controls on capital transactions. The "fully opened economy" was at last on the nation's agenda.

Simultaneously with the acceptance of these new international obligations, the economy itself began to decline into its worst postwar recession. During October 1964, the same month that Sahashi replaced

Imai as vice-minister, the recession began. At first it looked like a normal cyclical downswing caused by a balance of payments crunch and government controls on credit, a type of recession that Japan had experienced several times since the Korean War. However, on December 1, 1964, the Japan Special Steel Company declared that it was bankrupt and applied to the courts for relief under the Company Reorganization Law (Kaisha Saisei Hō). On March 6, 1965, the Sanyō Special Steel Company followed suit, announcing that it could not cover its debts of some ¥50 billion. This was the biggest bankruptcy that had yet occurred in postwar Japan. Two months later the Yamaichi Securities Company reported that it too was unable to meet its debts and was going under; it was saved only by a drastic, government-secured loan program. Finally, in June and July the government abandoned its sixteen-year policy of balanced budgets and began to issue bonds to cover deficit financing of counterrecession expenditures. Fiscal policy had finally replaced Japan's long reliance on monetary policy alone.

Under these circumstances analysts began to argue that this was not a "normal" recession but instead a "structural recession" caused by the "distortions" of high-speed growth. The structural recession thesis was associated above all with economists around Prime Minister Satō, who replaced Ikeda in November 1964, and with MITI.[31] In retrospect it appears that the thesis was somewhat overstated and was motivated as much by Satō's political need to find an issue to use against Ikeda as by any fundamental changes in the economy. The causes of the recession were, first, the uncertainty that followed liberalization, assumption of IMF article 8 status, and entry into the OECD; second, rising labor costs due to a drying up of the supply of young workers; third, the government's tight money policies; and fourth, continued overcapacity due to excessive, keiretsu-driven investment.

For all of their coolness to the Special Measures Law, political leaders such as MITI Minister Fukuda had feared that something like this would happen. During mid-1964 Fukuda provided Sahashi with one of his greatest satisfactions. On June 26, 1964, he told the cabinet that the motivations and purposes of the Special Measures Law had all been sound, that the idea of the "cooperation formula" contained in the bill was a good one, and that it should be adopted as a tool of general industrial policy even though the law had failed to pass. MITI, he said, was going to set up cooperation discussion groups for synthetic textiles (actually created on October 26, 1964) and petrochemicals (December 19, 1964), and would entertain the possibility of establishing them for other industries suffering from excess capacity. These measures, he said, would be taken through the ministry's residual powers of "administrative guidance"—a term that had first appeared in a MITI annual report only during fiscal 1962—and not on the basis of any particular law.[32] On July 18, 1964, a month after Fukuda made this speech, Ikeda reshuffled his cabinet and replaced Fukuda with Sakurauchi Yoshio, the son of a prewar MCI minister (1931) and a leader of the Kōno faction (Nakasone faction after Kōno's death in July 1965). Sakurauchi continued as MITI minister in the Satō cabinet but was replaced by Miki Takeo in June 1965. It was thus Sakurauchi, Miki, and Sahashi who had to combat the recession by implementing the ideas of the Special Measures Law through administrative guidance.

The institution of administrative guidance has done more than any other Japanese practice to spread the belief around the world that the Japanese government-business relationship is based upon some underlying, possibly culturally derived, national mores that have no parallels in other countries. The London *Economist* defines administrative guidance as "Japanese for unwritten orders"; and Prof. Uchida Tadao of Tōdai writes that "the Diet is almost powerless in . . . determining economic programs in this country as such authority actually has been transferred to the administrative sector, particularly government offices."[33] Many foreigners have protested. "What bothers our manufacturers," says Ernst Hermann Stahr of the Union of German Textile Manufacturers, "is that it's not really a matter of Japanese competitiveness, but a maze of impenetrable government supports and subsidies. Our people feel that whatever they do, the Japanese will just lower their prices."[34] It was administrative guidance that gave MITI the reputation during the 1960's of being the "Ministry of One-Way Trade."[35] On the other hand, a Japanese analyst writes, administrative guidance "is what makes Japan's business tick. It is what made this country the world's third industrial nation. It is one of the pillars that support Japan Incorporated."[36]

There is nothing very mysterious about administrative guidance. It refers to the authority of the government, contained in the laws establishing the various ministries, to issue directives (*shiji*), requests (*yōbō*), warnings (*keikoku*), suggestions (*kankoku*), and encouragements (*kanshō*) to the enterprises or clients within a particular ministry's jurisdiction.[37] Administrative guidance is constrained only by the requirement that the "guidees" must come under a given governmental organ's jurisdiction, and although it is not based on any explicit law, it cannot violate the law (for example, it is not supposed to violate the Antimonopoly Law). During the 1950's administrative guidance was rarely mentioned in connection with MITI's actions because most of its orders, permissions, and licenses were then firmly based on explicit control laws. Administrative guidance came to be openly practiced and discussed during the 1960's, and then only because MITI lost most of its explicit control powers as a result of liberalization and the failure to enact the Special Measures Law. In a sense, administrative guidance was nothing more than a continuation by MITI of its established practices through other means. All Japanese observers concur in Shiroyama's conclusion. "After the failure of the Special Measures Law, the only thing left was administrative guidance."[38]

Administrative guidance differs from orders issued in accordance with, for example, the Foreign Exchange and Foreign Trade Control Law in that it is not legally enforceable. Its power comes from government-business relationships established since the 1930's, respect for the bureaucracy, the ministries' claim that they speak for the national interest, and various informal pressures that the ministries can bring to bear. The old Japanese proverb used to describe this threat of governmental retaliation is "To take revenge on Edo by striking at Nagasaki," meaning that the bureaucracy has the means to get even with a businessman who refuses to listen to its administrative guidance.[39] As we shall see below, MITI has on occasion retaliated with force against an enterprise that rejected its advice.

In some of its forms administrative guidance is indistinguishable from a formal legal order by the government. An example is guidance through policy statements (*shidō yōkō*). This refers to the obligation of the public to pay attention and respond in good faith to properly drawn and published policies of the government, although penalties for noncompliance have never been specified. The most famous case of this form of administrative guidance occurred during the early 1970's, when the city of Musashino in the suburbs of Tokyo issued a policy statement saying that housing contractors who built large projects had to cooperate in providing or helping to buy land on which to build elementary schools. When a contractor ignored these guidelines, the city capped the water and sewage lines he had built for the project with concrete. The contractor took the city to court, but the court upheld the city.[40] Generally speaking, few objections are possible when administrative guidance is couched in terms of the national interest. The press likes to cite the case of a city bank executive who called on the Ministry of Finance to protest that his bank could not absorb the full quota of government bonds assigned to it by administrative guidance. A Banking Bureau official replied, "So you think your bank can survive even after Japan collapses? Go back and tell your president exactly what I said."[41] Sahashi was particularly adept at and inclined to use this kind of defense of his administrative guidance.

The problems of administrative guidance begin when it is suspected that a ministry is not neutral in an issue it is supposed to be arbitrating, or when it has been captured by the people it is supposed to be regulating, or when its administrative guidance is really only a governmental cloak (kakuremino) hiding an otherwise illegal cartel, or when the deliberation councils in which administrative guidance is carried out have been packed with people leaning in a certain direction. There is no ready relief from such malpractices when they are suspected. Several protests against administrative guidance on these grounds erupted during the 1970's, as we shall see in the next chapter.

During the recession of 1965 the main form of MITI's administrative guidance was investment coordination done in "cooperative discussion groups." Whatever businessmen or their representatives may have said in the Diet about MITI, Sahashi, or the Special Measures Law, in private they welcomed these cartels to stave off the consequences of their own preemptive investment and the weakening of demand during the recession. On January 29, 1965, the discussion group for petrochemicals decided that new ethylene-producing facilities for fiscal 1965 and 1966 should be limited to 350,000 tons, and that firms already established in the industry should be the only ones to develop such facilities. And on March 18, 1965, the synthetic textiles discussion group agreed on a formula for new acrylic fibers facilities that would keep output below 30 tons per day. In May 1965 MITI set up a paper pulp industry discussion group, and in November 1966, one for the ferroalloys industry. Other industries employed the specialized committees of the Industrial Structure Council for the same purpose, and the council ultimately replaced the discussion groups as the place where most industrialists and financiers got together to agree on how much each was going to invest in what kinds of plants and equipment.

Another important form of administrative guidance during this period was the promotion of mergers. Sometimes this meant nothing more than MITI's bringing the parties together and endorsing their union before the FTC. The biggest such merger was the reamalgamation on June 1, 1964, of the three companies that had come into being after SCAP broke up the old Mitsubishi Heavy Industries. However, sometimes more was needed to achieve a merger than mere verbal encouragement. During fiscal 1963 the Japan Development Bank set aside some ¥3 billion (enlarged to ¥6 billion during 1964) for "structural credit" loans to large firms that merged. The government had long used easy financing to encourage mergers among medium and smaller enterprises; now it extended such funds to the automobile, petrochemical, and alloy steel industries. In the merger of the Nissan and Prince automobile companies, which was finally consummated on August 1, 1966, Nissan is alleged to have received a reward in the form of an $11.1 million loan from the JDB.[42] The government justified this kind of largesse as part of its export promotion policies, since economies of scale lowered the prices of export products. As Hollerman notes, "It is ironic that whereas zaibatsu dissolution was undertaken by the occupation authorities in the name of economic democracy, their reconstruction is now being pursued in Japan in the name of import liberalization."[43] Sahashi credits Minister Sakurauchi with bringing off the Nissan-Prince merger, but most observers believe that Sahashi himself did most of the work.[44]

These months of "structural recession," mergers, and administrative guidance led up to and conditioned Vice-Minister Sahashi's last hurrah—the fight he had with the Sumitomo Metals Company of Osaka because it refused to abide by his administrative guidance. Steel, in Inayama Yoshihiro's words, is the "rice of industry," and the steel industry has long been regarded by knowledgeable observers as the "honor student" of the Japanese government-business relationship.[45] During the mid-1960's, however, MITI was having some problems with its prize pupil. Because the Yawata works had been founded as a state enterprise (which in 1934 became the major participant in Japan Steel, a public corporation), four of the "big six" steel companies (Yawata, Fuji, Nippon Kōkan, Kawasaki, Sumitomo, and Kobe) distrusted MITI's impartiality on the grounds that it had a soft spot in its heart for its "true children," Yawata and Fuji, the successors to Japan Steel after SCAP broke it up. Moreover, relations with the steel industry were delicate. All of the big six firms had high-ranking former MITI officials on their boards of directors—except for Sumitomo, which refused on principle to hire bureaucrats. But even so it was hard to give direct orders to the industry because so many of its executives were top leaders in business organizations such as Keidanren and Keizai Dōyūkai.

There were two main problems in the administration of the steel industry: coordination of investment for new blast furnaces and converters, and coordination of production in order to maintain prices at a reasonable level. Inayama of Yawata had long held that avoidance of price fluctuations in the steel industry was in the national interest, both to ensure that the industry could schedule repayments on the loans for its huge investments and to avoid the ripple effect that price instability in steel had on the rest of the economy. From the era of priority production just after the war down to approximately 1960, MITI had exercised detailed control over investments in the steel industry through the plans of the Industrial Rationalization Council and through the policy use of the Foreign Capital Law. In 1960 Vice-Minister Matsuo (who went to Nippon Kōkan after his retirement) had proposed a steel industry law to establish an investment-coordination cartel as an exception to the Antimonopoly Law, but the industry had rejected it in favor of self-coordination, legalized by MITI's alleged supervision but actually carried out by the Japan Steel Federation. By 1965 this attempt at self-regulation had broken down, and overcapacity in the steel industry combined with the recession threatened to bankrupt some of the biggest firms in the nation.

The immediate issue was a MITI recommendation to reduce production (*kankoku sōtan*) designed to prevent a collapse of steel prices. The ministry "recommended" (ordered) that for the second quarter of fiscal 1965 (July to September) each company cut its production by 10 percent based on its share of total output during the second half of fiscal 1964 (October 1964 to March 1965). All of the "big six," including Sumitomo, went along with this. Then, on November 9, 1965, MITI ordered that this reduction be continued into the third quarter (the trough of the recession hit in October). Sumitomo refused to accept this administrative guidance on the grounds that it was the only company among the big six that had met its MITI-assigned export quota for the first half of the fiscal year, and it charged that the biggest operators, Yawata, Fuji, and Nippon Kōkan, had diverted some of the steel supposedly produced for export into the domestic market. Sumitomo argued that MITI's base for determining market shares failed to take account of export performance of the various companies and was biased against the newer, better-managed firms in the industry—such as Sumitomo.

The president of Sumitomo Metals, Hyūga Hōsai, was an old hand at this sort of thing. He had served Sumitomo continuously since his graduation from Tōdai Law in 1931 and had gained experience in the governmental bureaucracy at first hand as secretary to Minister of Finance Ogura Masatsune (of Sumitomo) in the third Konoe cabinet (1941). During 1965 he was the leading figure in the Osaka branch of

Keizai Dōyūkai. He had no difficulty whatsoever in controlling his enthusiasm for MITI's intervention in the steel industry, which he believed had always favored Yawata and Fuji.

On November 18, 1965, after Hyūga's initial opposition, MITI Minister Miki—himself an LDP faction leader, holder of the record as the longest continuously elected member of the Diet, and a future prime minister—got on the telephone and, according to Hyūga, promised that if Sumitomo would go along with the production cut through at least the third quarter, he would act favorably on Sumitomo's investment plans for its big Wakayama steel works (the company intended to add a fourth blast furnace and a fourth and fifth rotary furnace, or converter). Sahashi had not been directly involved in this dispute un til Hyūga's defiance of MITI, and both he and Miki are vague on whether they consulted each other before Miki's call.*

However, on November 19, the day after Miki's call, Sahashi also contacted Hyūga and told him that unless Sumitomo backed down, he would use the Import Control Ordinance (Yu'nyū Bōeki Kanri Rei, cabinet order 414 of 1949) to restrict imports of coking coal for the company to precisely the amount necessary to produce its authorized quota and not a shovelful more. Sahashi here revealed MITI's most authoritarian side, and when the whole matter became public, the press generally backed Sumitomo as the underdog. Hyūga held a press conference in Osaka where he said that since it was his company that was spending the money and taking the risks, he did not see that it was any concern of the government how much the company produced. (This was, of course, not entirely candid, since Sumitomo had profited as much as any other company from government-backed financing and government-guaranteed loans from the World Bank.) More pointedly, however, Hyūga added that MITI favored firms that had ex-MITI bureaucrats working for them, and that it appeared to him as if Vice-Minister Sahashi had overruled Minister Miki. "Which one of them is the minister?" he asked the gathered Osaka reporters. This was promptly transformed by the national press into big headlines—SAHASHI, MINISTER; MIKI, VICE-MINISTER—that stuck in the public mind as a slogan. (This case is similar to the

---

* According to Sahashi, Miki's telephone call was merely a matter of courtesy from a senior politician to an influential constituent. His "promise" was extremely vague—an example of what is called *kanchō yōgo* (literally, "official jargon," but meaning a government official's saying yes to a citizen's request as a matter of politeness but with the implication that the official has no intention of doing anything about the request). Hyūga, in Sahashi's view, deliberately misunderstood Miki's meaning. See Matsubayashi Matsuo, ed., *Kaikoroku, sengo Tsūsan seisaku shi* (Memoirs: postwar MITI policies; Tokyo: Seisaku Jihō Sha, 1973), p. 141.

disputes between Minister Ogawa and Vice-Minister Yoshino in 1936 and between Minister Kobayashi and Vice-Minister Kishi in 1941.)

Sahashi was embarrassed—he and Miki had a good relationship—but he stuck to his guns and won. On January 11, 1966, Sumitomo claimed that it had not rebelled against administrative guidance but had only sought an exception because of its superior export performance, and said that it would go along with the others. Its imports of an indispensable raw material were promptly restored. Leaders of the steel industry had worked behind the scenes to achieve this compromise, and Sumitomo's export quota was also raised.

There were several consequences of this famous incident. Most important, the contretemps had so rattled the entire steel industry and business community, as well as exposing to public view procedures that were normally secret, that the elders of business and government determined to alter the structure of the industry itself by merging the Yawata and Fuji steel companies into one clear industry leader. In March 1970 New Japan Steel, the world's largest steel company, came into being after a lengthy and often fierce fight with the Fair Trade Commission. We shall return to MITI's role in this famous merger in the next chapter.

A less important but no less revealing consequence was Sumitomo Metals' acceptance of its first amakudari bureaucrat. Three years after the incident, in 1969, Hyūga invited retiring MITI Vice-Minister Kumagai Yoshifumi to join Sumitomo Metals' board of directors. Kumagai had worked briefly for Sumitomo before entering MITI and therefore was more acceptable to the firm than a bureaucrat it did not know. In June 1978 Hyūga moved up to the chairmanship, and Kumagai became president of Sumitomo Metals. Hyūga had obviously learned that his otherwise excellent company lacked one important capability in its executive suite: the bureaucratic skills of a MITI insider.[46]

Only three months after his victory over Sumitomo, Sahashi himself decided that he had exhausted his usefulness. He declared, however, that he would not take any of the three paths of amakudari normally followed by high-ranking officials in retirement. He did not want to enter private enterprise because the presence of an outsider only annoyed the long-service employees and interfered with their own chances for promotion. He did not want to enter politics because he was disillusioned with politicians. And he did not want to go to a government corporation, because there he would have to take orders from some vice-minister, and that did not suit him. Sahashi therefore spent the next six years doing economic research and writing a series of very useful and candid books. In 1972 he finally took a position as chairman of the Leisure Development Center, a MITI-sponsored association to promote the tourist and recreation industries. When I met him in 1974, he appeared the very model of an international tourist executive: ensconced in an office surrounded with tropical fish in tanks, recently returned from a visit to the South Pacific, and dressed in a white safari suit, he answered my questions frankly, and passionately defended his beloved MITI. He was not known to the press as "Mr. MITI" (*Misutā Tsūsan-shō*) for nothing.

The demobilization of the Japanese economy really only began during the early 1960's with trade and exchange liberalization; the statement in the 1956 *Economic White Paper*, "We are no longer living in the days of postwar reconstruction," was about five years premature. Until trade liberalization was forced on it, Japan had operated a totally closed economy in which all of its contacts with the rest of the world were mediated and brokered in government offices. Trade liberalization began—it did not end—a complicated process of opening the Japanese economy to the full range of commercial and competitive pressures that affect all of the world's market economies. Not until 1980, when the Foreign Capital Law of 1950 was finally abolished, could it be said that Japanese economic demobilization was more or less complete. Although the Japanese economy prospered enormously from the global trends toward trade and capital liberalization, the actual process of removing Japan's controls was a harrowing one for both Japan and its trading partners. The period from approximately 1960 to 1980 left scars, as we shall see in the next chapter, that twenty years later were still affecting the Japanese-American alliance.

In January 1981 the special commission of distinguished Japanese and American leaders—the "wisemen"—who had been appointed in May 1979 by Prime Minister Ōhira and President Carter to examine factors affecting the long-term economic relationship between the two countries, issued its report. Under the general subject "Japan's Market: Open or Closed?" the wisemen discussed administrative guidance:

One of the most difficult aspects of the Japanese economic system for non-Japanese to understand is the nature of the government-business relationship. The more embracing set of consultations between the private and public sectors and less of an adversary relationship than in the United States lend substance in some American eyes to the concept of a "Japan, Inc." This image presents a very false and misleading impression of the Japanese economy. It is also very harmful to United States–Japan economic relations because it creates the false impression that Japan can manipulate exports and imports at will. Business does not meekly respond to government fiat nor is government the creature of business. Most Japanese, however, do acknowledge the existence of government reliance on administrative guidance, usually describing the informal means by which government attempts to influence business without resorting to legislative or regulatory measures as would be the case in the United States.[47]

As this chapter has sought to show, administrative guidance became a salient feature of the Japanese government-business relationship only in the context of trade liberalization and MITI's failure to provide a new legal basis for its guidance activities. Until then the government's role in economic decision-making had been guaranteed by its management of the foreign exchange budget. After that budget was abolished, the government continued to play its traditional role just as always—but without its old explicit power to compel compliance through control of an industry's or an enterprise's foreign trade.

The government's role in the economy, either before or after trade liberalization, has never been highly constrained by law. To be sure, the Japanese economic system rests on a legal foundation—but usually on short, very general laws, the Special Measures Law being a good example. The actual details are left to the interpretation of bureaucrats so that the effects can be narrowly targeted. And large areas of economic activity are covered by neither general laws nor detailed cabinet or ministerial orders, but are left to administrative guidance. The power of administrative guidance is rather like the grant of authority to a military commander or a ship captain to take responsibility for all matters within his jurisdiction. Administrative guidance is a perfectly logical extension of the capitalist developmental state, with its emphasis on effectiveness rather than legality.

The power of administrative guidance greatly enhances the ability of Japanese economic officials to respond to new situations rapidly and with flexibility, and it gives them sufficient scope to take initiative. The Japanese have unquestionably profited from the elimination of legal middlemen and the avoidance of an adversary relationship in public-private dealings. Needless to say, this cozy relationship between officials and entrepreneurs is open to abuse—and, as we shall see in the next chapter, it has on occasion been abused. But given the general developmental imperatives of postwar Japan, the public has been willing to accept the trade-off between bureaucrats occasionally exceeding their mandate and quicker and more efficient economic administration. As the degree of trade and capital liberalization increased, administrative guidance declined, but it will never disappear completely from the Japanese scene, given the public's awareness of Japan's economic vulnerability and its acceptance of the need for governmental coordination of economic activities.

As the last of the old-style industrial-policy bureaucrats, Sahashi worked hard to mitigate the effects of liberalization and to continue high-speed growth as long as possible. Following his period in office, MITI encountered a storm of criticism of its activities, and the cooperative relationship between government and business began to crack under demands by the private sector for the restoration of self-control. However, shortly after the first "oil shock" of 1973–74, MITI again found a call for its services—to lead third-stage knowledge-intensive industrialization and to correct many abuses that had accompanied the renewal of self-control. The ministry also underwent an internal reform and redefinition of the qualities of a MITI official. Unlike Sahashi and his fellows of the older generation, the new MITI official was to be experienced in international affairs, adept at foreign languages, and as much at home with trade administration as with industrial policy. In contrast to Sahashi's self-description as a "domestic-use-only bureaucrat," his successors were "cosmopolitan nationalists."

The passing of the Kishi-Shiina line did not mean the end of high-speed growth. Whereas Japanese productivity had grown at a rate of 9.5 percent on an average annual basis between 1950 and 1967, it increased to 10 percent during 1967–73 and held steady at 8.3 percent during 1978–79, following the severe effects of the oil shock. By the end of the 1970's Japan and its ally, the United States, together produced each year about 35 percent of the total new output of the planet and engaged in almost 20 percent of the world's total trade. Japan had become a rich nation. The real legacy of people like Sahashi was not their "control bureaucrat" mentality but their having shown the nation how to change its industrial structure in order to meet changes in the economic environment, and how to do so without relinquishing the advantages of either democracy or competition. Thanks to MITI, Japan came to possess more knowledge and more practical experience of how to phase out old industries and phase in new ones than any other nation in the world.

EIGHT

Internationalization

D URING the decade from the recession of 1965 to the recession
after the first "oil shock" (1974), the paths of MITI and of Japan
first diverged and then came back together again. Japan attained the zenith of its postwar economic growth, but MITI suffered
from a classic case of the greatest bureaucratic infirmity of all—
fulfillment of mission and loss of function. One issue after another
plagued the ministry in this era—industrial pollution, revolts against
its administrative guidance, charges of corrupt collusion with big
business, inflation, public dismay at some of the consequences of its
industrial location policy (especially the virtual depopulation of some
Japan Sea coast prefectures, such as Shimane, and the overcrowding
of the Tokyo-to-Kobe industrial zone), and serious damage to relations with Japan's main economic partner, the United States, because
of trade imbalances, an undervalued yen, and Japanese procrastina-
tion in implementing capital liberalization.

By the mid-1970's the ministry began to show renewed strength: it
successfully redefined its mission, changed its personnel, gave itself a
new structure, and shed the parts of its heritage that were no longer
relevant—and all the while it reasserted those elements that Japan
still needed. The oil crisis and all of its ramifications gave the ministry
a new lease on life. MITI's primary problem at the time was to understand what changes were needed, to answer its critics, and to hold off
rivals, such as the Ministry of Finance, who saw advantages for themselves in MITI's weakened influence. One official characterized 1968–
69 as the worst year in MITI's history, and Vice-Minister Morozumi
Yoshihiko (1971–73) referred to the years leading up to the basic reform of the ministry in July 1973 as a "long, dark tunnel."[1]

It all began with capital liberalization. After Japan had joined the OECD in 1964—with more reservations to the OECD's capital liberalization code than any of the sixteen other members except Spain and Portugal—the country seemed to forget that reasonably free movement of capital among the signatory nations was one of the OECD's fundamental goals. However, there were many foreigners who were quick to remind the Japanese that they had agreed to end restrictions on direct foreign investment in the Japanese economy. Japan gained several advantages from membership in the OECD, including greater ease in floating its securities in overseas markets; and it was itself, of course, a major investor in Korea, Taiwan, and Southeast Asia. The slowness of Japanese compliance first came up in May 1965 at the Japanese-American Financial Leaders Conference. Demands that Japan liberalize were made again in July at the Japanese-American Joint Committee on Trade and the Economy, repeated in December at the Business International convention in Tokyo, and repeated again in February 1966 at the OECD itself.[2]

The very thought of capital liberalization struck terror in the hearts of MITI officials and Japanese industrial leaders. In their view trade liberalization had meant only meeting world competition in terms of products (quality, design, price, and so forth), a level at which Japan had worked out the successful strategy of importing technology from Europe and America, combining it with Japanese labor power, and then offering to the market products that were able to compete profitably with those of other countries. But capital liberalization meant competition at every level of an enterprise—in technology, capital resources, managerial skills, and all the rest. The low levels of capitalization of Japanese firms, a consequence of the indirect financing system invented during the capital shortage of the Korean War period, made them easy targets for foreign acquisition. The issue, of course, was nationalistic rather than economic—the belief on the part of some Japanese that the United States had for all intents and purposes "bought" Western Europe—and was about to buy Japan, as well.

MITI had long feared that some such catastrophe might easily occur, and during the recession of 1965 (particularly after the bankruptcy of Sanyō Special Steel), it began to deride what it called Japan's "cherry-blossom-viewing and sake-drinking economy," by which it meant numerous low equity, over-invested firms wholly dependent upon government-guaranteed bank loans.[3] If such firms could not even survive a domestic recession in a hothouse economy, how were they going to compete with the Fords, du Ponts, and IBMs of the world? The ministry argued that the solution to these problems was to promote large-scale mergers in order to produce concentrations of economic power on a par with the United States and West Germany. It wanted to reduce the "big six" steel companies to, say, two or three, and the automobile manufacturers from ten (Daihatsu, Fuji, Honda, Hino, Isuzu, Mitsubishi, Nissan, Suzuki, Tōyō Kōgyō, and Toyota) to two (Nissan and Toyota). The problem with this approach was that it was hard to merge Japanese firms, given their company unions, lifetime employment systems, and keiretsu affiliations. Moreover, such a policy would put MITI squarely on the side of big business, or even worse, of zaibatsu business. Some observers reinterpreted MITI's old slogan of "scrap and build" (first applied to the coal industry) to mean "scrap medium and smaller enterprises" and "build Mitsubishi Heavy Industries."[4] As it turned out, MITI had less to fear from medium and smaller enterprises than it did from some very big businesses themselves. And it had forgotten all about the Fair Trade Commission.

Before these problems developed, MITI got an assist from the top leaders of business, but for reasons more connected with the Sumitomo Metals Company incident than with capital liberalization itself. Inayama Yoshihiro, the president of Yawata Steel, had been so appalled by the "Sahashi, minister; Miki, vice-minister" controversy and the public squabbling over market shares in the steel industry that in January 1966 he proposed to Nagano Shigeo, president of Fuji Steel, that they merge their two companies. This would produce one steel company so large that it would create a genuine hierarchy in the industry, and, he hoped, conditions of stable oligopoly. Nagano responded favorably. In order to create a forum in which these negotiations could be pursued, in March 1966 the leaders of the main industrial federations formed a policy board, or "business general staff," named the Industrial Problems Research Association (Sangyō Mondai Kenkyū Kai, called "Sanken" for short). The big steel merger was Sanken's greatest achievement (it became inactive thereafter), but its formation coincided with the rise of the capital liberalization issue, and the association therefore decided to address the problem of mergers for all major industries as well as for steel.[5]

In its fully elaborated form Sanken brought together leaders from steel, electric power, chemicals, machinery, textiles, trading, finance, and securities, plus representatives of medium and smaller enterprises. Its guiding intellectual orientation was provided by Nakayama Sohei (b. 1906), since 1961 the president of the Industrial Bank of Japan (Nihon Kōgyō Ginkō) and probably the greatest go-between of modern Japanese business. He took charge of a committee to make recommendations for the reorganization of Japanese industry in order to end "excessive competition" and to prepare to meet the challenges of capital liberalization. The Nakayama Committee, augmented by bureaucrats from MITI and the EPA, worked on its report between July 1966 and June 1967. When it was completed, the report called for either mergers or "cooperation" in seven industries: steel, automobiles, machine tools, computers, petroleum refining, petrochemicals, and synthetic textiles. The committee's main contribution was to provide a rationale for the Yawata-Fuji merger, but its influence can be seen in many other areas, including both MITI's ultimately abortive efforts to reorganize the automobile industry and its very successful measures to link the electronics and machine tool industries.[6]

While these analytic activities were underway, MITI was also busy preparing countermeasures to hold off liberalization until the basic phases of the reorganization could be accomplished. In January 1967 the ministry set up a Capital Transactions Liberalization Countermeasures Special Committee (Shihon Torihiki Jiyūka Taisaku Tokubetsu Iinkai) within the Industrial Structure Council to hear and endorse what it proposed to do. This committee joined with another special committee set up by the Ministry of Finance's Foreign Capital Council (Gaishi Shingikai) and came up with a vast tangle of rules and procedures that had the effect of turning Japan's capital "liberalization" into a strictly pro forma acquiescence in international conventions.

Some of these rules included the 100 percent liberalization of only those industries in which foreign competition was unlikely (sake brewing, motorcycles, and the manufacture of *geta*, or Japanese wooden clogs, are the famous examples), the limitation of direct investment in other industries to joint ventures with at least 50 percent Japanese participation, the limitation of equity ownership in established firms to 20 percent, the selective designation of industries to be liberalized, the omission of vital segments from allegedly liberalized industries (the television industry was declared liberalized, except that foreigners could not produce color sets or use integrated circuits; the steel industry possessed eight of the ten largest blast furnaces on earth, but foreigners were prohibited from supplying the precise kind of steel needed by the automobile industry), the requirement that at least half of the directors in a joint venture must be Japanese nationals, and so forth endlessly. As if these measures were not enough, all proposed joint ventures or wholly owned subsidiaries remained subject to screening and approval by MITI under either the Foreign Exchange and Foreign Trade Control Law or the Foreign Capital Law if they involved the introduction of foreign technology into Japan.[7] (It is hard to imagine a joint venture or subsidiary that would not include the introduction of some form of technology or know-how).

On June 6, 1967, the cabinet adopted these principles and with great fanfare proclaimed the "first round" of capital liberalization on July 1. This opened up some 50 industries, 17 at 100 percent and 33 at 50 percent, to foreign participation. There can be no doubt that this initial effort was a purely cosmetic public relations gesture. All the industries liberalized were ones in which a Japanese enterprise controlled more than 50 percent of the market, or in which most of the products were sold exclusively to the Japanese government (railroad cars), or for which no Japanese market existed (corn flakes). Genuine capital liberalization came to Japan only slowly, and not through MITI's initiative but as a consequence of the weakening of the ministry and the growing realization on the part of industry that it had to "internationalize" if it was to avoid isolation. Ironically enough, by the time the economy was fully liberalized in the late 1970's, the big investors were not the Americans or the Europeans but the Arab oil sheiks.[8]

MITI was engaged on many fronts during this period. The Yawata-Fuji merger, which Sanken and MITI kept totally secret until 1968, required all the influence the ministry could muster to get past the FTC and the other steel companies. MITI also had its difficulties in bringing off mergers in such competitive fields as automobiles and textiles, and the foreigners were not kept quiet for long by the limited liberalization of 1967. However, MITI's abilities to deliver on its policies during the late 1960's were attenuated by internal factional struggles. Sahashi's wrangle with Sumitomo Metals was the true cause of his retirement as vice-minister, but some politicians who wanted him out made a public issue of another incident that they contended showed MITI's arrogance and Sahashi's unsuitability.

As vice-minister, Sahashi had appointed Kawahara Hideyuki (class of 1941) as chief secretary. Kawahara had been one of Sahashi's closest associates for many years and an outstanding MITI official (he was one of the first to identify the pollution problem as serious). On February 27, 1966, Kawahara suddenly took ill and died, and Sahashi authorized a formal, state-financed funeral for him at Tokyo's Tsukiji Honganji (a major Buddhist temple). This led to some petty complaints in the Diet about the small funerals provided for politicians as compared to the elaborate rites for Kawahara. The incident embittered Sahashi but also put the ministry on notice that the politicians were gunning for him and for the type of MITI official he represented.[9]

Before his retirement Sahashi was able to name Kawahara's replacement as chief secretary, but Minister Miki made it clear that he himself would choose Sahashi's own successor. The next chief secretary was Ōjimi Yoshihisa (March 1966 to May 1968), a transitional figure in that he was sometimes thought of as a member of the "Sahashi faction" (he had headed the Industrial Structure Investigation Office in the Secretariat at the time of the Special Measures Law), but he was also more oriented than Sahashi to the problems of Japan in the world economy. He became the last vice-minister (1969–71) to have some claim to represent the old "Kishi-Shiina" orientation. For the position of vice-minister after Sahashi, Miki chose Yamamoto Shigenobu, a former chief of the International Trade Bureau and an official who, having served overseas in the Bangkok embassy, was in 1966 director of the Medium and Smaller Enterprises Agency. When Yamamoto took over as vice-minister, he in turn selected Kumagai Yoshifumi as his chief of the Enterprises Bureau, and for the period May 1968 to November 1969 Kumagai succeeded Yamamoto as vice-minister.

In addition to all their pending policy problems, this post-Sahashi team of Yamamoto, Kumagai, and Ōjimi had to devote a great deal of attention to the internal problems of factions and lowered morale that had persisted since the Sahashi-Imai fight. By all accounts Yamamoto performed brilliantly; he is one of the most fondly remembered vice-ministers. He set out systematically to put industrial faction officers in international faction posts and vice versa, a policy that also reflected his own background as a specialist in promoting Japan's export trade in heavy machinery and high-value-added products rather than textiles and sundries (he was, significantly, the first vice-minister whose amakudari was to the automobile industry, where he became in 1968 the executive director of Toyota Motors). Typical of Yamamoto's personnel policy was the appointment of Miyazawa Tetsuzō, who had a background in heavy industry but no overseas service, to be director of the International Trade Bureau; and his appointment of Morozumi Yoshihiko, whose background included service in Paris and the Enterprises Bureau, to be chief of the Mining Bureau.

These policies worked well enough for the time being, but bickering within the ministry continued about Sahashi's policies. Old industrial-policy cadres insinuated that the new leaders were not true "raised-in-the-ministry samurai" (like Sahashi) and that they were inclined to pursue a "foreign appeasement" policy in the face of the demands for capital liberalization. These charges often caused early leaders of the "international faction" to go out of their way to be tough, as for example in the United States–Japan textile negotiations, in order to refute the accusations that they were predisposed to placate foreigners. After Yamamoto retired and Kumagai became vice-minister, the leaders of the ministry decided that the old Sahashi faction had to go. Kumagai appointed Morozumi chief secretary (May 1968 to November 1969), and he carried out a thorough purge of Sahashi's younger associates. No member of the Sahashi faction prospered in the ministry (with the possible exception of Ōjimi, who was really an independent) after Sahashi himself left the scene.

It is important to understand that this internal factional struggle interacted with and influenced MITI's various policies during this period. The new leaders of the ministry did not differ much from Sahashi on fundamentals, but most of them had served overseas, were well versed in the "culture" of international commerce (which involved institutions such as the IMF, GATT, and the OECD, and trends such as capital liberalization), and they were sensitive to the new, high-technology industries that were shortly to succeed steel, chemicals, and textiles. In contrast to men such as Sahashi, they are accurately described as "cosmopolitan nationalists." They were also the leaders who reformed the ministry in 1973 and who led Japan out of the oil shock.

However, at the time they were establishing their supremacy, they were extremely vulnerable to internal charges that they were caving in to politicians, consorting with foreigners, or otherwise letting down MITI's old traditions. To the extent that they responded to these internal complaints, they left themselves open to external attack from politicians and bureaucrats in other ministries, to charges that they were out of touch with the times, arrogant as the reform bureaucrats of the old school, in favor of policies that were damaging to Japan's foreign relations, and subservient to big business. Nonetheless, when Miki passed over Sahashi's chief of the Enterprises Bureau, Shimada Yoshito, for vice-minister and named Yamamoto instead, a new mainstream was established within the ministry. It produced a clear line of descent among the vice-ministers that was markedly more internationalist in orientation than the line of descent Sahashi had set up for the 1955–66 period. This new lineage went from Yamamoto to Kumagai to Ōjimi to Morozumi to Yamashita Eimei to Komatsu Yūgorō.

During the spring of 1966 Vice-Minister Yamamoto had welcomed the ideas for mergers, particularly the big steel merger, coming from Sanken; and he had set out to prepare the way for them with the Fair Trade Commission. On November 28, 1966, he received formal FTC assent to mergers that breached the commission's rule against combinations giving a single enterprise more than a 30 percent market share in an industry. The commission also accepted the necessity of "investment coordination" as an exception to the Antimonopoly Law in order to confront the threats coming from abroad.[10] Yamamoto justified these measures in terms of the need to improve the industrial structure before the full force of capital liberalization hit the economy. He was delighted when, in January 1968, Yawata and Fuji came to terms. It looked like the "merger of the century" and was, of course, also the recreation of the prewar and wartime Japan Steel Corporation.

On April 17, 1968, however, thanks to a slip of the tongue by President Nagano of Fuji Steel, the *Mainichi shimbun* and the *Nikkan kōgyō* newspapers broke the story that a Yawata-Fuji merger was in the works. This scoop generated a public furor that was rivaled only by the controversy over the Special Measures Law four years earlier. A group of economists at Tokyo University led by Professor Uchida Tadao met and issued a formal statement arguing that the proposed steel merger was economically unsound and would lead to monopolistic price increases. Uchida also contended that "what is really significant about the case is the absence of concern for the legal, economic, and social implications of so large a merger, as well as the widespread belief that the acts of private enterprises are not based on their own independent decisions but on the administrative guidance of MITI."[11] Uchida was particularly concerned that the Japanese public did not understand the economic need for competition and for defending it through the legal system.

The Fair Trade Commission listened to all of this and on January 27, 1969, clarified its position on the legal requirements for mergers. The commission did not necessarily oppose mergers that resulted in the formation of the largest enterprise in an industry—so long as it could be convinced that the new corporation would be unable to compel its competitors to follow its pricing decisions simply because of its size. On this basis, a month later (February 24) the commission formally declared that it would approve the Yawata-Fuji merger only if each company divested itself of certain key subsidiaries that, if retained, would give the new company price control over the steel industry. Inayama and Nagano resisted this decision, even though Sanken's Nakayama had already warned them that sales of some facilities would be unavoidable, and tried to mobilize political influence against the FTC. As a consequence, on May 7, 1969, the FTC for the first time in its existence went to the Tokyo High Court and got a restraining order against a merger. The fat was now definitely in the fire.

During June 1969 the Tokyo High Court held public hearings on the merger; the FTC presented its position, as did the professors, the companies, consumer groups, and related industries—and MITI in the person of Sakon Tomosaburō, chief of the Steel Industry Section in MITI's Heavy Industries Bureau, who made the unfortunate public comment that in this court the "laymen are judging the professionals." The press covered the hearings extensively. On October 30, 1969, the court finally ruled that the merger could proceed only if Fuji sold one of its plants to Nippon Kōkan and Yawata turned over one of its installations to Kobe Steel. Both companies reluctantly complied, and New Japan Steel, the world's largest steel company, formally came into being on March 31, 1970. Three years later, on May 30, 1973, former MITI Vice-Minister Hirai Tomisaburō, who had retired in 1955 and entered Yawata, became president of the country's largest enterprise. Although Hirai was widely respected as a leader of the steel industry, this elevation of a former bureaucrat to the top position of a company long associated with the government led some to see a trend toward excessive bureaucratic influence in the economy.[12]

MITI, of course, was totally identified with the steel merger, if for no other reason than that the chief executives of the new company, including Ojima Arakazu, Inayama Yoshihiro, Hirai Tomisaburō, and Tokunaga Hisatsugu, were all former MCI or MITI officials. Because of this and several other issues that came to a head at precisely the same time that the steel case ended up in court, MITI was subjected to some of the most withering criticism it had ever endured in its long history. The contemporaneous foreign criticism of the ministry— James Abegglen's term "Japan, Inc." and the London *Economist*'s references to "notorious MITI"—never fazed MITI officials, but domestic criticism was taken seriously. The main issues raised by domestic critics, in addition to the steel merger, were environmental damage, overcrowding, alleged collusion with big business, and a host of other side effects of high-speed growth that the public demanded be addressed. And as if this were not enough, right in the midst of all these problems the ministry experienced the most serious revolt ever against its administrative guidance, a blow that signified a genuine turning point in its relations with big business.

The issue of industrial pollution and environmental damage had numerous facets. At its worst it referred to the appearance of the Minamata and *itai-itai* "diseases," caused respectively by mercury poisoning of the waters around Minamata village in Kumamoto prefecture by the Chisso Fertilizer Company and cadmium poisoning in Toyama prefecture and other locations. (In September 1969 the chief of the Tokyo Mine Safety Office, a division of MITI, committed suicide when cadmium contamination was confirmed in Gunma prefecture.)[13] Only slightly less serious was the so-called Yokkaichi asthma that seemed to afflict everyone in the big petrochemical complexes at Yokkaichi and Tokuyama. As the press revealed, many of these conditions had actually been diagnosed as early as 1955 but had elicited no governmental corrective measures. The blame was laid squarely at MITI's door.

More politically significant because they affected so many people were air pollution in all the major cities (it was predicted that a chic, well-designed gas mask would soon become as indispensable an item of personal daily use as the umbrella), and automobile and truck accidents (because of inadequate expenditures on highways and alleged insensitivity to safety in automobile design). Noise, crowding, and the shortage of land for housing in the big cities also led many to question the value of high-speed growth. Organizations of local residents and consumers were created to protect such things as "sunshine rights," that is, the right of a resident not to have all sunshine blocked by an intervening high-rise. The word *kōgai* ("pollution," or more literally, "public wound") appeared in the newspapers every day.

During 1967 the Diet enacted the Pollution Countermeasures Basic Law (Kōgai Taisaku Kihon Ho, number 132 of August 3), which set standards for seven kinds of pollution: air, water, soil (added in 1970), noise, vibration, subsidence, and offensive odors. However, on MITI's insistence the Diet modified article 1 of the Ministry of Welfare's draft law to add that antipollution measures must be "in harmony with the healthy development of the economy."[14] This effectively gutted the law. But as pollution problems intensified, the politicians ultimately had no choice but to overrule the ministry. The result was the famous "pollution Diet" (*kōgai kokkai*, the 64th session, November 24 to December 18, 1970), which passed some fourteen antipollution laws and removed the phrase "in harmony with the economy" from the basic law. MITI had finally gotten the point; on July 1, 1970, it renamed its Mine Safety Bureau the Environmental Protection and Safety Bureau (Kōgai Hoan Kyoku) and increased its budget for dealing with industrial pollution problems from ¥274 million (1970) to ¥638 million (1971). A decade later MITI was to be credited with carrying out one of the most effective industrial cleanup campaigns in history, and in the process it also developed a thriving new industry in antipollution devices.[15] But in 1970 no one was thanking it, nor did many think that it could do the job.

In addition to being held responsible for the pollution problem, MITI was also blamed for damaging relations with the United States.

The Nixon administration, elected in 1968, was publicly committed to obtaining limitations on Japanese exports of synthetic textiles to America, just as the Kennedy administration had earlier negotiated an "orderly marketing agreement" covering cotton textiles. Both administrations were responding to political demands from the American Textile Manufacturers Institute, who used the potent argument that imports were putting many of the blacks among their employees out of work. (It should be noted that Japan has consistently and successfully prohibited imports of leather goods on the grounds that these would compete with the domestic industries of the *burakumin*, a dispossessed minority in Japanese society.)

Nixon thought he could arrange a quid pro quo since Prime Minister Satō had made a major political issue out of the return of Okinawa. At the Satō-Nixon summit conference in Washington (November 19–20, 1969) Nixon agreed to the precise terms Satō wanted for the return of Okinawa (without nuclear weapons), in return for which he thought he had received a promise from Satō to bring synthetic textile exports under control. The Japanese press also thought so, since it invented the slogan *ito o utte, nawa o katta* ("selling thread to buy rope," meaning "trading textiles for Oki*nawa*") to characterize Satō's diplomacy toward the United States.[16]

Satō, as it turned out, could not deliver on his promise because of obstruction by both the textile industry and MITI. From September 15 to 19, 1969, a MITI on-site inspection team had toured the United States to determine the extent, if any, of damage to domestic spinners and weavers from Japanese imports. Led by Takahashi Shukurō, the chief of MITI's Textiles Bureau, and composed of the chiefs of the First Market Section, the Fibers and Spinning Section, the Textiles Export Section, and other officials, this mission concluded that the American textile industry was thriving and that the damage caused by imports was nil. For all practical purposes this remained the Japanese position for the next two years—through what was to become one of the most unproductive interactions between two allies in the postwar world, what Maeda Yasuyuki would later characterize as the "quagmire negotiations."[17]

The textile dispute between Japan and the United States was only the most public and the noisiest of several economic clashes. Many of the other disputes, like that concerning textiles, also seemed to focus on MITI as the culprit. For example, following capital liberalization, MITI received a proposal from the Texas Instruments Company, which wanted to open a wholly owned subsidiary in Japan to manufacture integrated circuits. MITI sat on the proposal for some 30 months, claiming that it was giving the request "careful consideration." It then decided that the U.S. company would be permitted no more than a 50 percent ownership in conjunction with Japanese interests, that it would have to license its technology to Japanese competitors, and that it would have to limit its output until Japanese companies were better able to compete.[18] Similarly, at the time of the reversion of Okinawa, the Gulf Oil Company proposed building a refinery in Okinawa as a way of gaining access to the Japanese retail market. MITI said Gulf could not do so unless it had a Japanese partner, and when it looked as if Gulf might link up with Idemitsu Petroleum, MITI warned Idemitsu off.[19] Other issues included television exports (on June 9, 1970, Zenith charged that the Japanese were dumping TV sets in the United States, and MITI Minister Miyazawa Kiichi all but conceded the point by acknowledging that Japanese television receivers cost more in Japan than outside the country), grapefruit imports (during December 1968, the United States asked for liberalization of imports of grapefruit, tomatoes, ham, sausage, beef, and other agricultural products, but the Agriculture Ministry took a page out of MITI's book and refused), and above all joint ventures in the automobile industry.[20]

With the hindsight of a decade the automobile controversy of the late 1960's seems almost laughable (during 1979 Japan sent 2.1 million cars to the United States, while the United States sent 16,224 to Japan).[21] Realistically, the issue was never one of imports of American automobiles: American manufacturers made no effort to develop models that would appeal to the Japanese market, the Japanese tariffs were too high, and American cars were too big and too expensive to operate in Japan. The issue was the desire of the American Big Three auto firms to buy into Japanese automotive companies as part of their global manufacturing and marketing strategies. Throughout late 1967 and 1968, following the first round of capital liberalization, executives of Ford, General Motors, and Chrysler were in Japan seeing whether they could find partners for joint ventures. Meanwhile, MITI was doing its best to merge the smaller auto firms into keiretsu built around either Nissan or Toyota. As we saw in the last chapter, Sahashi had already succeeded in merging Nissan and Prince, and MITI was now extracting promises from all the other producers not to contemplate joint ventures with the Americans unless they first talked it over with the ministry. Just to make sure that nothing went wrong, MITI also mobilized its amakudari network in the auto industry: Yamamoto

Shigenobu at Toyota, Yamazaki Ryūzō (a former chief of the International Trade Bureau) at Nissan, Suganami Shōji (a former chief of the Commercial Affairs Bureau of MCI) at Hino, and several others.

Unfortunately for MITI, however, it had no "old boy" contact at Mitsubishi Motors (Mitsubishi Heavy Industries before June 1, 1970) for the simple reason that Mitsubishi, of all the old zaibatsu, was the most rigorous in excluding former bureaucrats from its ranks (with one or two exceptions in Mitsubishi Trading). Moreover, as the largest and most distinguished keiretsu in the country, Mitsubishi was definitely displeased by MITI's policy of building only two auto empires, Toyota and Nissan, which left it out of this business. Mitsubishi was also less fearful of foreigners than were the trade and industry bureaucrats: Mitsubishi Petroleum had long been associated with Getty Oil; the keiretsu had entered into numerous joint ventures (Caterpillar Mitsubishi, Mitsubishi-York, Mitsubishi-TRW, Mitsubishi-Mallory, Mitsubishi-Monsanto, and so forth); and, given Mitsubishi's huge financial resources, the Japanese side in any auto deal was more likely to buy out its foreign partner than the other way around.

The stage was thus set for the biggest shock MITI ever received in its history, the announcement of May 12, 1969, that Vice-President Makita Yoichirō of Mitsubishi Heavy Industries had returned from Detroit with an agreement with Chrysler to create a new automobile company (Mitsubishi would contribute an initial capital of ¥46 billion, or 65 percent, and Chrysler ¥16.1 billion, or 35 percent). Yoshimitsu Hisashi, the incumbent chief of the Heavy Industries Bureau, said that the announcement hit him like water poured into his ear while he was sleeping (*nemimi ni mizu da*, that is, like a "bolt from the blue"), and Vice-Minister Kumagai declared himself appalled.[22]

The fallout from the Mitsubishi-Chrysler agreement was enormous. The politicians and the businessmen immediately read it as a declaration of independence by some big businessmen from MITI. On October 14, 1969, the cabinet decided to speed up the liberalization of automotive capital, now scheduling it for October 1971. The government would not approve the Mitsubishi-Chrysler deal until that time, but when the time arrived it could stall no longer. During the autumn of 1969 Mitsubishi opened assembly lines for a car called the "Colt Gallant Hardtop," which it proudly showed off to Chrysler distributors who visited Japan as a delegation during EXPO 70, the big international exposition sponsored by MITI. As soon as the date for liberalization had passed, the joint venture was put into effect and Chrysler began to sell the Mitsubishi car in the United States as the

"Dodge Colt." As a result Mitsubishi promptly moved ahead of Tōyō Kōgyō to become Japan's number three automaker (and, as it turned out a decade later, when the U.S. number three auto manufacturer had to seek governmental assistance to stay in business, the most profitable division of Chrysler).

MITI was humiliated. Vice-Minister Kumagai was forced to call on business leaders and say that if private enterprise wanted to enter into tie-ins with foreigners, MITI would offer no objections. MITI had thought that it had a merger between Mitsubishi and Isuzu all wrapped up as a result of an agreement initialed on June 19, 1968. That naturally fell through given the new developments, and Isuzu promptly accepted another 65:35 joint venture with General Motors. MITI had more leverage over Isuzu than it did over the financially and politically powerful Mitsubishi, and it therefore rewrote the Isuzu-GM agreement in order to ensure that GM did not obtain control of the company. But MITI's plans for reorganizing the automobile industry were clearly in a shambles.[23]

From a broader perspective MITI was probably lucky that these developments took place when they did. Toyota and Nissan, MITI's chosen leaders of the industry, were never in any danger of losing their positions; the joint ventures eased some of the American pressure on Japan to liberalize; and the capital that flowed to Mitsubishi and Isuzu energized them both, providing more jobs for auto workers, suppliers, and trading companies alike (C. Itoh is Isuzu's trading company, while Mitsubishi Shōji serves Mitsubishi Motors). But regardless of how one judges the outcome of this famous incident, credit for liberalizing the automobile industry in Japan must go to Mitsubishi and not to MITI or any other element of the Japanese government.

The Mitsubishi coup led to a period of genuine confusion and turmoil within the ministry. On May 26, 1969, in an interview with the *Nihon keizai* newspaper, MITI Minister Ōhira Masayoshi said that the ministry would not interfere with what it perceived to be a new "private-sector industrial guidance model" (*minkan shudō-kata*), as distinct from the old "governmental industrial guidance model" (*seifu shudō-kata*).[24] This comment set off a debate within MITI and the industrial world that lasted until the oil shock in the autumn of 1973. Officials within MITI were divided on the proposed new formula for industrial policy; retired "seniors" expressed their dismay; business leaders said that it was high time; and commentators of every hue and description contributed their opinions. Some argued that MITI had been "bitten in the hand by its pet dog," that "the grown son [industry] tends to forget to thank his parents [MITI] for their loving care" (this comment from Sahashi), and that the ministry was in danger of being reduced to the status of the U.S. Department of Commerce (in a word, a mere handmaiden of big business; this according to MITI, which has always claimed to represent the national interest and not the interests of industry).

On the other hand, numerous critics arose to reply that MITI had become "neurotic," that it was acting like industry's "overprotective mama," that it had become nothing more than a bureaucratic *sōkaiya* (a bully or claque hired by some managements to prevent stockholders from asking annoying questions at annual meetings), that it had shown appalling bureaucratic apathy toward the pollution problem, and that it was time for enterprises to stop "weeping in front of MITI's gate." [25]

Within the ministry Amaya Naohiro, the head of the Planning Office in the Secretariat (October 1968 to June 1971), published an important treatise answering many of the ministry's critics but also calling for a "new MITI" and a "new approach to industrial policy." Amaya is MITI's best-known "house theorist." In January 1962, while serving as assistant chief of the General Affairs Section in the Secretariat, he became famous for a paper entitled "What Do the Times Require of Us?" This was a forcefully argued defense of Sahashi's "public-private cooperation formula" and of the ministry's new emphasis on reform of the "industrial structure" as its basic policy line. Because he was then a young official, the "first Amaya thesis" struck some senior officials as a little too strong for their tastes—some called him a "cheeky squirt" (*kozō*)—and he was quietly transferred to the Japanese consulate in Sydney until 1966. By 1980 he was vice-minister for international affairs, a new post created in 1976 directly under the MITI vice-minister.

The "second Amaya thesis"—formally entitled "Basic Direction of the New International Trade and Industry Policy" (Shin Tsūsan Seisaku no Kihon Hōkō of June 1969)—argued that the ministry must respond to changes in the public's values concerning further high-speed growth. In Amaya's view this change had occurred because Japan was beginning the transition from an advanced industrial society to a postindustrial society, and the country therefore required a change of industrial structure every bit as profound and as difficult to achieve as the heavy and chemical industrialization of the 1950's and 1960's.

Some of the characteristics of this new industrial structure would be (1) the growth of the tertiary sector (services) and the systematic enlargement of consumer goods enterprises, (2) robot-operated factories for the processing of raw materials, (3) the pyramidization of enterprises serving the high-technology assembly industries, (4) a technological revolution in the medical and educational sectors, and (5) many other developments associated with "knowledge-intensive industries." He candidly acknowledged that the ministry should lead the campaign toward internationalization, the fight against pollution, and efforts to raise the levels of product safety and consumer protection. He also accepted the "private-sector industrial guidance model," although he did not spell out what this implied.[26]

The second Amaya thesis contains the nucleus of what would eventually emerge as MITI's policies governing the shift of the industrial structure during the 1970's. The first in-house reactions to it, however, were mixed. The "private-sector industrial guidance model" seemed to imply the abandonment of the vertical industrial bureaus oriented to micro policy in favor of horizontal functional bureaus oriented to macro policy. This many officials were unwilling to concede. Vice-Minister Kumagai held that industrial policy itself meant governmental intervention at the micro level; anything else was mere economic policy.[27] His view ultimately prevailed, although the vertical bureaus were much better camouflaged after the reform of 1973 than they had been during high-speed growth.

Other officials preferred their own euphemisms for what Amaya had spelled out. For example, Morozumi insisted that economic growth should continue but that what should now be stressed was not speed but the "utilization of growth" for the good of the whole society. He was concerned that the new MITI policy not become so oriented to social issues that it neglect the nurturing of new industries. He also recognized that too great a social welfare commitment by MITI would raise unmanageable jurisdictional disputes with other ministries. He also explicitly rejected any European or American notion of a static international division of labor; Japan, he said, would have to compete in the computer, aviation, and space industries, and he was not willing to concede these to any other country.[28]

In light of all the comment on the "private-sector industrial guidance model," the ministry asked the Industrial Structure Council to recommend a new industrial policy for the 1970's. Not surprisingly, since he was in charge of the research efforts, the council confirmed and expanded many of Amaya's ideas. The new policy was published in May 1971. It acknowledged that high-speed growth had caused such problems as pollution, inadequate investment in public facilities, rural depopulation, urban overcrowding, and so forth. It proposed adding two new standards to those already in existence for determining what industries were appropriate for the new industrial structure. In addition to a high income elasticity of demand and a high growth rate of productivity, these were an "overcrowding and environmental standard" and a "labor content standard." These new standards meant that the ministry would try to phase out industries that contributed to overcrowding and pollution and replace them with high-technology, smokeless industries ranking very high on the value-added scale. The objective was what was termed a "knowledge-intensive industrial structure" (*chishiki shūyaku-kata sangyō kōzō*), the main components of which would be machines controlled by integrated circuits, computers, robot development of ocean resources, office and communications machinery, high fashion (including furniture), and management services such as systems engineering, software, and industrial consulting. In order to implement and administer these policies, a complete reform of the ministry was also recommended, which Vice-Minister Morozumi (June 1971 to July 1973) undertook to carry out.[29]

If during the spring of 1971 the Industrial Structure Council's proposals seemed somewhat visionary and long range, before the summer was over most of the conditions on which they were predicated would be outdated. Two MITI ministers, Ōhira and Miyazawa (November 1968 to July 1971), had exhausted their usefulness in trying to solve the Japanese-American textile dispute. In July 1971 Prime Minister Satō asked the LDP faction leader Tanaka Kakuei to take over and give it a try. Tanaka was a party politician but with a difference. Not only was he not a former high-ranking bureaucrat, he did not even have a university education. He was a self-made millionaire in the construction, railroad, and real estate businesses; and he had been a member of the Diet from his native Niigata prefecture since 1947, when he was first elected at the age of 29. Ten years later Kishi had appointed him postal minister, which made him one of the youngest cabinet members in Japan's history, and in 1962, when he was 44, Ikeda named him minister of finance (July 1962 to June 1965).

After performing well in that critical post, Tanaka went on to become secretary-general of the LDP, where he won Prime Minister Satō's respect for his skill in managing two general election victories for the party (January 1967 and December 1969). At the Ministry of Finance and subsequently at MITI he became known as an activist minister, one who told bureaucrats what he wanted done, used them as his own personal brain trust, and often won their respect and loyalty because of his intelligence and generosity.[30] He was well known for his unusually sharp memory, and the press nicknamed him the "computerized bulldozer." He also had a lot of money of his own, received more of it because of his powerful positions within the party and government, and spent it effectively to enlarge his faction in the Diet—all of which ultimately led to his downfall.

Shortly after Tanaka took over at MITI, the "Nixon shocks" occurred. It is unclear to this day whether President Nixon and National Security Adviser Kissinger were retaliating against Prime Minister Satō because of his failure to deliver on the textiles-for-Okinawa deal, or whether they simply overlooked Japan in the midst of their other troubles (Kissinger has acknowledged that it took him five years to gain some understanding of Japanese political processes).[31] Nixon and Kissinger did feel that they had reason to be irritated with Japan: capital liberalization was proceeding at a snail's pace, demands that Japan revalue its obviously undervalued currency were consistently rebuffed, the Vietnam War was causing the American balance of payments to hemorrhage, the textile dispute simmered on, and the American press was becoming sharply critical of Japan (see, for instance, the *Time Magazine* of March 2, 1970, on Japan's "hothouse economy," and the *Business Week* of March 7, 1970, on "Japan, Inc.").

Whatever the case, in July 1971 the Nixon administration unveiled its basic shift in United States' policy toward the People's Republic of China without coordinating this démarche in any way with its leading East Asian ally; and on August 16, 1971, it suspended convertibility of the U.S. dollar into gold and put a 10 percent surcharge on imports into the American market. On August 28, 1971, the Bank of Japan cut the yen free from the exchange rate that Dodge had created in 1949; and on December 19, 1971, following conclusion of the Smithsonian agreement ending fixed exchange rates, revalued the yen upward by 16.88 percent to US$1 = ¥308. Even before these dramatic developments, Japanese analysts were publishing books on the "Japanese-American Economic War" and saying that "the age of Japanese-American cooperation will never return." This turned out to be vastly overstated, but no one knew that during 1971 and 1972.

Tanaka capitalized brilliantly on the Nixon shocks. He openly championed Japanese recognition of Peking—his slogan was "Don't miss the boat to China"—and this ruined Prime Minister Satō's chances of continuing in office. It also effectively blocked Satō's intended successor from becoming prime minister: Fukuda Takeo had suffered the misfortune of being appointed Foreign Minister only a fortnight before the dramatic shift in Washington-Peking relations. (The Chinese communists indirectly helped Tanaka by launching a strident campaign against Satō, claiming that he was attempting to revive Japanese militarism, and stating that they would not deal with him or anyone associated with him as Japanese prime minister.)

On October 15, 1971, Tanaka adroitly ended the textile dispute by giving the Nixon administration what it wanted while also coming up with a ¥200 billion "relief program" for the Japanese textile industry (including governmental purchase of surplus machines, compensation for losses in exports, and long-term low-interest loans for "production adjustment" and occupational change).[32] Tanaka also offered the country new leadership on the overcrowding problem. Following the second Amaya thesis of 1969, the ministry had set some of its bright young officials to investigate the seriousness of that problem. They discovered that fully 73 percent of the nation's total industrial production was concentrated in a narrow belt along the east coast, and that some 33 million people lived within 30 miles of the three largest cities (Tokyo, Osaka, and Nagoya). This meant that 32 percent of the nation's population was living on 1 percent of the land area.

They also came up with such startling statistics as the fact that during rush hours Tokyo's traffic moved at only 5.6 miles per hour (2.5 m.p.h. along some routes), that the city had only 12 percent of its land area given over to roads (compared to 43 percent in Washington, D.C. or 23 percent in London), and that during the 1960's some 22 rural prefectures had suffered drastic declines in population (several communities in Tanaka's native Niigata prefecture were discovered to have all-female fire departments). To deal with these problems, MITI proposed a vast and very expensive program of industrial relocation, including building bullet-train networks all over the country, connecting Shikoku and Hokkaido to the main island through a system of monumental bridges and tunnels, and providing strong tax incentives to get industries to move out of the Tokyo-Kobe corridor.

The official in charge of these plans was Konaga Keiichi, who from October 1969 to July 1971 was chief of the Industrial Location Guidance Section in the Enterprises Bureau. When Tanaka became MITI minister in July 1971, he appointed Konaga his personal secretary, and Konaga was the ghost writer for Tanaka's best-selling book *Nihon rettō kaizō ron* (A plan to remodel the Japanese archipelago).[33] The book was published in June 1972, just a month before the LDP convention at which Tanaka planned to contest the party presidency (and, thus, the prime ministership) with Fukuda Takeo. A rewritten and spruced up version of MITI's original plan, it sold more than a million copies and helped ensure Tanaka's victory. On July 7, 1972, Tanaka moved from MITI to the prime minister's office, and he named as MITI minister Nakasone Yasuhiro, another party politician, LDP faction leader, and last-minute ally of Tanaka's in the LDP election contest (the press suggested that a large sum of money had passed between them).

The installation of the Tanaka cabinet seemed to mark a real turning point in Japanese politics. In contrast to the consistent domination of the government by former bureaucrats, Tanaka offered a cabinet made up of younger party politicians, including men who had experience in telling the bureaucracy what they wanted done, had no compunctions about blaming the bureaucracy for policy mistakes, and were "activist" in a way that ministers had not been since Ikeda's time. They were, however, so activist on one front—spending public money—that they contributed to a revival of bureaucratic government following the oil shock.

Tanaka accomplished many things—above all, the normalization of relations between Japan and China. But almost from the outset his administration led to serious inflation—a period of what the public came to call "crazy prices." Tanaka's industrial relocation policy was not the primary cause, and many of his big construction projects were desperately needed in any case (even though some people charged that Tanaka's background as a construction industry tycoon gave him more than a political interest in them). The root cause of "crazy prices" was Japan's public finance system and the divided responsibility among politicians and bureaucrats for managing it. In this sense, crazy prices were as much a side effect of the high-speed growth era as overcrowding and pollution. By the end of Tanaka's rule the country was reviving terms not heard since the occupation—economic control (keizai tōsei) and economic police (keizai keisatsu).[34]

The problem was excess liquidity. The Ministry of Finance had never believed that Japan could actually be forced to relinquish its trade advantage in an undervalued currency, and the value it set in late 1971 for the yen against the dollar still left the yen considerably undervalued (the yen was not allowed to float until after 1973). Many firms, however, were doing business on the basis of an internal, more highly valued exchange rate and pocketing the difference. As the *Mainichi* noted, "From about the middle of 1972, Japanese industries had been conducting trade at the rate of ¥270–¥280 to the dollar, and by selling the earned dollars to the Bank of Japan at a rate of ¥301 to the dollar, they earned an extra ¥20 per dollar."[35] In addition, the government-sponsored investment boom of the late 1960's had once again left industry with considerable overcapacity. As a result, investment slumped throughout the first half of the 1970's, and because of the danger of foreign protectionism the old relief valve of an export drive was also not as readily available as it had been ten years earlier. On March 31, 1970, the government even took the cosmetic step of changing the name of the old Supreme Export Council to the Trade Council. Continuing protectionism by Japan also caused problems in that the government prohibited importers from spending their cash on certain commodities, such as lumber, in order to protect domestic industries.

Into this economic milieu the Tanaka government pumped money as the government had never done before, both because of its industrial dispersal program and because it believed it had to pay off industries that claimed to have been damaged by capital liberalization, the "Nixon shocks," or the settlement of the textile dispute. MITI itself acknowledges an increase of ¥234 billion in the general account and investment budgets during the month following the Nixon shocks of 1971 (allegedly to save medium and smaller enterprises), and Tanaka cowed the Ministry of Finance's normally independent Budget Bureau into giving him everything he wanted. On Tanaka's orders Budget Bureau Director Aizawa Hideyuki increased the fiscal 1973 budget over the previous year by some 24.6 percent.[36] As John Campbell argues, "The major real effect of [Tanaka's dispersal] plan seems to have been simply to provide a justification for high spending, allowing the Liberal Democrats and even the Ministry of Finance to throw a cloak of virtue and high purpose over a budget which, in the final analysis, was little more than the largest pork-barrel in the history of Japanese public finance."[37]

The resultant inflationary conditions resembled nothing so much as the price spiral during World War I that led up to the rice riots. Again, just as in 1917 the general trading companies were in the forefront of the speculative boom. Above all other enterprises, the trading companies had too much cash sitting idle and no place to spend it. They began investing in land, which caused real estate values to appreciate in an unprecedented manner. For example, Mitsubishi Trading Company purchased the old premises of the NHK broadcasting station in the heart of Tokyo for ¥6 million per square meter, several times higher than the officially valued price, which brought a wave of criticism down on the trading company's head. Still, it had the money, and real estate was the best hedge against inflation.[38]

Serious political problems developed when the general trading companies began to speculate in daily necessities and hold them off the market in anticipation of further price rises. Just as in 1917 the press and the public began to suspect that cornering a market (kaishime) and holding goods off the market (urioshimi) were the root causes of the crazy prices. When during the second half of 1973 steel prices shot up, criticism began to focus on monopolies and cartels, which were supposed to be illegal but were known to be flourishing under the protection of MITI's administrative guidance. Many consumers' groups began to argue that the "private-sector industrial guidance model" boiled down to a "zaibatsu guidance model," the avoidance of which had been the original justification during the 1930's for turning industrial guidance over to the government.

On March 10, 1973, the new Price Regulation Section of the Economic Planning Agency introduced a draft law in the Diet entitled the "Temporary Measures Law Against the Kaishime and Urioshimi of Daily Life Commodities" (Seikatsu Kanren Busshi no Kaishime oyobi Urioshimi ni tai suru Rinji Sochi ni kan suru Hōritsu) to give the government new power to control prices. The debate over this law brought forth criticism of MITI and of big business every bit as devastating as that at the time of the "pollution Diet." The Diet passed and began to enforce the law (number 48) on July 6, well before the oil crisis complicated these problems.[39]

It was also right in the middle of the period of "crazy prices," and only three months before the first oil shock, that MITI unveiled its organizational "new look." Through a basic rewriting of the MITI establishment law (number 66 of July 25, 1973), Minister Nakasone and Vice-Minister Morozumi reshuffled the ministry in a way intended to placate its critics, allow it to deal with the new problems, and protect its proven capabilities. It was the first comprehensive revision of MITI's structure since 1952 and was known within the ministry as the "reform of the century."

In essence Morozumi retained both the International Trade and Trade Promotion bureaus but renamed them; changed the name of the Enterprises Bureau to the Industrial Policy Bureau and gave it new sections for Industrial Structure and Business Behavior; merged the old Light and Heavy Industries bureaus into a new Basic Industries Bureau (metals and chemicals combined); created a new Machinery and Information Industries Bureau that put electronics, computers, automobiles, and general machinery under one administration (we shall return to this grouping later); transformed the old Textiles Bureau into the Consumer Goods Industries Bureau; and set up a new external agency, the Natural Resources and Energy Agency (NREA), which combined the administration of petroleum, coal, energy conservation, and public utilities (including nuclear power generation) into one powerful unit. (Appendix B includes a chart of MITI's "new structure," or "face lift," as some critical journalists put it.)[40]

Morozumi retired on the day the new structure was enacted and turned over its implementation to Yamashita Eimei (class of 1943, former first secretary in the Canadian embassy, deputy director of the Heavy Industries Bureau, and chief of the Chemical, International Trade, and Enterprises bureaus). On October 6, 1973, the "Fourth Middle Eastern War" (as the Japanese call it) erupted. Ten days later six countries of the Organization of Petroleum Exporting Countries raised their oil prices by 21 percent, and on October 20 six Middle Eastern nations suspended shipments of oil to nations supporting Israel. The "oil shock"—a considerably more important event than what the Japanese press had called the "Nixon shocks"—hit Japan and the world with stunning force. On November 16, 1973, the cabinet enacted its "Emergency Petroleum Countermeasures Policy," which ordered crash conservation programs; and Japanese political leaders, including MITI Minister Nakasone, set out on trips to the Middle East to try to win friends among nations they had not paid much attention to in the past. Japan was the world's largest petroleum importer and totally dependent on the Middle East. (One of the projects that Nakasone agreed to build in the area in order to cement relations was a $3 billion petrochemical complex at Bandar Shahpur—Bandar Khomeini after the 1979 revolution—in Iran. Ironically enough, Vice-Minister Yamashita Eimei, who became an executive of the Mitsui Trading Company after his retirement, ended up being in charge of building it. Cost overruns, the turmoil of the revolution, and damage done during the war between Iran and Iraq may have turned it into one of the most expensive foreign-aid efforts the Japanese have ever undertaken.)[41]

The significance of the oil shock for purposes of this study lies in the fact that it once again reminded the Japanese people that they need their official bureaucracy. The country had had a governmental energy policy in one form or another ever since the Meiji Restoration, and the energy problems of the 1970's provided MITI, in the words of the *Mainichi*, with a "once in a lifetime opportunity" to regain its previous authority—a challenge that it met with great skill and ingenuity.[42]

The ministry's immediate problem was the impact of the oil crisis on the already "crazy" prices. First heating oil began to rise in price and then to disappear altogether from the market. Then toilet paper and next household detergents became scarce. The public became convinced that industrial cartels were using the crisis in order to make huge profits. An atmosphere similar to that at the time of the rice riots gripped the country. Minister Nakasone set up a command post inside MITI that he manned himself with his bureau chiefs and his chiefs of the Paper and Pulp Industry Section in the Consumer Goods Industries Bureau (in charge of toilet paper) and the Chemical Products Section in the Basic Industries Bureau (in charge of detergent). When the taxi drivers went on strike because of a shortage of liquefied petroleum gas, or housewives rioted in Osaka because of a shortage of kerosene, or long lines were discovered in front of supermarkets that allegedly had toilet paper for sale, the MITI leaders tried to send emergency shipments to calm the panic buying. Old industrial policy bureaucrats reared on the slogan that "steel is the rice of industry" now found themselves preoccupied with consumer goods and irate housewives. The leaders of the ministry, who had begun their careers during the occupation, said that it reminded them of the days of the Economic Stabilization Board, when MCI exercised control over all commodities.[43]

Out of this confusion came two new laws: the Emergency Measures Law for the Stabilization of the People's Livelihood (Kokumin Seikatsu Antei Kinkyū Sochi Hō, number 121 of December 22, 1973) and the Petroleum Supply and Demand Normalization Law (Sekiyu Jukyū Tekiseika Hō, number 122, also of December 22). They gave MITI broad powers to demand reports from wholesalers and retailers on their supplies, to establish standard prices for designated commodities, to draw up plans for the supply of consumer products, and to fine violators. Nakamura compares the petroleum law specifically with Yoshino's trade control law of September 1937, and Kakuma sees in both 1973 laws a return to at least the time of Sahashi's Special Measures Law.[44] In essence the new laws legalized MITI's administrative guidance and formally recognized that administrative guidance was in the national interest. Neither law created a "third control era," as some feared they would, but they did begin to tip the balance in Japan from "self-control" back toward "state control."

And yet during 1973, with the country experiencing a 29 percent inflation rate, the question of whether MITI's administrative guidance served the national interest or only the interests of big business remained intensely controversial. It was the Fair Trade Commission that placed this question squarely in the limelight. On October 24, 1972, Prime Minister Tanaka had named a most unusual and independent former bureaucrat, Takahashi Toshihide (chief of the Ministry of Finance's Banking Bureau from April 1963 to June 1965, the period during which the bureau was engaged in constant conflict with Sahashi over the Special Measures Law), as chairman of the Fair Trade Commission. Takahashi simply believed that it was his job to defend the Antimonopoly Law, even though it had been widely ignored in recent years. He was also convinced that the economic events of 1972 and 1973 were related to this flouting of the Antimonopoly Law.

Takahashi could have chosen any of several industries to make his point (steel, for example), but because of the oil crisis he chose the petroleum refining and distribution industry. On November 27, 1973, officials of the Fair Trade Commission raided the offices and demanded to see the books of the Petroleum Association of Japan and of twelve petroleum companies. According to the FTC, "The on-the-spot inspection was made to investigate a report that the oil companies raised the prices of their products and restricted supplies under the initiative of the association." [45]

On February 19, 1974, based on the documents his inspectors had collected, Takahashi charged the association and the companies with operating an illegal price cartel and turned the case over to the Tokyo High Public Prosecutor's Office. This was a sensational development—Takahashi's picture was on the cover of most national magazines that week—and it became even more sensational when the petroleum companies replied that anything they had done in concert had been in accordance with MITI's administrative guidance.

The prosecutors called in numerous MITI officials, including Iizuka Shirō, then director of the Basic Industries Bureau and formerly in charge of administrative guidance over the petroleum industry, and questioned them closely about their intentions in administrative guidance, what role the Petroleum Association played in it, and numerous other questions MITI was not pleased to have aired in the newspapers. Vice-Minister Yamashita met the press and angrily denied that MITI condoned illegal acts; he argued that the oil companies' prices would have gone up twice as much if the ministry's administrative guidance had not prevented it. But MITI was definitely on the defensive, and its defense was not helped when, on April 16, 1974, the *Asahi* printed the names of 50 former MITI officials, including 5 former vice-ministers, who were employed as amakudari executives throughout the oil industry. [46]

On May 28, 1974, the prosecutors indicted the Petroleum Association, the twelve companies, and seventeen of their executives, charging that they had criminally violated articles 3 and 8 of the Antimonopoly Law—to wit, that between December 1972 and November 1973 the executives had met some five times and concluded illegal agreements among themselves to raise prices and withhold products from the market. MITI was not charged, nor was administrative guidance mentioned in the indictment, but the defendants made it clear that both would form the heart of their defense. The executives each faced a maximum penalty of three years in jail or a ¥500,000 fine.[47]

So began the famous "black cartel" (*yami karuteru*) case. According to the press the women of the Housewives' Federation repeatedly shouted "banzai" on hearing the news of the indictments, but Keidanren was definitely displeased. FTC Chairman Takahashi said that the indictments should serve as a warning to others. MITI indicated that its administrative guidance had been "betrayed" by the oil companies, and that it planned to review the entire matter for future policy action. In a press conference Vice-Minister Yamashita also said that he hoped Japanese industrialists would not "lose their motivation" and become "desperate" as a result of the indictments.

The case was the first criminal prosecution for a violation of the Antimonopoly Law since its enactment, and the first instance of a government official criticizing administrative guidance in the line of duty since the practice had begun. However, more important than the case itself—which dragged on in the courts until 1980, when the Tokyo High Court finally ruled that MITI was not authorized to cause companies to restrict production through administrative guidance—was FTC Chairman Takahashi's attempt to strengthen the Antimonopoly Law. On September 18, 1974, the FTC published its proposed revisions, including one giving the FTC power to order companies to desist from cartels and to lower prices (under the AML as it then stood, the commission could only issue warnings). It also proposed strengthening the rules on splitting companies that had achieved near monopoly control over their industries, authorization of prosecutions for price fixing on the basis of circumstantial evidence alone, and several other changes.[48]

Even though Keidanren and MITI bitterly opposed the AML revision, the FTC case was given a boost when in November a scandal broke over Prime Minister Tanaka's expenditures of huge sums of money in the July election for the upper house and over charges that he had profited personally from his tenure in office—and, worse, that he had not reported the details to the tax authorities. No legal action was taken against him, but on November 26 he resigned as prime minister. Because the LDP had fallen to a new low in public esteem, Vice-President Shiina Etsusaburō of the LDP turned to Miki Takeo (MITI minister when Sahashi was vice-minister); among politicians Miki was known to the public as "Mr. Clean." Among his several efforts to refurbish the party's tarnished image in the wake of Tanaka's rule by money-power politics (*kinken seiji*), Miki championed Takahashi's law in the Diet.[49]

Unfortunately for Miki and Takahashi, the prime minister's sponsorship was not enough. The lower house passed the AML revision bill in order to save the prime minister's face, but it did so only on the understanding that Shiina would arrange to have it killed in the upper house, which he did. In February 1976, Takahashi resigned because of frustration and illness. However, as he left the scene, economic critics hailed him as the most colorful and effective chairman in the history of the FTC; and the LDP, now suffering from the thinnest of majorities in both houses, discovered that his proposed revision of the Antimonopoly Law was popular with the public. Thus, on June 3, 1977, a much watered-down version of Takahashi's law was enacted; the law made it somewhat harder for companies to operate blatantly illegal cartels, and it gave the FTC limited authority to break up monopolies.[50]

The effect on MITI of the black cartel case and the revision of the Antimonopoly Law was to put the ministry on notice that administrative guidance must be used in the interests of the nation and the people, and that the ministry should guard against abuses of its power. MITI had some trouble accepting this message, but it eventually got the point. As former Vice-Minister Morozumi said in a lecture to his juniors in the bureaucracy, as irritating as it can sometimes be, officials are duty bound to act within the law and on the basis of law.[51]

Under the pressure of all these external events and of its own internal reform, the ministry at last began to internationalize. During 1974 the new Industrial Structure Section in the Industrial Policy Bureau, led by the partly Harvard-educated economist Namiki Nobuyoshi, wrote new plans for the industrial structure that went well beyond both Amaya's 1969 thesis and the Industrial Structure Council's 1971 plan. The new plans also took account of the oil crisis, the economic conflicts with the United States and Europe, the public's changed attitude toward economic growth, and the current recession.

On November 1, 1974, the ministry published its first "long-term vision" of the industrial structure, a document it revised annually for the rest of the decade and published for public discussion. The statement set stringent standards for energy conservation and petroleum stockpiling, spelled out in detail what a "knowledge-intensive industrial structure" would look like, identified protectionism as a serious threat and demanded that Japan "internationalize" for its own good, and in general explained to the public and the politicans where Japan stood economically and where it had to go in order to continue to prosper. The vision also introduced the concept of a "plan-oriented market economy." This is essentially Sahashi's old "public-private co-operation formula" as institutionalized within the government; it gives the Industrial Structure Council the responsibility for annual co-ordination of budget priorities, investment decisions, and research and development expenditures.[52]

Capital liberalization was finally achieved in the years following the first "vision" statement. On May 1, 1973, the government had announced that Japan was "100 percent liberalized"—except that it still protected some 22 industries as exceptions, still applied all the old rules about joint ventures and subsidiaries, and still maintained numerous administrative restrictions on both trade and capital transfers ("nontariff barriers," as they are called). Four of the exceptional industries were the standard "sacred cows" of all countries—agriculture, mining, oil, and retail trade—and one was leather goods, included in order to protect the livelihood of a Japanese underclass, the burakumin. But the other 17 were the new strategic industries that MITI was nurturing.

Computers were the best-known case. Since the late 1960's MITI had poured money into domestic computer research, pushed companies into keiretsu, licensed foreign technology, and held off the competition—in short, MITI had formulated and administered a standard development program on the pattern of the 1950's. Its creation of the Machinery and Information Industries Bureau reflected this campaign: the bureau specifically linked computers and machines in order to prepare the way for the industries that the ministry had identified as export leaders after automobiles—semiconductors, numerically controlled machine tools, robots, and advanced consumer electronic goods such as videotape recorders. However, by the mid-1970's MITI realized that protectionism could no longer be used as one of its policy tools, and it therefore scheduled full liberalization of the computer industry for April 1, 1976. Most of the other 17 exceptional industries were opened at the same time, as was retail trade.

The next major sign of internationalization was the ministry's decision to dismantle its main statutory powers, the Foreign Exchange and Foreign Trade Control Law of 1949 and the Foreign Capital Law of 1950. On November 11, 1979, almost 30 years to the day after SCAP approved it as a temporary measure, the Diet enacted MITI's revision of the Trade Law. This revision, which went into effect a year later, abolished the Foreign Capital Law, altered the language of the "basic purpose" of the Trade Law from "prohibition in principle" to "freedom in principle," and reduced the powers of the government to residual rights of intervention in the economy in the event of balance of payments difficulties or other emergencies.[53] With a global trade surplus during 1977 of some $17.5 billion, which was a 77 percent increase over 1976, Japan could finally afford to lower its guard somewhat.

The new economic conditions of the 1970's also afforded MITI opportunities to exercise many of the old functions that it had perfected over the previous 50 years. For example, during the late 1970's it was busy creating cartels in the "structurally depressed industries" (textiles, rubber, steel, nonferrous metals, shipbuilding, and some petrochemicals) in order to allocate market shares to be scrapped and the number of employees to be retrained or pensioned. Based on the Temporary Measures Law for the Stabilization of Designated Depressed Industries (Tokutei Fukyō Sangyō Antei Rinji Sochi Hō, of May 15, 1978), MITI established a ¥10 billion fund (¥8 billion from the Development Bank and ¥2 billion from industry) for paying firms to scrap excess facilities; and it also obtained an exception to the Antimonopoly Law (opposed by the FTC) for "investment-limiting cartels" and mergers whose purpose was to reduce excess capacity. It all seemed quite familiar.[54]

On the positive front, during the years after the oil shock the ministry converted most electric power generation from oil to liquefied natural gas, liquefied petroleum gas, or coal. It also increased nuclear power generation by some 58 percent as of 1980; it shifted about half of the nation's 43 blast furnaces from heavy oil to coke and tar (and planned to convert all of them); it cut oil imports by better than 10 percent from 1973 levels; it stockpiled more than a hundred days' supply of petroleum; it diversified sources of supply away from the Middle East (notably to Mexico); and it commissioned the fashion designer, Mori Hanae, to create an "energy conservation look" (*shōene rukku*) for men during summertime—a tieless, short-sleeved, safari suit—in order to cut air-conditioning costs. During July 1979 MITI Minister Ezaki Masumi had himself photographed wearing one of the new suits and ordered MITI officials to shift to them; the Ministry of Finance, however, turned down the "energy conservation look" for its own officials as too undignified.

Despite the turmoil that swirled around the ministry during the 1970's, by the end of the decade its leaders had reason to be satisfied. Japan had more than fulfilled the long-range goal its bureaucrats had set for the country after the war; it had indeed caught up with Western Europe and North America. The lives of all Japanese had been transformed from the poverty of the 1930's and the death and de-struction of the 1940's to some of the highest levels of per capita income on earth. During the decade Japan's economy had also weathered two petroleum crises and emerged in stronger condition, despite the fact that Japan remained the most vulnerable of the world's economies to commercial interruptions.

Acknowledgment of and respect for Japan's achievements were uni-versal. The *Times* of London (July 21, 1980) declared that Japan had emerged as "the world's leading industrialized nation." MITI leaders were not complacent; they continued vigorously to shape Japan's in-dustrial structure for the future. But the attainment of a per capita GNP approximately the same as that of the other advanced industrial democracies clearly marked the end of an era. The future problems of the Japanese economy now begin from an entirely new premise: Japan is one of the world's rich nations. This achievement has also generated major interest throughout the world in how Japan grew so fast and for such a long period of time, a subject of particular interest in the United States, which is increasingly concerned to revitalize its own economy. The question repeatedly asked by Japan's economic partners and competitors is What are the lessons to be learned from Japan's recent economic history?

NINE

A Japanese Model?

THE HISTORY of the modern state has been one of continuous enlargement of the state's functions. From its traditional concern with defense, justice, and communications, it has expanded to encompass education; physical, mental, and moral health; birth control; consumer protection; ecological balance; the elimination of poverty; and, ultimately, in totalitarian social systems (as the term implies), the attempt to eliminate the distinction between state and society. In totalitarian systems the state tries to do everything. We began this book by distinguishing between the regulatory state and the developmental state, but these hardly exhaust the functions of the state in the late twentieth century. Today there are welfare states, religious states, equality states, defense states, revolutionary states, and so forth. All of this is a way of saying that the innumerable things a state does can be arranged in rough rank order according to its priorities, and that a state's first priority will define its essence. It is possible, of course, that these priorities will change, thereby changing the nature of the state, and that in some periods a confusion in priorities will cause different parts of the state to operate at cross-purposes.

The effectiveness of the Japanese state in the economic realm is to be explained in the first instance by its priorities. For more than 50 years the Japanese state has given its first priority to economic development. This does not mean that the state has always been effective in achieving its priorities throughout this period, but the consistency and continuity of its top priority generated a learning process that made the state much more effective during the second half of the period than the first. Some of the Japanese state's policies for economic development, such as the imperialism of the Pacific War, were disastrous, but that does not alter the fact that its priorities have been consistent. A state attempting to match the economic achievements of Japan must adopt the same priorities as Japan. It must first of all be a developmental state—and only then a regulatory state, a welfare state, an equality state, or whatever other kind of functional state a society may wish to adopt. This commitment to development does not, of course, guarantee any particular degree of success; it is merely prerequisite.

Given that Japan's state priorities have been remarkably consistent during the middle of the twentieth century, one must quickly add that Japan's record in achieving its priorities has been mixed. This is not to question the great and lasting achievements of the Japanese economy after 1955. The nation's economic strength at the end of the 1970's and its collective wisdom concerning what is necessary to support 115 million people with few natural resources at a per capita GNP of around $9,000 to $10,000 1978 dollars suggest that Japan should be able to maintain its own population in the manner it has come to expect, and also to contribute to the welfare of others, for many decades to come. It is rather to stress that the high-growth system cannot be reduced to any particular device or institution, to the rate of saving, or the employment system, or the banking system; and that the high-growth system certainly was not the invention of any single person or party at a particular time. Japan's achievements were the result of a tortuous learning and adaptation process that in the present context began with the financial panic of 1927 and ended with the adjustments in the wake of the oil shock of 1973.

The high-growth system, like the basic priorities of the state, was not so much a matter of choice for Japan as of necessity; it grew out of a series of economic crises that assailed the nation throughout the Shōwa era. The most obvious of these, in addition to the financial panic of 1927 and the oil shock, include the invasion of Manchuria in 1931, the fascist attacks on capitalism during the 1930's, the war with China from 1937 to 1941, the Pacific War, the collapse of the economy in 1946, the Dodge Line of 1949, the post–Korean War recession of 1954, the trade liberalization of the early 1960's, the recession of 1965, the capital liberalization of 1967–76, and the health and safety crises of the early 1970's. It is of course gratifying that Japan ultimately gained a powerful conception of how to achieve its priorities and then applied this conception with rigor and thoroughness. But it would be to reason in an ahistorical and ill-informed manner to fail to note that

Japan's high-growth system was the product of one of the most painful passages to modernity any nation has ever had to endure.

It may be possible for another state to adopt Japan's priorities and its high-growth system without duplicating Japan's history, but the dangers of institutional abstraction are as great as the potential advantages. For one thing, it was the history of poverty and war in Japan that established and legitimized Japan's priorities among the people in the first place. The famous Japanese consensus, that is, the broad popular support and a willingness to work hard for economic development that have characterized the Japanese during the 1950's and 1960's, is not so much a cultural trait as a matter of hard experience and of the mobilization of a large majority of the population to support economic goals. The willingness of the Japanese to subordinate the desires of the individual to those of the group is markedly weakening as generations come on the scene who have no experience of poverty, war, and occupation. To date Japan has not faced the egalitarian problems of other states for the simple reason that all Japanese were made equally poor by the war and postwar inflation and because, for all practical purposes, it bans immigration into its social system.

The priorities of the Japanese state derive first and foremost from an assessment of Japan's situational imperatives, and are in this sense a product not of culture or social organization or insularity but of rationality. These situational imperatives include late development, a lack of natural resources, a large population, the need to trade, and the constraints of the international balance of payments. It may be possible to borrow Japan's priorities and institutions, but the situational nationalism of its people during the 1950's and 1960's is something another people would have to develop, not borrow. During the 1920's and 1930's Japan tried to solve the economic problems it faced by handing over to the state the responsibility for economic development. It goes without saying that what the state did during the 1930's made the situation worse, not better, but the fact that there may have been preferable alternatives to the ones adopted does not detract from the rationality of the priorities. The same situational imperatives still exist in Japan today, even though they have been mitigated by overseas investment, trade surpluses, diversification of markets, and so forth. Nurturing the economy has been a major priority of the Japanese state because any other course of action implied dependency, poverty, and the possible breakdown of the social system. Regardless of the drastic changes of political regime that have occurred during the course of the Shōwa era, economic priorities have always been at or near the top of the state's agenda, and this is a constant that is unlikely to change.

Perhaps surprisingly, in light of the determined efforts of the American occupiers to change Japanese economic institutions, a considerable degree of continuity also exists throughout the Shōwa era in the means adopted by the state to achieve economic development. The great discontinuity is of course in the discredited reliance on military force to achieve economic security via imperialism. This failed so disastrously that after 1945 it was totally repudiated. But this does not mean that the strictly economic development policies attempted during the militarist era were or should have been repudiated. Instead of being rejected, they came to form a repertoire of policy tools that could be used again after peace and independence had been attained. There is actually nothing surprising about this: just as the activism of the postwar American state had its roots in the New Deal and just as the totalism of the postwar Soviet state had its roots in the Stalinism of the First Five Year Plan, so the developmentalism of the postwar Japanese state had its roots in the economic initiatives of the 1930's. In this sense the experience of the 1930's and the 1940's was not by any means totally negative for postwar Japan; these were the years in which the managerial tools of the developmental state were first tested, some being rejected and others proving useful. Overcoming the depression required economic development, war preparation and war fighting required economic development, postwar reconstruction required economic development, and independence from U.S. aid required economic development. The means to achieve development for one cause ultimately proved to be equally good for the other causes.

There are striking continuities among the state's various policy tools over the prewar and postwar years. Yoshino and Kishi discovered industrial rationalization during the late 1920's as a means to overcome the recession; their protégés Yamamoto, Tamaki, Hirai, Ishihara, Ueno, Tokunaga, Matsuo, Imai, and Sahashi applied it again during the 1950's and 1960's to achieve modern, competitive enterprises. During both periods the state attempted to replace competition with cooperation, while not totally losing the benefits of competition. Governmental control over the convertibility of currency lasted uninterruptedly from 1933 to 1964, and persisted even after that time in attenuated forms. The Petroleum Industry Law of 1934 is the precise model for the Petroleum Industry Law of 1962. The plans and planning style of the Cabinet Planning Board were carried over to the

Economic Stabilization Board and the Economic Planning Agency, particularly in their use of foreign exchange budgets to implement their plans. MITI's unique structural features—its vertical bureaus for each strategic industry, its Enterprises Bureau, and its Secretariat (derived from the old General Affairs Bureau of MCI and the General Mobilization Bureau of MM)—date from 1939, 1942, and 1943, respectively. They continued to exist in MITI down to 1973 unchanged in function and even, in some cases, in name. Administrative guidance has its roots in the Important Industries Control Law of 1931. Industrial policy itself was, of course, as much a part of the Japanese governmental lexicon in 1935 as it was in 1955.

Perhaps the greatest continuity is in terms of the people who executed the state's industrial policy. Yoshino, Kishi, Shiina, Uemura, and virtually all other leaders of politics, banking, industry, and economic administration were prominent in public life before, during, and after the war. The continuities between MCI and MITI are not only historical and organizational but also biographical. The late 1970's marked the end of an era, but the change above all was a change of generations: the top leaders of the bureaucracy were no longer men who had experienced service during wartime and the postwar occupation. The new officers of MITI during the 1980's will be young Japanese born during the 1960's, and their easy familiarity with peace and prosperity makes them different from all other Japanese born during the preceding years of the twentieth century.

The wrenching changes that MITI was forced to undertake during the late 1970's were caused at least in part by the fact that the ideas of the people who had guided Japan's economy from approximately 1935 to 1965, the generation that is typified by Sahashi, were no longer adequate to the new problems facing the nation and the ministry. The old cadres had been first of all managers of heavy and chemical industrialization. But the 1970's and beyond demanded specialists in managing an already industrialized economy whose very weight gave it global responsibilities. It is to MITI's credit that it produced such leaders, and that they set out to engineer a new change of industrial structure, one that emphasized postindustrial "knowledge-intensive" industries. The greatest assurance of their likely success in such a difficult venture, however, was the fact that they had been reared in an organization that had already changed the industrial structure once before.

The fundamental problem of the state-guided high-growth system is that of the relationship between the state bureaucracy and privately owned businesses. This problem erupted at the very outset of industrial policy in the schemes of Yoshino's Temporary Industrial Rationality Bureau, and it persisted uninterruptedly down to the Mitsubishi revolt and to the Fair Trade Commission's attack on MITI's administrative guidance cartel for the petroleum-refining industry. It is a problem that will never disappear; it is inherent in the capitalist developmental state. Over the past 50 years Japan developed and attempted to implement three different solutions to this problem—namely, self-control, state control, and cooperation. None of them is perfect, but each is preferable to either pure laissez faire or state socialism as long as forced development remains the top priority of the state.

Self-control means that the state licenses private enterprises to achieve developmental goals. The typical institution is the state-sponsored cartel, in which the state authorizes cartels in industries it designates as strategic but then leaves to the enterprises themselves the task of fashioning and operating the cartel. This was the approach adopted for the Important Industries Control Law of 1931, and for the steel industry from the public sales system of 1958 to the Sumitomo Metals Company incident of 1965. The primary advantage of this form of government-business relationship is that it affords the greatest degree of competition and private management in the developmental state system. Its greatest disadvantage is that it leads to control of an industry by the largest groups in it (as in zaibatsu domination), and to the likelihood of divergence between the interests of the big operators and the interests of the state (as, for example, in the wartime "control associations"). This form of government-business relationship is the one typically preferred by big business.

State control refers to the attempt to separate management from ownership and to put management under state supervision. It was typically the form of the relationship preferred by the "reform" (or "control") bureaucrats of the late 1930's and by the whole state bureaucracy during postwar reconstruction and the early stages of high-speed growth. Its principal advantage is that the state's priorities take precedence over those of private enterprise. Its primary disadvantages are that it inhibits competition, and therefore tolerates gross inefficiency in the economy, and that it fosters irresponsible management. The closest Japanese approximations to it occurred in Manchuria, in the prewar and wartime electric power generating industry, in the wartime munitions companies, in the postwar coal industry, and in the hundred or more public corporations of contemporary Japan. The inefficiencies of state control are commonly blamed for the poor performance of Japanese industry during the Pacific War.

The third form of the government-business relationship, that of public-private cooperation, is by far the most important. Although all three forms occurred throughout the entire 50 years of this study (depending primarily on variations in the political power of the state and private enterprise), the broad pattern of development since the late 1920's has been from self-coordination to its opposite, state control, and then to a synthesis of the two, cooperation. The chief advantage of this form is that it leaves ownership and management in private hands, thereby achieving higher levels of competition than under state control, while it affords the state much greater degrees of social goal-setting and influence over private decisions than under self-control. Its principal disadvantage is that it is very hard to achieve. It flourished in Japan during the 1950's and 1960's primarily because of the failure during the 1930's and 1940's of both of the other modes of the government-business relationship. During high-speed growth Japanese-style government-industrial cooperation came as close to squaring the circle—to achieving social goal-setting without the disadvantages of socialism—as any form of mixed economy among all the historical cases.

The chief mechanisms of the cooperative relationship are selective access to governmental or government-guaranteed financing, targeted tax breaks, government-supervised investment coordination in order to keep all participants profitable, the equitable allocation by the state of burdens during times of adversity (something the private cartel finds it very hard to do), governmental assistance in the commercialization and sale of products, and governmental assistance when an industry as a whole begins to decline.

This form of the government-business relationship is not peculiarly or uniquely Japanese; the Japanese have merely worked harder at perfecting it and have employed it in more sectors than other capitalist nations. The so-called military-industrial complex in the United States, to the extent that it identifies an economic relationship and is not merely a political epithet, refers to the same thing. If one were to extend the kinds of relationships that exist between the U.S. Department of Defense and such corporations as Boeing, Lockheed, North American Rockwell, and General Dynamics to other sectors of industry, and if one were also to give the government the power to choose the strategic sectors and to decide when they were to be phased out, then one would have a close American approximation of the postwar Japanese system. The relationship between government and business in the American national defense industries—including the unusual management and ownership arrangements for the nuclear weapons laboratories and the existence of such official agencies as the former Atomic Energy Commission and the National Aeronautics and Space Administration—is thought by Americans to be exceptional, whereas it was the norm for Japan's leading industrial sectors during high-speed growth. It is also perhaps significant that aviation, space vehicles, and atomic energy are all sectors in which the United States is preeminent, just as Japan is preeminent in steel production, ship-building, consumer electronics, rail transportation, synthetic fibers, watches, and cameras.

As noted earlier, the cooperative government-business relationship in the capitalist developmental state is very difficult to achieve and maintain. Even with such deeply entrenched social supports for cooperation as a shared outlook among government and industrial leaders because of common education (for instance, at Tōdai Law) and an extensive cross-penetration of elites because of early retirement from government service and reemployment in big business, the Japanese have difficulty in keeping public-private cooperation on the tracks. Industry is quite willing to receive governmental assistance, but it does not like government orders (as the steel and automobile industries illustrate). Government is often frustrated by the excessive competition and preemptive investment of industries it is trying to foster (as the petrochemical and textile industries illustrate). Nonetheless, the Japanese have worked hard to create cooperative relationships and have developed numerous unusual institutions through which to pursue them. These include the official "deliberation councils" such as the Commerce and Industry Deliberation Council of 1927, the Cabinet Advisers Council of 1943, the Industrial Rationalization Council of 1949, and the Industrial Structure Council of 1964; MITI's vertical bureaus and the corresponding officially sanctioned trade associations for each industry; the temporary exchange of officials between the state and private enterprise (for example, the posting of young MITI officers to Keidanren headquarters); the formal "discussion groups" implemented in the wake of the failure of the Special Measures Law; and the practice of administrative guidance, in which government officials and representatives of banking and industry can coordinate their activities unconstrained by law and lawyers.

In addition, the Japanese have fostered social supports for cooperation. We have already mentioned two of them—the essentially bureaucratic education of both public and private managers and the extensive "old boy" networks. It should not be thought that these are the only social supports or that they are not duplicable in other societies. They would be very hard to duplicate in other societies, since they rest on long-entrenched practices, but they are not pure cultural givens. As this book has sought to show, there was more consensus and cooperation in Japan during the 1950's than during the 1930's, which suggests that the reasons for this difference are to be found in changed historical circumstances and political consciousness and not in something as relatively unchanging as cultural mores. Some other social supports for government-business cooperation include the virtual impotence of corporate stockholders because of the industrial financing system; a work force fragmented among labor aristocrats enjoying semilifetime employment, temporaries, small-scale subcontractors, and enterprise unions; a system of collecting private savings through the postal system, concentrating it in government accounts, and investing it in accordance with a separate, bureaucratically controlled budget (FILP); some 115 government corporations covering such high-risk areas as petroleum exploration, atomic power development, the phasing out of the mining industry, and computer software development (these corporations are the successors to the national policy companies of the 1930's, the eidan of the wartime era, and the kōdan of the occupation); and a distribution system that serves not only to retail goods but also to keep the unemployed, the elderly, and the infirm working, thereby weakening demands for a welfare state in Japan.

In Japan, as compared with the United States, one of the most powerful social supports for private managers' cooperation with the government is that Japanese managers enjoy freedom from being judged exclusively in terms of short-term financial performance. Just as the essential spirit of Japanese industrial policy after the late 1920's lay in the search for ways to replace competition with cooperation without a drastic loss in efficiency, the industrial rationalization campaigns sought criteria of good management other than short-term profitability. These included the maintenance of full employment, increased productivity, expansion of market share, cost reduction, and the management of long-term innovation.

Morita Akio, chairman of Sony Corporation, believes that the emphasis on profitability has been a major cause of American industrial decline. He asserts, "The annual bonus some American executives receive depends on annual profit, and the executive who knows his firm's production facilities should be modernized is not likely to make a decision to invest in new equipment if his own income and managerial ability are judged based only on annual profit."[1] Morita believes that the incentive structure of postwar Japanese business has been geared to developmental goals, whereas the incentive structure of American business is geared to individual performance as revealed by quick profits. The result is not simply a lack of long-term planning in the United States but also exorbitant executive salaries, private corporate aircraft, palatial homes, and other major discrepancies between the rewards of labor and management. In postwar Japan the living standards of top executives and ordinary factory workers have differed only slightly (Morita observes that the American president of Sony's U.S. subsidiary makes more in corporate salary than Morita himself receives from Sony). On the other hand, it might be noted that managers in Japan have access to corporate entertainment funds of a size unparalleled in any other economy. The National Tax Agency calculated that during 1979 corporate social expenses amounted to some ¥2.9 trillion, or $13.8 billion, which meant that corporate executives were spending $38 million per day on drink, meals, golf fees, and gifts for their colleagues and customers.[2]

The point is that Japan's more flexible means of evaluating managers contributes to smoother labor-management relations than in some other countries and also avoids disincentives to cooperate with other enterprises and with the government. These Japanese practices came into being as a result of postwar conditions. According to Morita, "There is nothing in Japanese history to suggest that smooth labor-management relations came naturally"; prewar Japanese capitalism was "stark in its exploitation of labor." The postwar leveling of all Japanese incomes because of inflation and national adversity made possible the relative equality of rewards that existed during high-speed growth, as well as the emphasis on measures other than profitability for managerial performance. These social conditions are of considerable advantage to Japan in competing with countries such as the United States, but obviously they would be very difficult to transplant: although the salaries of American managers might be reduced, the institution of some other measure of performance than short-term profitability would require a revolution in the American system of allocating savings to industry through stock markets.

The priorities and social supports for cooperation among the Japanese might not be replicable in other societies, but it is easy to imagine that they might be matched—that is, a different society might be able to manipulate its own social arrangements in ways comparable to those of postwar Japan in order to give top priority to economic development and to provide incentives for public-private cooperation. If this were the case, then such a society would need an abstract model of the Japanese high-growth system to use as a guide for its own concrete application. Specialists on modern Japan will differ as to the precise elements and the weight to be attached to each element in such a model, but the following, based on the history of MITI, is my own estimation of the essential features of the Japanese developmental state. For purposes of this discussion, I stipulate that Japan's particular history would not have to be reexperienced, and that the social inputs of popular mobilization and the incentives to cooperate already exist in the society trying to emulate Japan (assumptions that are not necessarily realistic, as this study has sought to demonstrate).

The first element of the model is the existence of a small, inexpensive, but elite bureaucracy staffed by the best managerial talent available in the system. The quality of this bureaucracy should be measured not so much by the salaries it can command as by its excellence as demonstrated academically and competitively, preferably in the best schools of public policy and management. Part of the bureaucracy should be recruited from among engineers and technicians because of the nature of the tasks it is to perform, but the majority should be generalists in the formulation and implementation of public policy. They should be educated in law and economics, but it would be preferable if they were not professional lawyers or economists, since as a general rule professionals make poor organization men. The term that best describes what we are looking for here is not professionals, civil servants, or experts, but managers. They should be rotated frequently throughout the economic service and retire early, no later than age 55.

The duties of this bureaucracy would be, first, to identify and choose the industries to be developed (industrial structure policy); second, to identify and choose the best means of rapidly developing the chosen industries (industrial rationalization policy); and third, to supervise competition in the designated strategic sectors in order to guarantee their economic health and effectiveness. These duties would be performed using market-conforming methods of state intervention (see below).

The second element of the model is a political system in which the bureaucracy is given sufficient scope to take initiative and operate effectively. This means, concretely, that the legislative and judicial branches of government must be restricted to "safety valve" functions. These two branches of government must stand ready to intervene in the work of the bureaucracy and to restrain it when it has gone too far (which it undoubtedly will do on various occasions), but their more important overall function is to fend off the numerous interest groups in the society, which if catered to would distort the priorities of the developmental state. In the case of interests that cannot be ignored, deflected, or satisfied in symbolic ways—or upon which the perpetuation of the political system depends—the political leaders must compel the bureaucracy to serve and manipulate them.

A non-Japanese example of the kind of relationship we are looking for would be something like the American legislative branch's relationship to the wartime Manhattan Project or to the postwar nuclear submarine development program. The political system of the developmental state covertly separates reigning and ruling: the politicians reign and the bureaucrats rule. But it must be understood that the bureaucrats cannot rule effectively if the reigning politicians fail to perform their positive tasks, above all, to create space for bureaucratic initiative unconstrained by political power.

There are several consequences of this type of political system. One is that groups without access to the system will on occasion take to the streets to call attention to their disaffection (this occurred in Japan in 1960 in the anti–security treaty riots, in the student revolts of the late 1960's, in the demonstrations against the new Tokyo airport and the government's nuclear ship project, and in the campaign against industrial pollution). These demonstrations may arise out of important interests that cannot be indefinitely ignored by the state, or they may simply reflect demands for political participation. Whatever the case, when they occur the political leaders are called upon to exercise "safety valve" functions, forcing the bureaucracy to alter priorities just enough to calm the protesters but taking most of the "heat" of the demonstrations themselves. Clever politicians will anticipate eruptions of this sort (Satō Eisaku's strategy for the renewal of the security treaty in 1970). As long as the developmental projects are succeeding and their benefits are being equitably distributed, the political leaders should be able to deal with these problems symptomatically. Projects to call attention to the development effort and to instill pride in its successes may also be recommended (the Japanese Olympics of 1964, EXPO 70).

A major political difference between the capitalist developmental state and the communist dictatorship of development is that the capitalist state simply ignores the nonstrategic sectors of the society, whereas the communist state attempts directly and forcibly to demobilize them. The first is preferable because it avoids the unintended consequences of the presence of large numbers of police and the full apparatus of repression, which is not only wasteful of resources but is also incompatible with effective international commerce. This is certainly one lesson the Japanese learned from the 1940's.

The Japanese political system should also be distinguished from the bureaucratic-authoritarian regimes of Argentina, Brazil, Chile, and Uruguay. In these states the ruling elites seek to promote industrialization by excluding from power the previously mobilized economic groups and by developing collaborative relationships with multinational corporations. They do this through a technocratic political arrangement that relies heavily on coercion to enforce the rules of the game.[3] Japan differs in that it is a democracy in which the politicians are chosen by the votes of the majority; its stability has rested on the ability of the ruling political party to forge a coalition of voters committed to economic growth and effective management. During high-speed growth this coalition reflected the widespread recognition of Japan's situational imperatives; during the early 1970's the coalition began to weaken markedly, but it appears to have been reinvigorated by the energy crisis and the acceptance of the need for a new shift of industrial structure. Until very recent times the Japanese also have not been hospitable to collaboration with foreign capital. The Korean developmental state, by contrast, seems to share some of the bureaucratic-authoritarian characteristics and should to that extent be distinguished from the postwar Japanese case.

Postwar Japan also differs from the market-socialist states (chiefly Yugoslavia and Hungary), where various experiments have been undertaken to try to synthesize market economics with political control. The contradictory tensions inherent in these systems are more like those of Japan during the period of attempted state control (the late 1930's and 1940's) than they are like Japan after it had regained its independence and launched high-speed growth based on public-private cooperation.[4]

In addition to occasional protest demonstrations, a probable further consequence of the capitalist developmental system will be the periodic occurrence of "corruption" scandals. These arise because of the separation between reigning and ruling and because of the opportunities this condition gives some insiders to exploit the development programs. As long as these scandals occur primarily among politicians and not among bureaucrats, and as long as the development effort is proceeding to the benefit of the society as a whole, these scandals will be tolerated as unfortunate but not too serious imperfections in the overall system. However, if they occur among the bureaucracy, they signal the need for quick surgery and reconstitution of the system.

The third element of the model is the perfection of market-conforming methods of state intervention in the economy. In implementing its industrial policy, the state must take care to preserve competition to as high a degree as is compatible with its priorities. This is necessary to avoid the deadening hand of state control and the inevitable inefficiency, loss of incentives, corruption, and bureaucratism that it generates. It is probable that the market-conforming methods that actually work cannot be discovered a priori but will have to emerge from conflict between the managers of the state and the managers of the privately owned strategic industries. A cooperative relationship between the state and private enterprise is not a natural one: the state inevitably will go too far, and private enterprise inevitably will resent state interference in its decisions. When either the state or private enterprise becomes clearly dominant over the other, as occurred in Japan during the late 1940's (state dominance) and during the early 1970's (private-enterprise dominance), development will falter. One clear lesson from the Japanese case is that the state needs the market and private enterprise needs the state; once both sides recognized this, cooperation was possible and high speed growth occurred.

Japan offers a panoply of market-conforming methods of state intervention, including the creation of governmental financial institutions, whose influence is as much indicative as it is monetary; the extensive use, narrow targeting, and timely revision of tax incentives; the use of indicative plans to set goals and guidelines for the entire economy; the creation of numerous, formal, and continuously operating forums for exchanging views, reviewing policies, obtaining feedback, and resolving differences; the assignment of some governmental functions to various private and semiprivate associations (JETRO, Keidanren); an extensive reliance on public corporations, particularly of the mixed public-private variety, to implement policy in high-risk or otherwise refractory areas; the creation and use by the government of an unconsolidated "investment budget" separate from and not funded by the general account budget; the orientation of antitrust policy to developmental and international competitive goals rather than strictly to the maintenance of domestic competition; government-conducted or government-sponsored research and development (the computer industry); and the use of the government's licensing and approval authority to achieve developmental goals.

Perhaps the most important market-conforming method of intervention is administrative guidance. This power, which amounts to an allocation of discretionary and unsupervised authority to the bureaucracy, is obviously open to abuse, and may, if used improperly, result in damage to the market. But it is an essential power of the capitalist developmental state for one critical reason: it is necessary to avoid overly detailed laws that, by their very nature, are never detailed enough to cover all contingencies and yet, because of their detail, put a strait jacket on creative administration. One of the great strengths of Japanese industrial policy is its ability to deal with discrete complex situations without first having to find or enact a law that covers the situation. Highly detailed statutes serve the interests primarily of lawyers, not of development. The Japanese political economy is strikingly free of lawyers; many of the functions performed by lawyers in other societies are performed in Japan by bureaucrats using administrative guidance.

The Japanese of course rely on law, but on short and highly generalized laws. They then give concrete meaning to these laws through bureaucratically originated cabinet orders, ordinances, rules, and administrative guidance. All bureaucracies, the Japanese included, are inclined to abuse this rule-making authority (compare, for example, the chaos of rules churned out by the American Internal Revenue Service); but the answer to this problem seems to lie in finding better bureaucrats, not in eliminating their discretionary powers. In the case of flagrant bureaucratic abuse, the offended party may have to turn to the courts—something that the Japanese began to do during the 1970's more than in the past (for example, in the pollution suits and in the FTC's resort to the courts in the Yawata-Fuji merger case and the black cartel case). Nonetheless, compared to the participants in other systems, the Japanese seek to avoid litigation, relying instead on tailor-made government solutions to concrete problems (as in the Maruzen Oil Company case), and thereby avoiding legal impact on sectors that do not need it. At its best Japanese administrative guidance is comparable to the discretionary authority entrusted to a diplomat negotiating an international agreement. Success depends upon his skill, good sense, and integrity, and not on a set of legal requirements that no matter how well crafted can never truly tell a negotiator what to do.

The fourth and final element of the model is a pilot organization like MITI. The problem here is to find the mix of powers needed by the pilot agency without either giving it control over so many sectors as to make it all-powerful or so few as to make it ineffective. MITI itself came into being through a fortuitous process of accretion. MCI originated from the separation of agricultural and commercial-industrial administration. It developed by adding industrial functions while shedding commercial ones, obtained a planning capability when the Cabinet Planning Board was merged with its General Affairs Bureau in MM, and gained complete control over energy only when coal, petroleum, and electric power administration were combined during the MM era. The war also provided the ministry with micro-level intervention powers through its Enterprises Bureau. MITI itself finally resulted from the union of MCI and the apparatus for controlling international trade (the BOT). MITI has never had jurisdiction over transportation, agriculture, construction, labor, or finance, although it has had a strong influence over them, particularly over finance, through such institutions as the Japan Development Bank. The fight over Sahashi's Special Measures Law revolved primarily around MITI's efforts to extend its jurisdiction to cover industrial finance.

It is obviously a controversial matter to define the scope of the pilot agency. MITI's experience suggests that the agency that controls industrial policy needs to combine at least planning, energy, domestic production, international trade, and a share of finance (particularly capital supply and tax policy). MITI's experience also suggests the need not to be doctrinaire; functions can and should be added and subtracted as necessary. The key characteristics of MITI are its small size (the smallest of any of the economic ministries), its indirect control of government funds (thereby freeing it of subservience to the Finance Ministry's Bureau of the Budget), its "think tank" functions, its vertical bureaus for the implementation of industrial policy at the micro level, and its internal democracy. It has no precise equivalent in any other advanced industrial democracy.

These four elements constitute only a model, and a sketchy one at that. There are obviously numerous social and political consequences of this structure, including normative and philosophical ones, that any society considering adopting it should ponder carefully. As has been said repeatedly, the Japanese did not so much adopt this system of political economy as inherit it. Among its various implications, one in particular should be mentioned; the capitalist developmental state generates a pattern of conflict that differs in many ways from that in other democracies.

Japan's is a system of bureaucratic rule. As S. N. Eisenstadt pointed out more than a generation ago, all known bureaucratic regimes generate two kinds of conflict: struggles within the bureaucracy, and struggles between the bureaucracy and the central political authorities.[5] This case study of MITI offers numerous illustrations of each. Jurisdictional disputes among agencies over policy, appropriations, and priorities are the very lifeblood of the Japanese bureaucracy. MCI came into being in part because of a struggle between the agricultural and the industrial bureaucrats. During the 1930's MCI's reform bu-

reaucrats allied themselves with the military against old-line ministries such as Finance and Foreign Affairs to advance their industrial
development schemes. However, during the war MCI and MM civilians clashed constantly with the military bureaucrats. MITI was born
of a struggle between the Foreign Affairs and industrial bureaucrats.
High-speed growth saw MITI constantly pitted against the Fair Trade
Commission and, to a lesser but probably more important extent, the
Ministry of Finance. All the established ministries compete with each
other to extend their influence over the smaller agencies (Economic
Planning, Defense, Environment, and the others) and to place their
transferees in positions of influence throughout the government.

This kind of conflict fulfills important functions for the developmental state; not least of all, it invigorates the bureaucracy, giving it a
strong esprit de corps and providing competitive checks to compla-
cency, bureaucratic rigidity, and arrogance. The greatest threat to a
bureaucrat's security comes not from the political world or private-
interest groups but from other bureaucrats. On the other hand, conflicts among bureaucrats can also cause slow decision-making, distortions in policy to accommodate competing bureaucratic interests, and
avoidance of high-risk problems. There is no way to avoid these
drawbacks entirely, and coordination (*chōsei*) of the bureaucracy is
easily the most frustrating and time-consuming, yet critical, task of
the leaders of the state.

The Japanese have developed several innovative practices to try to
mitigate bureaucratic competition. One is to give the jobs of initial
policy formation and coordination to younger, not-so-exposed officials, a tactic that leaves their seniors in the position of appearing only
to approve policies coming from below. Senior officials can thus help
make and coordinate decisions without being constrained by attribu-
tions of personal authorship. Another useful practice is the recruitment of ministers and other senior political leaders from among former senior bureaucrats, thereby giving powers of coordination to
leaders with expert knowledge of the bureaucracy, "old boy" connections, and hierarchical relations with serving bureaucrats. (This practice can, of course, merely raise the bureaucratic infighting to a higher
level, as occurred in the case of Yoshida versus MITI). Still another
Japanese practice is the use of the budgetary process to effect coordination, which requires that budget-making be kept in bureaucratic
hands and greatly elevates the influence of the Ministry of Finance. A
fourth innovation is the use of bureaucratic proxies to try to effect coordination, as in the deliberation councils. Other practices of bu-

reaucratic competition and coordination common to all state systems occur prominently in Japan, including leaks to and bureaucratic manipulation of the press, selective briefing of favored politicians, the maintenance of secrecy concerning the actual norms of bureaucratic life, and so forth.

The other kind of conflict—that between the bureaucracy and political authorities—is equally common. The effective functioning of the developmental system requires a separation between reigning and ruling, but the separation itself is never formally acknowledged (it is *ura*, not *omote*; implicit, not explicit). As a result, boundary problems are inevitable, and serious conflict occurs when the political leaders believe the bureaucracy is exceeding its powers (as during the 1930's) or when the bureaucracy believes the politicians are exceeding theirs (as during the "Fukuda typhoon" or under the regime of Prime Minister Tanaka Kakuei). MITI's history reveals numerous examples of this type of conflict: the fight between MCI Minister Ogawa and Yoshino and Kishi; the fight between zaibatsu-connected ministers and the reform bureaucrats; the fight between MCI Minister Kobayashi and Kishi and the "reds" of the Cabinet Planning Board; the fight between Tōjō and Kishi during 1944 (although perhaps this is a better example of intrabureaucratic conflict); the fight between Yoshida and Shirasu on the one hand and the leaders of MCI on the other at the time of the creation of MITI; and the involvement of politicians in the Imai-Sahashi dispute.

Most of the practices used to mitigate struggles among bureaucrats are also suitable for mitigating struggles between bureaucrats and politicians. The norm is the attempt to avoid or to privatize conflict. This is often achieved by combining the perspectives of each side in one leader. Japan's most important postwar politicians—Yoshida, Kishi, Ikeda, Satō, Fukuda Takeo, and Ōhira—were all former senior bureaucrats. Although it is natural that political leaders would be found among such an intrinsic elite as the Japanese higher bureaucracy, their utilization in postwar Japan has certainly contributed to the effective operation and coordination of the Japanese developmental state.

This exercise in model building is not intended either to detract from Japanese achievements or to recommend the Japanese model to others. The history of MITI actually reveals a harder lesson than either of these; for all of Japan's alleged borrowing from abroad, the Japanese political genius rests in the identification and use of their own political assets. The development of MITI was a harrowing process, but its special characteristics and the environment in which it works arise from the special interaction of the Japanese state and society. The Japanese built on known strengths: their bureaucracy, their zaibatsu, their banking system, their homogeneous society, and the markets available to them. Such postwar reforms as the elimination of the military from political life, the rationalization of the zaibatsu, the strengthening of the Diet, and the equalization of social classes were all important, but the institutions of the Japanese developmental state are products of Japanese innovation and experience.

This suggests that other nations seeking to emulate Japan's achievements might be better advised to fabricate the institutions of their own developmental states from local materials. It might suggest, for example, that what a country like the United States needs is not what Japan has but, rather, less regulation and more incentives by the government for people to save, invest, work, and compete internationally. The Japanese learned to cooperate effectively with each other as a matter of national survival; the wars and economic miseries of the 1940's compelled them to maintain what were essentially wartime degrees of social and economic mobilization well into the 1960's. Lacking a comparable consensus on goals, the United States might be better advised to build on its own strengths and to unleash the private, competitive impulses of its citizens rather than add still another layer to its already burdensome regulatory bureaucracy.

Such an American policy may, however, be unrealistic for the longer term. Given the need for the United States to maintain the military balance among the nuclear powers; to reinvigorate its economy; to achieve coordination among its environmental, energy, welfare, educational, and productive policies; and to stop living off its capital; Americans should perhaps also be thinking seriously about their own "pilot agency." Above all the United States must learn to forecast and to coordinate the effects of its governmental policies. Agricultural policy has for too long been left outside any integrated economic strategy; commercial and economic representatives have for too long endured second-class status in the State Department's hierarchy; domestic regulatory actions have for too long been taken without a prior cost-benefit analysis of their economic impact; and a growing legal thicket has for too long replaced goal-oriented, strategic thought in economic affairs. These are some of the things that an economic pilot agency might tackle in the United States. It is not clear that the United States could ever free such an apparatus from the constraints imposed by congress, the courts, and special interest groups; but if economic mobilization becomes a national priority, then MITI will be an important institution to study and think about. As Peter Drucker has put it, "The exception, the comparatively rare service institution that achieves effectiveness, is more instructive than the great majority that achieves only 'programs.'"[6]

APPENDIXES

APPENDIX A

The Political and Administrative Leadership of the Trade and Industry Bureaucracy, 1925-1975

Ministers	Vice-ministers

I. MINISTRY OF COMMERCE AND INDUSTRY (Shōkō-shō), 1925–1943

First Katō Takaaki Cabinet, June 11, 1924–August 2, 1925 (Coalition)

1. Takahashi Korekiyo, 4/1/25–4/17/25 (Seiyūkai)	1. Shijō Takafusa, 4/1/25–4/10/29
2. Noda Utarō, 4/18/25–8/2/25 (Seiyūkai)	

Second Katō Takaaki Cabinet, August 2, 1925–January 30, 1926 (Kenseikai)

3. Kataoka Naoharu, 8/2/25–1/30/26 (Minseitō)

First Wakatsuki Cabinet, January 30, 1926–April 20, 1927 (Minseitō)

Kataoka Naoharu, 1/30/26–9/14/26

4. Fujisawa Ikunosuke, 9/14/26–4/20/27 (Minseitō)

Tanaka Giichi Cabinet, April 20, 1927–July 2, 1929 (Seiyūkai)

5. Nakahashi Tokugorō, 4/20/27–7/2/29 (Seiyūkai)	2. Mitsui Yonematsu, 4/10/29–7/2/30

Hamaguchi Cabinet, July 2, 1929–April 14, 1931 (Minseitō)

6. Tawara Magoichi, 7/2/29–4/14/31 (Minseitō)	3. Tajima Katsutarō, 7/2/30–12/21/31

Second Wakatsuki Cabinet, April 14, 1931–December 13, 1931 (Minseitō)

7. Sakurauchi Yukio, 4/14/31–12/13/31 (Minseitō)

Inukai Cabinet, December 13, 1931–May 26, 1932 (Seiyūkai)

8. Maeda Yonezō, 12/13/31–5/26/32 (Seiyūkai)	4. Yoshino Shinji, 12/21/31–10/7/36

(Adm.) Saitō Cabinet, May 26, 1932–July 8, 1934 (national unity)

9. Nakajima Kumakichi, 5/26/32–2/9/34 (Furukawa zaibatsu)

Ministers	Vice-ministers

10. Matsumoto Jōji, 2/9/34–7/8/34 (House of
    Peers)

(Adm.) Okada Cabinet, July 8, 1934–March 9, 1936 (national unity)
11. Machida Chūji, 7/8/34–3/9/36 (Minseitō)

Hirota Cabinet, March 9, 1936–February 2, 1937 (bureaucratic)
12. Kawasaki Takukichi, 3/9/36–3/27/36
    (Minseitō)
13. Ogawa Gōtarō, 3/28/36–2/10/37
    (Minseitō)
        5. Takeuchi Kakichi,
           10/7/36–12/22/36
        6. Murase Naokai,
           12/22/36–10/19/39

(Gen.) Hayashi Cabinet, February 2, 1937–June 4, 1937 (bureaucratic)
14. (Vice Adm.) Godō Takuo, 2/10/37–6/4/37

First Konoe Cabinet, June 4, 1937–January 5, 1939 (national unity)
15. Yoshino Shinji, 6/4/37–5/26/38
16. Ikeda Seihin, 5/26/38–1/5/39 (Mitsui
    zaibatsu)

Hiranuma Cabinet, January 5, 1939–August 30, 1939 (bureaucratic)
17. Hatta Yoshiaki, 1/5/39–8/30/39
    (ex-bureaucrat)

(Gen.) Abe Cabinet, August 30, 1939–January 16, 1940 (national unity)
18. (Vice Adm.) Godō Takuo,
    8/30/39–1/16/40
        7. Kishi Nobusuke,
           10/19/39–1/4/41

(Adm.) Yonai Cabinet, January 16, 1940–July 22, 1940 (national unity)
19. Fujihara Ginjirō, 1/16/40–7/22/40 (Mitsui
    zaibatsu)

Second Konoe Cabinet, July 22, 1940–July 18, 1941 (national unity)
20. Kobayashi Ichizō, 7/22/40–8/31/40
    (Mitsui zaibatsu)
    Kawada Isao, 8/31/40–11/2/40 (concur-
    rently minister of finance)
    Kobayashi Ichizō, 11/2/40–4/4/41 (Mitsui
    zaibatsu)
        8. Ojima Arakazu,
           1/4/41–10/21/41
21. (Adm.) Toyoda Teijirō, 4/4/41–7/18/41

Third Konoe Cabinet, July 18, 1941–October 18, 1941 (national unity)
22. (Adm.) Sakonji Seizō, 7/18/41–10/18/41

(Gen.) Tōjō Cabinet, October 18, 1941–July 22, 1944 (bureaucratic)
23. Kishi Nobusuke, 10/18/41–10/8/43
        9. Shiina Etsusaburō,
24. Tōjō Hideki, 10/8/43–11/1/43
           10/21/41/–10/8/43
    (concurrently prime minister)
       10. Kishi Nobusuke,
           10/8/43–11/1/43

Ministers	Vice-ministers

II. MINISTRY OF MUNITIONS (Gunju-shō), 1943–1945

1. Tōjō Hideki, 11/1/43–7/22/44 (concurrently prime minister)

   1. Kishi Nobusuke, 11/1/43–7/23/44

(Gen.) Koiso Cabinet, July 22, 1944–April 7, 1945

2. Fujihara Ginjirō, 7/22/44–12/19/44 (Mitsui zaibatsu)

   2. Shiina Etsusaburō, 7/23/44–7/28/44
   3. Takeuchi Kakichi, 7/28/44–4/10/45

3. Yoshida Shigeru, 12/19/44–4/7/45 (ex-bureaucrat)

(Adm.) Suzuki Cabinet, April 7, 1945–August 17, 1945

4. (Adm.) Toyoda Teijirō, 4/7/45–8/17/45

   4. Shiina Etsusaburō, 4/10/45–8/25/45

(Prince) Higashikuni Cabinet, August 17, 1945–October 9, 1945

5. Nakajima Chikuhei, 8/17/45–8/25/45 (Seiyūkai)

III. MINISTRY OF COMMERCE AND INDUSTRY (Shōkō-shō), 1945–1949

1. Nakajima Chikuhei, 8/26/45–10/9/45

   1. Shiina Etsusaburō, 8/26/45–10/12/45

Shidehara Cabinet, October 9, 1945–May 22, 1946 (conservative)

2. Ogasawara Sankurō, 10/9/45–5/22/46

   2. Toyoda Masataka, 10/12/45–6/14/46

First Yoshida Cabinet, May 22, 1946–May 24, 1947 (conservative)

3. Hoshijima Nirō, 5/22/46–1/31/47

   3. Okuda Shinzō, 6/14/46–2/12/47

4. Ishii Mitsujirō, 1/31/47–5/24/47

   4. Okamatsu Seitarō, 2/12/47–11/8/48

Katayama Cabinet, May 24, 1947–March 10, 1948 (socialist coalition)

5. Mizutani Chōzaburō, 5/24/47–3/10/48

Ashida Cabinet, March 10, 1948–October 15, 1948 (socialist coalition)

Mizutani Chōzaburō, 3/10/48–10/19/48

Second Yoshida Cabinet, October 15, 1948–February 16, 1949 (conservative)

6. Ōya Shinzō, 10/19/48–2/16/49

   5. Matsuda Tarō, 11/8/48–5/24/49

Third Yoshida Cabinet, February 16, 1949–October 24, 1952 (conservative)

7. Inagaki Heitarō, 2/16/49–5/24/49

Ministers	Vice-ministers

IV. MINISTRY OF INTERNATIONAL TRADE AND INDUSTRY
(Tsūshō Sangyō-shō), 1949–1975

1. Inagaki Heitarō, 5/25/49–2/17/50   1. Yamamoto Taka-
                  yuki,
2. Ikeda Hayato, 2/17/50–4/11/50   5/25/49–3/31/52
3. Takase Sōtarō, 4/11/50–6/28/50
4. Yokoo Shigemi, 6/28/50–7/5/51
5. Takahashi Ryūtarō, 7/5/51–10/30/52

                  2. Tamaki Keizō,
                  3/31/52–11/17/53

Fourth Yoshida Cabinet, October 30, 1952–May 21, 1953 (conservative)
6. Ikeda Hayato, 10/30/52–11/29/52
7. Ogasawara Sankurō, 11/29/52–5/21/53

Fifth Yoshida Cabinet, May 21, 1953–December 9, 1954 (conservative)
8. Okano Kiyohide, 5/21/53–1/9/54

                  3. Hirai Tomisaburō,
                  11/17/53–11/25/55
9. Aichi Kiichi, 1/9/54–12/9/54

First Hatoyama Cabinet, December 10, 1954–March 19, 1955 (conservative)
10. Ishibashi Tanzan, 12/10/54–3/19/55

Second Hatoyama Cabinet, March 19, 1955–November 22, 1955 (conservative)
Ishibashi Tanzan, 3/19/55–11/22/55

Third Hatoyama Cabinet, November 22, 1955–December 22, 1956 (LDP)
Ishibashi Tanzan, 11/22/55–12/22/56 4. Ishihara Takeo,
                  11/25/55–6/15/57

Ishibashi Cabinet, December 23, 1956–February 25, 1957 (LDP)
11. Mizuta Mikio, 12/23/56–2/25/57

First Kishi Cabinet, February 25, 1957–June 12, 1958 (LDP)
Mizuta Mikio, 2/25/57–7/10/57

                  5. Ueno Kōshichi,
                  6/15/57–5/13/60
12. Maeo Shigesaburō, 7/10/57–6/12/58

Second Kishi Cabinet, June 12, 1958–July 15, 1960 (LDP)
13. Takasaki Tatsunosuke, 6/12/58–6/18/59
14. Ikeda Hayato, 6/18/59–7/15/60

                  6. Tokunaga Hisatsu-
                  gu, 5/13/60–7/7/61
First Ikeda Cabinet, July 19, 1960–December 8, 1960 (LDP)
15. Ishii Mitsujirō, 7/19/60–12/8/60

Second Ikeda Cabinet, December 8, 1960–December 9, 1963 (LDP)
16. Shiina Etsusaburō, 12/8/60–7/18/61

                  7. Matsuo Kinzō,
                  7/7/61–7/23/63

Ministers	Vice-ministers
17. Satō Eisaku, 7/18/61–7/18/62	
18. Fukuda Hajime, 7/18/62–12/9/63	8. Imai Zen'ei, 7/23/63–10/23/64

Third Ikeda Cabinet, December 9, 1963–November 9, 1964 (LDP)
    Fukuda Hajime, 12/9/63–7/18/64
19. Sakurauchi Yoshio, 7/18/64–11/9/64

        9. Sahashi Shigeru, 10/23/64–4/25/66

First Satō Cabinet, November 9, 1964–February 17, 1967 (LDP)
    Sakurauchi Yoshio, 11/9/64–6/3/65
20. Miki Takeo, 6/3/65–12/3/66

        10. Yamamoto Shigenobu, 4/25/66–5/25/68

21. Kanno Watarō, 12/3/66–2/17/67

Second Satō Cabinet, February 17, 1967–January 14, 1970 (LDP)
    Kanno Watarō, 2/17/67–11/25/67
22. Shiina Etsusaburō, 11/25/67–11/30/68

        11. Kumagai Yoshifumi, 5/25/68–11/7/69

23. Ōhira Masayoshi, 11/30/68–1/14/70

        12. Ōjimi Yoshihisa, 11/7/69–6/15/71

Third Satō Cabinet, January 14, 1970–July 7, 1972 (LDP)
24. Miyazawa Kiichi, 1/14/70–7/5/71

        13. Morozumi Yoshihiko, 6/15/71–7/25/73

25. Tanaka Kakuei, 7/5/71–7/7/72

Tanaka Cabinet, July 7, 1972–December 9, 1974 (LDP)
26. Nakasone Yasuhiro, 7/7/72–12/9/74

        14. Yamashita Eimei, 7/25/73–11/8/74
        15. Komatsu Yūgorō, 11/8/74–7/27/76

Miki Cabinet, December 9, 1974–December 24, 1976 (LDP)
27. Kōmoto Toshio, 12/9/74–12/24/76

APPENDIX B

Internal Organization of the Ministry, Selected Dates, 1925-1973

1. MINISTRY OF COMMERCE AND INDUSTRY, 1925

Minister
Parliamentary vice-minister
Vice-minister
    Secretariat (Daijin Kanbō)
        Secretarial Section (Hishokan, Hisho-ka)
        Documents Section (Bunsho-ka)
        Statistics Section (Tōkei-ka)
        Accounting Section (Kaikei-ka)
    Commercial Affairs Bureau (Shōmu Kyoku)
        Commercial Policy Section (Shōsei-ka)
        Trade Section (Bōeki-ka) [1]
        Stock Exchange Section (Torihiki-ka)
        Insurance Section (Hoken-ka) [2]
    Industrial Affairs Bureau (Kōmu Kyoku)
        Industrial Policy Section (Kōsei-ka)
        Industrial Enterprises Section (Kōgyō-ka)
        Industrial Business Section (Kōmu-ka)
    Mining Bureau (Kōzan Kyoku)
        Mining Policy Section (Kōsei-ka)
        Mining Enterprises Section (Kōgyō-ka)
    External Bureaus:
        Patent Bureau (Tokkyo Kyoku)
        Iron and Steel Works (Seitetsu-jo)

1. Changed to bureau, May 3, 1930; to external bureau, July 14, 1937.
2. Changed to department (bu), May 27, 1927; to bureau, May 8, 1935.

2. MINISTRY OF COMMERCE AND INDUSTRY, June 16, 1939

Minister
Vice-minister
  Secretariat (Daijin Kanbō)
    Secretarial Section (Hisho-ka)
    Documents Section (Bunsho-ka)
    Accounting Section (Kaikei-ka)
    Research Section (Chōsa-ka)
    Intelligence Section (Hōdō-ka)
    Laws and Ordinances Examination Committee (Hōrei Shinsa Iin)
  General Affairs Bureau (Sōmu Kyoku)
    General Affairs Section (Sōmu-ka)
    Production Expansion Section (Seisan Kakujū-ka)
    Materials Coordination Section (Busshi Chōsei-ka)
  Minerals Bureau (Kōsan Kyoku)
    Mining Administration Section (Kōsei-ka)
    Gold Mining Section (Sankin-ka)
    Copper Mining Section (Sandō-ka)
    Nonferrous Metals Section (Hitetsu Kinzoku-ka)
  Machinery Bureau (Kikai Kyoku)
    General Machinery Section (Ippan Kikai-ka)
    Transportation Machinery Section (Yusō Kikai-ka)
    Precision Machinery Section (Seimitsu Kikai-ka)
  Textiles Bureau (Sen'i Kyoku)
    General Affairs Section (Sōmu-ka)
    Cotton Industry Section (Mengyō-ka)
    Wool Products Section (Yōmō Seihin-ka)
    Synthetic Textiles Section (Jinzō Sen'i-ka)
  Iron and Steel Bureau (Tekkō Kyoku)
    Iron and Steel Manufacturing Section (Seitetsu-ka)
    Coordination Section (Chōsei-ka)
    Special Steel Section (Tokushukō-ka)
  Chemical Bureau (Kagaku Kyoku)
    Inorganic Section (Muki-ka)
    Organic Section (Yūki-ka)
    Synthetic Section (Gōsei-ka)
  Management Bureau (Kanri Kyoku)[3]
    General Affairs Section (Sōmu-ka)
    Life Insurance Section (Seimei Hoken-ka)
    Casualty Insurance Section (Songai Hoken-ka)
    Stock Exchange Section (Torihiki-ka)
    Commercial Affairs Section (Shōji-ka)
  Promotion Department (Shinkō Bu)[4]
    General Affairs Section (Sōmu-ka)

3. A combination of the old Commercial Affairs and Insurance bureaus, it was abolished altogether in December, 1941, and its powers transferred to the Finance Ministry.
4. Predecessor of the Enterprises Bureau; see Chapter 5.

Trade Associations Section (Shōgyō Kumiai-ka)
Industrial Associations Section (Kōgyō Kumiai-ka)
Facilities Section (Shisetsu-ka)
Financing Section (Kin'yū-ka)
External Bureaus:
   Trade Bureau (Bōeki Kyoku)
   Price Bureau (Bukka Kyoku)
   Fuel Bureau (Nenryō Kyoku)
   Patent Bureau (Tokkyo Kyoku)

3. MINISTRY OF INTERNATIONAL TRADE AND INDUSTRY,
   May 25, 1949

Minister
Vice-minister
Superintendent of international trade (Tsūshō-kan)
   Secretariat (Daijin Kanbō)
      Secretarial Section (Hisho-ka)
      General Affairs Section (Sōmu-ka)
      Accounting Section (Kaikei-ka)
      Welfare Section (Kōsei-ka)
      Regional Affairs Section (Chihō-ka)
      Liaison Section (Shōgai-ka)
      Public Information Section (Kōhō-ka)
      Deliberation Councils Office (Shingi-shitsu)
      Research and Statistics Department (Chōsa Tōkei Bu)
   International Trade Bureau (Tsūshō Kyoku)
      Trade Policy Section (Tsūshō Seisaku-ka)
      Materials Coordination Section (Busshi Chōsei-ka)
      Export Section (Yushutsu-ka)
      First Import Section (Yunyū Daiichi-ka): the sterling bloc
      Second Import Section (Yunyū Daini-ka): North and South America,
         continental Europe, the Middle East
      Third Import Section (Yunyū Daisan-ka): Asia
      Markets Section (Shijō-ka)
      Trade Research Section (Tsūshō Chōsa-ka)
   International Trade Promotion Bureau (Tsūshō Shinkō Kyoku)
      Promotion Section (Shinkō-ka)
      Trade Auditing Section (Tsūshō Kansa-ka)
      Agricultural and Fisheries Products Section (Nōsuisan-ka)
      Control Section (Kanri-ka)
      Export Inspection Section (Yushutsu Kensa-ka)
      Facilities Section (Shisetsu-ka)
      Accounting Department (Keiri Bu)
   International Trade Enterprises Bureau (Tsūshō Kigyō Kyoku)
      Enterprises Section (Kigyō-ka)
      Industrial Finance Section (Sangyō Shikin-ka)
      Reconstruction Section (Fukkō-ka)

Industrial Labor Section (Sangyō Rōdō-ka)
Special Procurements and Reparations Department (Chōtatsu Baishō Bu)
International Trade Textiles Bureau (Tsūshō Sen'i Kyoku)
 Textiles Policy Section (Sensei-ka)
 Textiles Export Section (Sen'i Yushutsu-ka)
 Cotton Textiles Section (Mengyō-ka)
 Silk Section (Kengyō-ka)
 Synthetic Textiles Section (Kagaku Sen'i-ka)
 Linen and Wool Section (Mamō-ka)
 Clothing Section (Irui-ka)
 Finished Textiles Section (Seihin-ka)
 Inspection Section (Kansa-ka)
International Trade General Merchandise Bureau (Tsūshō Zakka Kyoku)
 Packaging Sundries Section (Hōsō Zakka-ka)
 Sundries Export Section (Zakka Yushutsu-ka)
 Daily Use Materials Section (Nichiyōhin-ka)
 Paper Industry Section (Shigyō-ka)
 Rubber Section (Gomu-ka)
 Ceramics Section (Yōgyō-ka)
 Construction Materials Section (Kenzai-ka)
 Leather Goods Section (Hikaku-ka)
 Wooden Products Section (Mokuseihin-ka)
International Trade Machinery Bureau (Tsūshō Kikai Kyoku)
 Machine Policy Section (Kisei-ka)
 Machinery Export Section (Kikai Yushutsu-ka)
 Industrial Machines Section (Sangyō Kikai-ka)
 Agricultural and Daily Livelihood Machines Section (Nōrin Minsei-ka)
 Electric Machinery Section (Denki Kikai-ka)
 Cast and Forged Products Section (Chūtanzōhin-ka)
 Electric Communications Machines Department (Denki Tsūshin Kikai Bu)
 Rolling Stock Department (Sharyō Bu)
International Trade Chemical Bureau (Tsūshō Kagaku Kyoku)
 Chemical Policy Section (Kasei-ka)
 Organic Section (Yūki-ka)
 Inorganic Section (Muki-ka)
 Alcohol Section (Arukōru-ka)
 Fats and Oils Section (Yushi-ka)
 Chemical Fertilizer Department (Kagaku Hiryō Bu)
International Trade Iron and Steel Bureau (Tsūshō Tekkō Kyoku)
 First Iron and Steel Section (Tekkō Daiichi-ka)
 Second Iron and Steel Section (Tekkō Daini-ka)
 Raw Materials Section (Genryō-ka)
 Scrap Recovery Section (Kaishū-ka)
External Bureaus:
 Resources Agency (Shigen Chō)
  Secretariat (Chōkan Kanbō)
  Coal Control Bureau (Sekitan Kanri Kyoku)
  Coal Production Bureau (Sekitan Sangyō Kyoku)
  Mining Bureau (Kōzan Kyoku)

Mine Safety Bureau (Kōzan Hoan Kyoku)
Electric Power Bureau (Denryoku Kyoku)
Patent Agency (Tokkyo Chō)
Medium and Smaller Enterprises Agency (Chūshō Kigyō Chō)[5]
Industrial Technology Agency (Kōgyō Gijutsu Chō)[6]

4. MINISTRY OF INTERNATIONAL TRADE AND INDUSTRY,
   September 1, 1952

Minister
Vice-minister
  Secretariat (nine sections, one office, and one department; 1200 officials)
  International Trade Bureau (14 sections; 428 officials)
  Enterprises Bureau (9 sections; 282 officials)
  Heavy Industries Bureau (12 sections; 204 officials)
  Light Industries Bureau (10 sections and one department; 253 officials)
  Textiles Bureau (7 sections; 112 officials)
  Mining Bureau (4 sections; 94 officials)
  Coal Bureau (5 sections; 121 officials)
  Mine Safety Bureau (3 sections; 58 officials)
  Public Utilities Bureau (12 sections; 302 officials)
  Regional International Trade and Industry Bureaus and Mine Safety Inspection Departments (5,135 officials)
External Bureaus:
  Patent Agency (672 officials)
  Medium and Smaller Enterprises Agency (166 officials)
  Institute of Industrial Technology (4,422 officials)

5. MINISTRY OF INTERNATIONAL TRADE AND INDUSTRY,
   July 25, 1973

Minister
Parliamentary vice-minister (2)
Vice-minister
Private secretary to the minister
  Secretariat (Daijin Kanbō)
    Secretarial Section (Hisho-ka)
    General Affairs Section (Sōmu-ka)
    Accounting Section (Kaikei-ka)
    Regional Affairs Section (Chihō-ka)
    Public Information Section (Kōhō-ka)
    Data Processing Administration Section (Jōhō Kanri-ka)
    Welfare Administrator (Kōsei Kanri-kan)
    Research and Statistics Department (Chōsa Tōkei Bu)

5. Founded August 2, 1948.
6. Founded August 1, 1948.

International Trade Policy Bureau (Tsūshō Seisaku Kyoku)
    General Affairs Section (Sōmu-ka)
    The Americas–Oceania Section (Beishū Taiyōshū-ka)
    West Europe–Africa–Middle East Section (Seiō Afurika Chūtō-ka)
    South Asia–East Europe Section (Minami Ajia Tōō-ka)
    North Asia Section (Kita Ajia-ka)
    Trade Research Section (Tsūshō Chōsa-ka)
    International Economic Affairs Department (Kokusai Keizai Bu)
    Economic Cooperation Department (Keizai Kyōryoku Bu)
International Trade Administration Bureau (Bōeki Kyoku)
    General Affairs Section (Sōmu-ka)
    Export Section (Yushutsu-ka)
    Import Section (Yunyū-ka)
    Agricultural and Marine Products Section (Nōsuisan-ka)
    Foreign Exchange and Trade Finance Section (Kawase Kin'yū-ka)
    Export Insurance Planning Section (Yushutsu Hoken Kikaku-ka)
    Long-Term Export Insurance Section (Chōki Yushutsu Hoken-ka)
    Short-Term Export Insurance Section (Tanki Yushutsu Hoken-ka)
Industrial Policy Bureau (Sangyō Seisaku Kyoku)
    General Affairs Section (Sōmu-ka)
    Research Section (Chōsa-ka)
    Industrial Structure Section (Sangyō Kōzō-ka)
    Industrial Finance Section (Sangyō Shikin-ka)
    Business Behavior Section (Kigyō Kōdō-ka)
    International Enterprises Section (Kokusai Kigyō-ka)
    Commercial Policy Section (Shōsei-ka)
    Commercial Affairs Section (Shōmu-ka)
    Consumer Economy Section (Shōhi Keizai-ka)
    Price Policy Section (Bukka Taisaku-ka)
Industrial Location and Environmental Protection Bureau (Ritchi Kōgai Kyoku)
    General Affairs Section (Sōmu-ka)
    Industrial Relocation Section (Kōgyō Saihaichi-ka)
    Industrial Location Guidance Section (Ritchi Shidō-ka)
    Industrial Water Section (Kōgyō Yōsui-ka)
    Environmental Protection Planning Section (Kōgai Bōshi Kikaku-ka)
    Environmental Protection Guidance Section (Kōgai Bōshi Shidō-ka)
    Safety Section (Hoan-ka)
    Mine Safety Section (Kōzan-ka)
    Coal Mine Safety Section (Sekitan-ka)
Basic Industries Bureau (Kiso Sangyō Kyoku)
    General Affairs Section (Sōmu-ka)
    Iron and Steel Administration Section (Tekkō Gyōmu-ka)
    Iron and Steel Production Section (Seitetsu-ka)
    Nonferrous Metals Section (Hitetsu Kinzoku-ka)
    Chemical Products Safety Section (Kagakuhin Anzen-ka)
    Basic Chemical Products Section (Kiso Kagakuhin-ka)
    Chemical Products Section (Kagaku Seihin-ka)
    Chemical Fertilizer Section (Kagaku Hiryō-ka)
    Alcohol Industry Department (Arukōru Jigyō Bu)

Machinery and Information Industries Bureau (Kikai Jōhō Sangyō Kyoku)
   General Affairs Section (Sōmu-ka)
   International Trade Section (Tsūshō-ka)
   Industrial Machinery Section (Sangyō Kikai-ka)
   Cast and Forged Products Section (Chūtanzōhin-ka)
   Electronics Policy Section (Denshi Seisaku-ka)
   Data Processing Promotion Section (Jōhō Shori Shinkō-ka)
   Electronics and Electrical Machinery Section (Denshi Kiki Denki-ka)
   Automobile Section (Jidōsha-ka)
   Weights and Measures Section (Keiryō-ka)
   Aircraft and Ordnance Section (Kōkūki Buki-ka)
   Vehicle Section (Sharyō-ka)
   Machinery Credit Insurance Section (Kikai Hoken-ka)
Consumer Goods Industries Bureau (Seikatsu Sangyō Kyoku)
   General Affairs Section (Sōmu-ka)
   International Trade Section (Tsūshō-ka)
   Fiber and Spinning Section (Genryō Bōseki-ka)
   Textile Products Section (Sen'i Seihin-ka)
   Paper and Pulp Industry Section (Shigyō-ka)
   Household and Miscellaneous Goods Section (Nichiyōhin-ka)
   Recreation and Miscellaneous Goods Section (Bunka Yōhin-ka)
   Ceramics and Construction Materials Section (Yōgyō Kenzai-ka)
   Housing Industry Section (Jūtaku Sangyō-ka)
   Textile Inspection Administrator (Sen'i Kensa Kanri-kan)
External Bureaus:
  Natural Resources and Energy Agency (Shigen Enerugī Chō)
   Secretariat (Chōkan Kanbō)
   Petroleum Department (Sekiyu Bu)
   Coal Mining Department (Sekitan Bu)
   Public Utilities Department (Kōeki Jigyō Bu)
  Patent Agency (Tokkyo Chō)
  Medium and Smaller Enterprises Agency (Chūshō Kigyō Chō)
  Industrial Technology Agency (Kōgyō Gijutsu In)

APPENDIX C

The Bureaucratic Careers of Vice-Ministers Sahashi and Imai

1. SAHASHI SHIGERU

April 1937	Enters MCI as member of class of 1937. Total of 19 in class. Class association named Tokuwa Kai.
4/37–1/38	Assigned to Industrial Business Section, Industrial Affairs Bureau.
1/38–10/41	Army service in China: accounting officer first lieutenant.
10/41–11/46	Assigned to the Silk and Wool Section, Textiles Bureau, MCI; Iron and Steel Bureau, MM; Nagoya Munitions Superintendent's Office, MM; Iron and Steel Section, Mining Bureau, MCI (simultaneously chairman, Commerce and Industry Workers' Union).
11/46–5/47	First section chief appointment: chief, Labor Section, General Affairs Bureau, MCI.
5/47–12/48	Chief, Paper Industry Section, Textiles Bureau (on 6/19/47 the section was transferred to the Daily Necessities Bureau).
12/48–8/51	Chief, Cotton Textiles Section, Textiles Bureau, MCI-MITI.
8/51–8/52	Chief, General Affairs Department, Sendai MITI Bureau.
8/52–7/54	Chief, Coal Policy Section, Coal Bureau.
7/54–6/57	Chief, Secretarial Section, Minister's Secretariat.
6/57–6/60	Deputy chief, Heavy Industries Bureau.
6/60–7/61	Chief, Heavy Industries Bureau.
7/61–7/63	Chief, Enterprises Bureau.
7/63–10/64	Director, Patent Agency.
10/64–4/66	Vice-minister.
4/66–4/72	Sahashi's "rōnin" (unemployed samurai) period.
4/72–	Chairman of the board, Leisure Development Center, a MITI-sponsored association serving the tourism industry.

2. IMAI ZEN'EI

April 1937	Enters MCI as member of class of 1937.
4/37–9/46	Assigned to Trade Bureau; Temporary Materials Coordination Bureau; Textiles Bureau, MCI-MM.
9/46–6/47	First section chief appointment: chief, Distribution Section, Coal Agency, MCI.
6/47–10/49	Chief, Supply and Demand Section, Production Bureau, Economic Stabilization Board.
10/49–2/51	Chief, First Import Section, International Trade Bureau, MITI.
2/51–6/51	Chief, Trade Policy Section, International Trade Bureau.
6/51–8/52	First secretary, Japanese Embassy, Washington.
8/52–7/54	Chief, Trade Policy Section, International Trade Bureau.
7/54–6/56	Chief, General Affairs Section, Minister's Secretariat.
6/56–8/58	Chief, Promotion Department, Medium and Smaller Enterprises Agency.
8/58–2/61	Chief, Textiles Bureau.
2/61–7/62	Chief, International Trade Bureau.
7/62–7/63	Director, Patent Agency.
7/63–10/64	Vice-minister.
11/65–	Executive director and then (5/66) president, Japan Petrochemicals; chairman, Petroleum Committee, Industrial Structure Council.

NOTES

NOTES

Complete authors' names, titles, and publication data for the works cited in short form are given in the Bibliography, pp. 367–80.

ONE

1. One of the most prominent Japanese economists, Shinohara Miyohei, subsequently acknowledged that he had not always understood or approved of government policy but that with hindsight he had changed his mind. See Shinohara. For the influence of the London *Economist*'s book, see Arisawa, 1976, p. 371.
2. William W. Lockwood, "Economic Developments and Issues," in Passin, p. 89; Uchino Tatsurō, *Japan's Postwar Economic Policies* (Tokyo: Ministry of Foreign Affairs, 1976), p. 6.
3. Arisawa, 1937, p. 4
4. Kindleberger, p. 17.
5. See Gotō.
6. Richard Halloran, *Japan: Images and Realities* (New York: Knopf, 1970), p. 72.
7. Hadley, p. 87.
8. *Consider Japan*, p. 16.
9. Haitani, p. 181.
10. Kaplan, p. 14.
11. Ruth Benedict, *The Chrysanthemum and the Sword* (Boston: Houghton Mifflin, 1946), p. 316.
12. Titus, p. 312.
13. See Chen.
14. Hugh Patrick, "The Future of the Japanese Economy: Output and Labor Productivity," *The Journal of Japanese Studies*, 3 (Summer 1977): 239.
15. *Ibid.*, p. 225.
16. Sahashi, 1972, p. 190.
17. Philip H. Trezise, "Politics, Government, and Economic Growth in Japan," in Patrick and Rosovsky, p. 782.
18. Campbell, pp. 2, 200. Slight Diet alterations of the budget also occurred in 1977 and 1978, during the period of thin majorities for the LDP.
19. Industrial Structure Council, *Japan's Industrial Structure: A Long Range Vision* (Tokyo: JETRO, 1975), p. 9.
20. Roberts, p. 439.
21. On the Three Sacred Treasures, see Shimada Haruo, "The Japanese Employment System," *Japanese Industrial Relations*, Series 6 (Tokyo: Japan Insti-

tute of Labor, 1980), p. 8. For background and bibliography, see Organization for Economic Cooperation and Development, 1977a.
22. Amaya, p. 18; Organization for Economic Cooperation and Development, 1972, p. 14.
23. Clark, p. 64.
24. On public corporations and the Fiscal Investment and Loan Plan, see Johnson, 1978.
25. Amaya, p. 20.
26. See, e.g., Richard Tanner Johnson and William G. Ouchi, "Made in America (Under Japanese Management)," *Harvard Business Review*, Sept.-Oct. 1974, pp. 61–69; and William McDonald Wallace, "The Secret Weapon of Japanese Business," *Columbia Journal of World Business*, Nov.-Dec. 1972, pp. 43–52.

27. Allinson, p. 178.   28. Tomioka, pp. 15–16.
29. M. Y. Yoshino, p. 17.   30. Ohkawa and Rosovsky, p. 220.
31. Amaya, pp. 9–69.
32. R. P. Dore, "Industrial Relations in Japan and Elsewhere," in Craig, p. 327.
33. Nakamura, 1974, pp. 165–67.   34. See Toda.
35. Hadley, p. 393.   36. Kaplan, p. 3.
37. Boltho, p. 140.   38. Yasuhara, pp. 200–201.
39. Louis Mulkern, "U.S.-Japan Trade Relations: Economic and Strategic Implications," in Abegglen et al., pp. 26–27.
40. Wolfgang J. Mommsen, *The Age of Bureaucracy: Perspectives on the Political Sociology of Max Weber* (New York: Harper Torchbooks, 1977), p. 64; Dahrendorf, 1968, p. 219; Dore, in Craig, p. 326; George Armstrong Kelly, "Who Needs a Theory of Citizenship?" *Daedalus*, Fall 1979, p. 25.
41. *The Bureaucratization of the World* (Berkeley: University of California Press, 1973), p. 147.
42. Amaya, p. 51.
43. For the signs of an incipient American industrial policy, see David Vogel, "The Inadequacy of Contemporary Opposition to Business," *Daedalus*, Summer 1980, pp. 47–58.
44. See Johnson, 1974; Johnson, 1975.
45. Shibagaki Kazuo, "Sangyō kōzō no henkaku" (Change of industrial structure), in Tokyo University, 1975, 8: 89.
46. See Drucker.   47. Allinson, pp. 34–35.
48. Henderson, p. 40.   49. Nettl, pp. 571–72.
50. Bell, p. 22, n. 23.
51. Ernest Gellner, "Scale and Nation," *Philosophy of the Social Sciences*, 3 (1973): 15–16.
52. Black, p. 171.
53. Tiedemann, p. 138.
54. Amaya, p. 1.
55. Kakuma, 1979a, p. 58; Nawa, 1975, p. 88.
56. Ozaki, 1970, p. 879.
57. MITI, 1957, pp. 3–4.
58. Nawa, 1974, p. 22.
59. On Taylorism, see Samuel Haber, *Efficiency and Uplift: Scientific Management in the Progressive Era* (Chicago, Ill.: University of Chicago Press, 1964).

Denis Healey describes "a new approach to improving our industrial performance," which he established in Great Britain in 1974 after he became Chancellor of the Exchequer. It actually boiled down to an attempt at industrial rationalization. See Denis Healey, *Managing the Economy*, The Russell C. Leffingwell Lectures (New York: Council on Foreign Relations, 1980), p. 29.

60. Gilpin, pp. 70–71.
61. See Ueno, p. 27.
62. *Can Pluralism Survive?* The William K. McInally Lecture (Ann Arbor: Graduate School of Business Administration, University of Michigan, 1977), p. 24.
63. Takashima Setsuo, p. 30.   64. Ueno, p. 14.
65. Ohkawa and Rosovsky, p. 200.   66. See Kodama.
67. Ohkawa and Rosovsky, p. 182.   68. Boltho, pp. 188–89.
69. Amaya, p. 78.
70. MITI, *Industrial Policy and MITI's Role* (Tokyo: MITI, 1973), p. 1.
71. In Arisawa, 1976, p. 133; and Nakamura, 1974, p. 164.
72. Arisawa, quoted in Obayashi, p. 69; Shiina, 1976, pp. 106–14.
73. Tanaka, pp. 655–56.
74. Maeda, 1975, p. 9.
75. Clark, p. 258.

TWO

1. See Johnson, 1980. Seidensticker's suggestion is contained in a letter of July 25, 1979.
2. Kakuma, 1979b, p. 171.
3. Japan Industrial Club, 2: 434.
4. See Obayashi. Cf. Berger, pp. 87–88.
5. Campbell, p. 137.   6. Weber, p. 1004, n. 12.
7. Black, pp. 55, 77.   8. Weber, p. 959.
9. Cf. Ide Yoshinori, "Sengo kaikaku to Nihon kanryōsei" (Postwar reform and the Japanese bureaucratic system), in Tokyo University, 1974, 3: 146.
10. Ide and Ishida, pp. 114–15.
11. For a theoretical discussion of this pattern in many late-developing nations, see Heeger.
12. See Iwasaki, pp. 41–50.
13. Kojima Kazuo, p. 26. See also Personnel Administration Investigation Council, p. 58.
14. Henderson, pp. 166, 195.
15. Isomura and Kuronuma, pp. 11–15, 18.
16. See Kanayama.
17. Black, p. 209.
18. Yamanouchi, pp. 85, 121–22, 181–82. For similar political uses of the phrase denka no hōtō, see *Sōri daijin*, pp. 56–57.
19. Duus and Okimoto, p. 70.
20. Craig, p. 7.
21. The basic source on the purge is Hans H. Baerwald, *The Purge of Japanese Leaders Under the Occupation* (Berkeley: University of California Press, 1959).

22. Satō, p. 60.
23. Amaya, p. 72.
24. Noda Economic Research Institute, p. 5.
25. Roser, p. 201.
26. See Ide Yoshinori, in Tokyo University, 1974, 3: 149–58.
27. For details, see Ōkōchi Shigeo, "Nihon no gyōsei soshiki" (The organization of administration in Japan), in Tsuji, 2: 94–99.
28. Kakuma, 1979b, p. 5 *et seq.*
29. "Shihai taisei no seisaku to kikō" (The policies and structure of the ruling system), in Oka, pp. 53–68.
30. Campbell, p. 128, n. 29.
31. Wildes, p. 92.
32. "Kanryō o dō-suru" (What about the bureaucracy?), *Chūō kōron*, Aug. 1947, p. 3.
33. Ōkubo, pp. 4–5.
34. Watanabe Yasuo, "Kōmuin no kyaria" (Careers of officials), in Tsuji, 4: 200; Satō, pp. 60–61.
35. Sugimori Kōji, "The Social Background of Political Leadership in Japan," *The Developing Economies*, 6 (Dec. 1968): 499–500.
36. Robert M. Spaulding, Jr., "The Bureaucracy as a Political Force, 1920–45," in Morley, p. 37.
37. For statistics on the numbers of cabinet and private bills introduced in the first thirty Diets under the Constitution of 1947, see Fukumoto, pp. 132–36. See also T. J. Pempel, "The Bureaucratization of Policy-making in Postwar Japan," *American Journal of Political Science*, 18 (Nov. 1974): 647–64.
38. See Ministry of Finance, Tax Bureau, p. 9; and Hollerman, 1967, p. 248. Odahashi Sadaju, former technical adviser to the House of Councillors Commerce and Industry Committee, declares that the shingikai have actually taken over the Diet functions of deliberating on laws. See Odahashi, p. 23. See also Yung H. Park, "The Governmental Advisory Commission System in Japan," *Journal of Comparative Administration*, 3 (Feb. 1972): 435–67. For studies of particular shingikai, see Yung H. Park, "The Central Council for Education, Organized Business, and the Politics of Education Policy-making in Japan," *Comparative Education Review*, 19 (June 1975): 296–311; and Michael W. Donnelly, "Setting the Price of Rice: A Study in Political Decisionmaking," in Pempel, pp. 143–200.
39. Interview with Sahashi Shigeru, Tokyo, Sept. 5, 1974.
40. "Nihon ni okeru seisaku kettei no seiji katei" (The political processes of policy-making in Japan), in Taniuchi, pp. 7–8.
41. Yamamoto, pp. 46–50, 74–78.
42. MITI Journalists' Club, Oct. 1963, p. 76. For the term kakuremino as applied to shingikai, see Yamamoto, p. 21.
43. Weber, p. 1416.
44. "Gendai yosan seiji shiron" (A sketch of modern budgetary politics), in Taniuchi, p. 107.
45. Campbell, p. 280.
46. Titus, p. 11.
47. Wildes, p. 113.
48. On income distribution, see Boltho, p. 163.

49. In Taniuchi, pp. 15–20.   50. Satō, p. 66.
51. Akimoto, p. 142.   52. Matsubayashi, 1976, p. 233.
53. Itō Daiichi, 1968, pp. 457–58.
54. Industrial Policy Research Institute, p. 264.
55. See Kusayanagi, May 1969, p. 165; Matsumoto, 1: 16; and Takeuchi, p. 14.
56. Akaboshi, p. 171.
57. Martin Landau and Russell Stout, Jr., "To Manage Is Not to Control," *Public Administration Review*, 39 (Mar.-Apr. 1979): 151.
58. Kusayanagi, Jan. 1969, p. 180.
59. "Tsūsan-shō ni miru gendai keibatsu kenkyū" (Research on modern keibatsu as seen in MITI), *Zaikai tenbō*, Aug. 1978, pp. 62–65.
60. Kubota, p. 50.   61. Matsubayashi, 1973, p. 85.
62. Nishiyama, pp. 109–14, 228–30.   63. Spaulding, p. 265, table 45.
64. See the preface by Kishi in Yoshino Shinji Memorial Society, *Yoshino Shinji*. For Kishi's high regard for Yoshino, see Kishi, Sept. 1979, p. 282.
65. "Amakudari" (Descent from heaven), *Shūkan yomiuri*, Sept. 4, 1976, p. 149.
66. Honda, 1: 164–69.
67. Shibusawa, p. 17. See also Konaka, pp. 99–125.
68. *Mainichi Daily News*, Apr. 8, 1974.
69. Clark, pp. 36–37.
70. Sakakibara, 1977a, pp. 31–32.
71. *Mainichi Daily News*, Apr. 8, 1974.
72. Kakuma, 1979b, p. 100.
73. Yoshino Shinji, 1962, pp. 242–50; Shiina, 1970, p. 212.
74. In Tsuji, 4: 179–81.
75. Kusayanagi, 1974, p. 126; Nawa, 1975, p. 80; and *Japan Times*, July 1, 1974. For a bibliography of Hayashi's numerous articles, see Ozaki, 1970.
76. Ōjimi and Uchida, p. 31.
77. MITI Journalists' Club, 1963a, p. 227.
78. Misonō, p. 13.
79. Takeuchi, p. 63.
80. Akimi, pp. 9–13; MITI Journalists' Club, 1956, pp. 266–69; and Akimoto, pp. 19–21.
81. The report that set off the incident of 1979–80 was Jin Itsukō, Oka Kuniyuki, and Murakami Masaki, "Kōdan, yakunin, giin, jigyōdan no ketsuzei 13-chō en kuichirashi" (How public corporations, bureaucrats, and Diet members gobble up 13 trillion yen of tax receipts), *Gendai*, Nov. 1979, pp. 80–110.
82. *Mainichi Daily News*, Jan. 6, 1976.
83. For a list of Japanese government corruption cases from 1872 to 1976, see Ōuchi Minoru, *Fuhai no kōzō, Ajia-teki kenryoku no tokushitsu* (The structure of corruption; characteristics of Asian political authority) (Tokyo: Daiyamondo Sha, 1977), pp. 193–96.
84. See, e.g., *Far Eastern Economic Review*, July 1, 1974, pp. 33–36; and *Japan Times Weekly*, Apr. 28, 1979, p. 5.
85. Fukumoto, pp. 157–59.
86. Takada Shin'ichi, "Tsūsan OB no zensangyō 'amakudari' bumpuzu"

("Amakudari" distribution map of former MITI officials), *Zaikai tenbō*, Aug. 1978, pp. 84–90.

87. See Ward Sinclair, "Good Grazing for Old Firehorses," *San Francisco Chronicle*, Feb. 10, 1980 (reprinted from the *Washington Post*). See also *Serving Two Masters: A Common Cause Study of Conflicts of Interest in the Executive Branch* (Washington, D.C.: Common Cause, 1976).

88. Hadley, p. 38.

89. Quoted by Shiba and Nozue, p. 32.

90. Amaya, p. 57.

91. Nakamura, 1969, p. 314.

92. For a complete list of the members of the Kayō-kai, see MITI Journalists' Club, 1963a, pp. 41–42, 266–76.

93. Iwatake, pp. 306–7; *Shūkan yomiuri*, Sept. 4, 1976, p. 149.

94. The basic source on this subject is Okōchi, in Tsuji, 2: 77–110.

95. Shinobu Seizaburō, "From Party Politics to Military Dictatorship," *The Developing Economies*, 5 (Dec. 1967): 666–84.

96. Sahashi, July 1971, p. 108.

97. Sakakibara, Nov. 1977, p. 73.

98. *Mainichi Daily News*, Aug. 2, 1974; *ibid.*, Jan. 10, 1976.

99. *Keizai seisaku*, p. 211.   100. See Johnson, 1977, pp. 235–44.

101. Honda, 2: 47.   102. Ōjimi and Uchida, p. 32.

103. *Mainichi Daily News*, Jan. 21, 1976; Honda, 2: 77.

104. Suzuki Kenji, "Keisatsu o shimedashite, Bōeichō o nottoru ōkura kanryō" (Freezing out the police: Ministry of Finance bureaucrats take over the Defense Agency), *Sandē mainichi*, July 30, 1978, pp. 132–34. For the background of the Self-Defense Forces, see Martin E. Weinstein, *Japan's Postwar Defense Policy, 1947–1968* (New York: Columbia University Press, 1971). See also Honda, 2: 121–55.

105. Shibano, pp. 131–39.

106. Watanabe Yasuo, in Tsuji, 4: 186.

107. Hollerman, 1967, pp. 160–61.

108. Sakakibara, Nov. 1977, p. 71.

109. For a study of these institutions, see Johnson, 1978.

110. MITI Journalists' Club, 1956, pp. 273–74.

111. Nawa, 1974, pp. 126–28. The ranks from step seven and below may vary from time to time. See also Nawa, Apr. 1976.

112. See *Kankai* Editorial Board, Oct. 1976; and Fukui Haruhiro, "The GATT Tokyo Round: The Bureaucratic Politics of Multilateral Diplomacy," in Blaker, pp. 101–2.

113. Akaboshi, pp. 164–72; Policy Review Company, 1970, s.v. "Tsūsan-shō," pp. 68–69.

114. Kakuma, 1979a, pp. 103, 107.

115. Japan Civil Administration Research Association, 1970, p. 153.

116. Kusayanagi, May 1969, p. 163.

117. "MITI and Japan's Economic Diplomacy—With Special Reference to the Concept of National Interest," unpublished paper for the Social Science Research Council Conference on Japanese Foreign Policy, Jan. 1974, p. 46.

118. Sahashi, 1971a, pp. 266–68.

119. Ozaki, 1970, p. 887.

120. Kakuma, 1979b, pp. 220, 223.

THREE

1. See James Q. Wilson, "The Rise of the Bureaucratic State," *The Public Interest*, 41 (Fall 1975): 77–103.
2. Kobayashi, 1977, p. 102 *et seq.*
3. Tiedemann, p. 139.
4. Horie Yasuzō, "The Transformation of the National Economy," in Tōbata, pp. 67–89.
5. See Roberts, p. 131. 6. See MITI, 1962, pp. 3–163.
7. In Tōbata, p. 87. 8. Kusayanagi, May 1969, p. 173.
9. Arisawa, 1976, p. 4; Odahashi, p. 139.
10. Yoshino Shinji, 1962, pp. 99–100; History of Industrial Policy Research Institute, 1975, 2: 3–5; Maeda, 1975, p. 9.
11. Yoshino Shinji, 1962, pp. 18–21, 34–35.
12. History of Industrial Policy Research Institute, 1975, 1: 10; 2: 124–27.
13. Honda, 2: 9–11; and Inaba, 1977, pp. 176–84. Incidentally, another illustrious figure who got a start on his life work in the old MAC was Yanagita Kunio (1875–1962).
14. Masumi, p. 172. 15. Japan Industrial Club, 1: 109.
16. Arisawa, 1976, p. 5. 17. Havens, p. 74.
18. See MITI, 1951, p. 61–63; MITI, 1962, pp. 170–80; MITI, 1964, pp. 38–40; MITI, 1965, pp. 7–9; Kakuma, 1979a, pp. 164–65; and Shiroyama Saburō, *Nezumi* (The rat) (Tokyo: Bungei Shunjū Sha, 1966). On kaishime, see Frank Baldwin, "The Idioms of Contemporary Japan," *The Japan Interpreter*, 8 (Autumn 1973): 396–409.
19. Shirasawa, pp. 28–33; Ann Waswo, *Japanese Landlords: the Decline of a Rural Elite* (Berkeley: University of California Press, 1977), pp. 117–18.
20. Takane, pp. 74–78; and Gotō.
21. Yoshino Shinji Memorial Society, pp. 207–10; Kakuma, 1979a, pp. 176–78; Nawa, 1974, pp. 18–19; and Kishi, in MITI, 1960, p. 95.
22. On Kobiki-chō, see Yoshino Shinji, 1965, p. 147 *et seq.*
23. Kakuma, 1979a, p. 163; Japan Industrial Club, 1: 111.
24. Japan Industrial Club, 1: 47–51.
25. *Fifty Years*, p. 18; and Roberts, pp. 240–42.
26. Yoshino Shinji Memorial Society, pp. 175–77, 188, 194–204; and Yoshino Shinji, 1962, pp. 43–44. On Kawai Eijirō's arrest, see Richard H. Mitchell, *Thought Control in Prewar Japan* (Ithaca, N.Y.: Cornell University Press, 1976), p. 158.
27. Arisawa, 1937, pp. 6, 42–47; Yoshino Shinji, *Waga kuni kōgyō no gōrika* (The rationalization of our country's industries) (Tokyo, 1930).
28. Arisawa, 1976, pp. 66–68; and Arisawa, 1937, pp. 67–80.
29. Havens, p. 80; Yoshino Shinji, 1962, pp. 124–28.
30. History of Industrial Policy Research Institute, 1975, 1: 145; 2: 44–45; and Yoshino Shinji, 1962, pp. 117–21.
31. Maeda, 1975, p. 9.
32. Kakuma, 1979a, pp. 184–85.
33. Nawa, 1974, p. 20.
34. See Chō; Fujiwara, pp. 322–23; Ōshima Kiyoshi, "The World Economic Crisis and Japan's Foreign Economic Policy," *The Developing Economies*, 5,

(Dec. 1967): 628–47; Hugh T. Patrick, "The Economic Muddle of the 1920's," in Morley, pp. 211–66; MITI, 1960, pp. 11–12; and Yasuhara, p. 30.

35. Kishi, Sept. 1979, p. 282; Nishiyama, pp. 129–32. The metric system did not replace all indigenous Japanese measures until 1959. Iwatake Teruhiko of MITI was the official responsible for completing the shift to metric. See Iwatake, pp. 122–24.

36. Shiroyama, Aug. 1975, p. 304.

37. Arisawa, 1976, p. 64.

38. Yoshino Shinji Memorial Society, p. 233.

39. Arisawa, 1976, p. 65.

40. Ōshima Kiyoshi (n. 34), p. 633; Arisawa, 1976, p. 20.

41. Quoted in Harari, pp. 47–48.

42. On Yoshino's succession to the vice-ministership, see Yoshino Shinji Memorial Society, pp. 233–50. On Kishi and the pay dispute, see Imai; Kurzman, pp. 110–11; and Yoshimoto, pp. 85–88. Some of the noncareer officials whom Kishi supported later transferred to work in the Manchukuo government, where they remained intensely loyal to Kishi. See Kakuma, 1979a, pp. 187–88. After Kishi returned from Europe, the pay dispute erupted again. Although the Hamaguchi cabinet ordered the pay cut in October 1929, the Wakatsuki cabinet actually carried it out only on May 27, 1931. Kishi clashed with MCI Minister Sakurauchi, and this time Kishi's sempai from the same feudal han, Matsumura Giichi of the House of Peers and also parliamentary vice-minister of MCI, had to be called in to force Kishi to back down. See Watanabe Yasuo, "Nihon no kōmuinsei" (Japan's public service system), in Tsuji, 2: 127–29; Kōno; and Robert M. Spaulding, Jr., "The Bureaucracy as a Political Force, 1920–45," in Morley, pp. 53–55.

43. Yoshino Shinji, 1935, p. 313.

44. Maeda, in Arisawa, 1976, p. 64.

45. The Major Export Industries Association Law of 1925 was amended in 1931 and 1934 to broaden its scope and give the cartels powers to compel compliance by outsiders. MCI's powers of supervision were also strengthened. The unions of medium and smaller enterprises exercised control primarily over the textile, knitwork, enamelware, celluloid, match, toy, fertilizer, and printing industries.

46. Hadley, p. 330.

47. MITI, 1964, p. 54. For the text of the law and a detailed analysis of each article, see pp. 47–73.

48. Yoshino Shinji, 1962, pp. 213–14; Arisawa, 1976, p. 93; Fujiwara, pp. 352–53; and Takase Masao.

FOUR

1. For the text of the Munitions Industries Mobilization Law, see MITI, 1964, pp. 25–29. On "state of incident," see the *New York Times*, Mar. 16, 1938.

2. History of Industrial Policy Research Institute, 1975, 2: 270–71.

3. See Peattie, p. 67.

4. On Uemura, see *Kankai* Editorial Board, Mar. 1976.

5. For the text of the law, see MITI, 1964, pp. 36–37.

6. Fujiwara, pp. 384–85.
7. Ministry of Finance, Secretariat, pp. 52–55, 67, 71, 74–79, 101–2, 151, 173, 182–83; Yasuhara, p. 32.
8. Osaka *Asahi shimbun*, July 21, 1928; quoted by Yamamura Katsurō, "The Role of the Finance Ministry," in Borg and Okamoto, p. 291.
9. Anderson, pp. 84, 93.
10. See History of Industrial Policy Research Institute, 1978; and Katō, p. 24.
11. On the Teijin case, see Roberts, pp. 294–95; Arthur E. Tiedemann, "Big Business and Politics in Prewar Japan," in Morley, pp. 294–96; and Yoshida Shigeru Biography Publication Committee, p. 72. (Note that this Yoshida Shigeru is a different person from the man who became prime minister after the war.)
12. Nakamura, 1974, pp. 30–31.
13. Ide and Ishida, p. 110.
14. Yoshino Shinji, 1962, pp. 356, 367–69.
15. Arisawa, 1976, pp. 113–19; Katō Toshihiko, "Gunbu no keizai tōsei shisō" (The military's economic control ideology), in Tokyo University, 1979, vol. 2, *Senji Nihon keizai* (The wartime Japanese economy), pp. 67–110.
16. Shiina, 1976.
17. Yoshino Shinji, 1962, pp. 277–78.
18. Yoshida Biography Committee, p. 76.
19. Arisawa, 1976, p. 147; Itō Mitsuharu; and Ōsawa, pp. 204–28.
20. On Ogawa and his purge of MCI, see Akimi, pp. 144–45; Kakuma, 1979a, p. 221; Kishi, Sept. 1979, pp. 282–83; Kurzman, p. 118; Shiroyama, Aug. 1975, p. 306; and Yoshimoto, pp. 92–96.
21. Yoshino Shinji, 1962, pp. 281, 285–89.
22. See Murase Memorial Editorial Committee, pp. 105–10, 698, 711–15; and MITI, 1960, pp. 92–94.
23. Yoshino Shinji, 1962, pp. 290–91.
24. Nakamura, 1974, pp. 21–23; Peattie, pp. 208–17. Peattie notes the influence of Soviet economic planning on the Manchurian five year plan.
25. See Tajiri, pp. 113–14; MITI, 1960, 101–2; Shiina, 1970, pp. 186–87; Shiina, 1976, pp. 107–8; Kishi, Sept. 1979, pp. 284–88; and Kishi, in *Tsūsan jyānaru*, May 24, 1975, p. 21.
26. Domestic Political History Research Association, p. 129. Tanaka Shin'ichi, the subject of this monograph, was an official with the South Manchurian Railroad until 1937, when he joined one of Ayukawa's Mangyō firms. From there he transferred to the Cabinet Planning Board, and from there to MM, MCI, and MITI.
27. Kakuma, 1979a, pp. 167–69, 195–96. For the law itself, see MITI, 1964, pp. 88–89. Kogane Yoshiteru also participated in drafting the law. See Nishiyama, pp. 103–8.
28. MITI, 1964, p. 238.
29. Yamamura, in Borg and Okamoto, pp. 288–89, 300.
30. History of Industrial Policy Research Institute, 1975, 2: 171–73. See also Yoshitomi, pp. 148–55.
31. Industrial Policy Research Institute, p. 234; MITI, 1960, pp. 123–24.
32. Shiroyama, Aug. 1975, p. 307; Berger, pp. 123–24.
33. Yoshino Shinji Memorial Society, pp. 295–99. See also Yoshino's pamphlet of late 1937, *Nihon kokumin ni uttau* (Report to the Japanese people).

34. Yoshino Shinji, 1962, pp. 365–66; History of Industrial Policy Research Institute, 1975, 2: 176–77.
35. Nakamura, 1974, p. 44.
36. MITI, 1964, p. 141.
37. History of Industrial Policy Research Institute, 1975, 2: 271.
38. For a table of the 41 most important imperial ordinances derived from the law, see Arisawa, 1976, p. 156.
39. It might be noted that *busshi dōin keikaku* is also the technical Japanese term for Soviet-type planning. See Ueno, p. 16. Concerning the original Japanese butsudō, Itō comments that "conceptually, it was a plan for materials mobilization, budgeting in materials in place of what was formerly expressed with currency." Itō Mitsuharu, p. 361.
40. On the influence of the butsudō and Soviet precedents, see Nakamura, 1974, pp. 24, 164–67; MITI, 1964, p. 124; and Tanaka, p. 655. Publication of the book by Tanaka was sponsored by Inaba Hidezo, Tokunaga Hisatsugu, Sahashi Shigeru, and other leaders of postwar industrial policy.
41. Tanaka, p. 11.
42. Arisawa, 1976, pp. 149–52; Inaba, 1965, pp. 22, 40–44.
43. Inaba, 1965, pp. 26, 59; Itō Mitsuharu, p. 362; and Tanaka, preface.
44. Two MITI vice-ministers have drawn attention to their work on the butsudō—Hirai Tomisaburō (*Tsūsan jyānaru*, May 24, 1975, pp. 28–30) and Ueno Kōshichi (MITI, 1960, p. 123). Ueno specifically mentions Sakomizu Hisatsune as a central figure in creating and executing the butsudō.
45. Nakamura, 1974, p. 63.
46. Yoshino Shinji Memorial Society, pp. 310–12.
47. Shiroyama, Aug. 1975, p. 308.
48. In Morley, p. 311.
49. Maeda, 1968, pp. 31–32; Kumagai, quoted in Suzuki Yukio, 1969, pp. 92–93.
50. MITI, 1964, p. 148.
51. See Miyake.
52. See "Nihon keizai no saihensei to Ryū Shintarō," in Gotō Ryūnosuke, *Shōwa kenkyū kai* (The Shōwa Research Association) (Tokyo: Keizai Ōrai Sha, 1968), pp. 225–34.
53. See Arisawa, 1976, pp. 200–203; Nakamura, 1974, pp. 95–102; and MITI, 1964, pp. 444–49. For an interesting defense of the Economic New Structure, see Tsukata.
54. Anderson, pp. 149, 154.
55. Kakuma, 1979a, p. 231; and Imai.
56. Fujiwara, p. 446.
57. Inaba, 1965, pp. 55–80; and Inaba, 1977.
58. On Inaba's connection with the Kyōchō Kai, see Inaba, 1977. Yoshida Shigeru, the first director of the Cabinet Research Bureau, was also affiliated with the Kyōchō Kai, and he brought from it to the Research Bureau Inaba, Katsumata, and Minoguchi Tokijirō, a prominent professor of economics at Hitotsubashi University after the war. On the Kyōchō Kai, see Japan Industrial Club, 1: 103.
59. For the text of the ordinance and a chart of the most important control associations and their presidents, see MITI, 1964, pp. 458–65, 508.
60. Shiroyama, Aug. 1975, pp. 311–12.
61. Bisson, p. 3.   62. Peattie, p. 219.

FIVE

1. Cohen, p. 54.
2. MITI, 1964, p. 501.
3. Arisawa, 1937, pp. 45–46 and note.
4. Kakuma, 1979a, pp. 238–39.   5. MITI, 1965, pp. 164–65.
6. MITI, 1964, p. 488.   7. Tanaka, pp. 25, 111.
8. Hadley, p. 124.
9. See Important Industries Council. This work includes an informative article by Yamamoto Takayuki, then chief of the Production Expansion Section in the General Affairs Bureau. It also includes a list of key corporate personnel. In addition, see Tsukata, pp. 34–42.
10. MITI, 1965, p. 275.
11. See MITI, 1960, pp. 104–5; and *Tsūsan jyānaru*, May 24, 1975, p. 25.
12. Supreme Commander for the Allied Powers, Monograph 48, "Textile Industries," p. 73.
13. For the text of this policy, as well as the two ordinances, see MITI, 1964, pp. 562–72. See also Kakuma, 1979a, pp. 237–38.
14. Cohen, p. 56.
15. Tanaka, p. 260; and Maeda, in Arisawa, 1976, p. 212.
16. Bisson, p. 96.
17. MITI, 1964, p. 524.
18. *Radio Report on the Far East*, no. 28 (Aug. 31, 1943), p. A20.
19. On Fujihara's secret appointment, see *ibid.*, no. 34 (Nov. 24, 1943), p. A1; for his critique, see MITI, 1964, p. 525.
20. The most important primary source on the Munitions Ministry and the Munitions Companies Law is Kitano. Kitano worked in MCI and the Ministry of Munitions from 1926 to 1946; he retired as chief of MCI's Mining Bureau. From November 1943 to November 1944 he was chief of the Documents Section in the Munitions Ministry. On the nationalization of the munitions factories during the last weeks of the war, see MITI, 1965, p. 382 (s.v. entries for June 8 and July 10, 1945); and Roberts, p. 362.
21. Bisson, pp. 116, 202.
22. Nawa, 1974, p. 28.
23. Ōkōchi, "Nihon no gyōsei soshiki" (The organization of administration in Japan), in Tsuji, 2: 92–93.
24. Kishi, Oct. 1979, pp. 298–99.
25. See Imai. See also Tajiri, p. 115.
26. The full details of the postwar recreation of MCI have never been revealed by the participants. For Yamamoto's and Shiina's comments, see MITI, 1960, pp. 49, 103, 114. Nawa Tarō of the *Asahi shimbun*, writing under both his own name and his pseudonym of Akaboshi Jun, has supplied the information about the other participants. See Nawa, 1974, p. 29; and Akaboshi, pp. 15–16. Nawa is probably mistaken about Hirai's being present; according to Hirai himself, he worked in Singapore from 1942 to December 1945. See *Tsūsan jyānaru*, May 24, 1975, p. 29. For evidence of the deep hostility to the military within MM, see the memoirs of Sahashi, 1967, pp. 74–76.
27. Supreme Commander for the Allied Powers, Monograph 13, "Reform of Civil Service," pp. 24–25.
28. *Ibid.*, p. 27.

29. For a discussion of how close SCAP came to producing a communist revolution in Japan, see Johnson, 1972.
30. For a breakdown of the ranks within Japanese companies, see JETRO, *Doing Business in Japan* (Tokyo: JETRO, 1973), p. 9. For a biography of Yoshida, see J. W. Dower, *Empire and Aftermath: Yoshida Shigeru and the Japanese Experience 1878–1954* (Cambridge, Mass.: Harvard University Press, 1979).
31. Hadley, p. 72.
32. "U.S. Banker Honored Here," *Japan Times*, Sept. 20, 1975.
33. *Tsūsan jyānaru*, May 24, 1975, pp. 44–45.
34. See MITI, 1972, p. 19.
35. Hata, p. 373; MITI Journalists' Club, 1956, p. 15.
36. Ichimada's name is difficult to romanize; his family name sometimes appears as Ichimanda and his given name as Hisato. I have used the form given in *The Yoshida Memoirs*, p. 255. On Yoshida's offer of the Finance portfolio to him, see Shioguchi, p. 32; and Abe, pp. 109, 239, 255.
37. See, inter alia, Kakuma, 1979a, pp. 248–49, 264; Matsumoto, 2: 95; MITI Journalists' Club, 1956, pp. 249–51; and MITI Journalists' Club, 1963a, p. 16.
38. On SCAP's belief that a "planned economy was necessary" for Japan, see Shiroyama, Aug. 1975, p. 313. For SCAP's affinities with the socialist Katayama government, see Haji, p. 235.
39. Kakuma, 1979b, p. 14.
40. *Fifty Years*, p. 215.
41. Quoted in Nakamura, 1974, p. 154.
42. For Ichimada's connection with Whitney, see Shioguchi, pp. 31, 248–50.
43. On the RFB, see Arisawa, 1976, pp. 286–89.
44. On coal policy, see History of Industrial Policy Research Institute, 1977a, pp. 4–61. The author of this important monograph is Takahashi Shōji of Mie University. See also Kojima Tsunehisa; and Katō, pp. 28–30. For Okamatsu's recollections of the "food for coal" policy, see MITI, 1960, pp. 109–10.
45. On MCI's Planning Office and priority production, see the memoirs of Kojima Keizō, in Industrial Policy Research Institute, p. 256.
46. The basic source on the ESB is Economic Planning Agency, 1976, pp. 24–73, including Arisawa's recollections, pp. 405–7.
47. On an American precedent for the ESB, see MITI, 1962, p. 349.
48. On the purge of Ishibashi, see Watanabe, pp. 51–55; Wildes, p. 138; and *The Yoshida Memoirs*, p. 93.
49. See "Yamaguchi hanji no eiyō shitchōshi" (The death of Judge Yamaguchi because of insufficient nutrition), in *Shōwa shi jiten*, pp. 283–84.
50. On the coal nationalization law, see Arisawa, 1976, p. 291; and MITI, 1965, p. 446. Takahashi Hikohiro notes that the only people who were enthusiastic about the nationalization of coal were MCI bureaucrats. See his "Shakaitō shuhan naikaku no seiritsu to zasetsu" (The establishment and collapse of the Socialist party cabinet), in *Iwanami kōza*, p. 286. In 1975, twenty-eight years after he worked on the law and while he was serving as president of the nation's largest enterprise (Japan Steel), Hirai Tomisaburō still spoke fondly of coal nationalization and how he had worked hard to achieve it. See *Tsūsan jyānaru*, May 24, 1975, p. 29.

51. For Kudō's comment, see Kakuma, 1979b, p. 29. For Ikeda's, see Shioguchi, p. 112. See also Japan Development Bank, p. 484; and Ikeda.

52. See Akaboshi, p. 16.

53. Cohen, p. 431.

54. Supreme Commander for the Allied Powers, Monograph 50, "Foreign Trade," p. 152. (This monograph was declassified only on February 27, 1970.)

55. Bōeki-chō translates literally as "trade agency," but the BOT itself used the title "Board of Trade" on its stationery and other official documents. For the creation of the BOT, see MITI, 1965, p. 414; and MITI, 1971, p. 361.

56. For Toyoda's recollections, see MITI, 1960, pp. 105–6; and *Tsūsan jyānaru*, May 24, 1975, p. 24.

57. Japan External Trade Organization, p. 3.

58. Inaba, 1965, pp. 218–37. See also Fukui Haruhiro, "Economic Planning in Postwar Japan: A Case Study in Policy Making," *Asian Survey*, 12 (Apr. 1972): 330–31.

59. Kakuma, 1979a, pp. 13–14, 253–55; MITI, 1960, p. 113 (Matsuda Tarō's recollections); Nawa, 1974, p. 33; and Shiroyama, Aug. 1975, p. 314.

60. See Shioguchi, pp. 40–42.

61. For Inagaki's speech, see MITI, 1962, pp. 386–87.

62. See Ozaki, 1972; and MITI, 1971, pp. 390–99.

63. MITI, 1962, pp. 448–49.

64. Supreme Commander for the Allied Powers, Monograph 50, "Foreign Trade," p. 110.

65. Hollerman, 1979, p. 719.

66. Charles S. Maier, *Recasting Bourgeois Europe* (Princeton, N.J.: Princeton University Press, 1975), pp. 580, 582.

SIX

1. Nakamura, 1969, p. 313.

2. Japan Development Bank, p. 17.

3. See Johnson, 1972.

4. Supreme Commander for the Allied Powers, Monograph 47, "The Heavy Industries," p. 120.

5. Boltho, p. 55*n*.

6. Note John Campbell's comment: "Not only was Ikeda an expansionist, but he had a far more activist conception of his office with respect to domestic policy in general and the budget in particular than any prime minister since Yoshida and until Tanaka." Campbell, p. 233.

7. See Chalmers Johnson, "Low Posture Politics in Japan," *Asian Survey*, 3 (Jan. 1963): 17–30.

8. See MITI Journalists' Club, 1956, p. 42; Kakuma, 1979b, p. 84; and Abe, p. 255.

9. Itō Daiichi, 1968, p. 465.

10. Broadbridge, p. 88.

11. Watanabe, p. 234.

12. See MITI, *Tsūshō sangyō-shō nempō* (fiscal 1949), p. 129 (hereafter cited as MITI, *Nempō*).

13. As an example of the misplaced cultural explanation, note the following: "Neither profitability nor common financing or trading activities explain the grouping of firms along the keiretsu lineage. The basic motivation for the grouping of keiretsu firms lies in sociological factors. The tendency to form a group is an inherent part of Japan's cultural tradition." Haitani, p. 124.

14. Ikeda, pp. 148–50.

15. See "Mergers Revive Trade Concerns Splintered in Japan in Occupation," *New York Times*, Dec. 7, 1952; and "Broken-up Concerns in Japan to Reunite," *New York Times*, Mar. 31, 1955.

16. MITI, *Nempō* (fiscal 1954), p. 80; MITI, 1965, pp. 573–75; and MITI Journalists' Club, 1956, p. 42.

17. Abegglen and Rapp, p. 430.

18. The standard work on the alleged incompetence of Japanese planners is Watanabe Tsunehiko, "National Planning and Economic Development: A Critical Review of the Japanese Experience," *Economics of Planning*, 10 (1970): 21–51.

19. Japan Development Bank, p. 23.

20. See the memoirs of Tamaki Keizō, in MITI, 1960, p. 116; and the comments of Hayashi Shintarō, in *Ekonomisuto* Editorial Board, 1: 99–101. See also Japan Development Bank, p. 28.

21. Supreme Commander for the Allied Powers, Monograph 39, "Money and Banking," p. 42.

22. MITI, *Nempō* (fiscal 1950), p. 151. Note that these annual reports were prepared well after the fiscal year they covered; thus, for example, the report for fiscal 1950 bears a preface dated October 1, 1951.

23. For the membership of the JDB's board, see Japan Development Bank, p. 52.

24. See "Sharp Increase in Post Office Savings Upsets Banks and Worries Bank of Japan," plus editorial, *Japan Economic Journal*, Oct. 7, 1980. See also Ministry of Finance, Tax Bureau, pp. 27, 41.

25. MITI Journalists' Club, 1956, p. 24; Endō, 1966, pp. 174–75.

26. Japan Long Term Credit Bank, pp. 4–5.

27. Endō, 1966, p. 179. See also Fujiwara, p. 426; and Shibagaki Kazuo, "Sangyō kōzō no henkaku" (Change of industrial structure), in Tokyo University, 1975, 8: 88.

28. Boltho, p. 126. For figures on the size of FILP and comparisons of it with both the general account budget and GNP, see Johnson, 1978, pp. 83–84.

29. For the term *Gaimu-shō no demise*, see Policy Review Company, 1968, p. 118; for the term "dark age," see Akimoto, p. 39.

30. See Yamamoto's memoirs, in MITI, 1960, p. 115; Shiroyama, Aug. 1975, p. 315; and Takase Sōtarō Memorial Association, p. 1067.

31. For the number of personnel in MITI's various units, see MITI, 1975, p. 95.

32. Sahashi, 1967, pp. 79, 87–88, 120–26. Sahashi refers to the union he headed as the "firing committee" (*kubikiri iinkai*).

33. On the Nagayama case, see Akimi, pp. 76–77, 148–51; Akimoto, p. 43; MITI Journalists' Club, 1956, pp. 258–59; and Nawa, Apr. 1976. Nagayama went to Shōwa Oil and Mitsubishi Yuka because, as chief secretary, he had

been closely involved in the sale of the old naval fuel depot at Yokkaichi to zaibatsu interests. Both Shōwa Oil and Mitsubishi Yuka are located at Yokkaichi.

34. For the text, see MITI, 1972, pp. 42–44. See also Tsuruta Toshimasa, "Sangyō seisaku to kigyō keiei" (Industrial policy and enterprise management), in Kobayashi, 1976, p. 138.

35. See Ueno, pp. 23, 221 *et seq.* The subtitle of this book is "A Study of Economic Laws and Administration and Their Effects."

36. MITI, *Nempō* (fiscal 1949), p. 128; (fiscal 1950), p. 148; (fiscal 1951), pp. 145–49; and (fiscal 1952), p. 164.

37. Noda Nobuo, pp. 27–28. On the reverse flow of American management techniques, see "U.S. Firms Worried by Productivity Lag; Copy Japan in Seeking Employee's Advice," *Wall Street Journal*, Feb. 21, 1980; and the important follow-up letter of Martin Bronfenbrenner, "How Japanese Firms Pick Their Workers," *Wall Street Journal*, Mar. 10, 1980.

38. Noda Nobuo, p. 24; Sakaguchi, p. 175; and the eulogy of Ishikawa, written by Deming, in Federation of Economic Organizations, pp. 264–67. The 1980 recipient of the Deming Prize was the Fuji Xerox Co. See *Wall Street Journal*, Oct. 16, 1980.

39. MITI, *Nempō* (fiscal 1951), p. 148; and (fiscal 1952), p. 136.

40. Supreme Commander for the Allied Powers, Monograph 50, "Foreign Trade," p. 130.

41. Ariga Michiko, "Regulation of International Licensing Agreements under the Japanese Antimonopoly Law," in Doi and Shattuck, p. 289.

42. MITI, *Nempō* (fiscal 1951), p. 149.

43. MITI, 1957, pp. 13–14.

44. Sahashi, 1972, p. 160.

45. See Arisawa, 1976, pp. 344–47; Akimi, pp. 49–53; and MITI, 1970, p. 502. For an example of a later MITI official needling Ichimada because of his opposition to the Kawasaki project, see Amaya, pp. 75–76.

46. On the World Bank loans, see MITI, 1972, p. 101. On the reaction to them, see the memoirs of Ōbori Hiromu, who went to Washington to help negotiate the loans, in Industrial Policy Research Institute, p. 238; and MITI Journalists' Club, 1956, pp. 47–48.

47. See Hirai's comments in *Tsūsan jyānaru*, May 24, 1975, p. 29. See also Ōnishi, p. 12.

48. Akimi, p. 78; Akimoto, pp. 19–21; and MITI Journalists' Club, 1956, pp. 66–87.

49. See "Kurabu kisha hōdan" (Free discussion by Press Club journalists), *Tsūsan jyānaru*, May 24, 1975, p. 50.

50. Supreme Commander for the Allied Powers, Monograph 26, "Promotion of Fair Trade Practices," pp. 95, 101.

51. *Ibid.*, p. 60.

52. On the Bridgestone case, see Hewins, p. 310; on the du Pont–Toray case, see Senba Tsuneyoshi, "Sengo sangyō gōrika to gijutsu dōnyū" (Postwar industrial rationalization and the import of technology), in History of Industrial Policy Research Institute, 1977a, pp. 118–19.

53. Supreme Commander for the Allied Powers, *Historical Monographs*, vol. X, part C, "Elimination of Private Control Associations," p. 85. This mono-

graph is not included in the set microfilmed, renumbered, and made generally available by the U.S. National Archives; it was microfilmed by the National Archives on June 4, 1974, at the special request of the author.

54. See, e.g., MITI, 1969a, p. 6.

55. Maeda, 1975, p. 14.

56. "New Japanese Law Sanctions Cartels," *New York Times*, Sept. 27, 1953.

57. On the steel industry's "public sales system" see Nawa, 1976a, pp. 146–54; Sahashi, 1967, pp. 180–85; and "Gyōsei shidō no jittai o arau" (Probing the realities of administrative guidance), *Tōyō keizai*, Apr. 6, 1974, pp. 31–33. Ariga Michiko, a long-time staff member of the FTC and the first woman to become a commissioner (1967–72), refers to the steel sales system as an "emasculation" of the AML. See the interview with her, "Kazaana aita dokkinhō" (The AML riddled with holes), *Ekonomisuto* Editorial Board, 1: 226–54, particularly pp. 243–44.

58. MITI, *Nempō* (fiscal 1957), pp. 100–101; (fiscal 1958), p. 100; and (fiscal 1959), p. 99.

59. Sahashi, 1971a, pp. 266–75; Sahashi, 1972, pp. 18–19.

60. Kakuma, 1979b, p. 106.

61. Economic Planning Agency, 1976, pp. 75–76; and Ōnishi, p. 13. Kusayanagi Daizō touches on the origins of the heavy and chemical industrialization policy in *Bungei shunjū*, Aug. 1974, pp. 112–13.

62. For the text of the MITI plan, see MITI, 1962, pp. 499–501.

63. See Hirai's comments on Okano and Ishibashi, in Matsubayashi, 1973, pp. 31–34, 41–42; and Industrial Policy Research Institute, p. 247.

64. Quoted in *Consider Japan*, p. 56.

65. See Shibagaki Kazuo, in Tokyo University, 1975, 8: 89.

66. Japan External Trade Organization, pp. 2–68, 951–52. The JETRO Establishment Law is printed in an English translation, pp. 935–43.

67. See "How Foreign Lobby Molds U.S. Opinion," *San Francisco Chronicle*, Sept. 15, 1976. Between 1959 and 1962 the New York office of JETRO also employed the services of former New York governor Thomas E. Dewey as a lobbyist. See Japan External Trade Organization, p. 78.

68. *Ekonomisuto* Editorial Board, 1: 100–105; Japan External Trade Organization, p. 49; *Fifty Years*, p. 273; MITI Journalists' Club, 1956, pp. 88–101; and Stone, pp. 147–48.

69. Nakamura, 1969, p. 309.

70. *Ekonomisuto* Editorial Board, 1: 51–52.

71. See Kakizaki.

72. Ministry of Finance, Tax Bureau, p. 84.

73. *Ekonomisuto* Editorial Board, 1: 27–28.

74. *Ibid.*, pp. 24–25.

75. Kakizaki, p. 83; Ministry of Finance, Tax Bureau, pp. 84–91.

76. MITI, *Nempō* (fiscal 1956), p. 109.

77. *Ibid.* (fiscal 1964), p. 62.

78. Tsuruta Toshimasa, in Kobayashi, 1976, p. 148.

79. *Ekonomisuto* Editorial Board, 1: 36–38.

80. On the petrochemical industry, see inter alia, MITI, 1969b, pp. 317–24 (basic policy statements); *Ekonomisuto* Editorial Board, 2: 98–148 (government-business relationships); and Senba Tsuneyoshi, in History of Industrial Policy Research Institute, 1977a, pp. 100–114 (licensing and import of

technology). For the dispute over the sale of state property, see Industrial Policy Research Institute, pp. 126, 246; and Arisawa, 1976, p. 244 (where it is argued that the sale of government installations during the 1950's was more important than the famous Meiji sales during the 1880's).

81. Arisawa, 1976, pp. 375, 390.
82. MITI, *Nempō* (fiscal 1961), p. 112.
83. Kakuma, 1979b, p. 131.
84. For the text of the plan, see *Ekonomisuto* Editorial Board, 1: 172–74.
85. Chandler.
86. Otis Cary, ed., *War-Wasted Asia, Letters, 1945–46* (Tokyo: Kōdansha International, 1975), p. 193.

SEVEN

1. For Sahashi's background, see his autobiography, *Ishoku kanryō*, 1967; and Sahashi, 1972, pp. 158–62.
2. Note that the term *ishoku kanryō* (exceptional bureaucrat) was also applied before the war to Wada Hiroo, the Agriculture Ministry official who was arrested in the Cabinet Planning Board incident and who headed the Economic Stabilization Board during the occupation. See Inaba, 1977, p. 178. For the phrase "samurai among samurai," see Matsubayashi, 1973, p. 138. For *gebaruto kanryō*, see Kusayanagi, May 1969, p. 162. For *kaijin Sachan*, see Kusayanagi, 1974, p. 115. See also Suzuki Yukio, 1969, p. 62.
3. Sahashi, 1967, p. 207.
4. MITI Journalists' Club, Oct. 1963, p. 76.
5. *Ekonomisuto* Editorial Board, 1: 72–74; MITI Journalists' Club, 1956, pp. 190–94.
6. *Ekonomisuto* Editorial Board, 1: 142–43.
7. Sahashi, 1967, p. 215. See also Kakuma, 1979b, pp. 131–36.
8. For a photograph of the *Sakura Maru* and a story about it, see "Japan's Floating Fair Finds Success in Europe," *New York Times*, Aug. 10, 1964. For the loan of the *Sakura* to the United States, see "Japanese Get Chance to Buy U.S. Goods at U.S. Prices," *Los Angeles Times*, Oct. 30, 1978.
9. See Sahashi, 1967, pp. 191–207; and Akimoto, pp. 80–82.
10. Interview with Imai, *Ekonomisuto*, Sept. 14, 1976, p. 78.
11. *Ibid.*, p. 79.
12. Komatsu, p. 23.
13. Shiroyama, 1975a, pp. 86–87. On the rates of liberalization, see MITI, 1965, pp. 698, 703.
14. Arisawa, 1976, p. 443; MITI Journalists' Club, Oct. 1963, p. 74.
15. Sahashi, 1967, p. 248.
16. See Ōta Shin'ichirō (MITI Secretariat, Planning Office), "Sangyō kōzō seisaku" (Industrial structure policy), in Isomura, 1972, pp. 312–15; MITI, 1969a, p. 11; MITI, 1972, pp. 128–31; and MITI, *Nempō* (fiscal 1961), pp. 75–76, 109–10.
17. Industrial Structure Investigation Council, ed., *Nihon no sangyō kōzō*.
18. Akaboshi, pp. 73–82; MITI Journalists' Club, Oct. 1963, pp. 78–84; MITI Journalists' Club, 1963a, p. 39; and Itō Daiichi, 1967, pp. 78–104.
19. Maeda, 1975, p. 16; Arisawa, 1976, p. 443; and Suzuki Yukio, 1963.

20. For various analyses of Japanese "excessive competition," see Abegglen and Rapp; Aliber; Boltho, p. 61; and Hollerman, 1967, p. 162.
21. Takashima Setsuo.
22. On the number of MITI vice-ministers with experience in Europe but not in the United States, despite the weight of Japanese-American trade, see Endō, 1975, p. 110.
23. On Konaga and Uchida, see Kusayanagi, 1974, pp. 116–19.
24. Sahashi, 1967, pp. 245–51.
25. See Japanese Diet, pp. 2–4.
26. See the obituaries of Ishizaka Taizō in *Japan Times*, Mar. 7, 1975, and *San Francisco Chronicle*, Mar. 7, 1975.
27. MITI, 1969a, pp. 2, 11.
28. See Akaboshi, pp. 93–96; Sahashi, 1967, pp. 240–45; MITI Journalists' Club, 1963a, p. 38; and Resources Development and Management Research Council, p. 60, s.v. "Maruzen Oil Company."
29. The primary source on the "Fukuda typhoon," including the direct quotations in this and the following paragraphs, is MITI Journalists' Club, Oct. 1963.
30. Akimoto, pp. 91, 142–43; Kakuma, 1979b, pp. 34–46; Sahashi, 1967, pp. 257–68; and Policy Review Company, 1968, p. 89.
31. On the "structural recession" thesis, see Arisawa, 1976, pp. 465–67. For MITI's endorsement of this thesis, see MITI, *Nempō* (fiscal 1965), p. 64.
32. For Fukuda's speech, see MITI, *Nempō* (fiscal 1964), p. 59; for the first use of *gyōsei shidō*, see *ibid*. (fiscal 1962), p. 123.
33. *The Economist*, Nov. 10, 1979, p. 85; *Japan Economic Journal*, May 14, 1974.
34. *Newsweek*, Aug. 21, 1972.
35. Stone, p. 152.
36. "'Gyōsei Shidō' Gets Close Public Scrutiny," *Japan Times*, June 3, 1974.
37. Henderson, p. 202. See also Maeda, 1968, pp. 38–40.
38. Shiroyama, Aug. 1975, p. 317. See also Amaya, p. 79; and Yamamoto, p. 81.
39. Yamanouchi, p. 193.
40. *Ibid.*, pp. 47–49.
41. "Administrative Guidance," *Mainichi Daily News*, Jan. 8, 1976.
42. Hewins, p. 305. The main official source on mergers is MITI, Enterprises Bureau, ed., *Kigyō gappei* (Enterprise mergers) (Tokyo: Ōkura-shō Insatsu-kyoku, 1970).
43. Hollerman, 1967, p. 252.
44. Sahashi, 1967, pp. 294–95. See Nakayama Sohei's high estimate of Sahashi's contribution to this merger in *Ekonomisuto*, July 13, 1976, p. 87.
45. Nawa, 1976a, p. 141; "Gyōsei shidō no jittai o arau" (Probing the realities of administrative guidance), *Tōyō keizai*, Apr. 6, 1974, pp. 31–33.
46. The primary sources on the Sumitomo Metals Company incident are Sahashi, 1967, pp. 282–89; and Hyūga, in *Ekonomisuto* Editorial Board, 2: 67–74. See also Akaboshi, pp. 83–92; Akimoto, pp. 58–63; Industrial Policy Research Institute, pp. 117–19; Kakuma, 1979b, pp. 172–76; Nawa, 1976a, pp. 159–66; Yamamoto, pp. 82–84; and Yamanouchi, pp. 29–30. For citations on legal studies of the incident, see Yamanouchi, p. 53, n. 2. For Kumagai's amakudari, see Matsubayashi, 1973, pp. 182, 194.

47. *Report of the Japan-United States Economic Relations Group, Prepared for the President of the United States and the Prime Minister of Japan* (Washington, D.C.: Japan-U.S. Economic Relations Group, 1981), p. 61.

EIGHT

1. Quoted in Suzuki Yukio, 1969, pp. 49, 124.
2. MITI, *Nempō* (fiscal 1965), p. 69.
3. Nawa, 1974, pp. 39–40.
4. Kakuma, 1979a, pp. 73–75.
5. See Katō Hidetoshi, "Sanken: A Power Above Government," *The Japan Interpreter*, 7 (Winter 1971): 36–42; Nawa, 1976a, pp. 81–82, 265–66; and Yamamoto, pp. 74–75.
6. See the interviews with Nakayama Sohei, in *Ekonomisuto*, July 6 and 13, 1976.
7. For details, see Allan R. Pearl, "Liberalization of Capital in Japan, Parts I and II," *Harvard International Law Journal*, 13, nos. 1 and 2 (Winter and Spring, 1972): 59–87, 245–70.
8. See "Japanese Economy Attracts Oil Money," *Washington Post*, Oct. 5, 1980.
9. On the funeral controversy, see Kakuma, 1979b, pp. 47–49; Matsubayashi, 1973, p. 138; and Sahashi, 1967, pp. 299–306. See also the volume of the Kawahara Hideyuki Memorial Committee.
10. For the text and an analysis of the MITI-FTC agreement, see Ueno, pp. 24–26.
11. Ōjimi and Uchida, p. 31. See also Yamamoto's comments (on the *Mainichi* leak), in Matsubayashi, 1973, p. 166; and Nawa (on Uchida's group), 1974, p. 42.
12. See Urata.
13. Japan Civil Administration Research Association, 1970, p. 156.
14. Shibano, p. 27; Organization for Economic Cooperation and Development, 1977b, p. 29.
15. See "Japan: Environmentalism with Growth," *Wall Street Journal*, Sept. 5, 1980. On MITI's internal changes, see Policy Review Company, 1970, s.v. "Tsūsan-shō," pp. 127–29.
16. See Hanabusa, p. 123; and Nawa, 1974, p. 45.
17. Maeda, 1975, p. 17.
18. See "MITI: Japan's Economic Watchdog," *Business Week*, Aug. 19, 1967; and Suzuki Yukio, 1969, p. 47.
19. Hanabusa, pp. 184–89.
20. On price differentials of Japanese electrical appliances, see *ibid.*, p. 32; on grapefruit and other issues, see Kakuma, 1979b, pp. 214–20.
21. "Study on Trade Deficit with the Japanese," *Wall Street Journal*, Apr. 29, 1980. For the total number of vehicles produced in Japan between 1965 and 1977, as well as the number exported and imported each year, see Komatsu, p. 41.
22. Kakuma, 1979b, pp. 149–51; *Mitsubishi Group*, pp. 34–35; Suzuki Yukio, 1969, pp. 64–66; and Yamamoto, pp. 54–57, 88–91, 191, 200.
23. For Vice-Minister Kumagai's views of these events, see *Ekonomisuto* Editorial Board, 1: 276–77; and Matsubayashi, 1973, pp. 191–92.

24. See Industrial Policy Research Institute, pp. 29–30, 122–24; and Suzuki Yukio, 1969, pp. 66, 84–86.
25. Bitten in hand: Satō, p. 61. Grown son: Suzuki Yukio, 1969, p. 60. Department of Commerce: Yamamoto, pp. 60–61. Neurotic: Suzuki Yukio, 1969, pp. 45–46. Mama: Aoki, p. 143. Sōkaiya: Honda, 1: 41. Apathy: *Fifty years*, p. 398. Weeping: Kakuma, 1979a, p. 71.
26. Japan Civil Administration, 1970, p. 164; Nawa, 1975, p. 85; and Suzuki Yukio, 1969, pp. 31–32.
27. See the interview with Kumagai, in Suzuki Yukio, 1969, pp. 83, 92–93.
28. Matsubayashi, 1973, pp. 220, 223.
29. See Ōta Shin'ichirō, "Sangyō kōzō seisaku" (Industrial structure policy), in Isomura, 1972, pp. 312–15.
30. For former Vice-Minister of Finance Yoshikuni Jirō's high appraisal of Tanaka's abilities and character, see Matsubayashi, 1976, pp. 232–33.
31. "Kissinger Says It Took Him Five Years to Understand Japan," *Los Angeles Times*, Feb. 10, 1978.
32. See Destler, p. 305.
33. Published by Nikkan Kōgyō Shimbun Sha. In May 1973 the Simul Press brought out an English translation under the title *Building a New Japan: A Plan for Remodeling the Japanese Archipelago*.
34. *Tsūsan jyānaru*, May 24, 1975, p. 18.
35. *Fifty Years*, p. 372.
36. On MITI's 1971 budget increase, see MITI, *Nempō* (fiscal 1971), p. 65; and on Tanaka and Aizawa, see Satō, p. 63.
37. Campbell, p. 257.
38. See "Japan's 'Economic Animals,'" *Far Eastern Economic Review*, Mar. 26, 1973, pp. 32–33.
39. Ōnishi, p. 47; Komatsu, p. 148.
40. For the evolution of the old bureaus into the new ones, see Trade and Industry Handbook Compilation Committee, 1974, pp. 360–61. For a critique of the new structure, see Honda, 1: 35–38.
41. On Japan's initial reaction to the oil shock, see Johnson, 1976. On Bandar Shahpur, see the *Economist* (London), June 30, 1979, p. 82; and "Mitsui Plans to Finish Stalled Work in Iran on Petrochemical Unit," *Wall Street Journal*, May 7, 1980.
42. Quoted in Kakuma, 1979b, p. 269.
43. Aoki, pp. 139–40. On toilet paper, plus a photograph of a toilet paper queue, see Komatsu, pp. 152–55.
44. Nakamura, 1974, pp. 169–73; Kakuma, 1979b, p. 195. For outlines of the laws themselves, as well as details on modifications of them made by the Diet, see MITI Information Office, *News from MITI*, no. 73-55 (Dec. 15, 1973), no. 73-56 (Dec. 15, 1973), and no. 73-67 (Dec. 28, 1973).
45. "FTC Raids," *Japan Times*, Nov. 28, 1973.
46. The *Asahi* list is reprinted in Watanabe Yōzō, "Sekiyu sangyō to sengo keizaihō taisei" (The petroleum industry and the postwar structure of economic law), in Tokyo University, 1975, 8: 275. See also "Probe Into Oil Products Price-fixing," *Japan Times*, Mar. 14, 1974; "Prosecutors Probe," *ibid.*, Mar. 20, 1974; "Probers to Grill MITI," *ibid.*, Mar. 25, 1974; "MITI Role Questioned," *ibid.*, Apr. 16, 1974; "MITI Says Oil Industry's Acts Com-

pletely Lawful," *ibid.*, Apr. 17, 1974; "Prosecutors Get Oil Price Report," *ibid.*, May 8, 1974.

47. See *Nihon keizai shimbun, Asahi shimbun, Japan Times, Mainichi Daily News,* and *Wall Street Journal,* May 29, 1974. See also the *Asahi* series "Sekiyu karuteru" (Oil cartel), May 29 and 30, 1974; "Oil Companies Are Indicted" *Japan Economic Journal,* June 4, 1974; "Letter from Tokyo," *Far Eastern Economic Review,* June 3, 1974. On the progress and outcome of the case, see Kakuma, 1979b, pp. 154–70, 178–89; *Japan Economic Journal,* Oct. 21, 1980, editorial; *Japan Times Weekly,* Feb. 14, 1981.

48. "Antimonopoly Law," *Japan Times,* May 30, 1974; "MITI-FTC Dispute," *Mainichi Daily News,* June 29, 1974.

49. See Chalmers Johnson, "Japan: The Year of 'Money-Power' Politics," *Asian Survey,* 15 (Jan. 1975): 25–34; and Chalmers Johnson, "Japan 1975: Mr. Clean Muddles Through," *Asian Survey,* 16 (Jan. 1976): 31–41.

50. For a chronology of the AML revision, see Komatsu, p. 174; for Shiina's killing of the AML revision bill in 1975, see Nawa, 1976a, p. 94. See also "FTC Head Takahashi Quits," *Japan Times,* Feb. 6, 1976.

51. See Morozumi.

52. MITI, 1974, 268 pp. The 1975 updating, of some 398 pp., was published on Aug. 20, 1975. JETRO also brought out a translation of the first "vision plan" under the title *Japan's Industrial Structure: A Long Range Vision* (Tokyo: JETRO, 1975), as well as an English supplement to the 1975 version.

53. *News from MITI,* no. 79-34 (Dec. 20, 1979); *Look Japan,* Jan. 10, 1980.

54. See Saxonhouse.

NINE

1. Sam Jameson and John F. Lawrence, "U.S. Problem Not Labor but Managers—Sony Chief," *Los Angeles Times,* Oct. 29, 1980.

2. "Firms Go Wild on Expenses; Japan's Taxmen Indulgent," *San Francisco Examiner,* Jan. 6, 1981.

3. For an excellent critique of the bureaucratic-authoritarian model, see David Collier, ed., *The New Authoritarianism in Latin America* (Princeton, N.J.: Princeton University Press, 1979).

4. For details, see Ellen Comisso, *Workers' Control Under Plan and Market: Implications of Yugoslav Self-Management* (New Haven, Conn.: Yale University Press, 1979).

5. "Political Struggles in Bureaucratic Societies," *World Politics,* 9 (Oct. 1956): 20–36.

6. Drucker, p. 53.

BIBLIOGRAPHY

BIBLIOGRAPHY

If an individual author has two or more items listed under his name, they are arranged chronologically according to date of publication.

Abegglen, James C. "The Economic Growth of Japan." *Scientific American*, 222 (Mar. 1970): 31–37.

———, and Rapp, William V. "Japanese Managerial Behavior and 'Excessive Competition.'" *The Developing Economies*, 8 (Dec. 1970): 427–44.

——— et al. *U.S.-Japan Economic Relations*. Berkeley: University of California, Institute of East Asian Studies, 1980.

Abe Yasuji. *Ichimada Naoto den* (A biography of Ichimada Naoto). Tokyo: Tōyō Shokan, 1955.

Administrative Investigation Council (Gyōsei Chōsa Kai). *Kaku kanchō kyoka ninka jikō no seiri ni kan suru chōsashu* (Investigation report on the reduction of licenses and approvals by government agencies). Vol. 1, N.p., Jan. 21, 1926.

Akaboshi Jun (pseud. of Nawa Tarō). *Shōsetsu Tsūsan-shō* (MITI stories). Tokyo: Daiyamondo Sha, 1971.

Akimi Jirō. *Tsūsan kanryō, seisaku to sono jittai* (Trade and industry bureaucrats: policy and its reality). Tokyo: San'ichi Shobō, 1956.

Akimoto Hideo. *Shōsetsu Tsūsan-shō* (MITI stories). Tokyo: Futami Shobō, 1975.

Aliber, R. Z. "Planning, Growth, and Competition in the Japanese Economy." *Asian Survey*, 3 (Dec. 1963): 596–608.

Allinson, Gary D. *Japanese Urbanism: Industry and Politics in Kariya, 1872–1972.* Berkeley: University of California Press, 1975.

Amaya Naohiro. *Hyōryū-suru Nihon keizai, shin sangyō seisaku no bijon.* (The Japanese economy adrift: a vision of the new industrial policy). Tokyo: Mainichi Shimbun Sha, 1975.

Anderson, Irvine H., Jr. *The Standard-Vacuum Oil Company and United States East Asian Policy, 1933–1941.* Princeton, N.J.: Princeton University Press, 1975.

Aoki Kazuaki. "Tsūsan-shō no shōhisha shikō wa honmono ka" (Is there any substance to MITI's commitment to consumers?). *Seikai ōrai*, June 1975: 138–44.

Arisawa Hiromi. *Nihon kōgyō tōsei ron* (The control of Japanese industry). Tokyo: Yūhikaku, 1937.

———, ed. *Sengo keizai jūnen shi* (Ten-year history of the postwar economy). Tokyo: Shōkō Kaikan Shuppan-bu, 1954.

————, ed. *Shōwa keizai shi* (Economic history of the Shōwa era). Tokyo: Nihon Keizai Shimbun Sha, 1976.

Bartlett, Randall. *Economic Foundations of Political Power*. New York: Free Press, 1973.

Bell, Daniel. *The Cultural Contradictions of Capitalism*. New York: Basic Books, 1976.

Berger, Gordon Mark. *Parties Out of Power in Japan 1931–1941*. Princeton: N.J.: Princeton University Press, 1977.

Bieda, K. *The Structure and Operation of the Japanese Economy*. Sydney, Australia: Wiley, 1970.

Bisson, T. A. *Japan's War Economy*. New York: Institute of Pacific Relations, 1945.

Black, Cyril E., et al. *The Modernization of Japan and Russia*. New York: Free Press, 1975.

Blaker, Michael, ed. *The Politics of Trade: U.S. and Japanese Policymaking for the GATT Negotiations*. New York: Columbia University, East Asian Institute, 1978.

Boltho, Andrea. *Japan: An Economic Survey, 1953–1973*. London: Oxford University Press, 1975.

Borg, Dorothy, and Okamoto Shumpei, eds. *Pearl Harbor as History: Japanese-American Relations 1931–1941*. New York: Columbia University Press, 1973.

Broadbridge, Seymour. *Industrial Dualism in Japan*. Chicago: Aldine, 1966.

Campbell, John Creighton. *Contemporary Japanese Budget Politics*. Berkeley: University of California Press, 1977.

Chandler, Alfred D., Jr. "Industrial Revolutions and Institutional Arrangements." *Bulletin of the American Academy of Arts and Sciences*, 33 (May 1980): 33–50.

Chen, Edward K. Y. *Hyper-growth in Asian Economies: A Comparative Study of Hong Kong, Japan, Korea, Singapore, and Taiwan*. London: Macmillan, 1979.

Chō Yukio. "Exposing the Incompetence of the Bourgeoisie: The Financial Panic of 1927." *The Japan Interpreter*, 8 (Winter 1974): 492–501.

Clark, Rodney. *The Japanese Company*. New Haven, Conn.: Yale University Press, 1979.

Cohen, Jerome B. *Japan's Economy in War and Reconstruction*. Minneapolis: University of Minnesota Press, 1949.

Commerce and Industry Research Council (Shōkō Gyōsei Chōsa Kai), ed. *Shōkō-shō yōran* (MCI handbook). Tokyo: Shōkō Gyōsei Sha, 1941.

Consider Japan. Comp. by staff of the *Economist*. London: Duckworth, 1963.

Craig, Albert M., ed. *Japan: A Comparative View*. Princeton, N.J.: Princeton University Press, 1979.

Dahrendorf, Ralf. *Society and Democracy in Germany*. Garden City, N.Y.: Doubleday, 1967.

————. *Essays in the Theory of Society*. Stanford, Calif.: Stanford University Press, 1968.

Destler, I. M., Fukui Haruhiro, and Satō Hideo. *The Textile Wrangle: Conflict in Japanese-American Relations, 1969–1971*. Ithaca, N.Y.: Cornell University Press, 1979.

Doi Teruo and Shattuck, Warren L., eds. *Patent and Know-how Licensing in Japan and the United States*. Seattle: University of Washington Press, 1977.

Domestic Political History Research Association (Naiseishi Kenkyū Kai). *Tanaka Shin'ichi shi danwa sokkiroku* (Transcript of a conversation with Mr. Tanaka Shin'ichi). Tokyo: Naiseishi Kenkyū Kai, 1976.

Drucker, Peter F. "Managing the Public Service Institution." *The Public Interest*, 33 (Fall, 1973): 43–60.

Duus, Peter, and Okimoto, Daniel I. "Fascism and the History of Prewar Japan: The Failure of a Concept." *Journal of Asian Studies*, 39 (Nov. 1979): 65–76.

Economic Planning Agency. *New Long-range Economic Plan of Japan (1961–1970): Doubling National Income Plan*. Tokyo: The Japan Times, [1961?].

────── (Keizai Kikaku-chō), ed. *Gendai Nihon keizai no tenkai, Keizai Kikaku-chō 30-nen shi* (The development of the modern Japanese economy: thirty-year history of the Economic Planning Agency). Tokyo: Ōkura-shō Insatsu-kyoku, 1976.

Ekonomisuto Editorial Board, ed. *Sengo sangyō shi e no shōgen* (Interviews toward a history of postwar industry). Vols. 1, 2. Tokyo: Mainichi Shimbun Sha, 1977.

Endō Shōkichi. *Zaisei tōyūshi* (Fiscal investment and loan funds). Tokyo: Iwanami Shoten, 1966.

──────, ed. *Nihon keizai no gunzō* (Japanese economic groupings). Tokyo: Gakuyō Shobō, 1975.

Esman, Milton J. "Japanese Administration: A Comparative View." *Public Administration Review*, 7 (Spring 1947): 100–112.

Fahs, Charles B. *Government in Japan: Recent Trends in Its Scope and Operation*. New York: Institute of Pacific Relations, 1940.

Federation of Economic Organizations (Keizai Dantai Rengōkai), ed. *Ishikawa Ichirō tsuisōroku* (Recollections of Ishikawa Ichirō). Tokyo: Kashima Kenkyū-jo Shuppan Kai, 1971.

Fifty Years of Light and Dark: The Hirohito Years. Comp. by staff of the *Mainichi Daily News*. Tokyo: Mainichi Shimbun Sha, 1975.

Fujiwara Akira, Imai Seiichi, and Ōe Shinobu, eds. *Kindai Nihon shi no kiso chishiki* (Basic knowledge of modern Japanese history). Tokyo: Yūhikaku, 1972.

Fukumoto Kunio. *Kanryō* (Bureaucrats). Tokyo: Kōbundō, 1959.

Gilpin, Robert. *U.S. Power and the Multinational Corporation*. New York: Basic Books, 1975.

Gotō Shin'ichi. *Takahashi Korekiyo, Nihon no "Keinzu"* (Takahashi Korekiyo: the "Keynes" of Japan). Tokyo: Nihon Keizai Shimbun Sha, 1977.

Hadley, Eleanor M. *Antitrust in Japan*. Princeton: N.J.: Princeton University Press, 1970.

Haitani Kanji. *The Japanese Economic System: An Institutional Overview*. Lexington, Mass.: D. C. Heath, 1976.

Haji Fumio. "Ikeda Hayato ron" (On Ikeda Hayato). *Kankai*, 3 (Jan. 1977): 230–37.

Hanabusa Yoshihisa. *Nichi-Bei keizai sensō* (A Japanese-American economic war). Tokyo: Ēru Shuppan Sha, 1970.

Harari, Ehud. *The Politics of Labor Legislation in Japan*. Berkeley: University of California Press, 1973.

Hata Ikuhiko. "Japan Under the Occupation." *The Japan Interpreter*, 10 (Winter 1976): 361–80.

Havens, Thomas R. H. *Farm and Nation in Modern Japan*. Princeton: N.J.: Princeton University Press, 1974.

Heeger, Gerald. "Bureaucracy, Political Parties, and Political Development." *World Politics*, 25 (July 1973): 600–607.

Henderson, Dan Fenno. *Foreign Enterprise in Japan: Laws and Policies*. Tokyo: Tuttle, 1975.

Hewins, Ralph. *The Japanese Miracle Men*. London: Secker and Warburg, 1967.

History of Industrial Policy Research Institute (Sangyō Seisaku Shi Kenkyū-jo). *Shōkō gyōsei shi dankai sokkiroku* (Transcript of discussion meetings on the history of commercial and industrial administration). 2 vols. Tokyo: Tsūshō Sangyō Chōsa Kai Toranomon Bunshitsu. 1975.

————. *Taishō Shōwa jidai shōkō gyōsei nempyō* (Chronology of commercial and industrial administration in the Taishō and Shōwa eras). Tokyo: Tsūshō Sangyō Chōsa Kai Toranomon Bunshitsu, 1976a.

————. *Waga kuni daikigyō no keisei hatten katei*. (The formation and development of big business in our country). Tokyo: Tsūshō Sangyō Chōsa Kai Toranomon Bunshitsu, 1976b.

————. *Sangyō seisaku shi kenkyū shiryō* (Research materials on the history of industrial policy). Tokyo: Tsūshō Sangyō Chōsa Kai Toranomon Bunshitsu, 1977a.

————. *Shōkō-shō Tsūsan-shō gyōsei kikō oyobi kanbu shokuin no hensen* (Changes in MCI and MITI administrative organs and leading personnel). Tokyo: Tsūshō Sangyō Chōsa Kai Toranomon Bunshitsu, 1977b.

————. *Nenryō kyoku sekiyu gyōsei ni kan suru zadankai* (Discussion group on petroleum administration by the Fuel Bureau). Tokyo: Tsūshō Sangyō Chōsa Kai Toranomon Bunshitsu, 1978.

Ho, Alfred K. *Japan's Trade Liberalization in the 1960's*. White Plains, N.Y.: International Arts and Sciences Press, 1973.

Hollerman, Leon. *Japan's Dependency on the World Economy: The Approach Toward Economic Liberalization*. Princeton, N.J.: Princeton University Press, 1967.

————. "International Economic Controls in Occupied Japan." *Journal of Asian Studies*, 38 (Aug. 1979): 707–19.

Honda Yasuharu. *Nihon neo-kanryō ron* (On Japan's new bureaucrats). 2 vols. Tokyo: Kōdansha, 1974.

Ide Yoshinori and Ishida Takeshi. "The Education and Recruitment of Governing Elites in Modern Japan." In Rupert Wilkinson, ed., *Governing Elites: Studies in Training and Selection*. New York: Oxford University Press, 1969.

Ikeda Hayato. *Kinkō zaisei, senryōka sannen no omoide* (Balanced finance: recollections of three years under the occupation). Tokyo: Jitsugyō no Nihon Sha, 1952.

Imai Hisao. "Kenka Nobusuke, kanryō ichidai" (Nobusuke the quarreler: the life of a bureaucrat). *Kankai*, 2 (Nov. 1976): 104–12.

Important Industries Council (Jūyō Sangyō Kyōgikai), ed. *Sangyō Setsubi Eidan kaisetsu* (Explanation of the Industrial Facilities Corporation). Tokyo: Tōhō Sha, 1943.

Inaba Hidezō. *Gekidō sanjūnen no Nihon keizai*. (The Japanese economy through thirty years of upheaval). Tokyo: Jitsugyō no Nihon Sha, 1965.

————. "Kanryō to shite no Wada Hiroo" (Wada Hiroo as a bureaucrat). *Kankai*, 3 (Feb. 1977): 176–84.

Industrial Policy Research Institute (Sangyō Seisaku Kenkyū-jo), ed. *Tsūsan-shō 20-nen gaishi* (An unofficial twenty-year history of MITI). Tokyo: Sangyō Seisaku Kenkyū-jo, 1970.

Industrial Policy Study Group (Sangyō Seisaku Kenkyū Kai). *Sangyō seisaku no riron* (The theory of industrial policy). Tokyo: Keizai Hatten Kyōkai, 1967.

Industrial Structure Council, International Economy Committee (Sangyō Kōzō Shingikai, Kokusai Keizai Bukai), ed. *Nihon no taigai keizai seisaku* (Japan's foreign economic policy). Tokyo: Daiyamondo Sha, 1972.

Industrial Structure Investigation Council (Sangyō Kōzō Chōsa Kai), ed. *Nihon no sangyō kōzō* (Japan's industrial structure). 5 vols. Tokyo: Tsūshō Sangyō Kenkyū Kai, 1964.

Industrial Technology Research Committee (Sangyō Gijutsu Chōsa Iinkai), ed. *Gijutsu kaihatsu seido to Tsūsan-shō ōgata purojekuto* (The technological development system and MITI's large-scale projects). Tokyo: Sangyō Kagaku Kyōkai, 1974.

Ino Kenji and Hokuto Man. *Amakudari kanryō* (Descended-from-heaven bureaucrats). Tokyo: Nisshin Hōdō, 1972.

Inoue Kanae. *Taikei kanchō kaikei jiten* (Dictionary of official accounting). Tokyo: Gihōdō, 1973.

Invention Association (Hatsumei Kyōkai), ed. *Tokkyo-chō* (The Patent Agency). Tokyo: Kyōiku Sha, 1975.

Isomura Eiichi, ed. *Gyōsei saishin mondai jiten* (Dictionary of current administrative problems). Tokyo: Teikoku Chihō Gyōsei Gakkai, 1972.

——— and Kuronuma Minoru. *Gendai Nihon no gyōsei* (Contemporary Japanese administration). Tokyo: Teikoku Chihō Gyōsei Gakkai, 1974.

Itō Daiichi. "Keizai kanryō no kōdō yōshiki" (The behavioral pattern of economic bureaucrats). In Japan Political Science Association (Nihon Seiji Gakkai), ed., *Gendai Nihon no seitō to kanryō* (Contemporary Japanese political parties and the bureaucracy). Tokyo: Iwanami Shoten, 1967.

———. "The Bureaucracy: Its Attitudes and Behavior." *The Developing Economies*, 6 (Dec. 1968): 446–67.

Itō Mitsuharu. "Munitions Unlimited: The Controlled Economy." *The Japan Interpreter*, 7 (Summer-Autumn 1972): 353–63.

Itoh Hiroshi, ed. *Japanese Politics: An Inside View*. Ithaca, N.Y.: Cornell University Press, 1973.

Iwakawa Takashi. *Kyokai, Kishi Nobusuke kenkyū* (Godfather: research on Kishi Nobusuke). Tokyo: Daiyamondo Sha, 1977.

Iwanami kōza Nihon rekishi (Iwanami lectures on Japanese history). Vol. 22. Tokyo: Iwanami Shoten, 1977.

Iwasaki Uichi. "The Working Forces in Japanese Politics." Ph.D. Dissertation, Columbia University, 1921.

Iwatake Teruhiko. *Zuihitsu Toranomon* (Toranomon essays). Tokyo: Tsūshō Sangyō Chōsa Kai, 1960.

Japan Civil Administration Research Association (Nihon Minsei Kenkyū Kai), ed. *Kōkyū kanryō sōran* (General survey of higher bureaucrats). 2 vols. Tokyo: Hyōron Shinsha, 1970–71.

Japan Development Bank (Nihon Kaihatsu Ginkō). *Nihon Kaihatsu Ginkō 10-nen shi* (A ten-year history of the Japan Development Bank). Tokyo: Nihon Kaihatsu Ginkō, 1963.

Japanese Diet, House of Representatives (Nihon Kokkai Shūgi-in). *Shōkō iinkai kiroku* (Records of the Commerce and Industry Committee). 43rd Diet, May 21, 1963.

Japan External Trade Organization (Nihon Bōeki Shinkō Kai), ed. *Jetoro 20-nen no ayumi* (The twenty-year course of JETRO). Tokyo: Nihon Bōeki Shinkō Kai, 1973.

Japan Industrial Club, Fifty-year History Editorial Committee (Nihon Kōgyō Kurabu Gojūnenshi Hensan Iinkai), ed. *Zaikai kaisōroku* (Recollections of business leaders). 2 vols. Tokyo: Nihon Kōgyō Kurabu, 1967.

Japan Long Term Credit Bank, Industrial Research Association (Nihon Chōki Shin'yō Ginkō Sangyō Kenkyū Kai). *Jūyō sangyō sengo 25-nen shi* (Twenty-five-year postwar history of important industries). Tokyo: Sangyō to Keizai, 1972.

Japan Trade Research Association (Nihon Bōeki Kenkyū Kai). *Sengo Nihon no bōeki 20-nen shi* (Twenty-year history of postwar Japanese trade). Tokyo: Tsūshō Sangyō Chōsa Kai, 1967.

Johnson, Chalmers. *Conspiracy at Matsukawa.* Berkeley: University of California Press, 1972.

―――. "The Reemployment of Retired Government Bureaucrats in Japanese Big Business." *Asian Survey,* 14 (Nov. 1974): 953–65.

―――. "Japan: Who Governs? An Essay on Official Bureaucracy." *Journal of Japanese Studies,* 2 (Autumn 1975): 1–28.

―――. "The Japanese Problem." In Donald C. Hellmann, ed., *China and Japan: A New Balance of Power.* Lexington, Mass.: D. C. Heath, 1976.

―――. "MITI and Japanese International Economic Policy." In Robert A. Scalapino, ed., *The Foreign Policy of Modern Japan.* Berkeley: University of California Press, 1977.

―――. *Japan's Public Policy Companies.* Washington, D.C.: American Enterprise Institute, 1978.

―――. "*Omote* (Explicit) and *Ura* (Implicit): Translating Japanese Political Terms." *Journal of Japanese Studies,* 6 (Winter 1980): 89–115.

Kakizaki Norio. "Shingikai, kanryō e no hōshi no kiseki" (Deliberation councils: places of service to the bureaucracy). *Ekonomisuto,* July 31, 1979, pp. 82–87.

Kakuma Takashi. *Dokyumento Tsūsan-shō, I, "shinkanryō" no jidai* (Documentary on MITI, I: the era of the "new bureaucrats"). Kyoto: P.H.P. Kenkyū-jo, 1979a.

―――. *Dokyumento Tsūsan-shō, II, Kasumigaseki no yūutsu* (Documentary on MITI, II: the melancholy of Kasumigaseki). Kyoto: P.H.P. Kenkyū-jo, 1979b.

Kanayama Bunji. "Seiiki no okite, kanryōdō no kenkyū" (Rules of the sacred precincts: research on the way of the bureaucrat). *Chūō kōron* (July 1978): 230–45.

Kankai Editorial Board. "Enerugī gyōkai ugokasu Tsūsan OB gun" (MITI's old boy network that controls the energy industry). *Kankai,* 2 (Mar. 1976): 128–35.

―――. "Tsūshō kokka Nihon o ninau Tsūsan-shō" (MITI: the guide of Japan's destiny as a trading nation). *Kankai,* 2 (Oct. 1976): 152–57.

Kaplan, Eugene J. *Japan: The Government-Business Relationship.* Washington, D.C.: U.S. Department of Commerce, 1972.

Katō Takashi. *Shigen Enerugī-chō* (The Natural Resources and Energy Agency). Tokyo: Kyōiku Sha, 1974.

Kawahara Hideyuki Memorial Committee (Kawahara Hideyuki Shi Tsuitōshū Kankōkai), ed. *Utsukushii kokoro, Kawahara Hideyuki shi no tsuioku* (Beautiful spirit: recollections of Mr. Kawahara Hideyuki). Tokyo, 1968. Privately published.

Keizai seisaku no butaiura (Behind the scenes of economic policy). Comp. by the Economics Department (Keizai-bu) of *Asahi Shimbun*. Tokyo: Asahi Shimbun Sha, 1974.

Kindleberger, Charles P. *The World in Depression, 1929–1939*. Berkeley: University of California Press, 1973.

Kishi Nobusuke, Yatsugi Kazuo, and Itō Takashi. "Kankai seikai rokujūnen" (Sixty years in the bureaucratic and political worlds). *Chūō kōron* (Sept. 1979): 278–96.

————. "Shōkō daijin kara haisen e" (From MCI minister to the defeat). *Chūō kōron* (Oct. 1979): 286–304.

Kitano Shigeo. *Gunju-shō oyobi Gunju Kaisha Hō* (The Ministry of Munitions and the Munitions Companies Law). Tokyo: Takayama Shoin, 1944.

Kobayashi Masaaki. *Nihon no kōgyōka to kangyō haraisage* (The industrialization of Japan and the sale of government enterprises). Tokyo: Tōyō Keizai Shimpōsha, 1977.

———— et al. *Nihon keieishi o manabu* (The study of the history of Japanese enterprise management). Vol. 3. Tokyo: Yūhikaku, 1976.

Kodama Fumio. "A Framework of Retrospective Analysis of Industrial Policy." Institute for Policy Science Research Report No. 78–2. Saitama University, Graduate School of Policy Science. July 1978.

Kojima Kazuo. *Hōrei ruiji yōgo jiten* (A dictionary of synonymous terms in laws and ordinances). Tokyo: Gyōsei, 1975.

Kojima Tsunehisa. "Sengo no sekitan seisaku to sekitan sangyō" (Postwar coal policy and the coal industry). *Shosai no mado*, 252 (Apr. 1976): 1–7.

Komatsu Yūgorō. *Gekidō no tsūsan gyōsei, kaiko to tembō* (Trade and industry administration in upheaval: retrospect and prospect). Tokyo: Jihyōsha, 1978.

Konaka Yōtarō, ed. *Tōdai Hōgaku-bu* (The Law School of Tokyo University). Tokyo: Gendai Hyōron Sha, 1978.

Kōno Kōnosuke. *Sakurauchi-ke no hitobito* (Members of the Sakurauchi family). Tokyo: Nihon Jihō Sha, 1965.

Kubota Akira. *Higher Civil Servants in Postwar Japan*. Princeton, N.J.: Princeton University Press, 1969.

Kurzman, Dan. *Kishi and Japan*. New York: Obolensky, 1960.

Kusayanagi Daizō. "'Ikōgyō' Kobayashi Ataru no naimaku" (Behind the scenes of Kobayashi Ataru and his "influence industry"). *Bungei shunjū* (Jan. 1969): 178–88.

————. "Sahashi Shigeru, amakudaranu kōkyū kanryō" (Sahashi Shigeru: a senior bureaucrat who will not descend from heaven). *Bungei shunjū* (May 1969): 162–74.

————. "Tsūsan-shō, tamesareru sutā kanchō" (MITI: a star bureaucracy on trial). *Bungei shunjū* (Aug. 1974): 110–26.

Kyoto University, Research Institute on Law and Economy (Kyoto Daigaku Hōsei Keizai Kenkyūkai). *Kōmuin jiten* (Public officials' dictionary). Kyoto: Kōbunsha, 1949.

Langdon, Frank C. "Big Business Lobbying in Japan: The Case of Central

Bank Reform." *American Political Science Review*, 55 (Sept. 1961): 527–38.

MacDonald, Hugh H., and Esman, Milton J. "The Japanese Civil Service." *Public Personnel Review*, 7 (Oct. 1946): 213–24.

Maeda Yasuyuki. "Seisaku kainyū no henshitsu to tsūsan kanryō" (Decline of policy intervention and the trade and industry bureaucracy). *Keizai hyōron*, 17 (Feb. 1968): 29–40.

———. "Tsūshō sangyō seisaku no rekishi-teki tenkai" (The historical development of trade and industrial policy). *Tsūsan jyānaru* (*rinji zōkan*), May 24, 1975, pp. 8–18.

Magaziner, Ira C., and Hout, Thomas M. *Japanese Industrial Policy*. Berkeley: University of California, Institute of International Studies, 1981.

Marshall, Byron K. *Capitalism and Nationalism in Prewar Japan: The Ideology of the Business Elite, 1868–1941*. Stanford, Calif.: Stanford University Press, 1967.

Masumi Junnosuke. *Nihon seitō shi ron* (The history of Japanese political parties). Vol. 4. Tokyo: Tokyo Daigaku Shuppankai, 1968.

Matsubayashi Matsuo, ed. *Kaikoroku, sengo Tsūsan seisaku shi* (Memoirs: postwar MITI policies). Tokyo: Seisaku Jihō Sha, 1973.

———, ed. *Kaikoroku, sengo Ōkura seisaku shi* (Memoirs: postwar Ministry of Finance policies). Tokyo: Seisaku Jihō Sha, 1976.

Matsumoto Seichō. *Gendai kanryō ron* (On contemporary bureaucrats). 3 vols. Tokyo: Bungei Shunjū Sha, 1963–66.

Matsumura Yutaka. *Japan's Economic Growth, 1945–60*. Tokyo: Tokyo News Service, 1961.

Ministry of Finance, Secretariat, Research and Planning Section (Ōkura-shō Daijin Kanbō Chōsa Kikaku-ka), ed. *Ōkura daijin kaikoroku* (Memoirs of ministers of finance). Tokyo: Ōkura Zaimu Kyōkai, 1977.

———, Tax Bureau. *An Outline of Japanese Taxes, 1977*. Tokyo: Ministry of Finance, Printing Bureau, 1977.

Ministry of International Trade and Industry (MITI) (Tsūshō Sangyō-shō). *Tsūshō Sangyō-shō nempō* (MITI annual report). 26 vols. Tokyo: Tsūshō Sangyō-shō, 1949–. 1 vol. per fiscal year.

———. *Tsūshō sangyō gyōsei kikō enkaku shōshi*. (A short history of the development of the administrative structure for trade and industry). Tokyo: Tsūshō Sangyō-shō, 1951.

———. *Sangyō gōrika hakusho* (Industrial rationalization whitepaper). Tokyo: Nikkan Kōgyō Shimbun Sha, 1957.

———. *Shōkō-shō sanjūgonen shōshi* (A short history of the thirty-five years of the Ministry of Commerce and Industry). Tokyo: Tsūshō Sangyō Chōsa Kai, 1960.

———. *Shōkō seisaku shi* (History of commercial and industrial policy). Vol. 3, *Gyōsei kikō* (Administrative structure). Tokyo: Shōkō Seisaku Shi Kankō Kai, 1962.

———. *Shōkō seisaku shi* (History of commercial and industrial policy). Vol. 11, *Sangyō tōsei* (Industrial control). Tokyo: Shōkō Seisaku Shi Kankō Kai, 1964.

———. *Tsūshō Sangyō-shō shijū nen shi* (Forty-year history of MITI). Tokyo: Tsūsan Shiryō Chōsa Kai, 1965.

———. *Tsūshō Sangyō-shō nijū nen shi* (Twenty-year history of MITI). Tokyo: Tsūshō Sangyō-shō, 1969a.

———. *Shōkō seisaku shi* (History of commercial and industrial policy). Vol. 21,

Kagaku kōgyō (Chemical industry, part 2). Tokyo: Shōkō Seisaku Shi Kankō Kai, 1969b.

———. *Shōkō seisaku shi* (History of commercial and industrial policy). Vol. 17, *Tekkōgyō* (The steel industry). Tokyo: Shōkō Seisaku Shi Kankō Kai, 1970.

———. *Shōkō seisaku shi* (History of commercial and industrial policy). Vol. 6, *Bōeki* (Foreign trade, part 2). Tokyo: Shōkō Seisaku Shi Kankō Kai, 1971.

———. *Shōkō seisaku shi* (History of commercial and industrial policy). Vol. 10, *Sangyō gōrika* (Industrial rationalization, part 2). Tokyo: Shōkō Seisaku Shi Kankō Kai, 1972.

———. *Sangyō kōzō no chōki bijon* (A long-range vision of the industrial structure). Tokyo: Tsūshō Sangyō Chōsa Kai, 1974.

———. *Tsūshō sangyō gyōsei shihan seiki no ayumi* (The course of a quarter century of trade and industrial administration). Tokyo: Tsūshō Sangyō Chōsa Kai, 1975.

Misawa Shigeo. "Seiji kettei katei no gaikan" (Outline of the political decision-making process). In Japan Political Science Association (Nihon Seiji Gakkai), ed., *Gendai Nihon no seitō to kanryō* (Contemporary Japanese political parties and the bureaucracy). Tokyo: Iwanami Shoten, 1967.

Misono Hitoshi. "Keizai kanryō no kinō to kongo no hōkō" (The functions of the economic bureaucracy and its future course). *Keizai hyōron*, 17 (Feb. 1968): 8–19.

MITI Journalists' Club (Tsūsan-shō Kisha Kurabu). *Tsūsan-shō* (MITI). Tokyo: Hōbunsha, 1956.

———. *Tsūsan-shō no isu* (The chair of MITI). Tokyo: Kindai Shinsho Shuppankai, 1963a.

———. "Tsūsan-shō no kao, keizai kanryō no seitai" (The faces of MITI: the ecology of the economic bureaucrats). *Chūō kōron* (Oct. 1963): 72–86.

Mitsubishi Group. Comp. by staff of the *Mainichi Daily News*. 2nd. ed. Tokyo: Mainichi Shimbun Sha, 1971.

Miyake Haruteru. *Kobayashi Ichizō den* (A biography of Kobayashi Ichizō). Tokyo: Tōyō Shokan, 1954.

Morley, James W., ed. *Dilemmas of Growth in Prewar Japan*. Princeton, N.J.: Princeton University Press, 1971.

Morozumi Yoshihiko. "Shinkanryō-zō" (The image of the new bureaucrats). *Jinji-in geppō*, 27 (June 1974): 1–3.

Murase Naokai Memorial Editorial Committee (Murase Naokai Shi Tsuitōroku Hensan Iinkai), ed. *Murase-san no omoide* (Recollections of Mr. Murase). Tokyo, 1970. Privately published.

Nakamura Takafusa. "Sengo no sangyō seisaku" (Postwar industrial policy). In Niida Hiroshi and Ono Akira, eds., *Nihon no sangyō soshiki* (Japan's industrial organization). Tokyo: Iwanami Shoten, 1969.

———. *Nihon no keizai tōsei, senji sengo no keiken to kyōkun* (Japan's economic controls: experiences and lessons from the wartime and postwar periods). Tokyo: Nihon Keizai Shimbun Sha, 1974.

Nakasone Yasuhiro. *Kaizu no nai kōkai, sekiyu kiki to Tsūsan-shō* (At sea without charts: the oil shock and MITI). Tokyo: Nihon Keizai Shimbun Sha, 1975.

Nawa Tarō. *Tsūsan-shō* (MITI). Tokyo: Kyōiku Sha, 1974.

———. "Kankai jinmyaku chiri" (Geography of bureaucratic personnel relations). *Kankai*, 1 (Nov. 1975): 80–88.

———. *Inayama Yoshihiro*. Tokyo: Kokusai Shōgyō Shuppan, 1976a.

———. "Fukuzatsu na Tsūsan jinmyaku oyogikiru" (Wading through the complex MITI personnel connections). *Kankai*, 2 (Apr. 1976): 35–41.

———. "Kankai jinmyaku chiri, Tsūsan-shō no maki" (Geography of bureaucratic personnel relations: MITI). *Kankai*, 2 (Dec. 1976): 40–49.

——— et al. "Kurabu kisha hōdan" (Free discussion by the Press Club). *Tsūsan jyānaru (rinji zōkan)*, May 24, 1975, pp. 48–58.

Nettl, J. P. "The State as a Conceptual Variable." *World Politics*, 20 (July 1968): 559–92.

Nishiyama Mataji. *Kogane Yoshiteru den* (A biography of Kogane Yoshiteru). Tokyo: Teishin Kenkyū Kai, 1978.

Noda Economic Research Institute (Noda Keizai Kenkyū-jo). *Senjika no kokusaku kaisha* (The national policy companies during wartime). Tokyo: Noda Keizai Kenkyū-jo, 1940.

Noda Nobuo. *How Japan Absorbed American Management Methods*. Manila: Asian Productivity Organization, 1970.

Obayashi Kenji. "'Nihon Kabushiki Kaisha' no shukuzu, Sankōshin no kanmin kyōchō-buri" (The epitome of "Japan, Inc.": official-civilian cooperation in the Industrial Structure Council). *Nikkei bijinesu*, July 26, 1971, pp. 68–70.

Odahashi Sadaju. *Nihon no shōkō seisaku* (Japan's commercial and industrial policy). Tokyo: Kyōiku Shuppan, 1971.

Ohkawa Kazushi and Rosovsky, Henry. *Japanese Economic Growth: Trend Acceleration in the Twentieth Century*. Stanford, Calif.: Stanford University Press, 1973.

Ōjimi Yoshihisa and Uchida Tadao. "Nihon no kanryō gyōsei to kanmin kyōchō taisei (Japan's bureaucratic administration and the system of public-private cooperation). *Gendai keizai* (Sept. 1972): 26–37.

Oka Yoshitake, ed. *Gendai Nihon no seiji katei* (The political process of modern Japan). Tokyo: Iwanami Shoten, 1958.

Ōkubo Shōzō. *Hadaka no seikai* (The political world laid bare). Tokyo: Saimaru Shuppankai, 1975.

Ōnishi Yukikazu. *Keizai Kikaku-chō* (The Economic Planning Agency). Tokyo: Kyōiku Sha, 1975.

Organization for Economic Cooperation and Development. *The Industrial Policy of Japan*. Paris: OECD, 1972.

———. *The Development of Industrial Relations Systems: Some Implications of Japanese Experience*. Paris: OECD, 1977a.

———. *Towards an Integrated Social Policy in Japan*. Paris: OECD, 1977b.

Ōsawa Etsuji. *Denryoku jigyōkai* (The electric power industry). Tokyo: Kyōiku Sha, 1975.

Ōta Akira. "Tsūsan-shō no 'batsu' kenkyū" (Research on MITI's "factions"). *Hito to Nihon* (Oct. 1978): 38–46.

Ozaki, Robert S. "Japanese Views on Industrial Organization." *Asian Survey*, 10 (Oct. 1970): 872–89.

———. *The Control of Imports and Foreign Capital in Japan*. New York: Praeger, 1972.

———. *The Japanese: A Cultural Portrait*. Tokyo: Tuttle, 1978.

Passin, Herbert, ed. *The United States and Japan*. 2nd. rev. ed. Washington, D.C.: Columbia Books, 1975.

Patrick, Hugh, and Rosovsky, Henry, eds. *Asia's New Giant: How the Japanese Economy Works*. Washington, D.C.: Brookings Institution, 1976.

Peattie, Mark R. *Ishiwara Kanji and Japan's Confrontation with the West*. Princeton, N.J.: Princeton University Press, 1975.

Pempel, T. J., ed. *Policymaking in Contemporary Japan*. Ithaca, N.Y.: Cornell University Press, 1977.

Personnel Administration Investigation Council (Jinji Gyōsei Chōsa Kai), ed. *Kōmuin jinji gyōsei no hensen* (Civil official personnel administration in transition). Tokyo: Jinji Gyōsei Chōsa Kai, 1972.

Policy Review Company (Seisaku Jihō Sha), ed. *Tsūsan-shō, sono hito to soshiki* (MITI: its personnel and organization). Tokyo: Seisaku Jihō Sha, 1968.

———, ed. *Nihon no kanchō* (Japanese government agencies). Tokyo: Seisaku Jihō Sha, 1970–. Biennial.

Radio Report on the Far East. Comp. by U.S. Federal Communications Commission, Foreign Broadcast Intelligence Service. Washington, D.C., Aug. 17, 1942–Oct. 14, 1945.

Resources Development and Management Research Council (Shigen Kaihatsu Un'ei Chōsa Kai), ed. *Zaikaijin jiten* (Dictionary of business leaders). Tokyo: Shigen Kaihatsu Un'ei Chōsa Kai, 1973.

Rice, Richard. "Economic Mobilization in Wartime Japan: Business, Bureaucracy, and Military in Conflict." *Journal of Asian Studies*, 38 (Aug. 1979): 689–706.

Roberts, John G. *Mitsui*. Tokyo: Weatherhill, 1973.

Roser, Foster B. "Establishing a Modern Merit System in Japan." *Public Personnel Review*, 11 (Oct. 1950): 199–206.

Sahashi Shigeru. *Ishoku kanryō* (An exceptional bureaucrat). Tokyo: Daiyamondo Sha, 1967.

———. "Kanryō shokun ni chokugen suru" (Straight talk to the gentlemen of the bureaucracy). *Bungei shunjū* (July 1971): 108–15.

———. *Yūjō mugen* (Anxieties). Tokyo: Sangyō Shinchō Sha, 1971a.

———. *Nihon e no chokugen* (Straight talk to Japan). Tokyo: Mainichi Shimbun Sha, 1972.

Sakaguchi Akira. *Ishikawa Ichirō*. Tokyo: Kashima Kenkyū-jo Shuppankai, 1972.

Sakakibara Eisuke. "'Gyōsei kaikaku' no hinkon" (The poverty of "administrative reform"). *Shokun* (Nov. 1977): 68–78.

———. *Nihon o enshutsu-suru shinkanryō-zō* (A portrait of the new bureaucrats who run Japan). Tokyo: Yamate Shobō, 1977a.

Satō, Seiichirō. "Ōkura-shō no chinbotsu" (The sinking of the Ministry of Finance). *Shūkan bunshun*, May 26, 1977, pp. 56–66.

Saxonhouse, Gary R. "Industrial Restructuring in Japan." *Journal of Japanese Studies*, 5 (Summer 1979): 273–320.

Scalapino, Robert A. *Democracy and the Party Movement in Prewar Japan*. Berkeley: University of California Press, 1953.

Shiba Kimpei and Nozue Kenzō. *What Makes Japan Tick?* Tokyo: Asahi Evening News Co., 1971.

Shibano Kōichirō. *Kankyō-chō* (The Environment Agency). Tokyo: Kyōiku Sha, 1975.

Shibusawa Kijirō. *Kōkyū kōmuin no yukue* (The paths of higher officials). Asahi

Shimbun Chōsa Kenkyū Shitsu, Internal Report, no. 120. Tokyo, May 10, 1966.

Shiina Etsusaburō. Autobiographical article in Nihon Keizai Shimbun Sha, ed., *Watakushi no rirekisho* (My personal history). Vol. 41. Tokyo: Nihon Keizai Shimbun Sha, 1970.

———. "Nihon sangyō no daijikkenjō, Manshū" (Manchuria: the great proving ground for Japanese industry). *Bungei shunjū* (Feb. 1976): 106–14.

Shimomura Osamu. "Kōdō seichō to Nihonjin" (High-speed growth and the Japanese). *Bungei shunjū* (Feb. 1976): 126–34.

Shinohara Miyohei. "Isetsu, Nihon Kabushiki Kaisha ron" (Conflicting views on Japan, Inc.). *Ekonomisuto*, Nov. 5, 1976, pp. 104–14.

Shioguchi Kiichi. *Kikigaki, Ikeda Hayato* (Verbatim notes: Ikeda Hayato). Tokyo: Asahi Shimbun Sha, 1975.

Shirasawa Teruo. *Nōrin-shō* (The Ministry of Agriculture and Forestry). Tokyo: Kyōiku Sha, 1974.

Shiroyama Saburō. *Kanryō-tachi no natsu* (The summer of the bureaucrats). Tokyo: Shinchōsha, 1975a.

———. "Tsūsan kanryō jinbutsu shōshi" (A short history of the bureaucratic personalities in MITI). *Chūō kōron* (Aug. 1975): 303–19.

Shōwa shi jiten (Dictionary of Shōwa history). Tokyo: Mainichi Shimbun Sha, 1980.

Sōri daijin (The prime minister). Comp. by the Political Department (Seiji-bu) of *Yomiuri Shimbun*. Rev. ed. Tokyo: Yomiuri Shimbun Sha, 1972.

Spaulding, Robert M., Jr. *Imperial Japan's Higher Civil Service Examinations*. Princeton: N.J.: Princeton University Press, 1967.

Stone, P. B. *Japan Surges Ahead: The Story of an Economic Miracle*. New York: Praeger, 1969.

Sugimoto Eiichi. *Tsūshō Sangyō-shō* (MITI). Tokyo: Kyōiku Sha, 1979.

Supreme Commander for the Allied Powers. *History of the Nonmilitary Activities of the Occupation of Japan, 1945–1951*. 55 monographs. Washington, D.C.: National Archives, 1951.

Suzuki Kenji. "Keisatsu o shimedashite, Bōei-cho o nottoru Ōkura kanryō" (The police frozen out: Finance bureaucrats take over the Defense Agency). *Sandē mainichi*, July 30, 1978, pp. 132–34.

Suzuki Yukio. "Sangyō seisaku gyōkai saihen o meguru zaikai rīdā no ishiki to bihēbiyā" (Financial leaders' views and behavior concerning industrial policy and industrial reorganization). *Keizai hyōron*, 12 (May 1963): 34–45.

———. *Keizai kanryō, shin sangyō kokka no purodyūsā* (Economic bureaucrats: producers of the new industrial state). Tokyo: Nihon Keizai Shimbun Sha, 1969.

Tajiri Ikuzō, Takemura Yoshio, and Shioda Mitsuhiko. "Kishi Nobusuke kenkyū" (Research on Kishi Nobusuke). *Bungei shunjū* (July 1978): 100–168.

Takane Masaaki *Nihon no seiji erīto* (Japan's political elite). Tokyo: Chūō Kōron Sha, 1976.

Takase Masao. "Nihon ni okeru dokusen kiseihō no keifu" (The genealogy of monopoly regulation legislation in Japan). *Hōritsu jihō*, 46 (Jan. 1974): 76–87.

Takase Sōtarō Memorial Association (Takase Sōtarō Sensei Kinen Jigyōkai), ed. *Takase Sōtarō*. Tokyo: Toppan, 1970.

Takashima Setsuo. "Nihon no sangyō gyōsei to kyōchō hōshiki" (Japan's industrial administration and the cooperation formula). *Keizai hyōron*, 12 (May 1963): 26–33.

Takashima Tadashi. "Keizai kōsei no jitsugen to sangyō seisaku" (Industrial policy and the achievement of economic welfare). *Seikai ōrai* (July 1976): 114–25.

Takeuchi Naokazu. *Konna kanryō wa yamete-shimae* (Bureaucrats such as these should be fired). Tokyo: Nisshin Hōdō, 1978.

Tanaka Shin'ichi. *Nihon senji keizai hishi* (Secret history of Japan's wartime economy). Tokyo: Computer Age, 1974.

Taniuchi Ken et al. *Gendai gyōsei to kanryōsei* (Modern administration and the bureaucratic system). Vol. 2. Tokyo: Tokyo Daigaku Shuppankai, 1974.

Temporary Administrative Investigation Council (Rinji Gyōsei Chōsa Kai). *Gyōsei no kaikaku* (Reform of administration). Tokyo: Jiji Tsūshin, 1967.

Tiedemann, Arthur E. "Japan's Economic Foreign Policies, 1868–1893." In James W. Morley, ed., *Japan's Foreign Policy, 1868–1941*. New York: Columbia University Press, 1974.

Titus, David Anson. *Palace and Politics in Prewar Japan*. New York: Columbia University Press, 1974.

Tōbata Seiichi, ed. *The Modernization of Japan*. Tokyo: Institute of Asian Economic Affairs, 1966.

Toda Eisuke. "Mokuhyō o miushinatta Tsūsan kanryō" (MITI bureaucrats who have lost their objective). *Ekonomisuto*, May 31, 1977, pp. 24–29.

Tokyo University, Social Science Research Institute (Tokyo Daigaku Shakai Kagaku Kenkyū-jo), ed. *Sengo kaikaku* (Postwar reform). Vols. 3, 8. Tokyo: Tokyo Daigaku Shuppankai, 1974, 1975.

———, ed. *Fashizumu-ki no kokka to shakai* (State and society in the Fascist era). Vol. 2. Tokyo: Tokyo Daigaku Shuppankai, 1979.

Tomioka Tadao. *Chūshō Kigyō-chō* (The Medium and Smaller Enterprises Agency). Tokyo: Kyōiku Sha, 1974.

Trade and Industry Handbook Compilation Committee (Tsūsan Handobukku Henshū Iinkai), ed. *Tsūsan handobukku* (Trade and industry handbook). Tokyo: Shōkō Kaikan, [1965?]–1976. Published annually.

Tsuji Kiyoaki, ed. *Gyōseigaku kōza* (Lectures on the science of administration). Vols. 2, 4. Tokyo: Tokyo Daigaku Shuppankai, 1976.

Tsukata Ichizō. *Sangyō gōrika ron* (On industrial rationalization). Tokyo: Nihon Shuppan Sha, 1942.

Ueno Hiroya. *Nihon no keizai seido* (The economic system of Japan). Tokyo: Nihon Keizai Shimbun Sha, 1978.

Urata Tomoo. "Sangyōkai ni haishutsu-suru kanryō shusshinsha" (Ex-bureaucrats in the industrial world). *Keizai ōrai* (Oct. 1973): 146–53.

Watanabe Takeshi. *Senryōka no Nihon zaisei oboegaki* (Notes on Japanese finance under the occupation). Tokyo: Nihon Keizai Shimbun Sha, 1966.

Weber, Max. *Economy and Society*. Ed. by Guenther Roth and Claus Wittich. New York: Bedminster Press, 1968.

Wildes, Harry Emerson. *Typhoon in Tokyo: The Occupation and Its Aftermath*. New York: Macmillan, 1954.

Wilson, James Q. "The Rise of the Bureaucratic State." *The Public Interest*, 41 (Fall 1975): 77–103.

Yamamoto Masao, ed. *Keizai kanryō no jittai, seisaku kettei no mekanizumu* (Facts about economic bureaucrats: the mechanisms of policy determination). Tokyo: Mainichi Shimbun Sha, 1972.

Yamamura Kozo. *Economic Policy in Postwar Japan.* Berkeley: University of California Press, 1967.

Yamanouchi Kazuo. *Gyōsei shidō* (Administrative guidance). Tokyo: Kōbundō, 1977.

Yasuhara Kazuo. *Ōkura-shō* (The Ministry of Finance). Tokyo: Kyōiku Sha, 1974.

Yoshida Shigeru. *The Yoshida Memoirs.* Cambridge, Mass.: Houghton Mifflin, 1962.

Yoshida Shigeru Biography Publication Committee (Yoshida Shigeru Denki Kanko Henshū Iinkai). *Yoshida Shigeru.* Tokyo: Meikōsha, 1969.

Yoshimoto Shigeyoshi. *Kishi Nobusuke den* (A biography of Kishi Nobusuke). Tokyo: Tōyō Shokan, 1957.

Yoshino, M. Y. *The Japanese Marketing System.* Cambridge: Massachusetts Institute of Technology Press, 1971.

Yoshino Shinji. *Nihon kōgyō seisaku* (Japan's industrial policy). Tokyo: Nihon Hyōron Sha, 1935.

―――. *Nihon kokumin ni uttau* (Report to the Japanese people). Tokyo: Seikatsusha, 1937.

―――. *Shōkō gyōsei no omoide* (Recollections of commercial and industrial administration). Tokyo: Shōkō Seisaku Shi Kankō Kai, 1962.

―――. *Sazanami no ki* (A record of rippling waves). Tokyo: Ichigaya Shuppan Sha, 1965.

Yoshino Shinji Memorial Society (Yoshino Shinji Tsuitōroku Kankō Kai), ed. *Yoshino Shinji.* Tokyo, 1974. Privately published.

Yoshitomi Shigeo. *Gyōsei kikō kaikaku ron* (On reform of administrative organs). Tokyo: Nihon Hyōron Sha, 1941.

Zaikai tenbō Editorial Board. "'Tsūsan kanryō no seitai' tettei kenkyū" (Research in depth on the "mode of life of MITI bureaucrats"). *Zaikai tenbō* (Aug. 1978): 62–95.

INDEX

INDEX